SAGE was founded in 1965 by Sara Miller McCune to support the dissemination of usable knowledge by publishing innovative and high-quality research and teaching content. Today, we publish over 900 journals, including those of more than 400 learned societies, more than 800 new books per year, and a growing range of library products including archives, data, case studies, reports, and video. SAGE remains majority-owned by our founder, and after Sara's lifetime will become owned by a charitable trust that secures our continued independence.

Los Angeles | London | New Delhi | Singapore | Washington DC | Melbourne

INDIA'S FOREIGN POLICY

Thank you for choosing a SAGE product!
If you have any comment, observation or feedback,
I would like to personally hear from you.

Please write to me at **contactceo@sagepub.in**

Vivek Mehra, Managing Director and CEO, SAGE India.

Bulk Sales

SAGE India offers special discounts
for purchase of books in bulk.
We also make available special imprints
and excerpts from our books on demand.

For orders and enquiries, write to us at

Marketing Department
SAGE Publications India Pvt Ltd
B1/I-1, Mohan Cooperative Industrial Area
Mathura Road, Post Bag 7
New Delhi 110044, India

E-mail us at **marketing@sagepub.in**

Subscribe to our mailing list
Write to **marketing@sagepub.in**

This book is also available as an e-book.

INDIA'S FOREIGN POLICY

Surviving in a Turbulent World

Edited by
Arvind Gupta
Anil Wadhwa

Los Angeles | London | New Delhi
Singapore | Washington DC | Melbourne

Copyright © Arvind Gupta and Anil Wadhwa, 2020

All rights reserved. No part of this book may be reproduced or utilized in any form or by any means, electronic or mechanical, including photocopying, recording or by any information storage or retrieval system, without permission in writing from the publisher.

First published in 2020 by

SAGE Publications India Pvt Ltd
B1/I-1 Mohan Cooperative Industrial Area
Mathura Road, New Delhi 110 044, India
www.sagepub.in

SAGE Publications Inc
2455 Teller Road
Thousand Oaks, California 91320, USA

SAGE Publications Ltd
1 Oliver's Yard, 55 City Road
London EC1Y 1SP, United Kingdom

SAGE Publications Asia-Pacific Pte Ltd
18 Cross Street #10-10/11/12
China Square Central
Singapore 048423

Published by Vivek Mehra for SAGE Publications India Pvt Ltd. Typeset in 10.5/13 pt Berkeley by Zaza Eunice, Hosur, Tamil Nadu, India.

Library of Congress Cataloging-in-Publication Data

Names: Gupta, Arvind, editor. | Wadhwa, Anil, editor.
Title: India's foreign policy: surviving in a turbulent world/edited by
    Arvind Gupta, Anil Wadhwa.
Description: Thousand Oaks: SAGE Publications India Pvt Ltd, 2020. |
    Includes bibliographical references and index. |
Identifiers: LCCN 2020008947 (print) | LCCN 2020008948 (ebook) | ISBN
    9789353882952 (Hardback) | ISBN 9789353882969 (ePub) | ISBN
    9789353882976 (eBook)
Subjects: LCSH: India—Foreign relations.
Classification: LCC DS448 .I667 2020 (print) | LCC DS448 (ebook) | DDC
    327.54—dc23
LC record available at https://lccn.loc.gov/2020008947
LC ebook record available at https://lccn.loc.gov/2020008948

ISBN: 978-93-5388-295-2 (HB)

SAGE Team: Rajesh Dey, Vandana Gupta and Madurima Thapa

Contents

Acknowledgements ix

Chapter 1. Introduction
            by *Arvind Gupta* 1

PART A: DRIVERS AND TRENDS

Chapter 2. Indian Narrative in Emerging Multi-polar World:
            Some Reflections
            by *S. D. Muni*. 21

Chapter 3. National Security Determinants of Foreign Policy
            by *P. S. Raghavan*. 34

Chapter 4. Strategizing Soft Power Projection
            by *Veena Sikri* 45

Chapter 5. India and Multilateralism
            by *Asoke Kumar Mukerji* 62

Chapter 6. Leveraging International Cooperation in
            Science and Technology
            by *Arvind Gupta* 84

Chapter 7. Indian Narrative through the Cold War Era:
From Panchsheel to Détente
by *Vivek Prahladan* 100

Chapter 8. Rebalancing Foreign Policy and
Non-traditional Security Issues
by *Uttam Kumar Sinha* 115

Chapter 9. The Economic Dimension of India's Foreign Policy
by *Prasenjit K. Basu* 131

Chapter 10. Domestic Drivers of India's Neighbourhood Policy
by *Ashok Behuria* 152

Chapter 11. Intelligence and Foreign Policy:
India and the World in 2050
by *Vikram Sood* 164

PART B: RELATIONSHIPS

Chapter 12. India's Relations with the Great Powers
by *Rajiv Sikri* 179

Chapter 13. India's Relations with Its SAARC Neighbours
by *Satish Chandra* 194

Chapter 14. Political Economy of India's International Relations:
A New Path for Sustained Strategic Interlinkages
by *Arun K. Singh*.................................... 217

Chapter 15. Dealing with the Rising China
by *Sujit Dutta*.. 232

Chapter 16. Japan and India: Partners in Progress
by *Deepa Gopalan Wadhwa* 252

Chapter 17. India–Russia Ties:
Exploring Convergences and Divergences
by *Ajai Malhotra* 266

Chapter 18. Changing Landscape of Central Asia
by *D. P. Srivastava* 281

Chapter 19. India and West Asia:
           Promoting Security in a Turbulent Region
           by *Talmiz Ahmad*................................ 301

Chapter 20. India and Southeast Asia
           by *Anil Wadhwa* 324

Chapter 21. India and the European Union
           by *Gulshan Sachdeva* 338

Chapter 22. India and the Indian Ocean
           by *Yogendra Kumar* 357

Chapter 23. India's Tryst with Africa: India–Africa Contextualized
           by *Anil Trigunayat*............................. 373

Chapter 24. Latin America: A Long-term Partner for India
           by *R. Viswanathan*.............................. 392

About the Editors and Contributors 408
Index.. 420

Acknowledgements

This book is an outcome of several roundtable discussions held at the Vivekananda International Foundation (VIF) to discuss India's place in the world. Many of the authors participated in these discussions. I would like to thank all the contributors for their thoughtful articles.

We would like to thank Vivekananda International Foundation (VIF), which is an independent, non-partisan think tank dedicated to research on foreign policy, defence, national security, governance, economics and civilizational issues, to sponsor this research on foreign policy. As the world becomes multipolar and India begins to take its deserved place in the community of the nation, there is an urgent need to develop an Indian vision and narrative. Such a narrative should be based on India's own experience of dealing with the world over several millennia and Indian wisdom contained in numerous ancient texts. We have to remind ourselves that the world will not take us seriously unless we project a distinct Indian identity.

Our special thanks to Rajesh Dey for commissioning this book. Vandana Gupta deserves thanks for painstaking editing.

I would like to place on record my appreciation of the efforts put in by Sh. Ramphal Vashisth of the VIF in coordinating with the authors at the various stages of the preparation of this book.

I would also like to acknowledge the support given by Ambassador Anil Wadhwa in conceptualizing and preparing the manuscript.

Arvind Gupta

1

Introduction

Arvind Gupta

The NDA government, led by Prime Minister (PM) Narendra Modi, has returned with a massive mandate for another five years. In his previous term from 2014 to 2019, PM Modi gave a new direction to India's foreign policy. The emphasis was on deepening engagement, producing new security concepts and raising India's profile abroad. Considerable emphasis was placed on linking national security with foreign policy. Modi used global platform to highlight ancient Indian value *Vasudhaiva Kutumbakam* (the world is a family) in India's foreign policy. Recognizing the potential of Indian diaspora, he reached out to the Indians and the persons of Indian origin living abroad for achieving foreign policy objectives. He focused on strengthening strategic key strategic partnerships with the USA, Japan and Russia; managing China and highlighting the maritime dimension of India's foreign policy. Thus, Indo-US relations were deepened as India signed a number of foundational agreements, which would increase the interoperability between the militaries of the two sides. PM Modi's 'Neighbourhood First' policy witnessed not only significant improvement of ties with neighbours but also a shift away from SAARC to BIMSTEC. India shed its ambivalence and promoted the Quad (India, the USA, Japan and Australia) quadrilateral ties, which would put a certain pressure on China. The concept of Indo-Pacific was enthusiastically embraced by policymakers.

Another distinct feature of India's foreign policy during his first term was the highlighting link between India's foreign policy and domestic priorities. Thus, during his 50+ visits abroad, Modi promoted India as a destination for foreign investment, promoted the Make in India concept, took measures to improve the Ease of Doing Business to attract foreign industries and signed a number of defence cooperation agreements with other countries. At the multilateral level, India, along with France, took the lead to set up an International Solar Alliance to promote solar energy.

During Modi's first tenure, the security dimension of India's foreign policy was also given prominence. Thus, India signed a large number of defence cooperation agreements, established cyber security dialogues with many countries, focused on counterterrorism, held joint exercises with key part in countries, conducted an Anti-Satellite Test (ASAT), set up several maritime security cooperation dialogues and conducted '2+2' (Defence Minister plus External Affairs Minister) dialogues with key countries such as the USA.

India has been a victim of cross-border terrorism for a very long time. PM Modi took upon himself to bring a relentless focus on this problem. Anywhere he went, any fora he addressed, he emphasized on the need for the global community to come together to fight terrorism and expose those who promote and support terrorism. He also called for a UN Convention on Countering Terrorism.

Realizing the importance of personal chemistry, Modi established personal contacts with the world's top *leaders*, regularly attended the meetings of top multilateral fora such as the G20 and hosted a large number of world leaders to India. India also hosted several high-profile conferences with the leaders of Africa, BRICS, etc. These initiatives improved India's visibility at international fora and burnished its image.

All this was happening on the back of an expanding economy which grew at an annual rate of about 7 per cent. During the five years of PM Modi, India became a US$2.5 trillion economy, the fifth largest in the world. India is already the third largest economy in purchasing power parity (PPP) terms. Modi has set a target of making India a US$5 trillion economy by 2024. The target may look challenging but is achievable. The international financial institutions took note of India's growth, which at one point of time overtook that of China. India became the fastest growing economy of large size.

In Modi's first term, India got unprecedented international visibility. However, a close examination of the last five years shows that there were several areas where a lot more needs to be done. India could not make it to the Nuclear Supplier's Group because of China's consistent opposition. The China–Pakistan Economic Corridor (CPEC) project, an offshoot of China's Belt and Road Initiative (BRI), went ahead despite India's protests. India was more or less excluded from the efforts of the USA for peace negotiation in Afghanistan as the formerly opened dialogue with the Taliban. Pakistan-based terror groups continued to attack India. Relations with Pakistan touched a new low. In the unprecedented scenes of violence, India launched surgical strikes in Pakistan-occupied Kashmir and air strikes inside Pakistan on two different occasions against the terrorist camps.

Relations with China also suffered a downward slide when the militaries of the two sides came face to face at Doklam in 2017 for 72 days. The situation was controlled when the two leaders met for an informal summit at Wuhan and launched the so-called Wuhan spirit to promote friendship and cooperation. During the last few years, China has taken virtual control of the South China Sea and begun to expand its presence in several countries of the Indian Ocean. Many of India's partners welcomed and embraced the BRI, which is an instrument being used by the Chinese to enhance their footprint globally. China's influence in India's neighbourhood and the Indian Ocean increased as it continued with the modernization of the People's Liberation Army (PLA).

India's global exports increased at a slow pace while imports increased rapidly, thus widening the trade gap. India was unable to conclude the Regional Comprehensive Economic Partnership (RCEP) agreement within the stipulated time.

All said and done, first five years of Mr Modi were notable for many successes. They set stage for an ambitious foreign policy agenda in the second term of the government. India's large markets attracted many investors. Many countries were getting disillusioned with China and began looking for alternative destinations for investments. Thus, India was in a sweet spot.

What can we expect in the next five years? The global and regional environment is dynamic. Nothing ever remains static except the national interests. India has limited control over geopolitical factors that shape the external environment. Indian foreign policy should have the resilience to navigate the turbulent international scene and safeguard one's interests.

As the second term of PM Modi begins, the global and regional environment has become quite uncertain. Global and regional turbulence cannot be ruled out. The question is: what are the factors that will shape India's foreign policy in the next five years or so; and how will India cope up with the changing global and regional environment? Is India resilient enough, for example, to navigate through the choppy waters of international affairs which are being rocked by the deepening rivalries among the great powers? Is India well prepared to wither the likely shocks in the international economic environment? These are some of the questions which the various chapters in this book address.

Global Environment: A New Cold War?

The world has several powerful leaders at the helm of affairs. They follow highly nationalistic policies, keeping the interest of their countries above everything else. The multilateral institutions are showing signs of helplessness and even atrophy. A new balance of power is shaping in the world. On the one hand, the world is becoming multipolar with several countries rising simultaneously and the hegemonic US showing some signs of decline, and on the other hand, there are also signs of a new Cold War shaping up, this time between the USA and the contender China.

The shape of the new Cold War, if it happens, will be different from the 1945–1989 Cold War that was fought in the backdrop of a bipolar world. Unlike between the USA and the USSR, this time around, there is a great deal of interdependence among various countries, including between the USA and China. The 'new' Cold War will have a very strong technological dimension, as is seen in the US–China trade war. President Trump is honing the art of economic sanctions, taking it to newer heights, to not let the US hegemony slip. He has concluded that China and Russia are rivals. Economic tools are being used with greater purpose and resolve. Invoking national security concerns, the USA has put a ban on the supply of high-tech products and components on the Chinese tech giant Huawei, which has emerged as a world leader in 5G technologies. This shows that the new Cold War will have very strong economic and technological dimension. The global economy, which is now very well integrated after several decades of globalization, can be disrupted by the US–China trade war. The trade war can disrupt global supply chains and global economies. It can lead to a new balance of power, as happened during the 2008–2009 Financial Crisis. Even advanced countries will be seriously impacted as their economies are interlinked with global supply chains which run through several countries, including the USA and China. Intellectual property will be the new bone of contention. The trade war could easily spill into a much wider economic war, which in turn could have military implications as well.

The existing multilateral institutions are not strong enough to deal with the consequences of the US–China trade war. The inadequacy of the multilateral institutions to deal with issues between the two major powers is clearly exposed. We saw this when China unilaterally rejected the finding of the Permanent Court of Arbitration (PCA) on the South China Sea issue and went ahead to occupy the disputed islands citing historical claims and sovereignty. The solutions to big power issues will have to be essentially bilateral and will depend upon the whims and fancies of the political leadership on the two sides.

The USA and China are not the only two players in the global scene. Russia is presently weak economically but looking to restore its past glory. It makes no concessions to the unilateralism of the USA. There have been many episodes in Russia's long history when it was down and out, and yet it bounced back. President Putin, backed by the Russian public opinion, is playing the rather weak hand on the international scene. Yet Russia has a large nuclear arsenal, its military is being modernized, and the country is looking to develop its rich North and the Far East. Although spurned by Europe, it is clear that it has a major role to play in European affairs even if as an outsider. Russia has recovered a lot of ground in the Middle East through its calibrated intervention in Syria. It is trying to do so in Eurasia. As its relationship with the West has deteriorated, it has moved closer to China. The two are in a quite close relationship, but it must be realized that Russia would not be content with playing a junior role to China, which has been forced to do so at the present moment. Likewise, China would be wary of Russia with whom it has had highly strained relations in the past. Thus, Russia–China tango has its own weak points. The interplay between Russia, China and the USA will affect the global environment quite significantly in the next five years. Russia's decline, if it continues, will have serious impact on global security.

India will have to navigate through the uneven international landscape as a new balance of power shapes up. India cannot afford to ignore any of these countries for the other. China is a neighbour with whom India has a long unsettled border and many other issues. While the USA wants to contain China, and India would not mind if that happens, it does not have the wherewithal to do so alone. China and Russia would like to see the US influence in Asia decrease. They would also like India to be weaned away from the USA. Thus, India becomes a kind of a swing state in this big power geopolitical game. While India is closely tied with the USA and Japan through the Quad and Malabar exercises, it is also a member of non-US groupings such as BRICS, RIC and Shanghai Cooperation Organisation (SCO). India's challenge would be to navigate between the conflicting interests of these countries and groupings while ensuring at the same time that its own independence of decision-making and action is not jeopardized.

Naturally, India prefers a multi-polar world as it provides room for manoeuvre. It is beginning to develop the regional dimension in its foreign policy. By defining the Indo-Pacific concept broadly, PM Modi has redefined the contours of India's strategic geography which stretches from the Pacific Ocean to the eastern shores of Africa in the Indian Ocean. For the first time, India's security calculus places equal emphasis on continental and maritime dimensions. Indo-Pacific is a large geography through which a number of sea lines of communications (SLOC) pass. The freedom of navigation through the SLOC through which India's seaborne trade passes is vital for India's safety, security and prosperity. India has to play a commensurate role in safeguarding the SLOC. India's naval strength is not sufficient to do that alone. That is why teaming up with the USA, which is a global power, is becoming important for India. So Indo-US partnership, buttressed by the 'foundational' agreements which promote interoperability between the armed forces of the two countries, has become a necessity for India.

At the same time, India depends upon Russia and will continue to do so for several decades for its military hardware needs. The USA realizes that so long as India's dependence on Russia continues, India will be undecided between Russia and the USA and will tend to follow a middle path. The USA has begun to woo and persuade India to buy more of US equipment and reduce its dependence on Russian equipment. It has offered and sold some high-tech equipment including military aircraft and attack helicopters to India. A Defence Technology and Trade Initiative (DTTI) between the two countries to develop and jointly produce high-tech defence equipment is being developed. But more importantly, the USA has held out the threat of sanctioning India if the latter goes ahead and buys Russia's S-400 anti-missile antiballistic missile systems. India has ignored the US pressure and has gone ahead to sign an agreement with Russia for the purchase of S-400 missiles. It is not yet clear whether the USA will sanction India. The challenge before Indian diplomats would be to persuade the USA not to sanction India, citing strategic partnership between the two countries. S-400 issue is symptomatic of the difficulties that India will face in dealing with Russia and the USA at the same time as the distance between the two increases. India would hope that US–Russia relations improve. However, the US establishment is dead against any improvement in US–Russia relations. So India has a problem at hand.

In the years to come, such problems, when India would be caught in the cross-fires between various countries, would become more frequent. On many issues, India has generally maintained a middle course, sometimes a neutral line. However, it may be compelled to shed its ambiguities on many of these issues.

One more example of the conundrum that India would face is in the Middle East. In the next five years, the relationship between Iran and Saudi Arabia may deteriorate further, giving rise to tense situations. The USA and Saudi Arabia, backed by Israel, have teamed up to put an end to Iran's influence in the Middle East. Whether they would succeed is a different matter altogether. They are doing everything possible to undermine Iran's economy. The US sanctions on Iran and any other country which buys oil from Iran are calculated to weaken Iran economically and hoping that the economic difficulties would provoke the Iranian population to rise against the theocratic regime. Saudi Arabia has taken the lead to galvanize other Arab and Islamic countries to pressurize Iran. Iran on its part has reminded these countries that it has massive influence in various parts of the Middle East, on the Shia populations as well as in the Strait of Hormuz through which the Gulf oil passes. The attacks on oil tankers in the Gulf of Oman are symptomatic of the vulnerabilities of the region. The Civil War in Yemen has continued unabated. More such destabilizing events can happen in the next five years. The scenario of military conflict in the Gulf leading to a massive hike in oil prices cannot be ruled out.

India will be deeply affected by the turbulence in the Gulf region. Not only does it source two-thirds of its oil from the Gulf, but also nearly nine million Indian nationals work in the Gulf. Over the years, India has sought to maintain an equipoise between Iran on the one hand and Saudi Arabia on the other. The importance of Iran for India's foreign policy has gone up manifolds as India has started building a port in Chabahar to improve access to Central Asia and Afghanistan. The International North–South Transport Corridor (INSTC) is also important for India as it provides access to Commonwealth of Independent States (CIS) countries and Central Asian countries. None of this will materialize if Iran gets involved in a conflict with Saudi Arabia, the USA or Israel, which in turn could destabilize the entire Gulf region. India should be prepared to deal with the situation in the next five years.

India has revitalized its Look East Policy by upgrading it to the Act East Policy. However, Chinese inroads into the South China Sea have upset the geopolitical situation in the region quite considerably. The ASEAN countries are in no position to deal with a powerful and assertive China. They are also concerned that ASEAN centrality, which is critical for peace and stability, may be jeopardized by the new-found concepts such as Indo-Pacific, which brings confrontation between the USA and China to a head. They are in favour of the East Asia Summit (EAS) being strengthened as a forum to enforce a rule-based architecture in the region. Some of them continue to depend on the USA for their security. US–China clash, economic or otherwise, will impact our same countries badly. They are still not sure about India. They generally feel that India's power projection is still weak. Its economy is still inward-looking. They are concerned that India is blocking the conclusion of the RCEP. They are also alarmed by incidents such as Doklam which brought the militaries of India and China face to face. In the next five years, India will have to deal with ASEAN on their concerns on Indo-Pacific, India–China tensions, etc. They would rather see a strong India, but they don't find that India is taking enough initiatives in the ASEAN region either economically or militarily.

The strengthening of India–Japan strategic partnership is a high point of India's foreign policy of the last few years. Whether India–Japan partnership would develop a strong security dimension still remains to be seen. The quadrilateral ties between India, Japan, the USA and Australia have shown no great initiative in the last five years. The evolution of the Quad will be worth watching. India would need to have a clear vision with respect to the Quad. India is sensitive to Chinese concerns about the Quad and, hence not very forthcoming on its security dimension. How to deal with this ambiguity will be a major concern for the policymakers in the next five years.

Neighbourhood

If global uncertainties present big challenges to India's foreign policy, the neighbourhood is no less important. PM Modi has followed the Neighbourhood First policy which has shown some good results. India's engagement with Nepal, Bhutan, Sri Lanka, the Maldives, Bangladesh, Myanmar and Afghanistan has increased. PM Modi has placed a lot of emphasis on broad connectivity between India and its neighbours. He has also promoted BIMSTEC as a forum for sub-regional cooperation. Many initiatives have been started. However, implementation has been a problem. Indian Ministry of External Affairs would need to improve implementation of connectivity projects: old and new. The relationship with the Maldives, which had deteriorated considerably, has been retrieved. Relationship with Bangladesh, Sri Lanka and Nepal has also shown a positive outlook. The terror attacks in Sri Lanka and the political uncertainty within the country could pose some challenges for India in the next five years. Neighbourhood cannot be taken for granted. India would have to devote more resources, more diplomatic capital and greater engagement with the neighbourhood. In particular, India should develop engagement with younger people, women and other interest groups. India will need to find new models of engagement with the neighbourhood. It is essential that our knowledge about the neighbourhood is enhanced and updated. That would be a challenge in itself, given the inadequacy of resources and a general lack of urgency among the Indian agencies. This needs to be toned up.

Terror-sponsoring Pakistan will continue to pose a problem. Imran Khan has made Kashmir a central issue between India and Pakistan while India has been focusing on cross-border terrorism. The two visions do not match. India has made it clear that talks and terrorism do not go hand in hand. India will have to be better prepared to meet with the challenge of cross-border terrorism from Pakistan. Pakistan itself is undergoing a lot of turbulence as its economy is faltering and Imran Khan is facing domestic unrest. Economic difficulties could lead to internal discontent and open up the various fault lines within Pakistan. Pakistan army is unlikely to relent on its support for cross-border terrorism. India should be prepared to strengthen its own capabilities to deal with the challenge of terrorism, which is not going to disappear. In addition, the Pakistan-based terror groups would use social media and other means to radicalize the Indian youth. The radicalization of the youth is a global trend and taking hold of societies where this virus was not present earlier. India cannot underplay the role of radicalization in fomenting terrorism.

The Modi government in its second term has shown remarkable boldness. Its August 2019 decision to nullify through a presidential order the Article 370 of the Indian Constitution which provided a special status to the border state of Jammu and Kashmir has been perhaps the boldest move in the history of the troubled state. The government has taken a forward and progressive step to mainstream Jammu and Kashmir with India. The status of Jammu and Kashmir has been changed. The state has been converted into two union territories, one of Ladakh without a legislature and one of Jammu and Kashmir with a legislature. These changes will have significant impact on the domestic and foreign policy of the country.

Non-traditional Security

The nature of security challenges is changing. While many people have been warning about the growing salience of non-traditional security issues for many years, the scale and scope of the challenge are becoming visible now. Climate change is turning out to be an existing existential threat. Extreme weather events, connected with the global weather changes, climate changes, are becoming frequent, and India is not an exception. India's food energy and water security challenges are also huge. In most cases, such issues have been dealt with the help of internal domestic capacities. These challenges have a strong foreign policy dimension. The challenges cannot be dealt with without international cooperation. India has already taken some steps such as the setting up of International Solar Alliance to deal with the challenge of renewable energy. However, there has to be a systematic way of factoring in non-traditional security issues in foreign policy in the overall developmental and security strategy of the country. In the next five years, dealing with non-traditional security issues will be a major area of concern for Indian policymakers.

Economy

Economy and technology are essential components of a country's comprehensive national power. The global economic environment is highly uncertain. Although India is a growing economy, its share in global GDP and in global trade is still low. This constricts its influence in global arena. India will have to make strenuous efforts to increase its exports through a variety of measures such as trade facilitation. But even more important would be negotiations with other countries on higher level economic partnerships. There is a pressure from many countries on India to open up its economy, to adopt higher standards of intellectual property rights and to improve the Ease of Doing Business. India will have to make its economy more productive and competitive if it has to survive the global competition. That'll be a major task. Thus, the domestic actions get linked with external actions in a more direct way. Economic diplomacy would be successful only if the domestic economy is strong.

Technology

Technology will be an extremely important factor that will define the shape of the emerging world order. On this front, India would need to step up its game. It must produce critical technologies indigenously; otherwise, it would remain dependent on other countries and big companies for its needs. This would be a vulnerability in India's security metrics. 5G, a critical technology with massive security implications, is an example. India needs to spend more on R&D, innovation and human resources. It should improve science, technology engineering and mathematics education in the country. The need for high-technology skills is growing, and India must take timely steps to ensure that it does not lag behind in this area. India must develop as a technology hub with a lot of indigenous R&D. There is an urgent need to enhance the spending on R&D, which has languished at less than 1 per cent for many years. The quality of research in high-technology areas must also be improved. Universities must become the hub of innovation and creativity. Much more work needs to be done in this area.

Culture

Countries such as India and China are not simply nation states but are also civilizational states. Having had thousands of years of history, they have accumulated experience of dealing with the world. The values developed over millennia do not disappear overnight. The behaviour of countries is affected by the culture that they represent. In India's foreign policy, culture has played some role but not a strategic role. Time has come for India to build its own narrative in global affairs issues of global importance such as environment protection, conflict avoidance, peace and harmony. By and large, India has followed the Western script on these issues. PM Modi, in the last few years, has often drawn attention to India's rich civilization and culture, its scriptures and the values contained in its epics, which can be a rich source of inspiration for dealing with today's problems. India has been diffident in using its culture as a source of ideas. This must change. The UN recognition of 21 June as International Yoga Day has brought a spotlight on India's culture. It is important that this initiative should be continued as Indian culture has a lot to offer to the world, which is written with conflict and misery. The themes of *Vasudhaiva Kutumbakam* and *Sarve Bhavantu Sukhinah* (let there be peace for all) have been highlighted by PM Modi in his several speeches. Indian diplomatic effort to highlight the positive aspects of Indian culture must continue in the next five years. It is necessary to use culture for strategic purposes as many other countries are doing. How to do that needs to be thought through and followed through. A proper strategy needs to be devised for this purpose.

Domestic Priorities

Linking up foreign policy with domestic priorities is equally important. Except for a few Indian states, most others have either a land border or a coast. India's domestic policies are affected by what happens in the neighbourhood and abroad. The concept of the blue economy, which requires a high level of international cooperation, is important for India's prosperity. India also needs to improve ports infrastructure and its connectivity with the outside world. The safety of SLOC is important for India's trade, as mentioned earlier. Non-traditional security issues, including dealing with natural disasters, require international cooperation as was seen in the case of an earthquake in Nepal and cyclonic storms in Bangladesh and Myanmar. A large number of Indians work in the Gulf and other parts of the world. Political and economic developments in these countries also have an impact on Indian diaspora.

Border *management* issues are critical for good relations between India and its neighbours with whom it shares land and maritime boundaries. The unsettled border dispute with China is a major drag on India's security. The efforts to reach a settlement should be stepped up but without compromising India's core interest. At the same time, quality border management must be improved. The central and the border guarding forces, presently deployed in Indian borders, require much improvement. The coordination between the border guarding forces and other forces which are essentially under the control of the state or the central governments must improve. The illegal migration is a major security issue which must be tackled.

Indian states are also making efforts to attract foreign direct investment in order to promote their growth. Thus, the link between the domestic and foreign policy is clear. However, the role of the states in foreign policymaking needs to be factored in. The relationship between the government and the states, which is also improving insofar as foreign policy is concerned, needs to be institutionalized. Certain changes in the decision-making structures to allow greater say to the states in foreign policymaking can be considered.

Internal security issues also have a foreign policy impact. Cross-border terrorism is an example. However, other issues are the lack of an asylum's policy in India, the influx of refugees from conflict zones such as the Rakhine state, the weak security on the course, illegal fishing in Indian waters, etc. The use of social media to create internal disturbances has become all too common. This would be a challenge as well.

Implementation

In order to deal with these challenges, the method of decision-making and implementation will need to be reformed. The Ministry of External Affairs can at best be a facilitator. It has to work in tandem with other important ministries such as the Ministry of Defence, Ministry of Home Affairs, Ministry of Commerce and Ministry of Finance to deliver effective foreign policy. Implementational issues need to be addressed with far more vigour. This will require strengthening many of India's agencies such as the Exim bank and Shipping Corporation of India. The private sector will need to play a greater role in the implementation of foreign policy. Foreign policy should be treated as a whole of government enterprise rather than just being a responsibility of the Ministry of External Affairs.

In the years to come, defence diplomacy must be strengthened appreciably. The Ministry of Defence, the armed forces and the Ministry of External Affairs must work in a coordinated and synergetic fashion to take a military political approach to foreign policy. This will require many changes internally, such as setting up a military–political bureau in the midsection of Ministry of Defence to deal with defence diplomacy. The setting up of a cadre of defence diplomats would also be considered. A separate budget for defence diplomacy could be introduced.

This Book

India's foreign policy is a vast subject. No book can cover all dimensions entirely. Contributors to this book deal with only some of the important aspects of foreign policy.

In Part A, several critical issues having a bearing on India's foreign policy trajectory are discussed. Professor S. D. Muni advocates the need for building an Indian narrative on global and regional issues in an emerging multi-polar world. Such a narrative should reflect India's civilizational character developed over the past 5,000 years.

Ambassador P. S. Raghavan highlights the national security dimension of India's foreign policy, examining the role of the National Security Council and emphasizing that strengthening the institutions of national security must reflect in India's foreign policy.

Increasingly, it is being realized that soft power is as important as the hard power for achieving a country's foreign policy aims. India is blessed with considerable soft power which has not been used properly.

Ambassador Veena Sikri in Chapter 4 provides a detailed analysis of India's soft power projection. She provides suggestions for the strategizing soft power in India's context.

Ambassador Asoke Mukerji point outs that unilateral measures by the major powers pose a grave challenge to multilateralism. India has traditionally contributed to the democratization of multilateralism and must continue to do so.

Technology is already playing an important role in shaping the world. While India has creditable standing in global science and technology ranking, the innovation ecosystem in India remains weak, requiring nourishment. Arvind Gupta explores the status of science and technology and innovation in India and suggests how international cooperation can be leveraged to strengthen India's position.

Dr Vivek Prahladan, in Chapter 7, dives into the history of the concept of strategic autonomy in India's foreign policy. He says that the challenge before India will be how to adjust to the new distribution of power emerging in Eurasia.

Dr Uttam Kumar Sinha highlights the significance of non-traditional issues to India's national security. This is a neglected area. He points out that because non-traditional security issues are interlinked, the role of the state in providing security and development would have to be reframed.

The strong economic foundation is necessary for India to secure its place in the world. Scanning the different aspects of India's economy, Prasenjit Basu emphasizes that the continued vibrancy of the Indian economy is crucial to enhance India's voice in global affairs.

India has deep historical and cultural linkages with the countries in its neighbourhood. Dr Ashok Behuria points out that most countries have bits of India in them as India has bits of them in its entrails. He homes in on the domestic drivers of Indian foreign policy and how they shape the bilateral relations with the neighbours.

Effective foreign policy requires accurate intelligence inputs. Vikram Sood discusses the challenges to the intelligence operation working in tandem with foreign policy goals in the years ahead.

The chapters in Part B deal with India's key relationships. Examining the realities of international power politics and India's relations with the USA, Russia and China, Ambassador Rajiv Sikri feels that it is premature for India to think of itself as a leading power. There are many internal and external constraints which inhabit the rise of India to true great power status.

Ambassador Satish Chandra looks at India's relationship with its neighbours. He laments that despite commonalities between India and its neighbours, India does not know enough about them. China's increasing footprint in India's neighbourhood, the long-festering bilateral issues and serious governance deficit in many of these countries inhibit bilateral ties.

For the past 20 years, India and the USA have been engaged in developing a strategic relationship. Ambassador Arun Singh looks at Indo-US relations in the backdrop of global, economic and political flux. Indo-US ties are multidimensional, complicated and conditioned by regional and global factors. He suggests that India should seek a comprehensive approach to its ties with the USA taking into account the costs and benefits.

Development of a strategic partnership between India and Japan, driven by China's rise, has blossomed in the last few years. Asia's landscape will be impacted by how these relations develop. Ambassador Deepa Wadhwa examines the growth of the special strategic and global partnership between India and Japan. Both countries have felt the need to work together for the bilateral benefit and share strategic objective.

India has an extremely complex and difficult relationship with China. The rise of China has altered India's security environment a great deal. Unsettled boundary question will remain a source of insecurity for India. At the same time, the rise of China, its relationship with India's neighbours, its maritime ambition, all play a role in Sino-Indian relations. Professor Sujit Dutta examines the complexity of Sino-Indian relations.

The importance of Russia for India cannot be overstated despite the fact that India is building new partnerships such as with the USA. Ambassador Ajai Malhotra brings out the importance of the Russia factor in India's foreign and defence policy. He argues that India's bilateral ties with the USA and Russia need not be a zero-sum game. He suggests that at an opportune time, a well-prepared high-level meeting between India and Russia should be held to explore and identify common ground for working together.

India has adopted a proactive approach to Central Asia in the recent years. The relationship is constrained by the lack of connectivity. Ambassador Dinkar Srivastava highlights the importance of Central Asia for India. He brings out that the SCO reflects trends of cooperation and competition between Russia and China. China is using BRI to enhance its influence. SCO does not necessarily expand India's political space in the region. India must enhance connectivity through INSTC and development of the Chabahar Port.

The West Asia region is experiencing rapid change. The security environment there continues to worsen. Ambassador Talmiz Ahmad examines the security dynamic in the gulf in West Asia, which is critical for India's security and prosperity. He proposes that India should play an active role in shaping a diplomatic peace initiative for West Asian security in partnership with China and Russia. This is a novel idea whose time has come.

Analysing India's relationship with South East Asian countries, Ambassador Anil Wadhwa suggests that India should derive tangible economic benefit out of its engagement with the countries to its east. It should also leverage Act East Policy to develop its north-eastern region. In future, India will have to be nimble and quick in completing its ongoing connectivity projects in the east and undertake new projects.

India has a close relationship with European Union (EU). However, EU has been in turmoil due to Brexit, rise of China, rift with Russia and tension in relations with the USA. The refugee crisis has also hit EU badly. It is in this backdrop of uncertainty that India has to restructure in relation with EU and its institutions. Professor Gulshan Sachdeva provides a detailed analysis of the situation in EU and its relation with India. He identifies several areas such as climate change and technology where India and EU can build their partnership not neglecting trade and investment.

India's endorsement of Indo-Pacific will bring major changes in India's foreign policy. Ambassador Yogendra Kumar gives an overview of the importance of the Indian Ocean for India. He feels that there is much work ahead for India to shape a supportive maritime system in the Indian Ocean for securing peace stability and condition for its rapid socio-economic growth.

In the recent years, India has begun to focus on establishing multifarious partnerships with African countries. In the future, Africa will play a greater role in India's security and development. Ambassador Anil Trigunayat, in his chapter on Africa (Chapter 23), looks at India–Africa relations and warns that India can ill afford to let the African opportunities slip by.

Latin America is a relatively untapped region as far as India is concerned. Ambassador R. Viswanathan says that some Indians might think Latin America is less important for India because of the distance. He points out that India exports more to some Latin American countries than to neighbouring countries or traditional trade partners. He makes a strong case for India to pursue trade agreements with Mexico, Colombia and Peru.

The objective of the chapters is to give an advanced analysis of the different dimensions of India's foreign policy and also highlight the difficulties and challenges that lie ahead. Most chapters provide some kind of guidance on how these challenges can be met.

PART A

Drivers and Trends

Indian Narrative in Emerging Multi-polar World
Some Reflections

S. D. Muni

Westernized International Relations Studies

Any search for an Indian narrative in its foreign policy must start with the understanding of perspectives and elementary resources of foreign policy and international relations (IR) studies in India. As in other developing countries and the world as a whole, India and Indians for nearly the past hundred years have been studying IR in European- and Western-dominated academic framework. A close look at the syllabi on IR in the premier as well as state universities will focus on European renaissance, colonial and imperial orders, First and Second World Wars, post-Second World War developments, the Cold War and its end, etc. Contemporary IR theories and concepts are all studied as Western products, with exceptions here and there. The concept of power, which is so critical to the study of IR, is looked as a celebrated Western intellectual product seldom going beyond Machiavelli, Metternich or Morgenthau. Further, the concepts of power, understood largely in its coercive thrust, are celebrated as the principle and core concept of realism as compared to those of peace, coexistence and harmony in mutual engagements among nations.

This is both understandable and inevitable for two reasons. One is that the world politics has been dominated by the West and it is only fair to study all the landmarks and consequences of that dominance. But then, the world politics has also encountered various resistance and freedom movements against colonial and imperial rules, which figure in the curricula only in a scattered form and mostly taught without adequate depth and involvement. Second, there is a certain legitimacy dynamics of the sociology of knowledge. Knowledge gets generated and created as well as legitimized when endorsed and backed by the dominant system, dominant in crudely economic and political sense. One can recall the fact of higher value attached to research and academic publications of the West as compared to those in the developing world. At some stage or the other, we have all taken pride in appearing in such publications to establish our professional merit.

Even without questioning the IR intellectual traditions of nearly the past 300 years, say, up to the 17th or 18th century, a question naturally arises: If the world existed at all before the period of Western dominance? Was there anything which can be called as having a semblance of what we understand today as IR, before the Christ was born and Christianity, or for that matter Islam, was evolving as a civilizational system? And if so, what was the nature of that world order or global system as one may like to characterize it. The world then was dominated by the civilizational systems, that is, of Hinduism and Buddhism from Indian, Confucianism from Chinese, of Egyptian, Greek and Roman Empires. Culture and commerce flourished. Civilizations interacted and engaged with each other. Ideas regarding patterns of life, governance, art and architecture were exchanged and imbibed. Politics and diplomacy flowed through matrimonial alliances, and theories and concepts travelled through pilgrims and scholars. There were conflicts and contestations but no major war involving a large number of players. Not many serious attempts have been made to explore and define the characteristics and contours of the world as it then—before the rise of Europe—existed.

From the 1st century to the 17th century, the global economy and trade flows were dominated by India and China. Both these Asian giants put together accounted for more than 50 per cent of the global wealth. A chart prepared by Michael Cambalest, JP Morgan's chairman of marketing and investment strategy, shows that while India maintained a lead up to 1600 AD, China then took over until 1820 AD, when their collective primacy remained in place.[1] Both the countries then had extensive influence in Asia through their civilizational and commercial ties. China adopted Buddhism from India and then from 7th century onwards spread it to other Asian countries. Chinese used to refer to India as 'guru' (a teacher and philosopher country, the country of Shakya Muni, Buddha). It may be kept in mind that when India and China dominated the world economy together, they had no major competition or conflict between them. French and Dutch historians and their Indian students used to describe the South East Asian countries as 'Indianized states' or being part of 'Greater India' because of the impact India had on these countries. Both the Indian and the South East Asian civilizations deeply 'embraced' each other. They learned from each other and enriched each other.[2] India's Nalanda and Taxila universities were the centres of learning and enlightenment in Asia. Through spice trade, India also helped Islam to strike roots in South East Asian countries from the 11th century onwards. It may not be an exaggeration to say that by owning Islam, India contributed to its core concept through two of the theological schools, namely Deobandi and Barelvi, and reinforced its softer 'Sufi' content. Even today, it can be easily discerned that in India and its eastern extended neighbourhood, Islam is far more moderate in comparison to its radical Wahhabi version which is the source of much trouble in the world.

It is unfortunate that the IR of that period, of Asian dominance, is not in our course contents these days. It has not even been properly explored and systematically organized. Wonder if the present and future generations of IR scholars in India and Asia would have resources and inclination to map out the parameters of IR at that time. But if and when that is done, new insights into the Indian narrative on its global engagements as well as the dynamics of the then prevailing Asian order may emerge.

---

[1] Derek Thompson, 'The Economic History of Last 2,000 Years in Little Graph', *The Atlantic* (2012, 19 June). Available at https://www.theatlantic.com/business/archive/2012/06/the-economic-history-of-the-last-2–000-years-in-1-little-graph/258676/ (accessed on 20 November 2019).
[2] Amitav Acharya, *Civilisations in Embrace: The Spread of Ideas and the Transformation of Power, India and Southeast Asia in the Classical Age* (Heng Mui Keng Terrace: Institute of Southeast Asian Studies, 2013).
S. D. Muni and Rahul Mishra, *India's Eastward Engagement: From Antiquity to Act East Policy* (Thousand Oaks, CA: SAGE Publications, 2019, Chapter 1).

In Search of Indian Narrative

The dominance of the Western IR approach is being challenged now seriously and strongly. Recall Amitav Acharya's 2014 presidential address at the International Studies Association's annual meeting in which he stressed the need of broadening the IR by making it 'Global IR'. This could be done according to him by incorporating various national and regional studies and approaches all over the world. In some ways, what Acharya said was the revival of attempts made as early as the end of the 19th century and beginning of the 20th century to inject Indian narrative in the Westernized IR approach. In 1893, Swami Vivekananda's discourse on Hinduism at the Parliament of the World's Religions in Chicago, USA, conveyed the Indian narrative of peace and coexistence. In his address to the Americans as 'Brothers and Sisters', and message to the world that India has stood for 'tolerance and universal acceptance', the Indian concept of *Vasudhaiv Kutumbkam* (world–universe, as a family) was most forcefully introduced to the global audience.[3]

Then at the academic level, attempt to project an Indian narrative on IR could be seen in the writings of Benoy Kumar Sarkar, who in his article in *The American Political Science Review* in 1919 sought to construct the 'Hindu Theory of International Relations'. By referring to Kautilya's *Kamandakiya Nitisara, Shukra Niti, Athrava Ved*, etc., he explained how Hindus were also practising the principles of sovereignty, balance of power and strong state.[4] He was an ardent aggressive proponent of Hindu thought and culture, and an assertive nationalist. Earlier, in 1916, he also wrote *Chinese Religion through Hindu Eyes* and many other books where even authoritarian governance was endorsed. There were many historians and social scientists such as M. N. Chatterjee, V. S. Ram, P. N. Masaldan, B. M. Sharma and Dev Raj who had an engaging and competitive discourse from Indian perspective on the concepts and assessments of European IR. For instance, Ram and Masaldan questioned the 'civilizing mission' of the European colonial powers and argued that 'looking at the problem of peace from a purely

---

[3] *Business Standard*, 'Full Text of Swami Vivekananda's Chicago Speech of 1893' (2017, 11 September). Available at https://www.business-standard.com/article/current-affairs/full-text-of-swami-vivekananda-s-chicago-speech-of-1893-117091101404_1.html (accessed on 20 November 2019).

[4] Benoy Kumar Sarkar, 'Hindi Theory of International Relations: The Doctrine of Mandala (Sphere of Influence)', *The American Political Science Review* 13 (1919): 339–415. Available at http://www.jstor.org/stable/10.2307/1945958 (accessed on 20 November 2019).

European angle obscured the basic fact that war and conflict resulted from imperial urges'. In their writings and discourse, the 'European notions of world order' were 'provincialized'.[5] Commenting on the contributions of these scholars, a young analyst has aptly said:

> These histories reveal that the prevention of great power war did not, and does not, have a monopoly over the definition of the discipline. International thought was not the privilege of Europe and North America. Rather, it emerged in multiple locations as part of a global dialogue forged amidst the interests and experiences of empire, anti-imperial resistance, nationalist movements, and global intellectual networks. Indian scholars played an active role in this re-energised attempt to understand and document the 'international', presenting a stretched notion of disciplinary thought, one that incorporated emancipatory themes of race, anti-imperialism, transnational solidarity, and a re-imagined vision of post-imperial world order.[6]

There was also another group of Indian historians who explored the civilizational thrust of India's external engagements, particularly with the South East Asian countries and the Asia-Pacific region. They included scholars such as U. N. Ghoshal, R. C. Majumdar, O. C. Ganguli, Suniti Kumar Chatterji, Nilkanta Sastri and Kalidas Nag. This group was also associated with Dr Rabindranath Tagore. They brought to the light the strong civilizational connect between India and the Pacific and described the South East Asian countries as part of 'greater India', at least in the sense of cultural and civilizational links.[7] The underlying message of their historical explorations and studies was that India was a civilized country and did not believe in engagements involving conflicts and domination.

As it evolved and unfolded itself, India's struggle for Independence strongly reflected dimensions of Indian narrative in responding to the issues of then prevailing world order and non-colonial India's foreign policy. Strong opposition to colonialism, imperialism and racial discrimination, military alliances and wars were the key features of this narrative. Indian narrative was also reflected on some of the critical aspects of foreign policy where the independence struggle had an opinion different from that of the British India, such as the use of

---

[5] As quoted in Martin J. Bayly, 'The Forgotten History of India's International Relations' (ORF Issue Brief No. 210, 2017, November).

[6] Ibid.

[7] Kwa Chong Guan, ed., 'Early Southeast Asia Viewed from India: An Anthology of Articles', *Journal of the Greater India Society* (2013).

British troops in China, Persia and Mesopotamia, annexation of upper Burma and Khilafat Movement.[8] Indian Political Science Association (IPSA) established in 1938 provided an intellectual platform for scholarly articulation of foreign policy. Many illustrious figures such as Tej Bahadur Sapru, A. Appadorai and H. N. Kunzru were members of IPSA active on the foreign policy issues. There was also an attempt to institutionalize Indian foreign policy narrative with the formation of the Indian Council of World Affairs (ICWA). P. N. Sapru and H. N. Kunzru took the lead as they were frustrated with the British government controlled and Chatham House established Indian Institute of International Affairs (IIIA). Sir Tej Bahadur Sapru was appointed as the first president of the ICWA.[9] He was subsequently assisted by A. Appadorai as the secretary general of the ICWA. As an unofficial, non-political and academic organization, the ICWA used to organize seminars, discussions and international conferences to formulate and propagate public views on India's foreign policy. Nehru was supportive of the ICWA and made use of it in many ways both for his personal studies and for the benefit of the government. It also hosted India's major international conference such as the Asian Relations Conference in 1947 and International Conference on Indonesia in 1949, where independent India's views on critical global and Asian issues were articulated for concrete policy actions. Though officially supported by Nehru and the Indian government, the ICWA failed to establish Asian Relations Organisation. Nehru's support facilitated the ICWA's affiliation as observer at the important international conferences such as that of the Bretton Woods and Dumbarton Oaks where post-war global institutions such as the IMF, the World Bank and the UN Security Council were charted out. In 1955, the ICWA established Indian School of International Studies (ISIS) as an institution for scholarly research and studies on India's foreign policy. This emerged as the premier centre for international studies in India and is presently part of Jawaharlal Nehru University as the School of International Studies (SIS).

India's policy of non-alignment, though being denigrated in the present context, epitomized all the essential ingredients of Indian narrative in foreign policy, such as *Vasudhaiv Kutumbkam* and Peaceful Coexistence (*Pancasila* of Buddhist tenants). Reflecting the ethos and ideological thrust of India's struggle for independence, non-alignment disapproved of military alliances and war as a solution of world

---

[8] Bimal Prasad, *Origins of India's Foreign Policy* (1960).

[9] Vineet Thakur and Alexander E. Davis, 'A Communal Affair Over international Affairs: The Arrival of IR in Late Colonial India', *South Asia: A Journal of South Asian Affairs* 40, no. 4 (2017): 689–705.

problems. It provided a unique answer to the traditional balance of power approach by seeking to aggregate the power of the powerless in world affairs. It helped India maintain its strategic autonomy and make its mark in peacekeeping role (such as in Korea and Indo-China) and in creating an atmosphere of peace in the world at a time when the great powers displayed intensive rivalry and were following the pursuit of arms build-up.[10] Nehru, who was the principle propagator of non-alignment and India's foreign policy options in the pre- as well as post-Independence periods, had his thoughts rooted deeply into India's civilizational evolution and culture. His schooling in the European guild socialism and Western liberalism happily synthesized with the ideological thrust of India's composite culture. This is clearly evident from his pre-Independence writings such as *The Discovery of India* and the *Glimpses of World History* as well as from anti-colonial, anti-imperial, anti-racial and Asia-oriented foreign policy. He played a critical role in helping India's Asian neighbours fight for their independence and strive for democratic polities.[11] It may be interesting to recall that India's first International Buddhist Conference was organized in 1952 under Nehru's leadership.

This phase of projecting the Indian narrative at the Asian and global theatres, however, could not be consolidated as it did not last for long. There were many factors accounting for this failure. The strategic constraints imposed by India's partition and the Cold War, precipitating three wars of Kashmir in 1947–1948 and 1965 with Pakistan, and Himalayan border in 1962 with China, seriously dented the ideological élan of the Indian narrative. That led Nehru's successors such as Mrs Indira Gandhi to resort to greater pragmatism and use of power as became evident in the 1971 war with Pakistan that resulted in the creation of Bangladesh.[12] Mrs Gandhi and her successor son Rajiv Gandhi had proactive foreign policies and concentrated more on India's concrete and immediate interests than on the issues of world order. The integration of Sikkim in 1975, and interventions in Sri Lanka (1987–1990) and the Maldives (1988) were stark evidence of this. That the flavours and styles of Nehru's successors' policies were different

---

[10] K. P. Misra, 'Towards Understanding Non-alignment', *International Studies* 20, no. 1–2 (1981).

B. R. Nanda, ed., *India's Foreign Policy: Nehru Years* (New Delhi: Vikas Publishing House Pvt. Ltd, 1983).

[11] S. Gopal, *The Mind of Jawaharlal Nehru* (London: Orient and Longman, 1980).

[12] Surjit Mansingh, *India's Search for Power: Indira Gandhi's Foreign Policy, 1966–1982* (Thousand Oaks, CA: SAGE Publications, 1984).

from that of Nehru's should not lead us to assume that the former deviated from the core of Indian narrative. There is significant place of the use of force and war, though as the last resort, in India's 5,000 years of living experience. Refusal to surrender to unjust pressures, use of coercive instruments of state policy (*Dand* and *Bhed* in Kautilya's *Arthashastra*) and carry out *Dharma Yuddh* (righteous war), if and when required, are inherent parts of Indian narrative.

The intellectual discourse in India on IR and foreign policy also started changing after Nehru. Area studies, a concept flowing from the Cold War, spread and became an essential part of Indian IR studies. Those trained in Western academic traditions started debunking non-alignment describing Nehru as a woolly idealist. IR theories of the Western world started dominating IR teaching and research in India. Even some of the serious scholars of non-alignment such as A. P. Rana started casting it into the framework of 'decision-making' and behavioural paradigms of political science discourse.[13] During this period, foreign policy studies became too contemporary, bereft of its historical underpinnings. Writings of Nehru and references to India's Independence struggle became far and fewer, not to mention the civilizational aspects of Indian narrative. The Western IR with its realism, liberalism, constructivism, its linkage politics, decision-making behaviour and state characteristics became the principal poles to organize academic discourse. A band of enthusiastic young scholars joined hands with their Western mentors to declare that India lacked proper strategic culture and had no grand foreign policy strategy.[14]

The unfortunate aspects of this argument have been that India's strategic culture was being measured against the parameters of Western strategic benchmarks, and also that the contentions were not empirically substantiated. India's strategic culture must be assessed by critically examining the scriptures, political and historical mythologies and the oral traditions of narration that have often been stronger in India than its written texts. It must also be assessed by studying the rise and fall of Indian empires like those of the Guptas, Mauryas, Kanishkas, Cholas, Mughals, etc.; and studying the structures of defences created and wars fought, won and lost by the Mughals, Marathas, Rajputs, Sikhs, etc. How did India succeed in

---

[13] A. P. Rana, *Imperatives of Non-alignment: A Conceptual Study of India's Foreign Policy Strategy in the Nehru Period* (Noida: Macmillan, 1976).

[14] George Tanham, *Indian Strategic Thought: An Interpretive Essay* (Santa Monica, CA: RAND Corporation, 1992).
Kanti P. Bajpai and Amitabh Mattoo, eds., *Securing India: Strategic Thought and Practice* (New Delhi: Manohar Publishers and Distributors, 1996).

winning the Bangladesh War against the combined front of Pakistan, the USA and China? How could India employ democratic forces and institutions in smoothly achieving the integration of Sikkim? Strategic culture is not indicated only by winning wars, holding territories and deterring adversaries. Mutual accommodation and adjustments, even tactical surrenders and compromises, are also the parts of strategic grammar. Some of the arguments of 'India has no strategic culture' are now being countered by the study of Kautilya.[15]

The Emerging Multi-polar World Order and Indian Narrative

The prevailing post-Cold War world order is in a flux. There is general consensus on some of the key characteristics of this flux. To begin with, it is the US lack of will, not lack of capabilities, to sustain and reinforce the liberal global order that has ensured stability and broad peace since the end of the Second World War. This is evident in various ways. The USA has withdrawn from the Paris Climate Change commitment and also from the Nuclear arms control agreements with Russia. The US President Trump's position on European defence and security has pushed NATO in a crisis of confidence where the European leaders are debating to create their own defence mechanisms.[16] Reliability of the USA in the perception of the regional (Indo-Pacific) players such as Japan, Korea, Australia and India as a security guarantor has become all the more questionable despite the US repeated reassertions on its Asian rebalance strategy against the rising and assertive China.

China's rise and assertion is the result of global power shift from the West to the East both economically and militarily. Asian economies are growing faster and the Asian countries are acquiring greater security capabilities. China's aggressive stance on South China Sea maritime/territorial disputes has been widely resented in the Indo-Pacific region, and China's fast-growing naval capabilities and outreach, with deterrence capabilities even against the USA, in the Indian Ocean are invoking awe and anxiety among the affected countries. Its economic outreach through the Belt and Road Initiative and Asian Infrastructure Investment Bank (AIIB) is widely welcomed but no country in the

---

[15] Col. Gautam had initiated such a project to study Kautilya/Chanakya for its strategic relevance in contemporary times.

[16] Fabrice Pothier, *A European Army: Can the Dream Become a Reality* (London: IISS, 2019, 7 January). Available at https://www.iiss.org/blogs/analysis/2019/01/macron-european-army-reality (accessed on 20 November 2019).

region is prepared to endorse China's ambitions for hegemony and dominance. Russia which otherwise seems to be closer to China strategically in the region is also against Chinese hegemony and dominance. Regional major players such as India, Japan, Korea, Australia and Indonesia are working for a multi-polar Asia and a multi-polar world order.

Both globalization and multilateralism are under stress.[17] President Trump's 'America First' and United Kingdom's Brexit have deepened uncertainty in the global economic order. Trans-Pacific Partnership (TPP) agreement was shelved under US insistence, and smaller economic organizations such as SAARC have also become inactive under Pakistan's reluctance to engage with India creatively. Another important regional grouping Regional Comprehensive Economic Partnership (RCEP) is still struggling to be borne. Economic and identity-based assertive nationalism is posing serious challenges to multilateral institutions and engagements. Countries are finding bilateral geopolitical engagements more comfortable and effective in the pursuance of their respective national interests. The USA is happy dealing with North Korea on the nuclear issue. India, China and Japan have initiated bilateral channels to address their critical issues of concerns vis-à-vis each other.

In this world under flux, India has openly and boldly expressed its aspirations to be a leading, 'not only balancing', power. Soon after assuming the office of Foreign Secretary, Dr S. Jaishankar said in his Fullerton Lecture delivered at the International Institute for Strategic Studies (IISS London) Chapter in Singapore on 20 July 2015:

> Insofar as larger international politics is concerned, India welcomes the growing reality of a multi-polar world, as it does, of a multi-polar Asia. We, therefore, want to build our bilateral relationships with all major players, confident that progress in one account opens up possibilities in others. Also of note is the more regional approach to engagement, reflected in Prime Minister's recent visits to the Indian Ocean, Northeast Asia and Central Asia.... The transition in India is an expression of greater self-confidence. Its foreign policy dimension is to *aspire to be a leading power, rather than just a balancing power.* Consequently, there is also a willingness to shoulder greater global responsibilities. This was demonstrated recently in humanitarian

---

[17] Robert C. Feenstra and Alan M. Taylor, *Globalisation in an Age of Crisis: Multilateral Economic Cooperation in the Twenty-First Century* (Chicago, IL: University of Chicago Press, 2014).

assistance and disaster relief operations in Yemen and Nepal. It is also reflected in our role in peace-keeping and in keeping the maritime commons safe and secure ...

It is also underlined in this statement that India's preference in the emerging world is for a multi-polar order, underwritten by regional consolidation. What kind of Indian narrative will serve the requirements of such a world order? Dwelling on this aspect, Prime Minister Modi defined India's vision in the emerging world order as:

> All of this is possible, if we do not return to the age of great power rivalries I have said this before: Asia of rivalry will hold us all back. Asia of cooperation will shape this century. So, each nation must ask itself: Are its choices building a more united world, or forcing new divisions? It is a responsibility that both existing and rising powers have. Competition is normal. But, contests must not turn into conflict; differences must not be allowed to become disputes. Distinguished members of the audience, it is normal to have partnerships on the basis of shared values and interests. India, too, has many in the region and beyond...

> In conclusion, let me say this again: India's own engagement in the Indo-Pacific Region—from the shores of Africa to that of the Americas—will be inclusive. We are inheritors of Vedanta philosophy that believes in essential oneness of all, and celebrates unity in diversity एकमसत्यम, विप्रा:बहुदावदंति (Truth is one, the learned speak of it in many ways). That is the foundation of our civilizational ethos—of pluralism, coexistence, openness and dialogue. The ideals of democracy that define us as a nation also shape the way we engage the world...

> We will promote a democratic and rules-based international order, in which all nations, small and large, thrive as equal and sovereign we will work with others to keep our seas, space and airways free and open; our nations secure from terrorism; and our cyberspace free from disruption and conflict. We will keep our economy open and our engagement transparent. We will share our resources, markets and prosperity with our friends and partners. We will seek a sustainable future for our planet ...

> This is how we wish ourselves and our partners to proceed in this vast region and beyond. The ancient wisdom of the region is our common heritage. Lord Buddha's message of peace and compassion has connected us all. Together, we have contributed much to human civilization. And, we have been through the devastation of war and the hope of peace. We have seen the limits of power. And, we have seen the fruits of cooperation.

Prime Minister Modi's statement helps us to flag some of the critical components of the relevant Indian narrative. To begin with, India has to project its civilizational character in a definitive sense. This civilizational character has been shaped and enriched by diverse religious and cultural streams and varied historical experiences. Hindu–Buddhist contribution has been the biggest and strongest in this respect. Modi's statement refers to *Vedanta* philosophy of the Hindu tradition. Buddhism's non-violence and peace as core components further reinforce it. In general, Modi government's foreign policy has front-loaded its Hindu–Buddhist traditions for the projection of its soft power. There are also the components of non-religious culture such as yoga and Bollywood as parts of the Indian soft power package.

But India also is the birthplace of other religious and cultural streams such as Sikhism and Jainism. Islam came to India as an aggressor but got submerged into India under the Mughal Empire. In the course of its absorption in India, it was also reformed and, to some extent, redefined. Akbar's Din-e-Ilahi and Dara Shikoh's *Commingling of Two Oceans: Majma-ul-Bahrain* underlined the concept of unity in diversity in the midst of different religions and cultures flourishing in India. As already mentioned earlier, the *Deobandi* and the *Barelvi* schools as well as the streak of *Sufism* were India's distinct contributions to Islam that made it different from the Wahhabi–Salafi stream. India, thus, owned Islam and Islam was, in turn, Indianized. Therefore, the Indian state that has to be projected on the global stage is one of composite culture and a synthesized civilization. Besides being objective, the projection of composite, and not sectarian or truncated, culture is prudent in India's civilizational profile as there are Islamic countries in India's immediate and extended neighbourhood. The British ruled India for nearly 250 years and made it a colonial and imperial power. They made India look like an economically extractive and militarily aggressive and expansionist state to its Asian neighbours. But this experience has to be filtered out when reconstructing Indian heritage for engaging with the emerging world. The British came to rule and extract India. They left as soon as it became difficult for them to continue with their dominance. They did not become a part of India. Britain always remained their homeland.

Vasudhaiv Kutumbkam is one of the core Vedanta Sutra that defines India's approach to the world in a nutshell as already noted. This means that the world should be treated as a family, as belonging to one fraternity. The underlining principle of that is peaceful coexistence and mutual cooperation. Buddhist tenants of *Pancasila* (five principles) reinforce the axiom of peaceful coexistence. Nehru had made it a part of his approach to his Asian neighbours, especially China. This along with peace and non-violence of Jainism and the brotherhood notions of Islam and Sikhism also underlined the whole approach of non-alignment, disarmament and negotiated approach to conflict resolution. It was also under Nehru that India first convened the international conference of Buddhism to project India's civilizational character through its foreign policy. The core elements of this approach were reiterated in Modi's Shangri-La address in Singapore in June 2018. This approach encompasses building cooperation for co-prosperity, again like the concept of Security and Growth for All in the Region (SAGAR) coined by Modi. It lays down emphasis on promotion of trade, investments and cooperation in technological and diverse fields.

Emphasizing peaceful coexistence does not mean that the use of force and war has had no place in Indian narrative. The concept of *Dharma Yuddh*, both in its goals and conduct, has been a key component of Indian tradition. Ramayana and Mahabharata are seen as the epitomes of *Dharma Yuddh*. Sikhism celebrates righteous wars in the dictum of *Jo Lade Deenke Hait Veera Sohi* (the brave is the one who fights for the poor and the helpless). Ashoka had waged a brutal war against Kalinga, but that was not a righteous war, it was a war of annexation and dominance, of revenge and retribution. Ashoka himself detested the outcome of this war and sought solace in Buddhism. Such wars cannot be the part of Indian heritage to be projected. Fitting with this, India has a 'no first use' commitment in its Nuclear Doctrine. In the contemporary periods, India's interventions in helping Bangladesh emerge as a sovereign independent nation, as well as its interventions in Sri Lanka, both prior to and after the 1987 bilateral agreement, have been the examples of *Dharma Yuddh*. India's participation in UN-led peacekeeping also comes into the same category. So also the use of force in defence of one's territory, self-respect and long cherished values. Preparing for and acquiring capabilities to wage a *Dharma Yuddh*, defend oneself and credibly deter adversaries and enemies, both in the conventional and nuclear fields, should therefore be the essential parts of Indian narrative.

It can be summed up in the light of foregoing discussion that any credible Indian narrative for foreign policy in the emerging world order should emerge from a serious exploration of the evolution of Indian state through the past more than 5,000 years of civilizational layers. This is a task which is crying itself loudly to be undertaken by committed scholars and historians.

National Security Determinants of Foreign Policy

P. S. Raghavan

The foreign policy of a country is geared to further its national objectives. At a fundamental level, India's national objectives can be defined as achieving economic growth with equitable development, aiming to become a developed country in the shortest possible time frame. While this is a national effort, driven largely by domestic policies and actions, it may be facilitated or impeded by external influences. It is quite obvious as well that a secure domestic and external environment facilitates growth and development.

India's foreign policy, therefore, works to sustain a network of external relationships that promotes the best security environment for the country and maximizes the government's room for manoeuvre to pursue policies that, in its judgement, would put the country on the fastest path towards its national objectives.

A cardinal objective of national security management is a security equilibrium in the country's neighbourhood, characterized by mutual trust and cooperation. Cooperation is required to tackle inflows of arms, drugs and fake currencies across our borders, and to discourage neighbours from sheltering and arming insurgents who operate in our bordering states. From a broader perspective, a secure and stable neighbourhood enables an aspiring global power to interact with greater confidence with other major powers.

There are some complex realities in India's relations with its neighbours. As the largest country in South Asia by size, and economic and military strength, it has to deal with neighbours' 'small neighbour syndrome': an apprehension of abridgement of their sovereignty by political domination, economic influence or cultural affinities of the larger neighbour. With another big and strong country, China, in the neighbourhood, some of India's neighbours have tried to play one off against the other, to maximize their room for manoeuvre. Some have also tried to increase their leverage with India by giving refuge and assistance to Indian insurgents.

Bangladeshi politics is polarized between secular and radical forces, with the latter tending to seek inspiration from Pakistan. India-related issues, including sharing of river waters and transit facilities between East and Northeast India, have often got caught up in domestic Bangladesh politics. In Nepal, the struggle for identity and political representation of the Madhesi population has inevitably drawn in Indian political circles, causing other Nepalese elements to seek Chinese help to counter India's influence. Similarly, the Sri Lankan Tamils' agitation for more equitable representation in the country's polity finds sympathy in Tamil Nadu where a large number of Sri Lankan Tamil separatists have taken refuge. This has led some political elements in Sri Lanka to strengthen links with Pakistan and China.

These trends need to be countered by policies that promote mutually beneficial cooperation, address insecurities and dampen the motivation for blackmail vis-à-vis the other big neighbour. This also means willingness to make non-reciprocal concessions, provided core political, economic and security interests are protected.

Continuing tensions with Pakistan, exacerbated by cross-border incursions and Pakistan's arming and training groups for terrorist acts in India, are a perennial security threat, requiring imaginative foreign policy responses. Successive Indian governments have tried varying blends of dialogue with Pakistani governments and military responses to cross-border terrorism. Public sentiment, articulated in the media and by political forces, demands harsh responses to Pakistan-sponsored terrorism. At the same time, there is constant pressure from the USA and other Western countries for a dialogue to defuse tensions. The government has to formulate a Pakistan policy that it considers best suited for India's national security interests, steering carefully between domestic public expectations and foreign exhortations.

In the recent decades, Afghanistan (whose border with India is in Pakistan-occupied Kashmir) has become an arena of India–Pakistan rivalry. In Pakistan's calculus, Afghanistan provides it strategic depth vis-à-vis India. In the 1990s, its influence in the country gave it a wider territory for arming and housing anti-India terrorist elements. An active Indian presence in Afghanistan denies this opportunity to Pakistan. Hence, since the early 2000s, India has strengthened its partnership with Afghanistan, supporting its government's anti-terrorist and economic reconstruction efforts. This has predictably led Pakistan to sponsor terrorist attacks on Indian personnel and interests in Afghanistan.

Urging the USA, Europe, Russia and China to exert and sustain pressure on Pakistan to restrain its support for terrorism in India and Afghanistan is an important part of India's foreign policy towards these countries. This is distinct from an invitation to mediate, which India has strenuously opposed.

The one important neighbour of India, which is also one of the world's major powers, is China. Engaging with China will remain a critical foreign policy and national security challenge for India over decades. The 4,000+ km India–China border is still un-demarcated and there are a number of disputed pockets along the border, including in Jammu & Kashmir and areas around the India–Nepal–China and India–Bhutan–China tri-junctions. The claim to Arunachal Pradesh, that China has started pressing more vigorously over the past decade or so, is another major irritant.

Since the 1950s, China has extended political and military support to Pakistan, including assistance to its nuclear and missile programmes. In the recent years, it has strengthened its economic and military cooperation with other South Asian countries—Bangladesh, Nepal, Sri Lanka and the Maldives—trying to undermine India's influence with them. China sees India as a long-term strategic rival. There is a gap between India and China today, in economic and military strength. Analysts believe that China seeks to slow the narrowing of this gap and to keep India bogged down in its South Asian neighbourhood, so as to inhibit its global outreach. This analysis is validated by the US$62 billion China–Pakistan Economic Corridor, which will strengthen China's political and economic influence in Pakistan, besides establishing Chinese naval presence off India's West Coast.

At the same time, China is India's largest trade partner and a significant investor. It is a major supplier to India of pharmaceutical raw materials, solar panels, photovoltaic cells and smartphones. It has a near-monopoly over rare earth manufactures, which go into products from smartphones to cruise missiles. Its GDP is about 5 times that of India, its foreign exchange reserves about 10 times. It is a permanent member of the UN Security Council and a nuclear-weapon state.

India's China policy has to factor in both the interdependence and the asymmetry. This means cooperating with China on areas where it is of mutual benefit, even while firmly standing up for its core interests, as it did during the nearly two-month long India–China military stand-off in 2017 in the Doklam plateau near the India–Bhutan–China tri-junction.

Meanwhile, India needs to work quietly, but purposefully, to strengthen its position vis-à-vis China—building domestic economic and military strength, securing its influence with neighbours, pursuing convergences with Russia and the USA, and making common cause with other countries in China's neighbourhood, which have also been at the receiving end of China's assertiveness. China has asserted its territorial claims in the South China Sea by occupying claimed islands, changing facts on the ground, militarizing the area and ignoring the 2016 judgement of the Permanent Court of Arbitration, which did not accept the basis for China's claims.

India's Indo-Pacific strategy is shaped by these perspectives. India has important economic and security interests in the Indo-Pacific space—from the eastern shores of Africa to the Western shores of the USA. The share of foreign trade in India's GDP is over 40 per cent, and over 90 per cent of this trade is through the Indian Ocean, including most of its energy supplies. Protection of Indian Ocean sea lanes is, therefore, in India's vital economic interest. Terrorism, piracy, smuggling, human trafficking, territorial disputes and claims to global commons threaten India's security and strategic interests. These interests dictate that India should work against political, economic and military domination of this region by any country.

Most Western analysts and policymakers, as well as those in South East and East Asia, use the expression Indo-Pacific for the area from the east coast of India to the US Pacific Coast. The following paragraphs use that definition. The security and strategic issues in the Western Indo-Pacific are very different from those in the eastern part and require different approaches from an Indian perspective. This is touched upon in a subsequent section.

The recent resurrection of the India–US–Japan 'MALABAR' naval exercises in the Indian Ocean and of the India–US–Japan–Australia Quadrilateral Security Dialogue (the Quad) signalled the support of their participants for an inclusive security architecture in the Indo-Pacific. These initiatives need sustained follow-up and wider regional support to have an impact on the ground. There is also a growing realization that fundamental changes are required in the current security architecture, which dates back to the Cold War. The military rise of China and the Russia–China strategic partnership challenge the credibility of the US security umbrella, which was originally intended to counter a Soviet threat. Regional powers have to develop credible military capability, since the present extreme asymmetry in military strength in the region is not conducive to a security equilibrium. The thrust to strengthen Indian naval presence in the Indian Ocean should be seen in this context.

In addition to these initiatives, India's strategy includes building bilateral and plurilateral linkages to promote convergence of political approaches. Bilateral partnerships with Vietnam, Indonesia, Japan, Korea, Australia and others have strengthened. India has taken the initiative to impart fresh momentum to the Bay of Bengal Initiative for Multi-Sectoral Technical and Economic Cooperation (BIMSTEC) for enhancing regional connectivity and maritime security in this important enclave of the Indian Ocean. BIMSTEC includes India, Nepal, Bhutan, Bangladesh, Myanmar, Thailand and Sri Lanka. A dialogue of BIMSTEC National Security Advisors (NSAs) has been initiated to emphasize the importance of the security dimension of this partnership.

The resurgence of India–US relations in the 2000s reflected mutual economic and strategic interests. India's expanding market, its huge defence imports and its ambitious nuclear power expansion plans attracted US interest. From a broader strategic perspective, the USA recognized the increasing threat from China to its superpower dominance and saw a rising, democratic India as a useful strategic counterpoise. India welcomed the opportunity to attract US technologies and investments. The prospect of defence cooperation with the USA accorded with India's desire to dilute its near-total dependence on Russia for its military acquisitions and to access sophisticated US military technologies. The pivotal role of the USA in getting the Nuclear Suppliers Group to open up international civil nuclear cooperation with India cemented the India–US strategic partnership. The USA endorsed India's support for democracy and economic reconstruction in Afghanistan. To some extent, depending on the prevailing US priorities of the day, the India–US partnership encouraged US pressure on Pakistan to curb cross-border terrorism. But for India, as it grapples with the China-induced strategic challenges in its near and extended neighbourhood, the US stake in a strong India is the most important strategic underpinning of the India–US relationship.

India–US defence cooperation has reached unprecedented levels, with the signing of three of the four 'foundational agreements' that the USA normally concludes with its defence partners, and the US grant of the Strategic Trade Authorization-1 (STA-1) trading status to India, putting it on par with US allies for procurement of military technologies. At the same time, the intense US pressure on India to withdraw from 'significant defence transactions' with Russia, with the threat of sanctions under Countering America's Adversaries Through Sanctions Act (CAATSA), puts severe pressure on the India–US relationship, since it would have an impact on India's defence preparedness. Recently, there have also been differences on the bilateral trade imbalance. More worryingly for India, US moves for a precipitate disengagement from Afghanistan seem to be yielding a principal role to Pakistan for brokering an agreement with the Taliban. Concerns over CAATSA and the US course on Afghanistan need to be resolved in the context of the broader canvas of the India–US strategic partnership.

The India–Russia relationship is successor to the strong India–USSR relations of the Cold War years, which was characterized by solid Soviet support to India (most importantly in the UN Security Council) on its core political and security concerns, economic assistance for the industrialization of post-Independence India and extensive military assistance. The India–Russia strategic partnership is built on this foundation, with cooperation in defence, nuclear energy and hydrocarbons as core elements. Defence cooperation over the years has ensured that today, about 60–70 per cent of the weapons with the Indian armed forces are of Soviet or Russian origin. Despite the diversification of India's military acquisitions since 2000, Russia remains its principal supplier of sophisticated weaponry, with technology transfers and co-development of weapons systems enhancing the quality of the cooperation. Further, Russia is a permanent member of the UN Security Council with a veto, which it has used in the past for India's benefit. Its riches in natural resources offer economic opportunities for resource-hungry India.

Russia is a huge land mass to India's north, bordering much of its near and extended neighbourhood. Its actions in that neighbourhood—in Iran, Syria, Afghanistan and Central Asia—have an impact on India's interests. Strong India–Russia relations could ensure that these actions do not harm Indian interests. This is particularly relevant in the context of Russia–China relations, which have acquired deep strategic content, particularly as Russia's face-off with the West has intensified in the recent years. A vibrant defence and economic partnership with India could enhance Russia's resistance to Chinese pressures for acting against India's security interests. Through membership of Shanghai Cooperation Organisation (SCO, which includes Russia, China and four Central Asian countries) and a Free Trade Agreement with Eurasian Economic Union (EaEU, comprising Russia, Kazakhstan, Belarus, Kyrgyzstan and Armenia), India seeks to establish a political and economic presence in the strategically important region of Central Asia, bordering Iran, Afghanistan and Pakistan-occupied Kashmir, where Russia maintains a strong security presence and China is a dominant economic power.

In addition to these strategic considerations, terminating defence cooperation with Russia, under US pressure, is not a viable option for India, given the predominance of Russian weapons and equipment with India's armed forces. Disruption of the defence cooperation would be a hugely expensive proposition. As mentioned earlier, Russia is still the source of major weapons' platforms and cutting-edge technologies. A total shift from Russia to other suppliers would introduce serious vulnerabilities in India's defence for a considerable period. It would undermine the fundamental strategic premise of India–US relations of a strong India, with a robust foreign policy, which could hold its own in its near and extended neighbourhood, in the face of the inexorable expansion of China's economic and military influence. The challenge to India's diplomacy is to embed these perspectives in the framework of India–US relations.

The recent turbulences in global geopolitics, triggered by the acrimonious Russia–West stand-off, have not benefitted India's strategic interests. US sanctions against Russia have complicated India's effort to preserve its strategic autonomy in global affairs. They have driven Russia into a much closer embrace of China than their history of strategic rivalry would otherwise have permitted. The more recent US political and economic pressure on China will accentuate the new Russia–China convergences, unless it is accompanied by a less hostile posture against Russia.

It is not only India that is concerned about the potentially disruptive consequences for the world order of this distortion in the triangle of US–Russia–China relations. European and ASEAN countries, Japan and a number of other countries also share these concerns. India needs to work with these countries to try to shape this triangle in such a way as to maximize strategic autonomy and avoid being caught in the crossfire between them.

India has important political, economic and security interests in the West Asian region. About 8 million Indians work there, remitting about $40 billion annually to India. About 70 per cent of India's energy imports come from that region. There are important security interests too: West Asia has been a conduit for terrorists, terrorist financing and drugs coming into India. Major efforts have been made to strengthen India's relations with West Asian countries, with the political and economic cooperation reinforcing security and defence cooperation. Effective links have been established with a number of these countries to enable tracking of terrorist movements and their financing. India's relations in West Asia today transcend the religious, sectarian and political divides in that region. High-level political exchanges with Saudi Arabia, Iran, Qatar and Israel illustrate this point. Israel has become an important defence partner.

West Asia also offers a potentially significant trade route to Central Asia. The shortest land route through Pakistan is closed for obvious political and security reasons. The sea route via Europe is circuitous, time-consuming and expensive. A multimodal transport corridor—by sea from western Indian ports to Bandar Abbas or Chabahar port in Iran, and then by road or rail to Afghanistan, Central Asia or Russia—has been discussed with Russia, Iran and Azerbaijan. Trial runs have shown the commercial viability of all legs of this corridor. India is already developing terminals in Iran's Chabahar port. Some further railway infrastructure needs to be created. Completion of this project would now require negotiation with the USA, which has recently introduced fresh sanctions against Iran. This transport corridor will further India's strategic objectives in Afghanistan and Central Asia, which have been elaborated in the foregoing.

India's initiatives in West Asia have promoted its security interests in the Western Indian Ocean. As China seeks to expand its reach in this region through its Maritime Silk Road initiative, India has also strengthened partnerships with Indian Ocean littoral countries with a range of development assistance programmes. The Indian Ocean Rim Association, which has 22 member states, over half of them in the Western Indian Ocean, offers a platform for such cooperation. Prime Minister (PM) Modi announced in 2015 a partnership programme, Security and Growth for All in the Region (SAGAR), involving cooperative efforts for capacity building and security. The India–Japan initiative for an Asia–Africa Growth Corridor seeks to promote connectivity, infrastructure and development in the Indian Ocean. Transfer of an offshore patrol vessel to Mauritius and a maritime surveillance aircraft to Seychelles are examples of India's security cooperation in the region.

Issues relating to defence cooperation with Russia and threats of US sanctions draw attention to a major Indian security vulnerability. India is today among the world's largest importers of arms. Its indigenous defence manufacturing sector remains small and its defence exports are negligible. This situation generates intense international competition to capture India's defence market. It encourages blackmail, such as the threat of CAATSA. Dependence on external agencies for upgrades and spare parts of equipment exposes a vulnerability, particularly in times of crisis. Progressive indigenization of weapons manufacturing is, therefore, a national security imperative. It has to be built into defence acquisition policies. India should leverage its market size to extract the best possible technology transfer terms from defence suppliers so that over time, the country develops the capacity to develop and manufacture major weapons platforms. This effort has to be reinforced with a defence exports policy that makes indigenous defence manufacturing economically viable. Discussions on transfers of cutting-edge US or European defence technologies have not yet gone far, for various reasons, including concerns about their 'leakage' to other countries. The recent conclusion of the 'foundational agreements' and the US grant of STA-1 status to India may improve this picture. Even as India seeks to get military technologies from the USA, France and Israel, the Russian example sets the bar for the levels of technology that India should seek to extract from them.

The external linkages of national security challenges have resulted in an interlocking of foreign policy and national security perspectives. The external interactions of different sections of the political, economic, defence and security establishments have to be harmonized within the framework of a national security strategy. This is not a new reality, but has been brought into sharper focus by the new challenges created by the recent flux in great power relations. The global commons in oceans and in space are becoming areas of rivalry. Technology has facilitated the transnational reach of terrorism and organized crime, necessitating new patterns of cooperation between security agencies. It can also be used today to create major disruptions in distant countries: penetrating banking operations, destabilizing capital markets or disabling critical infrastructure. Developing broad bilateral security and political partnerships can help to forestall or thwart these threats or to mitigate their impact. Such partnerships can open doors to ensure security of critical materials supply and promote defence self-reliance through indigenization.

The effort to retain strategic autonomy of foreign policy involves give and take across sectors. Securing US understanding of India's defence cooperation with Russia or connectivity links through Iran may need meeting US political and economic interests elsewhere. The diversification of India's defence acquisitions, reducing Russia's total dominance, has to be compensated by broadening the base of India–Russia economic and energy cooperation, to ensure continued strong mutual stakes in that partnership. Optimal utilization of the billion dollar credit line, announced by PM Modi to promote development of the Russian Far East, will require innovative economic initiatives and financial mechanisms. India's Indo-Pacific strategy needs a blend of military interactions, connectivity projects, development cooperation and diplomatic initiatives—all of them in bilateral and multilateral formats. A multi-pronged approach has to be developed to protect India's technology, economic and security interests, in the face of the sharpening US–China divide on the global roll-out of fifth-generation (5G) communications technologies. Since India is a natural resource-deficient country, its external strategy needs to ensure the country's continued access to critical raw materials and energy resources, particularly in times of crises. International cooperation in space activities, geo-spatial information and technology security requires coordination with multiple departments and agencies.

A holistic approach to national security, including its external dimensions, was introduced in 1999, with the constitution of a National Security Council (NSC), chaired by the PM and including the Ministers of Home, External Affairs, Defence and Finance. The NSC is expected to develop long-term national strategies for internal and external security threats, the latter including those involving atomic energy, space and those arising from global economic, energy and ecological developments. The NSC is assisted by the NSA, who is its principal advisor on security issues. The NSA is also a part of the PM's Office, assisting the PM on foreign policy, defence, atomic energy and space issues (besides internal and external security); this emphasizes the interlinkages between these areas.

The NSA maintains regular contact with its counterparts in India's major partner countries. NSAs' dialogues, in bilateral and multilateral formats, have become standard features of global 'security diplomacy'. The level of information shared on sensitive security issues would depend on the state of bilateral relations; the obverse is that the tenor of the bilateral relationship can be qualitatively enhanced, if information-sharing on security issues becomes more intense. Perhaps the most graphic illustration of the complexity of security diplomacy is the participation of both Indian and Pakistani security experts in the Regional Anti-Terrorist Structure (RATS) of the SCO, which is meant to share information on terrorist threats in the region and to discuss ways of countering them.

The National Security Council Secretariat (NSCS), which functions under the direction of the NSA, collates and analyses intelligence and other inputs on developments impinging on national security, develops strategy papers after consultations with all stakeholders, facilitates inter-departmental coordination of actions and monitors implementation of major decisions on the strategic direction of India's foreign policy.

In 2017–2018, the mechanisms set up in 1999–2000 were reviewed and restructured, with an emphasis on domain knowledge and technical specialization. The NSCS is being enlarged and equipped with technology and analytical tools to strengthen its capacity to provide professionally sound advice to the political leadership.

The NSCS has played an important role in establishing the national cybersecurity architecture and coordinating the cybersecurity-related policies of the government. This includes cybersecurity dialogues with a range of countries, in bilateral and multilateral formats. These dialogues would provide useful security inputs for, inter alia, the government's 5G roll-out strategy. The NSCS represents India in the SCO-RATS. It is the Secretariat for multilateral NSA level dialogues including in BRICS (Brazil–Russia–India–China–South Africa), BIMSTEC, Russia–India–China dialogue on Afghanistan and the India–Maldives–Sri Lanka Maritime Trilateral. It coordinates bilateral NSA and Deputy NSA level dialogue with over 20 countries.

In today's circumstances, therefore, the making of foreign policy and the coordination of its implementation are no longer the sole preserve of the Ministry of External Affairs. A coherent pursuit of the country's national security objectives requires coordination between multiple stakeholders and an all-of-government approach that rises above sectoral interests. This needs directions from the apex political leadership so that sectoral interests of departments are trimmed in line with the larger national security interests. The newly reformed structures for national security management, which function under the direction of the apex political leadership, would provide valuable inputs for formulation of foreign policies that promote national security in all its dimensions and will play an important role in coordinating their implementation by the multiple actors in and outside government.

4

Strategizing Soft Power Projection

Veena Sikri

The Importance of Soft Power

A nation's power is defined by the 'the ability to alter the behavior of others to get what you want'.[1] Soft power is the ability to achieve this through 'attraction' rather than 'coercion' (hard power). Without, in any way, impeding or limiting the development of a nation's hard power, it is a sine qua non that strategizing soft power projection should be prioritized as the pathway of primary choice.

The terminologies of soft power projection have evolved in the 21st century. Yet these concepts and ideas are far, far older. Ancient Indian texts, notably Kautilya's *Arthashastra*[2] stated more than 2,000 years ago that 'the welfare of the State depends on an active foreign policy'.[3] The

---

[1] Joseph S. Nye, Jr, 'India and Soft Power'. Paper presented at the India Foundation Conference on Soft Power, New Delhi, 17–19 December 2018.

[2] Kautilya (Vishnugupta, Chanakya) wrote the *Arthashastra*, a comprehensive treatise on all aspects of statecraft, dated at its earliest to the 3rd century BCE. Surviving manuscripts may have been modified over time, with such changes estimated to have been made no later than 150 CE.

[3] Kautilya, *The Arthashastra*, edited, rearranged, translated and introduced by L. N. Rangarajan (New Delhi: Penguin Books India, 1992), 541 (6.2.1).

Arthashastra describes six measures of foreign policy (*sadgunya*) and four techniques (*chatur upaya*) in the conduct of foreign relations. The first *sadgunya* is *samdhi* (the policy of peace). The other five are *vigraha* (policy of hostility), *asana* (policy of keeping quiet), *yana* (marching on an expedition), *samsraya* (seeking another's protection) and *dvaidhibhava* (a dual policy of seeking peace with one and waging war against another). The first *upaya* is *sama* (the use of friendliness, persuasion, polite argument or reason). The other three are *dana* (the resort to gifts, concessions or compromises), *bheda* (or the fomenting of discord, dissensions and divisions through the use of propaganda and other means) and *danda* (the use of force when all else fails).

Samdhi and *sama*, identified as the pathways of primary choice, are the soft power equivalents. The remaining five *sadgunya* and three *upaya* represent different shades of hard power, since each of these includes some element of coercion.

The democratization of political power in the post-Second World War period has transformed soft power concepts from an essentially government-to-government (g-to-g) process to the one where the role of the public became increasingly important. Writing in 1946, British author and historian E. H. Carr categorized international power under three heads: military power, economic power and power over opinion.[4] In the ensuing years of the Cold War, overt efforts at influencing opinion across borders were derided as propaganda. Embassies and chanceries worked almost exclusively with governments. The concept of 'public opinion', far from being inclusive and open-ended, was limited to a close, often closed elite circle of owners and editors, advisers and opinion-makers. 'Power over opinion' was outsourced to these interest groups. In the absence of speedy means of communication, governments were able to play a far greater role in influencing public opinion in their respective countries, and across borders.

Gradually, the concept of public diplomacy took shape. The Edward Murrow Center for Public Diplomacy was the first set-up in the 1960s at the Fletcher School of Law and Diplomacy at Tufts University in Massachusetts, USA. The focus was on governments employing public media and social channels to influence the attitudes and actions of other governments.[5] By the early years of the 21st century, the focus of public diplomacy had moved away from governments to societies.

---

[4] Edward Hallett Carr, 'The Twenty Years' Crisis 1919–1939: An Introduction to the Study of International Relations' (London: MacMillan, [1939] 1946).

[5] Alan K. Henrikson, *What Can Public Diplomacy Achieve?* (Clingendael: Netherlands Institute of International Relations, 2006), 9.

'Public diplomacy seeks to promote ... national interest and national security through understanding, informing and influencing foreign publics and broadening dialogue between ... citizens and institutions and their counterparts abroad'.[6] Public diplomacy relates to all aspects of national life: political, economic, societal, cultural and military.

Public diplomacy activities have evolved through several phases.[7] The first, most basic, aspect of public diplomacy relates to news management, covering daily events and short-term news, putting out press releases and statements (including through Twitter and Facebook) and in other ways reacting to happenings in keeping with foreign policy and strategic priorities. This includes interacting with foreign and domestic media representatives. Most foreign offices assign high importance to this work, which is kept squarely within the foreign ministry structure. In India, this work is done through the External Publicity Division of the Ministry of External Affairs (MEA).

The second aspect of public diplomacy, moving towards cultural diplomacy, relates to strategic communications, aimed at managing perceptions about the country as a whole through carefully planned activities and events designed to reinforce the holistic image of the nation. This includes the political image of the country, but goes far beyond this to cover issues such as trade, tourism, investment, cultural relations and civilizational heritage. In India, the principle organizations for this aspect of public diplomacy remain the MEA and Indian Council for Cultural Relations (ICCR, an autonomous organization affiliated with MEA). However, there is a multiplicity of other agencies of the Government of India equally willing (and mandated) to take ownership of this task, such as the Ministry of Culture, Ministry of Human Resource Development and indeed almost all the line ministries dealing with individual sectors such as tourism, commerce and business development, among others. The key issue here is ensuring adequate coordination so that each activity reinforces the message about the nation, rather than splintering it.

The third and most enduring task of public diplomacy, squarely in the realm of cultural diplomacy, is to build long-term relationships with individuals, institutions and peoples in foreign nations in order to create understanding, recognition and appreciation of India's core

---

[6] Extracted from 'A Call for Action on Public Diplomacy', 2nd ed. (Washington, DC: Public Diplomacy Council, October 2005), 4.

[7] Mark Leonard (with Catherine Stead and Conrad Smewing), *Public Diplomacy* (London: The Foreign Policy Centre, 2002), 10–11.

civilizational values and contemporary developments, and to learn from theirs. This third dimension of public diplomacy is the core competency of ICCR. And it is this aspect of public diplomacy that has, in the 21st century, morphed into soft power projection.

The last decade of the 20th century saw the start of unimaginably rapid change with the information and communication technology (ICT) revolution heralding the dawn of the cyber-age. This has affected every aspect of our daily lives. Hitherto, people-to-people contacts across borders were comparatively slow and ponderous, and of negligible significance, least of all in influencing opinions. Today, mobile and Internet services have brought people to the centre of every opinion-building exercise. Virtual yet instantaneous e-connectivity has globalized services yet transformed the world into a global village. The ICT revolution combined with the spread of democracies across the world has made not just public opinion but individual opinion 'a measure as well as the source of power'.[8]

Before the ICT revolution, in foreign offices and embassies across the world, public and cultural diplomacy was seen as 'a support function, an adjunct or accessory service to major policy initiatives....'[9] Today, softpower projection has emerged as the single most elucidative element in achieving E. H. Carr's 'power over opinion'. Soft power projection is the key pillar of a successful foreign policy, fully on par with other pillars, be they political, economic or security-related. Strategizing soft power projection is now a vital task, critical for the achievement of national, regional and global policy objectives.

The Dimensions of India's Soft Power

The rubric of soft power is vast and comprehensive. Soft power includes civilizational heritage and traditional knowledge, language, literature, philosophy (including religions), education and academia, culture, cuisine, yoga, tourism and contemporary lifestyles, embracing in its ambit the 21st-century usage of social media through the Internet. For us in India, the unique aspect of soft power is the emotional bonding with and growing might (sociopolitical and economic) of the Indian diaspora.[10]

---

[8] Alan K. Henrikson, *What Can Public Diplomacy Achieve?* 2
[9] Ibid.
[10] In December 2016, Veena Sikri, as Chair of ICCR's Performance Audit Committee, authored the Report on 'India's Soft Power Projection through Cultural Diplomacy', where she first elucidated several of these ideas.

The essence of soft power is that its source lies outside the traditional format of g-to-g interactions that have hitherto been the fountainhead of diplomatic relations, bilateral or multilateral. Equally, the target audience for soft power projection also lies outside the normal formal ambit of diplomatic relations. The 'attraction' that is the essence of successful soft power projection is more like a meeting of the minds, an appeal to the inner self, be it a young student, a traveller, a teacher, a scientist or a philosopher. Soft power projection deals with universal truths, equally applicable to relationships within a family, within a community and within a nation. When extrapolated to the realm of transnational relationships, soft power projection can become the most potent and powerful, yet often underestimated and underutilized *astra* (weapon) in the armoury of diplomatic expertise.

In the turbulent 21st-century world, tranquillity and spiritual and physical well-being are at a high premium. The search for peace is paramount. And this search begins with the individual. Family structures have crumbled to the point of breakdown, and as a result, the crucial traditional role of the family in fostering ethical values and beliefs has greatly weakened. Modern educational systems have not fared much better in imbuing ethics. Adrift without these anchors, individuals seek individualistic pathways in the search for inner peace. The search is individual, yet the pathways are universal. Katha Upanishad, the major Sanskrit treatise dating to the 1st millennium BCE, recognizes this when it says 'those wise ones who see that the consciousness within them is the same consciousness within all beings attain peace'.

It is in this context that India's civilizational and philosophical heritage is being revisited by millions the world over. The celebration of the International Day of Yoga (IDY) on 21 June every year has refocused attention on the contemporary relevance of this heritage. The mounting global success of these celebrations reflects the increasing awareness on the need for inner peace together with the universal acceptance of meditation, yoga and spirituality as viable paths leading to success in this search. Prime Minister (PM) Narendra Modi, speaking in the UN General Assembly on 27 September 2014, inter alia introducing the proposal for the UN IDY, said:

> [Y]oga is an invaluable gift of India's ancient tradition. It embodies unity of mind and body; thought and action; restraint and fulfillment; harmony between man and nature; a holistic approach to health and well-being. It is not about exercise but to discover the sense of oneness with yourself, the world and the nature. By changing our lifestyle and creating consciousness, it can help in well-being.

India's soft power strengths are legion. India's is the oldest living civilization in the world, with an unbroken history going back many millennia. Ancient Indian ideas, traditions and value systems, ancient Indian epics and spiritual texts remain vibrant, relevant and followed by millions in India and abroad. The uniqueness of the living continuity of subcontinental India's civilizational heritage was immortalized in 1904 in a poetic composition by Muhammad Iqbal, later known as Allama Iqbal (1877–1938), the Urdu poet of undivided India, who is today the national poet of Pakistan. His poem, the Tarana-e Hind or 'Anthem of the People of Hindustan' is an ode to the incomparable beauty and resilience of India (Hindustan), reflecting the author's determined commitment to the composite, pluralistic culture of India, with Hindus, Muslims and followers of all faiths living together in peace and harmony.[11] Around 1945, this poem was set to music by renowned sitar maestro Pandit Ravi Shankar. Known across India by the first line of the poem 'Saare Jahan se Accha' (Hindustan, the best country in the world), this composition, with lyrics by Muhammad Iqbal, and music by Pandit Ravi Shankar, was adopted as the official quick march of the Indian Armed Forces and continues to be a favourite with schoolchildren across India.

In stanza 6, the poet says:

> *Mazhab nahin sikhata apas main bair rakhna,*
> *Hindi hain ham, watan hai Hindostan hamara*

(Approximate translation: Religion does not teach us to bear animosity among ourselves, we are of Hind, our homeland is Hindustan.)

In stanzas 7 and 8, Allama Iqbal says:

> *Unan-o-Misr-o-Ruma, sab mit gaye jahan se*
> *Ab tak magar hai baaqi naam-o-nishan hamara*
> *Kuch baat hai ki hasti mit-ti nahin hamari*
> *Sadiyon raha hai dushman daur-e-zaman hamara*

(Approximate translation: In a world in which ancient Greece, Egypt and Rome have all vanished, our own attributes [of Hindustan] live on

---

[11] Muhammad Iqbal recited the *Taraana-e-Hind* in 1905 at a public function at Government College, Lahore (now in Pakistan). This composition acquired immense popularity as an anthem of opposition to British colonial rule in undivided India and was later published as well. However, after the formation of the Muslim League in 1906, Muhammad Iqbal's views underwent a complete transformation and, in 1910, he composed another song for children 'Taraana-e-Milli' or 'Anthem of the Religious Community'.

today. There is something special in our existence that these [attributes] cannot be erased, even though for centuries, the time cycle of the world has been our enemy [invasions]).

The song 'Saare Jahan se Achha' embodies the continuing relevance of India's ancient wisdom and traditions. This is the living reality for the people of India and remains a major source of intellectual attraction for and study by foreign scholars.

I have referred to Kautilya's *Arthashastra* in the context of foreign policy and soft power projection. This treatise, described by some as 'The Science of Politics' and by others as 'The Science of Material Gain', covers all aspects of statecraft, including nature of government, law, civil and criminal court systems, ethics,[12] economics,[13] markets and trade, the methods for screening ministers, diplomacy, theories on war, nature of peace and the duties and obligations of a king. The *Arthashastra* texts incorporate philosophy and include ancient economic and cultural details on agriculture, mineralogy, mining and metals, animal husbandry, medicine, forests and wildlife. Beyond this, the *Arthashastra* emphasizes the need to empower the weak and poor in the kingdom and advises that 'the king shall provide the orphans, the aged, the infirm, the afflicted and the helpless with maintenance (welfare support). He shall also provide subsistence to helpless women when they are carrying and also to the children they give birth to'. Elsewhere, in Book 2, there is the specific suggestion that horses and elephants be looked after and be given food, when they become incapacitated from old age, disease or after war.

The details about village self-governance provided in the *Arthashastra*, the structure and autonomy of village assemblies (panchayats) as the most basic unit of the political and economic structure of the country, the role of the panchayat in supervising the affairs of the village, including dispute settlement, remain valid and almost unchanged even today! Taken as a whole, the *Arthashastra* reflects the prevailing strategic culture and comprehensive thinking of the times, with continued salience in dealing with contemporary issues.

Kautilya, the principal author of the *Arthashastra*, was a scholar at the ancient University of Taxila, founded around 1000 BCE, which flourished between 600 BCE and 500 CE, located in Punjab (Pakistan). Kautilya was the teacher and later advisor of Chandragupta Maurya, a man of humble origins, who founded the Mauryan Empire in the 4th

---

[12] https://en.wikipedia.org/wiki/Ethics (accessed on 21 November 2019).
[13] https://en.wikipedia.org/wiki/Economics (accessed on 21 November 2019).

century BCE. Among the most renowned rulers of India was the Mauryan Emperor Ashoka (3rd century BCE), whose edicts inscribed on stone pillars have been found throughout the realm. The Mauryan Empire has been the largest ever among all the empires India has known, covering a vast territory of 5 million sq. km. The vast dimensions of the Mauryan Empire establish the antiquity of the concept of India as one land and one nation.

The ancient name for India is Bharat, named after King Bharat, the ancestor of the Pandavas and the Kauravas, who battled with each other in the epic Mahabharata. King Bharat is said to have united all of India under his rule, and scientific calculations based on astrological references date the epic Mahabharata to the 5th or 6th millennium BCE. The concepts of Bharat (India) and *Bharatiyata* (Indianness) are ancient constructs, reflecting spiritual and material values that are shared across the land, regardless of intervening periods when the size of kingdoms and empires may have waxed or waned.

India is renowned for yoga and for the excellence of its cultural achievements as reflected through the diversity of the performing arts. All these are part of Indian traditional knowledge. The Sanskrit text, the Yoga Sutras of Sage Patanjali, dates back to the period prior to 400 CE. Sage Patanjali synthesized and organized the already ancient knowledge of yoga through the Yoga Sutras. The Sanskrit text *Natya Shastra*, attributed to Bharata Muni, is dated between 200 BCE and 200 CE. This is the most comprehensive and detailed treatise, a handbook on the dramatic arts, which includes dramatic composition, structure of a play, construction of a stage, genres of acting, body movements, make-up, costumes, musical scales, musical instruments and integration of music with art performances. It includes the theory of *Rasa* (aesthetics), detailing the moods the performer depicts. Entertainment is the desired effect of the performing arts, says the *Natya Shastra*, but not its primary goal. The primary goal is to transport the individual (audience) to another parallel reality, so that he can reflect on the spiritual and moral questions being raised. The tenets of the *Natya Shastra* remain relevant and are carefully studied and fully incorporated into performances by millions of students in India and abroad. The living, continuing reality of India's soft power, of India's tangible and intangible cultural heritage, is among the richest in the world.

Sushruta Samhita, the compendium of texts on medicine and surgery which includes the foundational text on Ayurveda, was written around the 1st millennium BCE by Sushruta, describing the work of his Guru, Divodasa. Aryabhata, considered among the earliest mathematician–astronomers, lived in Pataliputra (present-day Patna) in the 5th century CE during the Gupta Empire. His contributions include the place value system and zero, the approximation for pi, the description of the relativity of motion, including motions of the solar system.

In the 10th century CE, Abhinav Gupta (980–1018 CE) of Kashmir, a philosopher, mystic, poet, dramatist, wrote a commentary on the *Natya Shastra* (among many other prolific writings). This highlights the continuing study and interest in India's heritage, even a thousand years after the original texts were written. In the 11th century CE, Raja Bhoja (1010–1055), ruler in present-day Madhya Pradesh, a poet–philosopher king, was a prolific writer. Among many texts, he wrote the *Yuktikalpataru*, a treatise with multiple topics, including techniques of shipbuilding. Similarly, there are ancient treatises on Vastu Shastra, the science of architecture.

Ancient Indian ideas retain their salience and relevance in contemporary times. In this context, the concepts of *Vasudhaiva Kutumbakam* and *Sarva Dharma Sambhava* deserve special mention. The phrase *Vasudhaiva Kutumbakam* is from the Sanskrit text, the Maha Upanishad, considered by scholars to be the most ancient among the Vaishnava Upanishads, attached to the Atharvaveda. The full verse reads 'For those who live magnanimously, the entire world constitutes but a family'.[14] The words *Vasudhaiva Kutumbakam* are engraved in the entrance hall of the Parliament of India.

Vasudhaiva Kutumbakam highlights the global outlook of Indian sages and thinkers, placing society above self in every field of endeavour. This focus on the greater good (as opposed to just individual good or that of one's immediate family) is the key underlying thought. And this is not just altruism. Ultimately, keeping the interests of 'others' in mind will reap the best rewards for the self. The 'others' could be the *mohalla* or immediate neighbours, the village or town, the community as a whole and those living beyond national boundaries. In every way, this supports the concept of the global citizen. It recognizes that the common wealth of the world is a shared heritage, be this outer space, the oceans and seas, the mountains and minerals, the flora and fauna. Imbibing the spirit of *Vasudhaiva Kutumbakam* can contribute substantially in generating solidarity with the global community, and enhancing global responsibility, especially on issues such as climate change, global warming and achieving the Sustainable Development Goals (SDGs), in promoting concepts of universal peace and respect for

---

[14] Translated from the Maha Upanishad by Dr A. G. Krishna Warrier.

human rights, including conflict prevention, conflict resolution and all terrorism-related issues. Above all, *Vasudhaiva Kutumbakam* encourages a pluralistic society with compassion and tolerance, accommodating differences no matter whether these are based on religion or culture or language or ethnicity.

The ancient concept of *Sarva Dharma Sambhava* embodies the uniquely Indian approach to and understanding of secularism. *Sarva Dharma Sambhava* emphasizes equal respect for all religions, that all religions can and should coexist. As against the Western concept of secularism which focuses on the separation of Church and State, the essence of *Sarva Dharma Sambhava* is equidistance of the State from all religions. In 1893, Swami Vivekananda, speaking at the Parliament of the World's Religions in Chicago, had elaborated on this concept as an intrinsic part of India's civilizational tradition of accepting the greatness of all religions. India values religious harmony, he said, based on mutual respect and regard. In the tumultuous years leading up to the Independence of India from colonial rule, Mahatma Gandhi spoke and wrote at great length about *Sarva Dharma Sambhava*. For Mahatma Gandhi, the truth underlying all religions is the same, even though the pathways may be different.

History bears out India's commitment to the concept of *Sarva Dharma SamBahava*. India, already a rich mosaic of diversity in languages, cultural practices and ethnicities, has unhesitatingly embraced diversity of religions. India believes in retaining and absorbing diversity, not divesting it through imposition of uniformity. India has absorbed all religions into its fold. Jewish communities across the world have written extensively about their persecution in different lands, but have praised India where they received shelter in the state of Kerala, with no persecution or discrimination. Zoroastrians (Parsis) from the land of Persia, present-day Iran, received shelter in the state of Gujarat.

Traditional Indian knowledge systems remain alive because of their continuing acceptance by and relevance to all people, not just the rich and educated but the poorest of the poor. The people derive their value systems from the ancient knowledge that has come down to them through their ancestors, often by word of mouth from one generation to the next. The poor did not need to read books to imbibe this knowledge. Agricultural techniques, rainwater harvesting systems, nutrition and good health, weaving fabrics with natural dyes, every aspect of daily life in India continue to be influenced by traditional knowledge.

Across the world, people often wonder and express surprise at how India has emerged as the software or ICT superpower. Many in India attribute this to the millennia-old emphasis on the teaching of mathematics, especially pedagogy techniques, that have consolidated these skills at all levels, irrespective of levels of prosperity of the student.

It is vital to appreciate that India's traditional knowledge and management systems brought immense prosperity and wealth to every part of the nation, and every segment of society. Professor Angus Maddison[15] points out that in 1 CE India, united under the Mauryan Empire, accounted for 33 per cent of the world's population and 32 per cent of world's GDP, the highest in the world, ahead of China who was second. In 1000 CE, India accounted for roughly 28 per cent of the world's population and close to 28 per cent of world's GDP, still the highest in the world. It was the enormity of India's wealth that attracted invaders and colonizers. In 1500 CE, around the time the Mughals and European colonialists were arriving, India accounted for 25 per cent of the world population, and 24.36 per cent of world's GDP, second now to China under the Ming dynasty. For the next 200 years, under Mughal rule, India retained its share in world's GDP between 24 per cent and 25 per cent. Under colonial rule, India's economy was totally impoverished, with the share of world's GDP falling from 22.6 per cent of world GDP in 1700 (almost equal to Europe's share) to a low of 3.8 per cent in 1952, placing India among the poorest countries in the world in terms of per capita income.

Even in extreme poverty, India did not abandon or forget the three pillars, or three dimensions, of India's soft power, namely *continuity*, *living traditions* and *diversity*.

Strategizing Soft Power Projection

India's soft power heritage is an intrinsic and inalienable part of India's identity. This holds true for the country as a whole, and for each of its citizens. Understanding this heritage can contribute strongly to appreciating fellow citizens. In the context of foreign policy, explaining and projecting India's soft power is vital for other countries (governments, individuals and institutions) to understand India in a holistic and comprehensive manner. Strategizing soft power projection is essential to meet these objectives.

---

[15] Angus Maddison, *Contours of the World Economy, 1–2030 AD: Essays in Macroeconomic History* (Oxford: Oxford University Press, 2007).

Soft power projection within India and abroad may seem unrelated, but these are two sides of the same coin. Successful soft power projection in the context of India's foreign policy objectives can be achieved only if those tasked with doing so understand and appreciate these concepts as a part of their respective identities. It is important, therefore, that the sources of India's soft power, India's culture and heritage, are studied by one and all through the educational curriculum. Under colonial rule, the study of India's culture and heritage formed an insignificant part of the recommended educational curriculum. Swami Vivekananda said that education must provide 'life-building, man-making and character-forming assimilation of ideas'. Decades later, independent India's first Minister of Education, Maulana Abul Kalam Azad, pointed out how essential it is that schools in India sensitize the younger generation about ethics, the values of equality, justice and inclusiveness, and India's culture and diverse heritage. He laid emphasis on teaching about values drawn from all religions, so that the young could grow up appreciating diversity and the need for inclusiveness, embedding these in the individual psyche, thereby strengthening the nation's pluralist psyche. In independent India, even after 70 years, not enough has been done to broaden India's educational curriculum, especially on including the study of India's ancient and diverse heritage.

Indian universities and specialized institutions should encourage and facilitate rigorous research on India's history, culture and heritage, including ancient Indian concepts and ideas. Far too often, controversies are sought to be created because not enough rigorous research has been done on these ideas. And where such research has yielded positive results, such as on the reality of the ancient river Saraswati, there should be no hesitation in incorporating these results in the educational curriculum. Faculty-based research should be encouraged on the relevance of ancient Indian ideas in different contexts, including environmental studies, conflict resolution studies, history, philosophy, literature and aesthetics. Extensive research is vital if ancient Indian ideas and the multiple dimensions of India's diverse heritage are to be widely understood by Indians and foreign scholars and are to serve as a force multiplier for soft power projection.

Foreign scholars, deeply interested in India's ancient heritage, often refer to the lack of adequate research in this area. Such research is essential to elucidate and create appreciation for the universal relevance of key concepts, rather than linking these to any one religion. Facilities for the specialized study of India's diverse culture, heritage and languages should be accessible and easily available as a part of regular university curriculum in multiple faculties. As a natural corollary, there should be academic tie-ups with selected foreign universities in every major country: the USA, the UK, Japan, China, and also in South East Asia, Africa and Europe. Faculty exchange programmes can be developed so that modules on all aspects of India studies (ancient, medieval and contemporary) can be introduced at these universities once again with a multidisciplinary approach.

Coordinated education, research and training are the three ingredients needed within India to prepare for successful soft power projection abroad. Soft power projection needs detailed training and sensitization. Audiences and interests are different in each country, and these aspects need careful understanding and consideration. There can be no one-size-fits-all approach while planning for soft power projection. Achieving success in soft power projection is a complex task.

Soft power projection through diplomacy involves harnessing India's cultural and civilizational heritage to augment the country's strength on the global stage. Foreign policy constitutes the external dimensions of activity, based firmly within the context of achieving national goals and objectives, implementing the nation's vision of its own future within its borders, within its sub-region or region, and within the world polity. PM Narendra Modi has formally recognized and incorporated soft power projection as an essential dimension of his foreign policy doctrine, perhaps the first PM of India to have done so. In 2015, on completing one year in office, PM Modi declared the *Panchamrit* or five pillars of his foreign policy as:

- *Samriddhi* (economic prosperity)
- *Suraksha* (national security)
- *Samman* (dignity and honour of India and Indians)
- *Samvad* (greater engagement)
- *Sanskriti evam Sabhyata* (cultural and civilizational linkages)

The formal acceptance of cultural and civilizational linkages as an effective instrument of foreign policy is certainly a first, as is the recognition and inclusion of the Indian diaspora under *Sanskriti* and *Samman*. The concept of *Samvad*, too, is vital, since it brings in the focus on expanding engagement beyond the traditional g-to-g levels to include business, academia, scholars and the Indian diaspora. In short, the entire range of people-to-people linkages has been elevated and declared to be of substantive significance in achieving foreign policy objectives, including India's global aspirations.

PM Modi has made soft power projection through public and cultural diplomacy the centrepiece of his foreign visits. International interest in India is today at an all-time high, due in no small measure to the efficacy of the outreach launched during each of PM Modi's highly successful foreign visits. Leveraging this heightened interest into the successful attainment of India's national, regional and global objectives needs a sustained foreign policy effort with soft power projection through cultural diplomacy as one of its core pillars. The key question is whether this follow-up, this leveraging is being effectively implemented.

A relevant assessment of this is provided by Jonathan McClory, the creator and author of the annual *Soft Power 30* study, which ranks the world's top 30 countries in terms of soft power projection. Speaking in New Delhi in December 2018,[16] he explained that the *Soft Power 30* index is calculated each year through six sub-indices, measuring objective data on culture, digital, education, enterprise, government and global engagement. India's strongest assets, he says, are in digital, culture and government, with weaknesses in global engagement, education and enterprise. India has an overall ranking of 41 out of 60 countries based on these six sub-indices. International polling data are drawn from nationally representative surveys from 11,000 people in 25 countries, covering every region of the world. Survey respondents rate countries on the factors that drive perceptions of a foreign country, namely culture, foreign policy, liveability (cuisine, welcoming to tourists, visit for work or study) and technology exports. In the rankings based on perceptions, India ranks 43rd out of 60 countries. It is only on culture that perceptions about India place it in the top 30 of the world, at rank 23.

Jonathan McClory concludes that 'there seems to be a lack of understanding around what India wants from the world, and what it stands to contribute'. He calls for leveraging India's 'formidable cultural assets' by 'combining India's excellent digital reach with a greater international diplomatic presence'.

There is, indeed, universal appreciation and endorsement of India's soft power assets and capabilities, particularly in the fields of culture and civilizational heritage. However, the conclusion seems inescapable that the definition of soft power that shapes perceptions is much more comprehensive than just culture. It includes the contemporary

---

[16] Jonathan McClory, 'The Sleeping Giant: India's Soft Power Potential' at the Conference on Soft Power organized by India Foundation in New Delhi (full text carried in the *India Foundation Journal* [2019 March–April]).

relevance of classical Indian thought and ideas, and how these can shape outcomes in the modern world. Perceptions play a vital role in determining the success of soft power projection, and perceptions are influenced by a range of factors. These include perceptions about the effectiveness of India's foreign policy and its participation in global affairs; ease of traveling, studying or living in India; even the ease of obtaining a visa and the very experience of visiting the Indian Embassy or Indian Cultural Centre (ICC). Finally, there is little doubt that soft power projection is a major factor in determining the success or otherwise of a nation's foreign policy, and as such, it (soft power projection) should be incorporated as part and parcel of foreign policy planning.

Through the activities of ICCR (the autonomous organization under the MEA), India already has in place a formidable infrastructure for soft power projection. This includes (a) the network of close to 40 ICCs across the world, (b) chairs of Indian studies in foreign universities, for the establishment of which ICCR has concluded over 100 Memoranda of Understanding (MOUs) with leading universities and (c) the Foreign Students' Scholarships Programme, through which ICCR offers scholarships each year to more than 3,300 students from 137 countries to pursue higher studies in Indian universities and other recognized institutions of specialized studies, including in the field of culture. Effectively, ICCR is the Government of India's nodal agency for soft power projection.

Over the decades (ICCR was established in 1950), thousands of scholars, writers, creative and cultural personalities from every corner of the world have participated in these purposeful activities. Festivals of India have been held in numerous countries and reciprocal festivals have been convened in India. The planning of these activities and the tremendous effort in their implementation have been sincere and serious on all counts. Yet there is a mismatch somewhere between intended and achieved results. This can be gauged from the opinions expressed by participants, including foreign students, from the functioning of several among the chairs of Indian studies in foreign universities and from the activity outcomes of some among the ICCs.

In the recent years, special initiatives, especially the IDY have yielded outstanding success. Across the world, IDY has captured the imagination of youth and all those who seek well-being, while bringing into focus the universal and timeless relevance of ancient Indian ideas. This has rejuvenated the interest in civilizational heritage as the core of India's soft power. In order to build upon recent successes and strategize for the coming years, this is perhaps the right moment to review the coordinated functioning of the major institutions involved in soft power projection.

An important missing link in the programme planning for soft power projection is an effective impact assessment mechanism. Impact assessment should be built into every activity (chairs of Indian studies, foreign students scholarship programmes and others), since without it, repetition and consequent waste of resources become inevitable. The matrix for impact assessment is threefold for each country. First, clear identification of the target audience (for India) in that country, which includes both those who are already interested in India and those among whom interest is sought to be created. Second, identifying the aspects about India that are of key interest for the target audience. And third, synchronizing those aspects of India's soft power that are of interest to the target audience with those that are considered vital by India.

The impact assessment matrix is particularly relevant when soft power projection is accepted as one among the core pillars of foreign policy implementation. This greatly helps the implementing agency (in this case, ICCR) in effectively planning its activities and strengthening outcomes. If there is some hesitation in accepting the strategic significance of soft power projection, as seems to be the case with the MEA (India's foreign office), this can make the task of impact assessment more difficult for ICCR. The work of the ICCs goes on, but the key aspect of strategizing to maximize results is missing. Without soft power projection being among the core pillars of foreign policy planning and implementation, Heads of Mission do not attach adequate priority or importance to the task being done by the ICCs. On the other hand, once soft power projection is among the core pillars, Heads of Mission will be assessed, inter alia, on the targeted success of their work in this sector, which will certainly improve outcomes, including better coordination with ICCR.

To ensure funding for planned programmes, it will be in the interest of each Head of Mission to coordinate with ICCR and the relevant territorial division of the MEA in finalizing specific soft power projection plans each year. At present, annual plans are drawn up, but ensuring their implementation is an erratic process. Similarly, within each Mission, there will be a more coordinated approach towards soft power projection, with clearer division of responsibilities with hierarchal accountability than is the case at present.

The ICCs should be the coordinated single-point entity for soft power projection and related cultural diplomacy activities in Indian

Missions abroad. With the exception of consular matters, the ICC should function as the public face of the Indian Mission, covering all aspects such as education, yoga, AYUSH and teaching of Hindi, Sanskrit and other Indian languages. If experts are not available with the ICC, information should be at hand on how and where such facilities can be accessed. The ICCs should be digitally equipped to answer queries even on matters such as tourism. Outreach to universities and young audiences should be prioritized. As far as possible, the mandate and work of the ICCs should not be subject to the vagaries of short-term crises in bilateral relations.

ICCR, as the nodal agency for soft power projection, needs modernization of its cultural management skill sets. The effective management of financial resources to meet the core requirements of the ICCs is just one aspect. Responsiveness to multiple agencies, within India and abroad, is vital. Information retrieval through digitalization of all records, especially of foreign students who have studied in India, is yet another dimension. Coordination with the MEA and Heads of Missions, with universities across India and abroad, and with the wide spectrum of cultural personalities is essential yet exceedingly sensitive. Creating shared objectives and then working together to achieve them within time and financial constraints is daunting. ICCR's ability to meet these challenges is a crucial determinant of India's overall success in sift power projection.

Yoga, dance, music and interest in tourism are often the initial points of attraction (towards India) for foreign nationals. This includes, but is certainly not restricted to, the Indian diaspora or Indian expatriates. Leveraging this interest effectively needs a multifaceted approach, bringing in skills development, combined with contextualizing this interest in the far broader spectrum of India's knowledge systems, keeping in mind at all times the point of view and specific requirements of the person expressing the interest. In the words of Joseph Nye, 'soft power ... is often hard to use, easy to lose, and costly to re-establish'.[17]

---

[17] Joseph S. Nye Jr, 'Foreword', in *The Soft Power 30: A Global Ranking of Soft Power*, ed. Jonathan McClory (2016), 6.

India and Multilateralism

Asoke Kumar Mukerji

The growing recourse to unilateral measures by the major powers poses one of the gravest challenges to contemporary multilateralism. Multilateralism's core principle of international cooperation is essential to create a supportive external environment for India's national priorities. The rapid transformation of India, driven by its ambitious socio-economic development programmes, is anchored by its international trade. The fact that this trade accounts for as much as 40 per cent of India's gross domestic product (GDP)[1] today underscores the critical importance of the interlinkage between India's aspirations and the continued need for international cooperation through multilateralism.

India has been proactive in using multilateralism to meet its objectives. In the process, India has contributed significantly to the evolution of the multilateral system over the past century. It has taken initiatives, especially after its Independence from colonial rule in August 1947, to make the United Nations (UN) more responsive to ground realities. A core area of its activism has advocated the principle of equality in decision-making, which is the hallmark of its Independence and an integral part of the democratization of international relations.

---

[1] The World Bank, UNCTAD, and World Integrated Trade Solution, *India Trade Statistics*. Available at https://wits.worldbank.org/CountryProfile/en/IND (accessed on 9 December 2019).

The anomaly of a colony becoming a founder member of both the League of Nations and the UN is unique to India in international relations. As a signatory of the Treaty of Versailles on 28 June 1919,[2] India became a founder member of League and its General Assembly. This gave India a distinct legal status in contemporary international relations. India's signature on the Treaty was the direct outcome of India's massive military and financial contributions to the success of the Allied armies in the First World War.[3] Membership of the League also coincided with the opening of India's first diplomatic representation abroad, the Indian High Commission in London, created by the Government of India Act of 1919.[4]

India's foray into multilateral diplomacy began with its participation in the General Assembly of the League of Nations in 1920. The Indian delegation was led by the Indian High Commissioner in London.[5] India used its membership of the League's structures to gradually create its own imprint on multilateral affairs with an interest in the application of international cooperation. Four areas illustrate this aspect of India's early multilateral diplomacy.

The International Labour Organization (ILO) was created, like the League of Nations, by the Treaty of Versailles. India became a founder member of the ILO. Membership of the ILO had an impact on the evolution of labour standards in India. Prior to its Independence in August 1947, India ratified 13 ILO Conventions relating to decent working conditions of industrial workers (including women and children), the right to association of agricultural workers, seafarers and

---

[2] United States Library of Congress, *Treaty of Versailles*. Available at https://www.loc.gov/law/help/us-treaties/bevans/m-ust000002-0043.pdf (accessed on 9 December 2019).

[3] More than 1.4 million volunteer Indian soldiers took part in allied campaigns spread across Europe, Africa and Asia. India contributed about £300 million (equal in economic value to about £20 billion today), including a direct loan of £100 million to the United Kingdom in 1917. See Arvind Gupta, 'Indian Contribution to the First World War', *Journal of Defence Studies* 8, no. 3 (July–September 2014): 121–133. Available at http://www.idsa.in/system/files/jds/jds_8_3_2014_ArvindGupta_0.pdf (accessed on 9 December 2019).

[4] Universal Library, *The Govt. of India Act and Govt. Reports 1920*, Part III, Section 35 (Calcutta: N. N. Mitter, 1921). Available at https://ia800708.us.archive.org/33/items/govtofindiaact19029669mbp/govtofindiaact-19029669mbp.pdf (accessed on 9 December 2019).

[5] The Open University, *Formation of the League of Nations*. Available at http://www.open.ac.uk/researchprojects/makingbritain/content/formation-league-nations (accessed on 9 December 2019).

emigrants (including Indians taken abroad as plantation workers). These Conventions form part of the 43 ILO Conventions ratified by India so far,[6] creating a strong regulatory framework for India's objective of achieving the goal of 'decent work' and economic growth as part of Agenda 2030 on Sustainable Development.[7]

Two issues related to the conduct of India's multilateral diplomacy can be traced back to its membership of the ILO. One is India's ability to play a leadership role in multilateral gatherings. The leader of the Indian delegation, High Commissioner Sir Atul Chatterjee, ICS, became the first Indian to preside over the International Labour Conference (ILC) in 1927. He was also the first Indian to chair the ILO Governing Body in 1932–1933.[8] It was unprecedented for a non-self-governing country to play such a role, which contributed significantly to India's reputation as an active player in multilateral diplomacy.

The other issue was the participation of India in multilateral decision-making. India has been designated by the ILO General Assembly since 1922 as one of the ten countries of 'chief industrial importance' permanently represented on the ILO's Governing Body. The Body is a tripartite multi-stakeholder structure of governments, employers and workers. The other nine permanently represented governments are Brazil, China, France, Germany, Italy, Japan, the Russian Federation, the United Kingdom and the USA.[9] The ILO Governing Body has demonstrated the viability of taking decisions by consensus, or by majority vote, if there is no consensus, without any of the permanent members having a veto.

The second area relates to India's participation in the International Committee on Intellectual Cooperation (ICIC), established by the League in 1922.[10] The objective of the ICIC, which was strongly

---

[6] Government of India, Ministry of Labour and Employment, *India and the ILO*. Available at https://labour.gov.in/lcandilasdivision/india-ilo (accessed on 9 December 2019).

[7] International Labour Organization, *Decent Work and the 2030 Agenda for Sustainable Development*. Available at https://www.ilo.org/global/topics/sdg-2030/lang—en/index.htm (accessed on 9 December 2019).

[8] The Open University, *Formation of the League of Nations*.

[9] International Labour Organization, *Governing Body*. Available at https://www.ilo.org/global/about-the-ilo/how-the-ilo-works/governing-body/lang—en/index.htm (accessed on 9 December 2019).

[10] United Nations Research Guides, *League of Nations: Intellectual Cooperation*. Available at https://libraryresources.unog.ch/lonintellectualcooperation/ICIC (accessed on 9 December 2019).

promoted and supported by France, was to promote 'intellectual work and international relationships between scientists, researchers, teachers, artists and members of intellectual professions' in order to achieve 'international understanding between states as a means to preserve peace'.[11]

Eminent Indian intellectuals such as Professor D. N. Banerjee of Calcutta University, Professor Jagadish Chandra Bose, the founder of experimental science in India, and Dr Sarvepalli Radhakrishnan, contributed to the body's work. Dr Radhakrishnan was particularly active in bringing ideas and values from India's rich civilizational heritage to the emerging multilateral intellectual framework to sustain world peace. When the UN was created, the ICIC's work was transferred to UNESCO. Dr Radhakrishnan was accredited as independent India's first ambassador to UNESCO from 1946 to 1952.[12]

The third area of multilateral diplomacy from this period involved India's support for a French initiative to use multilateral legal instruments to counterterrorism. The League of Nations discussed and negotiated a Convention for the Prevention and Punishment of Terrorism.[13] The focus of the Convention was for members of the League of Nations to pass national legislation that would make terrorist acts extraditable offences in the event one of their nationals committed a terror act in a foreign jurisdiction. India was among the 24 countries of the League of Nations that signed the Convention in 1937. Britain did not sign the Convention. India was the only member of the League to ratify the Convention in January 1941. The disagreement of member states in the League and subsequently in the UN over how to apply the legal obligation to 'prosecute or extradite' resonates even today in India's campaign to get the UN General Assembly (UNGA) to adopt a Comprehensive Convention on International Terrorism (CCIT).

The fourth area of relevance for India's multilateral diplomacy was its participation in a series of discussions and negotiations that established the UN. The process for creating the UN was set in motion by

---

[11] United Nations Research Guide, *The League of Nations: Intellectual Cooperation*. Available at https://libraryresources.unog.ch/lonintellectualcooperation/ICIC (accessed on 9 December 2019).

[12] Constituent Assembly Members, *Sarvepalli Radhakrishnan*. Available at https://cadindia.clpr.org.in/constituent_assembly_members/sarvepalli_radhakrishnan (accessed on 9 December 2019).

[13] See https://www.un.org/counterterrorism/ctitf/en/international-legal-instruments (accessed on 9 December 2019). For further details, see https://www.wdl.org/en/item/11579/ (accessed on 9 December 2019).

President Franklin D. Roosevelt of the USA. Twenty-six allied nations fighting against the Axis powers were invited by the USA to a conference in Washington, DC, in January 1942.

The meeting was convened to get the endorsement of the group for endorsing the objectives of the Atlantic Charter, signed in July 1941 between the USA and the United Kingdom. These objectives included obligations not to seek territorial expansion; 'to seek the liberalization of international trade; to establish the freedom of the seas, and international labor, economic, and welfare standards'.[14] The Charter committed to the 'right of all peoples to choose the form of government under which they will live', including 'sovereign rights and self-government restored to those who have been forcibly deprived of them'.[15] At the 1942 Washington Conference, a 'Declaration by the United Nations' was signed by the 26 participating nations, including India.[16] This opened the door for India to become a founding member of contemporary multilateral organizations under the UN process, as an 'original' member under the UN Charter.[17]

India participated in the negotiations during the UN Monetary and Financial Conference at Bretton Woods in July 1944. The meeting decided to establish the International Monetary Fund (IMF) and International Bank for Reconstruction and Development (IBRD or World Bank) to 'sustain' the peace after the Second World War. India was an original signatory of the Bretton Woods Agreements.[18] It is useful to recall that in terms of significance in the global financial landscape, India was ranked 6th out of the 45 founding members of the IMF in

---

[14] United States Department of State, Office of the Historian, *The Atlantic Conference and Charter, 1941*. Available at https://history.state.gov/milestones/1937–1945/atlantic-conf (accessed on 9 December 2019).

[15] Yale Law School, Lillian Goldman Law Library, *Atlantic Charter, 14 August 1941*. Available at http://avalon.law.yale.edu/wwii/atlantic.asp (accessed on 9 December 2019).

[16] Yale Law School, Lillian Goldman Law Library, *Declaration by the United Nations* (1 January 1942). Available at http://avalon.law.yale.edu/20th_century/decade03.asp (accessed on 9 December 2019). India's Agent General in the USA, Sir Girija Shankar Bajpai, ICS, signed the Declaration on behalf of India.

[17] The United Nations, *Charter of the United Nations*, Article 3. Available at https://www.un.org/en/charter-united-nations/ (accessed on 9 December 2019).

[18] Ankit Mittal, 'How India Shaped International Monetary Policy at Bretton Woods', *LiveMint* (27 February 2016). Available at https://www.livemint.com/Sundayapp/OTKspkiceV5ipSvHgRaSVO/How-India-shaped-international-monetary-policy-at-Bretton-Wo.html (accessed on 9 December 2019).

1945, with a quota of US$400 million special drawing rights (SDRs). This placed it just below five self-declared permanent members of the UN Security Council. These quotas determined a country's financial contribution to the IMF, its voting power in IMF decisions and the limit of its access to IMF resources.[19]

When the UN Charter was negotiated, the core provisions regarding decisions on international peace and security in order to 'secure the peace' were agreed upon between the four allied military powers (the Republic of China, the United Kingdom, the Union of Soviet Socialist Republics and the USA). Despite having contributed over 2.5 million volunteer troops to fight in the allied armies in Europe, Asia and Africa during the Second World War, India was not a participant in these closed-door negotiations. The negotiations were spread out between October 1943 and February 1945.[20]

The draft UN Charter was shown to India, and the four British Dominions of Australia, Canada, New Zealand and South Africa, only between 4 and 13 April 1945 at a meeting hosted by the United Kingdom in London. Despite the participants calling for 'clarification, improvement and expansion' of some of the provisions of the draft Charter, the permanent members stood their ground.[21] The UN Conference on International Organization held in San Francisco between April and June 1945, attended by 50 nations, adopted the Charter,[22] including its controversial provision giving the five permanent members 'veto' rights in decision-making by the UN Security Council.[23]

Delegates from British India and India's princely states were part of the Indian delegation that participated in the San Francisco Conference.

---

[19] International Monetary Fund, *Articles of Agreement of the International Monetary Fund*, Article III.1, Schedule A. Available at https://www.imf.org/external/pubs/ft/aa/index.htm (accessed on 9 December 2019).

[20] United Nations, *Yearbook of the United Nations 1946–47*, p. 3 (New York, NY: United Nations). 'The Moscow Declaration on General Security' (October 1943) and subsequent negotiations at Dumbarton Oaks in 1944 and Yalta in 1945. Available at http://cdn.un.org/unyearbook/yun/chapter_pdf/1946–47YUN/1946–47_P1_SEC1.pdf (accessed on 9 December 2019).

[21] Ibid, 25. Australia's objections to the veto were overridden by the permanent members.

[22] Ibid, 9–10.

[23] United Nations, *Charter of the United Nations*, Article 27.3 (New York, NY: Department of Public Information). Available at https://www.un.org/en/charter-united-nations/ (accessed on 9 December 2019).

Led by Sir Arcot Ramaswami Mudaliar[24] and Sir V. T. Krishnamachari,[25] who signed the UN Charter on 26 June 1945, they acquiesced with the provisions of the Charter giving veto rights to the five permanent members of the UN Security Council. Indications that an independent India would not agree with such a stance were evident in the public speeches against the Indian position by Vijaya Lakshmi Pandit, who was present in San Francisco during the Conference.[26]

A new dynamism in India's participation in the UN became clearer in 1946, when the first session of the UNGA was held. India took its first major political initiative in the UN to give substance to the provisions of the Charter on non-discrimination by inscribing racial discrimination in South Africa on the agenda of the UNGA on 22 June 1946.[27] India's position reflected domestic sentiment that would make non-discrimination an integral part of the Indian Constitution.[28]

This initiative gathered momentum as more and more former colonies became independent and joined the 'anti-apartheid' movement. Ultimately, multilateral diplomatic measures used international cooperation, including using economic sanctions, to eventually bring about a multiracial South Africa through elections held in April 1994. President Nelson Mandela led a South African multiracial delegation for the first time to the UNGA in September 1994.

India's commitment to using international cooperation to protect fundamental human rights and freedoms through multilateral legal instruments became evident during the first session of the UNGA. Indian officials were aware of mass atrocity crimes committed during the Second World War, including the genocide perpetrated against Jews in Europe by Hitlerite Germany. As a member of the 17-nation UN War

---

[24] See https://www.unmultimedia.org/s/photo/detail/133/0001339.html (accessed on 9 December 2019).

[25] See https://www.unmultimedia.org/photo/detail.jsp?id=235/235929&key=13&query=viewed:%7B0%20TO%20999%7D&sf= (accessed on 9 December 2019).

[26] Julie Laut, 'The Woman Who Swayed America': Vijayalakshmi Pandit, 1945 (Venice: University of Venezia). Available at https://www.unive.it/pag/fileadmin/user_upload/dipartimenti/DSLCC/documenti/DEP/numeri/n37/05_Laut.pdf (accessed on 9 December 2019).

[27] United Nations, Nelson Mandela International Day, 18 July 2018. Available at http://www.un.org/en/events/mandeladay/un_against_apartheid.shtml (accessed on 9 December 2019).

[28] Government of India, Constitution of India, Article 15. Available at https://www.india.gov.in/sites/upload_files/npi/files/coi_part_full.pdf (accessed on 9 December 2019).

Crimes Commission between 1943 and 1948, India had participated in discussions on how to prevent and penalize such mass atrocity crimes.[29]

It was against this background that the suggestion of Raphael Lemkin, who coined the word 'genocide', for India to be one of the co-sponsors of a UN Convention against Genocide in the UNGA in 1946 met with a positive response from Vijaya Lakshmi Pandit, the leader of the Indian delegation.[30] The mandate for drafting a Convention against genocide was proposed by India, Cuba and Panama and adopted on 11 December 1946 by the General Assembly as Resolution 96(I). Within two years, the convention had been negotiated. It was the first multilateral legal document against mass atrocity crimes, adopted on 9 December 1948.[31]

This was followed by India's initiative in placing gender equality into the lexicon of the first multilateral treaty on human rights, the *Universal Declaration of Human Rights* (UDHR). India's freedom struggle had brought together both men and women into the process of overthrowing British colonial rule through non-violent means. One of the women activists was Hansa Mehta, who later became vice chancellor of M. S. University of Baroda.[32] She represented India in the UN Commission on Human Rights between 1947 and 1948. As the UN noted in March 2018:

> Hansa Mehta was a staunch fighter for women's rights in India and abroad. She is widely credited with making a significant change in the language of Article 1 of the UDHR, by replacing the phrase 'All men are born free and equal' to 'All human beings are born free and equal.[33]

---

[29] United Nations, Report No. E/CN.4/W.19, Ch. VI, A. (iii) (15 May 1948), 112–113. The 17 members were Australia, Belgium, Canada, China, Czechoslovakia, France, Greece, India, Luxemburg, Netherlands, New Zealand, Norway, Poland, South Africa, United Kingdom, the USA and Yugoslavia.

[30] Donne-Lee Frieze, ed., *Totally Unofficial. The Autobiography of Raphael Lemkin*, 123. Available at https://ia801606.us.archive.org/15/items/B-001–001–700/B-001–001–700.pdf (accessed on 9 December 2019).

[31] United Nations, Audiovisual Library of International Law, *Convention on the Prevention and Punishment of the Crime of Genocide* (Paris: United Nations, 9 December 1948). Available at http://legal.un.org/avl/ha/cppcg/cppcg.html (accessed on 9 December 2019).

[32] M. S. University Baroda, *Smt. Hansa Mehta, 1949–1958*. Available at http://www.msubaroda.ac.in/chancellor.php?action=vice_chancellor&id=12&only_brief=true (accessed on 9 December 2019).

[33] United Nations, Office of the High Commissioner for Human Rights, *The Role of Women in Shaping the Universal Declaration of Human Rights*

Sir Ramaswami Mudaliar of India was elected the first President of the Economic and Social Council (ECOSOC) of the UN in 1946. Under India's presidency, the ECOSOC mandated in February 1946 the launch of negotiations on international cooperation in trade and employment. Negotiators met in Havana between 21 November 1947 and 24 March 1948 at the UN Conference on Trade and Employment to finalize the creation of an International Trade Organization (ITO). The Havana Charter proposed to coordinate international cooperation in trade relations between countries in 'fields of employment, economic development, commercial policy, business practices and commodity policy', with a special focus on manufacturing, investment, market access and reduction of tariffs.[34]

The refusal of the US Congress to allow the USA to be part of the ITO led to a provisional agreement among 23 countries who had separately been negotiating tariff reductions in Geneva to enter into a 'General Agreement on Tariffs and Trade' (GATT) in October 1947.[35] India was a participant in these negotiations and became a founder member of the GATT.[36]

Another 48 years would pass before the objectives of the Havana Charter became part of the agreement establishing the World Trade Organization (WTO) on 1 January 1995. India is a founder member of the WTO. The WTO is anchored on the principle of one-country one-vote and a transparent dispute settlement mechanism (DSM)[37] whose decisions are accepted as binding by all members of the WTO.

The initial 15 years of the UN demonstrated the adverse impact on newly independent developing countries of the biggest contradiction

---

(6 March 2018). Available at https://www.ohchr.org/EN/NewsEvents/Pages/TheRoleWomenShapingUDHR.aspx (accessed on 9 December 2019).

[34] World Trade Organization, *The United Nations Conference on Trade and Employment, 'Final Act'* (April 1948). Available at https://www.wto.org/english/docs_e/legal_e/havana_e.pdf (accessed on 9 December 2019).

[35] World Trade Organization, *The General Agreement on Tariffs and Trade (GATT)* (1947). Available at https://www.wto.org/English/Docs_E/legal_e/gatt47_01_e.htm (accessed on 9 December 2019).

[36] India's GATT negotiations were conducted by Sir N. R. Pillai, who became independent India's first cabinet secretary in 1950. For further details, see World Trade Organization, *Understanding the WTO: The GATT Years: From Havana to Marrakesh* (Geneva: World Trade Organization). Available at https://www.wto.org/english/thewto_e/whatis_e/tif_e/fact4_e.htm (accessed on 9 December 2019).

[37] World Trade Organization, *Dispute Settlement*. Available at https://www.wto.org/english/tratop_e/dispu_e/dispu_e.htm (accessed on 9 December 2019).

in the UN Charter. This was the divergence between the Charter's provisions on decision-making in the UNGA (which is based on one-country one-vote)[38] and decision-making in the UN Security Council (based on the veto privilege of the five permanent members).[39]

The issue became compounded by the fact that in all the other subsidiary structures under the UNGA, such as the ECOSOC and later the Human Rights Council, decision-making was on the basis of one-country one-vote, making the veto-based decision-making process in the Security Council an aberration in the multilateral system.

India became one of the leaders in the UNGA to overcome this contradiction. Since decisions on the Security Council would need a two-thirds majority in the UNGA, the priority for developing countries such as India was to facilitate the entry of newly independent developing countries into the General Assembly. This was blocked by the Security Council, where permanent members decided as early as 1946 that applications for membership in the UN were a 'substantive issue' subject to their veto.[40]

From its first session in 1946 till 1953, when India's Vijaya Lakshmi Pandit was elected as the first woman and first Asian President of the UNGA, 'the General Assembly had adopted 806 resolutions. Of these, 12 were adopted by a majority vote. The remaining 794 were adopted by a vote of two-thirds or more of the Members present and voting, or unanimously'.[41] In contrast, the veto dominated decision-making in the Security Council, being used as an instrument for carving out (or denying) influence in the UNGA.[42]

Such obstacles to the democratization of multilateral relations were finally overcome by the unanimous adoption of the Decolonization

---

[38] United Nations, *Charter of the United Nations*, Article 18. Available at https://www.un.org/en/charter-united-nations/ (accessed on 9 December 2019).

[39] Ibid, Article 27.3.

[40] United Nations, *Repertory of Practice of United Nations Organs, The Security Council (1945–1954)*, para. 41. Available at http://legal.un.org/docs/?path=../repertory/art27/english/rep_orig_vol2_art27.pdf&lang=E (accessed on 9 December 2019).

[41] United Nations, *Repertory of Practice of United Nations Organs, The General Assembly (1945–1954)*, para 10. Available at http://legal.un.org/docs/?path=../repertory/art18/english/rep_orig_vol1_art18.pdf&lang=EF (accessed on 9 December 2019).

[42] United Nations, *Dag Hammarskjold Library, Security Council Veto List*. Available at https://research.un.org/en/docs/sc/quick (accessed on 9 December 2019).

Resolution, co-sponsored by India, by the UNGA in December 1960.[43] This decision represents the first major political achievement of the multilateral system after the adoption of the UN Charter in 1945.

The Decolonization Resolution put two issues relevant to India on the agenda of the UNGA. It catalysed the first amendments to the UN Charter through a voted resolution in the General Assembly to increase the number of non-permanent seats in the Security Council from 6 to 10, and the number of seats on the ECOSOC from 18 to 27.[44] The decision linked peace, security and development from the perspective of developing countries. It also focused on development through international cooperation that would preoccupy the General Assembly from 1964 till 2015, when Agenda 2030 with its 17 Sustainable Development Goals (SDGs) was adopted.[45]

India took the lead in creating a cohesive group within the General Assembly of newly independent developing countries. In 1964, the Group of 77 (G77) developing countries was formed. The General Assembly adopted a decision establishing a dedicated structure to respond to the development priorities of the G77 by creating the UN Development Programme (UNDP) in 1965.[46] India became the first Chair of the G77 in 1970–1971.[47]

Concerns within Western developed countries regarding the impact of industrialization and development on the environment led the UN to

---

[43] United Nations, *Declaration on Granting of Independence to Colonial Countries and Peoples*, UN General Assembly Resolution 1514 (XV) (14 December 1960). Available at https://www.un.org/en/decolonization/declaration.shtml (accessed on 9 December 2019).

[44] United Nations, *UNGA Resolution 1991* (XVIII) (17 December 1963). Available at https://documents-dds-ny.un.org/doc/RESOLUTION/GEN/NR0/186/66/IMG/NR018666.pdf?OpenElement (accessed on 9 December 2019). The UN General Assembly amended the UN Charter once again in 1971 to increase the representation of developing countries in the ECOSOC, creating a total of 54 elected seats in the body.

[45] United Nations, *Transforming Our World—Agenda 2030 for Sustainable Development* (September 2015). Available at https://sustainabledevelopment.un.org/post2015/transformingourworld (accessed on 9 December 2019).

[46] United Nations, UN General Assembly Resolution 2029, *Consolidation of the Special Fund and the Expanded Programme of Technical Assistance in a United Nations Development Programme* (22 November 1965). Available at https://documents-dds-ny.un.org/doc/RESOLUTION/GEN/NR0/217/92/PDF/NR021792.pdf?OpenElement (accessed on 9 December 2019).

[47] The Group of 77 at the United Nations, *About the Group of 77*. Available at https://www.g77.org/doc/ (accessed on 9 December 2019).

convene its first Conference on the Human Environment in Stockholm in July 1972.[48] Speaking at the conference, India stated, *inter alia*, that 'poverty is the biggest polluter'.[49] This led to a popular perception regarding a multilateral policy confrontation between development and environmental objectives.

India played an active role within the UNGA to converge these two issues into the concept of 'sustainable development'. The Brundtland Report on Sustainable Development was tabled at the World Conference on Environment and Development in 1987.[50] The concept of 'sustainable development' was formalized as multilateral policy at the historic 1992 Earth Summit held in Rio de Janeiro.[51] The Earth Summit played a major role in multilateral discussions and negotiation of a sustainable development agenda, which was mandated by the Rio+20 Summit of the UN held in 2012.[52]

The adoption of Agenda 2030 within a relatively short time span of two-and-a-half years between March 2013 and September 2015 represents another high point in the responsiveness of the General Assembly to ground realities.

Agenda 2030 resulted in making sustainable development an integrated universal framework, requiring the participation of all UN member states. It acknowledged the importance of nationally led efforts on the ground to achieve the targets of the SDGs. This significantly expanded the scope of international cooperation to impact on all aspects of human endeavour. At the same time, the need to support developing countries overcomes the handicaps of colonial rule for their

---

[48] United Nations, *United Nations Conference on the Human Environment* (Stockholm Conference, 2–16 June 1972). Available at https://sustainabledevelopment.un.org/milestones/humanenvironment (accessed on 9 December 2019).

[49] Indian National Congress, *Address to the United Nations Conference on the Human Environment* (14 June 1972). Available at https://www.inc.in/en/media/speech/the-human-environment (accessed on 9 December 2019).

[50] United Nations, *Report of the World Commission on Environment and Development: Our Common Future* (20 March 1987). Available at http://www.un-documents.net/ocf-cf.htm (accessed on 9 December 2019).

[51] United Nations, *United Nations Conference on Environment and Development*, Agenda 21 (3–14 June 1992). Available at https://sustainabledevelopment.un.org/content/documents/Agenda21.pdf (accessed on 9 December 2019).

[52] United Nations, *The Future We Want*, Annex, paragraph 2, (Rio de Janeiro, UN Conference on Sustainable Development 20–22 June 2012). Available at https://sustainabledevelopment.un.org/index.php?menu=1298 (accessed on 9 December 2019).

socio-economic development was recognized under the approach of 'common but differentiated responsibilities' in implementing Agenda 2030's SDGs.

Agenda 2030's integration of social and economic with environmental goals also met the objectives of the UN Charter 'to promote social progress and better standards of life in larger freedom'. The prioritization of the eradication of poverty as the overarching goal of Agenda 2030[53] by all UN member states represented a validation of India's view expressed at the 1972 Stockholm Conference on the Human Environment.

Third, by the negotiations between multi-stakeholders in nature involving governments, businesses, academia and civil society, Agenda 2030 acknowledged the incipient nature of change that had taken place in the world since the UN Charter was signed in 1945. Multi-stakeholder participation placed obligations on all participants to cooperate constructively in implementing the multilateral sustainable development policy, raising the profile and widening the impact of the principle of international cooperation.

For India, Agenda 2030 provides a direct interface between its national and multilateral development priorities, reflected in the work of NITI Aayog, which is the nodal point for implementing Agenda 2030 in India.[54] India's focus on sustainable development had been galvanized by the campaign for inclusive development (*Sabka Saath, Sabka Vikas*) during her general elections held in 2014. Consequently, several of the SDGs mirrored India's national development objectives. This was particularly applicable to the eradication of poverty, which became SDG 1, and was designated as the 'overarching' objective of Agenda 2030.

India's nationally declared objective of generating 175GW of renewable energy by 2022 contributed to SDG 7 on clean energy. Coupled with this was India's initiative, taken on the margins of the 2015 UN Framework Convention on Climate Change meeting in Paris, to launch an ambitious International Solar Alliance (ISA). The implementation of this proposal within 16 months in March 2018 and the meeting of the first General Assembly of the ISA in India in

---

[53] United Nations, *Transforming Our World*, Preamble and Para 2 of the Declaration.

[54] NITI Aayog, Government of India, *SDG Index, State/UT Ranking*. Available at https://sdgindiaindex.socialcops.com/YuJbcq9d44/state-ut-ranking/basic#3/23.00/81.26 (accessed on 9 December 2019).

October 2018 demonstrated India's capability and determination to give leadership and shape to international cooperation in environmental issues.

A similar approach was evident in Indian Prime Minister Narendra Modi's unusual proposal at the UNGA on 27 September 2014 for a multilateral decision on declaring 21 June as the International Yoga Day. The Prime Minister emphasized that

> Yoga embodies unity of mind and body; thought and action; restraint and fulfillment; harmony between man and nature; a holistic approach to health and well-being. It is not about exercise but to discover the sense of oneness with yourself, the world and the nature.[55]

In 2007, India had taken the initiative to have 2 October (Mahatma Gandhi's birthday) declared as an International Day of Non-Violence by the UNGA. The resolution had been adopted unanimously with 140 co-sponsors.[56] For the proposal to declare an International Yoga Day, the groundswell of support was spontaneous. Within 75 days, as many as 177 member states of the UNGA co-sponsored India's proposal, setting a record for decisions on declaring International Days by the UN. The unanimous Resolution adopted by the UNGA[57] implementing India's proposal reflected the depth of support among member states for international cooperation on issues reflecting the unity of mankind and harmony between man and nature. The decision recalled the significant advocacy of the unity of mankind made decades earlier by Dr Sarvepalli Radhakrishnan during his participation in the work of the ICIC and UNESCO on international intellectual cooperation.

Beyond the specific SDGs, India was able to integrate the use of appropriate technologies for sustainable development as an integral part of Agenda 2030.[58] This reflected India's own national priorities in this area, reflected in its Digital India programme.

---

[55] Narendra Modi, *Text of PM's Statement at UN General Assembly* (27 September 2014). Available at https://www.narendramodi.in/text-of-the-pms-statement-at-the-united-nations-general-assembly-6660 (accessed on 9 December 2019).

[56] United Nations, *UN General Assembly Resolution A/RES/61/271* (15 June 2007). Available at https://undocs.org/A/RES/61/271 (accessed on 9 December 2019).

[57] United Nations, *UN General Assembly Resolution A/RES/69/131* (11 December 2014). Available at https://undocs.org/A/RES/69/131 (accessed on 9 December 2019).

[58] United Nations, *Transforming Our World*, Para 41.

These achievements of India's multilateral diplomacy in implementing the principle of international cooperation through the General Assembly in the political, socio-economic and human rights spheres need to be placed in context. It is important to recognize that India has not always succeeded in its objectives in the General Assembly. The most well-known example of this for India is the adoption of the General Assembly Resolution endorsing the discriminatory Nuclear Non-Proliferation Treaty (NPT) of 1968.[59] The method in which the General Assembly adopted its decision on the NPT was a democratic and transparent one by recorded vote. India was unable to accept the outcome of the General Assembly's decision and decided not to become party to the NPT.

World leaders, when adopting Agenda 2030, had stressed that 'there can be no sustainable development without peace and no peace without sustainable development'.[60] The emphasis on peace brings the focus on decision-making in the UN Security Council, which has the primary responsibility to maintain international peace and security. In the Security Council, many decisions are not taken in a transparent and democratic manner, especially when permanent members invoke their veto privilege and take positions without giving any explanation.

For India, this anomaly directly impacts its engagement with multilateralism and its core interests. In recent years, non-participation in the decisions of the Security Council on issues related to India on its agenda has highlighted the need for India to become an equal participant in the Council's decision-making. Faced with the ineffectiveness of the Security Council in meeting its primary responsibility, world leaders had unanimously mandated 'early reform' of the Security Council in 2005.[61] The reason for prioritizing this reform is the fact that all member states have an obligation under Article 25 of the UN Charter to implement decisions of the Security Council, even when these decisions are taken in a non-transparent manner.

Issues relevant to India currently on the Security Council's agenda include countering terrorism, where India's proposals cannot be

---

[59] United Nations, *UN General Assembly Resolution 2273(XXIII)* (12 June 1968). Available at https://documents-dds-ny.un.org/doc/RESOLUTION/GEN/NR0/240/63/IMG/NR024063.pdf?OpenElement (accessed on 9 December 2019).

[60] United Nations, *Transforming Our World*, Preamble.

[61] United Nations, *UN General Assembly Resolution A/RES/60/1* (16 September 2005), para. 153. Available at http://www.un.org/en/development/desa/population/migration/generalassembly/docs/globalcompact/A_RES_60_1.pdf (accessed on 9 December 2019).

pursued directly by it, including in overcoming the veto power of permanent members such as China. At the same time, India is a member of specialized bodies such as the Financial Action Task Force (FATF), whose recommendations are integrated into Security Council resolutions on countering terrorism.

The Security Council takes decisions on the deployment of thousands of Indian troops contributed to volatile UN peacekeeping missions in South Sudan (UNMISS), the Democratic Republic of Congo (MONUSCO) and Golan Heights (UNDOF). Despite the clear provisions of Article 44 of the UN Charter giving the right to India as a troop contributing country to consult with the Security Council on the deployment of its troops, India has been kept out of the decision-making process by the permanent members.

Permanent members of the Security Council have, since 2011, used their privileged position to calibrate their interests in influencing the political end game in Afghanistan. This includes decisions taken by them to waive Security Council sanctions on listed Taliban figures identified for re-integration into the political process in Afghanistan. This has happened without the participation of India, which has invested over $3 billion into Afghanistan's infrastructure, including human resources development, and which faces a constant threat from terrorist elements incubated in the AfPak region.

Security Council decisions on Iran, including the implementation of the Joint Comprehensive Plan of Action on Iran's nuclear programme, have major implications for India's energy and connectivity initiatives, which revolve around Iran. Polarization between permanent members has created the space for a revival of unilateral extraterritorial legal measures by the USA, with serious implications for India's interests.

The situation in Yemen, where the ongoing Civil War on the agenda of the Security Council has been ignored by the permanent members, has grave implications for India. Yemen sits strategically on the major sea lane of communication through the Red Sea, which transports the bulk of India's foreign trade and digital data to the outside world, contributing to the transformation of India.

India's interest in participating on an equal basis in Security Council decision-making is also due to the impact of issues looming on the agenda of this body. These issues include the security of the cyber domain, where polarization between the permanent members on how to implement cybersecurity norms can lead to the fracturing or paralysis of cyberspace; the regulation of outer space, including its weaponization, where India has significant concerns; the security of the Blue Economy, which will impact the implementation of India's SAGAR Indian Ocean policy.

More than 70 years after its Independence from colonial rule, India needs to become part of the decision-making process in the Security Council. It should not continue to rely on the goodwill of some permanent members to achieve its national interests. How can this be achieved?

The process to reform the Security Council has a strong Indian influence. Following the expansion of the Security Council in 1965, non-permanent members, despite the increase in their numbers, had been unable to overcome the veto privilege of permanent members in taking decisions in the Security Council. India's Permanent Representative Brajesh Mishra led a successful effort of 10 developing countries on 14 November 1979 to seek greater equity and representation in the Security Council by putting this issue on the agenda of the General Assembly.[62]

In December 1992, India with 35 other members of the Non-Aligned Movement moved the General Assembly to ask the UN Secretary General (UNSG) to table a report on a 'possible review of the membership of the Security Council'.[63] Based on the report of the UNSG, the General Assembly decided in December 1993 to set up an Open-ended Working Group (OEWG) for member states to 'consider all aspects of the question of increase in the membership of the Security Council'.[64]

The historic mandate for Security Council reform given in 2005 by world leaders (including those representing the five permanent members) has been blocked by a small group of a dozen anti-reform

---

[62] United Nations, *Question of Equitable Representation on and Increase in the Membership of the Security Council*, UN Document No. A/34/246 (14 November 1979), submitted by Algeria, Argentina, Bangladesh, Bhutan, Guyana, India, Maldives, Nepal, Nigeria and Sri Lanka to the UN Secretary General. Available at http://www.un.org/en/ga/search/view_doc.asp?symbol=A/34/246 (accessed on 10 December 2019).

[63] United Nations, *Question of Equitable Representation on and Increase in the Membership of the Security Council*, UNGA Resolution No. A/RES/47/62 (11 December 1992). Available at http://www.un.org/documents/ga/res/47/a47r062.htm (accessed on 10 December 2019).

[64] United Nations, *Question of Equitable Representation on and Increase in the Membership of the Security Council*, UNGA Resolution No. A/RES/48/26 (3 December 1993). Available at http://www.un.org/documents/ga/res/48/a48r026.htm (accessed on 10 December 2019).

countries in the UNGA banded together as 'Uniting for Consensus',[65] led by China, who oppose any reform of decision-making by the five permanent members in the Security Council.

India, with like-minded pro-reform countries, has taken three initiatives to overcome this opposition. First, it pushed the decision of the UNGA to give formal structure to the mandate by launching intergovernmental negotiations (IGN) in 2007.[66] Second, it helped catalyse the UNGA decision in 2008 identifying five interlinked parameters for negotiations: categories of membership; the question of the veto; regional representation; size of an enlarged Security Council and working methods of the Council; and the relationship between the Council and the General Assembly.[67] Third, India led a concerted effort by 122 countries in the UNGA on 14 September 2015[68] to have a negotiating document adopted unanimously.[69]

Currently, momentum on Security Council reforms in the General Assembly has faltered. This is due to the 'missed opportunities by pro-reform States',[70] and the aggressive diplomacy of China,[71] which has

---

[65] Italy convenes this group, comprising of Argentina, Canada, Colombia, Costa Rica, Malta, Mexico, Pakistan, Republic of Korea, San Marino, Spain and Turkey.

[66] This group tabled a draft resolution for IGN, bearing the number A/61/L.69/Rev.1, because of which it is called the L69 group in the negotiations on UNSC reform in the UNGA. See http://www.un.org/en/ga/search/view_doc.asp?symbol=A/61/L.69/REV.1&Lang=E (accessed on 10 December 2019).

[67] United Nations, *Question of Equitable Representation on and Increase in the Membership of the Security Council and Related Matters*, UNGA Decision 62/557 (15 September 2008). Available at http://www.centerforunreform.org/sites/default/files/62%3A557.pdf (accessed on 10 December 2019).

[68] United Nations, *General Assembly Adopts, without Vote, 'Landmark' Decision on Advancing Efforts to Reform, Increase Membership of Security Council*. Available at http://www.un.org/press/en/2015/ga11679.doc.htm (accessed on 10 December 2019).

[69] C. S. Gharekhan, 'India's "Mission UN" on Track', *India Today* (16 September 2015). Available at http://indiatoday.intoday.in/story/india-mission-united-nations-on-track/1/475387.html (accessed on 10 December 2019).

[70] E. Courtenay Rattray, *A Security Council for the 21st Century: Challenges & Prospects* (IDSA Issue Brief, 20 July 2016. Available at http://www.idsa.in/issuebrief/a-security-council-for-the-21st-century_ecrattray_200716 (accessed on 10 December 2019).

[71] It is revealing, for example, that while the USA, UK, France and Russian Federation have endorsed India's permanent membership of the reformed UNSC, the PRC is the only permanent member not to have endorsed India's candidacy.

reportedly used 'levers of power and influence, including economic pressure'.[72] The result has seen an abrupt change of the IGN's successful Chairman, a distortion of the agreed parameters of text-based negotiations[73], and most significantly, a visible dilution[74] in the rock solid African Group support for the African president of the General Assembly's decision of September 2015.

As the UN moves to mark its 75th anniversary in 2020, reinvigorating the process of Security Council reform becomes a priority to ensure a supporting environment of peace for sustainable development. The most viable way to implement this priority would require tabling a draft resolution with 129 co-sponsoring member states for adoption by the General Assembly. This draft should reflect all the five areas agreed to for reform in the General Assembly decision of 2008. Contrary to public statements by responsible permanent members of the Security Council such as China, adopting such a resolution does not depend on 'comprehensive consensus'.[75] In 1998, the UNGA had unanimously decided that Security Council reform requires 'the affirmative vote of at least two thirds of the Members of the General Assembly'.[76] China is part of this unanimous decision. India has already reiterated that reform of the Security Council would require the UNGA to pass a resolution to amend the UN Charter.[77] It is time for India to take the lead in doing so.

It is possible to conceptualize three different scenarios for the achievement of this objective in the UNGA.

---

[72] Ibid.

[73] See http://www.un.org/pga/70/wp-content/uploads/sites/10/2015/08/17-May_Security-Council-Reform-17-May-2016.pdf (accessed on 10 December 2019).

[74] In October 2015, for example, the common position of India and Africa in favour of additional permanent seats in a reformed Security Council could not find any mention in the Delhi Declaration issued at the end of the India–Africa Summit. See 'Delhi Declaration', available at http://mea.gov.in/Uploads/PublicationDocs/25980_declaration.pdf (accessed on 10 December 2019).

[75] Xinhua, 'Chinese State Councilor Meets Co-chair of Inter-Governmental Negotiations on UN Security Council Reform (1 March 2019). Available at http://www.xinhuanet.com/english/2019-03/01/c_137861341.htm (accessed on 10 December 2019).

[76] United Nations, *Question of Equitable Representation on and Increase in the Membership of the Security Council and Related Matters*, UNGA Resolution A/RES/53/30 (1 December 1998).

[77] Ministry of External Affairs, India, *Reply to Lok Sabha Unstarred Question 631* (2 December 2015). Available at http://mea.gov.in/lok-sabha.htm?dtl/26094/Q+NO631+UNSC+REFORMS (accessed on 10 December 2019).

The 'traditional' scenario is for a consensus-based agreement.[78] This reflects a gradualist approach to reform, including the undemocratic veto mechanism in the UN Security Council. The initiative of France to limit the use of the veto on mass atrocity crimes could become a window towards this larger objective in the negotiations, although France has proposed limiting the use of the veto as part of a 'code of conduct' and not by amending the UN Charter.[79]

However, the likelihood of any consensus-based resolution on Security Council reform has receded significantly with the emergence of unilateralism as the preferred approach to international cooperation of major powers such as the USA, Russia, China and even the UK, which are all permanent members of the Security Council. In addition, the polarization between these major powers has made Security Council reform a part of their *inter se* differences, which has already impacted adversely the international peace and security.

A second scenario is more 'populist', involving the tabling of a draft UNGA resolution to be adopted by a two-thirds majority vote (129 out of 193 member states), essentially pitting the majority of the General Assembly's 188 member states against the five permanent members of the Security Council. Replacing the veto by majority voting would have to become the central focus of the IGN on Security Council reform under this scenario. This resolution would amend the decision-making provisions of the UN Charter on Security Council issues, including Article 27.3 on the veto, as well as Article 108 requiring the ratification of the amendments by all the five permanent members.

The third is a 'destructive' scenario. This would occur due to the outright rejection by the Security Council's permanent members to ratify the amendments proposed to the UN Charter by a successful UNGA resolution. Although such an outcome would temporarily paralyse the UN, it would catalyse the emergence of a new framework of

---

[78] United Nations, President of the General Assembly, *Inter-Governmental Negotiations on Security Council Reform* (27 March 2015). The document contains the conceptual framework for completing the reforms based on member-driven text-based negotiations. Available at https://www.un.org/pga/wp-content/uploads/sites/3/2015/03/270315_intergovernmental-negotiations-sc-reform.pdf (accessed on 10 December 2019).

[79] France Diplomatie, *Why France Wishes to Regulate the Use of the Veto in the UN Security Council*. Available at https://www.diplomatie.gouv.fr/en/french-foreign-policy/united-nations/france-and-the-united-nations-security-council/article/why-france-wishes-to-regulate-use (accessed on 10 December 2019).

'positive multilateralism' as the framework for international cooperation in the 21st century.

How can the General Assembly adopt a resolution on reforming the Security Council despite opposition from the five permanent members?

Since the core of the proposed resolution will go to the heart of the power of permanent members by addressing the question of the veto, it may be practical to seek co-sponsorship of the resolution by at least 129 member states before it is tabled in the General Assembly. A transparent campaign for co-sponsorship would successfully counter behind-the-scenes coercive diplomacy by permanent members. It was the adoption of such a transparent approach, facilitated by the global webcasting of UNGA proceedings in public glare that resulted in the unanimous adoption of the first draft text co-authored by 122 member states for Security Council reform in September 2015.[80]

Through advocating 'positive multilateralism', India would carry to a logical conclusion the thrust of its multilateral diplomacy since Independence in 1947, which is to make democratic decision-making and sustainable development the *raison d'être* of the multilateral system, endorsed by a vast majority of UN member states. The binding glue of such a network of 'positive multilateralism' could be Agenda 2030, which has been adopted unanimously by the General Assembly as a universally applicable framework. Such a development would integrate decision-making on peace, security and development as a new paradigm for the UN.

To implement such a vision, India should use the Raisina Dialogue platform that it initiated in 2016 in a coordinated manner. The scope and participants of the Dialogue need to be calibrated with the objective of providing a new 'Dumbarton Oaks' moment for drawing up an intellectual framework for 'positive multilateralism' for the 21st century. By encouraging a multi-stakeholder participatory approach, the Dialogue would address multilateral issues in an integrated manner, making the principle of international cooperation a living reality in the 21st century.

---

[80] United Nations, President of the General Assembly, *Draft Text for Inter-Governmental Negotiations* (31 July 2015). The position on abolition of the veto for all permanent members taken by the African Union, CARICOM and L-69 groupings may be seen on p. 14 of the Framework Document. Available at https://www.un.org/pga/wp-content/uploads/sites/3/2013/11/Security-Council-reform-IGN-31-July-2015.pdf (accessed on 10 December 2019).

India has a firm commitment to the principle of international cooperation. In this context, it is useful to recall the words of Prime Minister Narendra Modi in his first address to the UNGA in 2014. He said:

> India is a country that constitutes one-sixth of humanity, a nation experiencing economic and social transformation on a scale rarely seen in history. Every nation's world view is shaped by its civilization and philosophical tradition. India's ancient wisdom sees the world as one family. It is reflected in a tradition of openness and diversity, co-existence and cooperation. This is why India speaks not just for itself, but also for the cause of justice, dignity, opportunity and prosperity around the world. It is also because of this timeless current of thought that India has an unwavering belief in multilateralism.[81]

---

[81] Narendra Modi, *Text of the PM's Statement at the UN General Assembly* (27 September 2014). Available at https://www.narendramodi.in/text-of-the-pms-statement-at-the-united-nations-general-assembly-6660 (accessed on 10 December 2019).

Leveraging International Cooperation in Science and Technology

Arvind Gupta

Introduction

India has considerable achievements in using science and technology (S&T) for national security and development. All governments have given due attention to developing S&T infrastructure in the country and nurture programmes in atomic energy, space sciences, biotechnologies, information and communication technology (ICT), agricultural sciences, defence technologies, etc. Attention is being paid to develop applications of S&T in e-governance, health care, education, communications, infrastructure and many other areas. The results have been mixed. While India has a creditable position in global S&T rankings, the innovation ecosystem remains weak and undernourished.

Despite impressive achievements in developing peaceful uses of nuclear energy, space and agriculture, India cannot rest on its past laurels. It has to gear itself to meeting competition from other countries as well as global companies to remain in the race. Riding on new technologies, globalization is accelerating. Countries such as China have made impressive advances in conventional and newer areas of S&T. Many global companies are spending more on R&D than several countries put together. For instance Amazon spent $22.6 billion on R&D in 2018, which was more than that of Ireland. The competition for developing technologies for the 21st century in the areas of education, commerce, agriculture, health care, climate change, defence, etc., is becoming sharper. India will have to be flexible and nimble in adjusting to the rapid pace of technological advances. There is a danger that India will be swamped by technologies and products developed abroad and lose its advantage in strategic technologies.

India had an early start in harnessing in S&T, but it has not been able to capitalize on it in the S&T area. It is losing its vast market to global technology companies. This is reflected in huge imports of electronics hardware and appliances, mostly from China, into the country. India's economic e-commerce companies, which ride on high-technology platforms, are being bought by foreign companies. As the threat of climate change grows, new clean energy technologies and technologies to deal with water and land pollution will be needed. Its record in developing such technologies and commercializing them is at best patchy.

The battle over Intellectual Property Rights (IPRs) will define the contours of the 21st century. At the heart of US–China trade lies the sensitive issue of IPR 'theft'. Even a common device such as the cell phone or a printer has hundreds of patents into it. India's record in generating IPRs has certainly improved but is far below that of its competitors. Similarly, cybersecurity issues are rising in prominence not only in the military arena but also in civilian areas. India needs to pay greater attention to developing cybersecurity technology products and services indigenously. It is a matter of regret that despite its formidable prowess in the software area, India has not been able to develop its cybersecurity capabilities indigenously. Foreign companies are at the forefront of developing such technologies. They are positioning themselves to capture the global market. India should remain wary.

S&T requires a steady stream of youngsters who take up science as a career. Unfortunately, youth of India is attracted more to non-science disciplines than scientific disciplines. The quality of S&T education in India is also uneven despite the fact that many new colleges and universities have opened. The brain drain from India in the specialized areas of S&T and engineering is continuing unabated.

The importance of high-quality education from school to universities cannot be overestimated. Science, technology, engineering, mathematics and innovation education in India need to be vastly improved. There is a lot of work that needs to be done to change the rigid curricula, make education more relevant to the needs of a knowledge society and provide good quality, long-term careers in S&T. India needs to ensure that major science missions in the country generate jobs, create intellectual property and result in products and applications as well as new research. Science must be tightly integrated with national policies of development and security. All this needs to be done quickly and in a flexible manner.

India has been at the receiving end of technology export controls and sanctions in the past decade on account of its indigenous strategic and defence programmers. The atomic and space establishments have weathered the storm. Efforts to control the export of emerging technologies cannot be ruled out. This problem can only be tackled by ensuring that the indigenous development of S&T is given due attention and India sits at the leading export control regimes and has a say in shaping global norms and rules.

In India, science is still done predominantly in government institutions. Presently, about 65 per cent of R&D expenditure comes from government and the rest from the private sector. No wonder Indian companies do not figure in the world's top S&T companies. The share of the private sector in R&D needs to be improved vastly.

Science, R&D and innovation are becoming global. This is evident from the proposal of global scientific networks, existence of high visibility projects based on international cooperation, international collaboration in high-quality publications, emergence of global companies leveraging international expertise and the rise of global supply chain in the production of high-tech products. India will need to plug into global networks and supply chain. Presently, Indian institutions find it difficult to sustain international collaboration on their own.

In this chapter, we examine how international cooperation can be leveraged to use S&T for national objectives of growth, development and national security. The chapter argues that S&T should be closely integrated with the foreign policy objectives of the country.

Challenges

International cooperation can play a role in improving S&T infrastructure in the country, developing R&D alliances, making products for the global market, enhancing India's soft power and raising India's global profile. Over the years, India has developed a vast S&T cooperation programme with a large number of countries. India also participates in prestigious global science projects across the world. The contribution of Indian scientists, engineers and technologists has been recognized the world over. However, what benefits such international cooperation programme brings to the country needs to be properly assessed, documented and disseminated. Mere participation in scientific collaborations or having S&T cooperation agreements and Memoranda of Understanding (MoUs) with other countries is not sufficient. There should be a review of our scientific collaborations from a point of view of assessing their worthwhileness for national objectives of development and security.

How can international cooperation be leveraged to achieve national objectives? Today, when the problems of food, energy, water, pollution, industrial competitiveness, etc., are becoming more and more acute, our collaborations should be focused in these areas and provide answers to the burning problems which concern us. The world is at the cusp of a new revolution in technology with the emergence of technologies such as big data analytics, artificial intelligence, machine learning, gene editing, robotics, driverless cars, etc. Space technologies are also being integrated with other technologies and harnessed for growth, development and national security. The growth of cyberspace presents its own challenges. Emerging technologies are becoming strategic technologies with the wide-ranging application. Their use in education, food, commerce, energy, financial services and similar areas will revolutionize human lives. At the same time, there is a danger that if India does not develop these strategic technologies early, India may become dependent on others even for its basic requirements. This is already visible in the area of ICT. India has an advantage in this field but all the products and devices that it uses are developed abroad and are imported into the country in large numbers. Similarly, the emergence of new agricultural technologies and their aggressive marketing could have an adverse impact on Indian farmers who are still grappling with high input costs, rising debts and climate change. Innovations in marketing, which will change the nature of marketing, are an important area where India needs to be focused. E-commerce technologies are already impacting the traditional distribution and logistics networks.

Indian leaders have repeatedly asked scientists to align S&T with national needs and priorities, keeping the poorest of the citizens in focus. Improving the lives of the poorest sections of the population is a huge challenge which will require a balanced approach that maintains the right equilibrium between basic and applied science. The 21st-century challenges for India include maintaining robust economic growth, emerging as S&T power, harnessing S&T for India's growth, countering technology controls, leveraging vast Indian market, investing in S&T infrastructure, improving Science, Technology, Engineering and Mathematics (STEM) and emerging as innovation hub. There is also an urgent need to increase the share of high technology in trade, commerce and finance, withstand competition in the field of S&T, develop strategic technologies, raise S&T awareness in the country, generate jobs in the area of S&T, R&D and innovation, become a net exporter of S&T products and services, boost expenditure on R&D, enhance India's soft power, improve coordination among S&T agencies within the country and remain ahead of the curve in emerging technologies. The list is long and many more challenges can be added. Are we ready to meet these challenges?

Many of the challenges are domestic in nature. For instance, India needs to substantially raise its R&D expenditure which is languishing at about 0.7 per cent of the GDP for a long time. Expenditure on R&D needs to be raised to 2 per cent of the GDP as many experts have agreed. China, in contrast, spends about 2.5 per cent of GDP and has plans to increase it to 3 per cent of GDP. Even a country like Israel spends nearly 5 per cent of GDP on R&D. The top five companies in the world spend between 10 and 25 per cent of the revenue on R&D. This amounts over $100 billion. China has adopted a focused approach and is now in a position to capture the 5G global market in telecommunications. The Chinese company Huawei has been spending billions of dollars every year to develop new mobile technologies. We do not see such urgency or enthusiasm in any Indian company.

The problem in India has been that R&D has not been converted into prototypes, products and devices. The innovation ecosystem in the country which is driven by competition is weak. The technologies available in Indian labs have either been languishing or not been successfully converted into user-friendly products. The link between academia, government and commercial entities remains tenuous and uninspiring. How to strengthen this link is a major issue. India boasts of the third largest number of start-ups in the country. But the start-ups will wither away if they are not nurtured and supported in the beginning. This is already happening. Many foreign companies are buying Indian start-ups. This will be detrimental to India in the long run.

Indian Efforts

India has many policies to encourage R&D in the country. The Ministry of Science and Technology, the Ministry of Earth Sciences, the Ministry of Electronics and Information Technology and the Ministry of New and Renewable Energy are among the major ministries involved in scientific R&D. The leading agencies such as the Department of Science and Technology (DST), the Department of Biotechnology (DBT), the Department of Scientific and Industrial Research, the Department of Space and the Department of Atomic Energy have elaborate schemes and programmes. These have delivered good results. But India is not a leading S&T power yet. On many parameters of R&D, India's global rank is low. This lacuna needs to be addressed urgently.

The problem is that in India science is done essentially as a departmental piecemeal activity under different sets of policies. There is little coordination among the various departments, though this situation is beginning to change. There is no overall S&T policy, only a clutch of disparate policies. S&T is not a part of overall strategy for national development and national security. Thus, there is not much incentive for interdepartmental coordination. The success of schemes is usually judged in terms of the number of scholarships given, the amount of money spent and the number of events held. We need to assess the impact of the money spent on S&T on individual well-being, types of problems resolved and global influence gained.

The DST is the nodal agency for international cooperation in this area. At present, there are nearly 80 collaboration agreements with other countries. A sharp increase in the number of cooperation and collaboration MoUs has been witnessed in the recent past. A recent example is that of Israel–India Industrial R&D Corporation. A separate fund has been set up to drive the bilateral industrial R&D activity. This will help in achieving the desired research in the agreed time frame.

Besides, India is participating in leading global research programmes such as International Thermonuclear Experimental Reactor (ITER), Thirty Meter Telescope (TMT) and facility for anti-proton research, Large Hadron Collider, Laser Interferometer Gravitational-Wave Observatory (LIGO), Square Kilometre Radio Telescope, etc. India also has major national missions such as the National Supercomputing Mission[1] and Nano Science and Technology (Nano Mission). Similarly,

---

[1] The government has decided to launch ₹4,500 crore National Supercomputing Mission. This involves setting up of 73 interlinked supercomputers in different parts of country. The mission will be implemented by Centre for Development of Advanced Computing (C-DAC) and the Indian Institute of Science, Bangalore. This is a good example of interdepartmental cooperation. The supercomputing mission which will ride on the national knowledge network will support Make in India and Digital India programmes of the country. It may be mentioned that India has a global rank of 74 in supercomputing as

leading departments such as the DBT, the DST, the Department of Space and the Ministry of Electronics and Information Technology have impressive collaboration programmes. All this results in considerable activity. But as mentioned earlier, whether this adds up to a national strategy and problem-solving for the well-being of common man is doubtful.

IPR regimes are becoming more and more restrictive. This means in the future, which will be driven by knowledge, importing technologies and products will become difficult and more expensive. Therefore, India needs to develop its own innovation system.

In the past, fighting the technology control regime has been a major problem for India. Here, the MEA and other concerned departments such as the Department of Atomic Energy have collaborated to achieve positive results for India. After many years of struggle and help from the USA, India has become a member of the three leading export control regimes such as the Missile Technology Control Regime (MTCR), Wassenaar Arrangement and Australia Group. The membership of the Nuclear Suppliers Group (NSG) is still pending and has been held up due to the objections from countries like China and a few others. Similarly, India has also been a member of the Conference on Disarmament where issues like the production of fissile materials are to be discussed. India also participates in the International Atomic Energy Agency (IAEA), which is responsible for safeguards to prevent proliferation and promoting the peaceful uses of atomic and India has been a member of the governing board of the IAEA. In the area of space, India has been participating in UNCOPUOS committees which deliberate on the peaceful uses of outer space. As India becomes a major cyber power, its weight in global and regional organizations will also increase. One of the lacunae in the Indian system is that we do not have the manpower or the capacity to engage intensively with the leading issues in the area size of technology at the global level. Indian participation in many of these organizations is weak, often perfunctory and merely routine. For instance, India has been found wanting in participating in organizations which develop standards in various technology fields. This is a serious shortcoming which needs to be addressed.

---

compared to China, which is number 1. See, Money Control, *Govt to Launch ₹4,500 cr National Supercomputing Mission* (2015, 25 March). Available at https://www.moneycontrol.com/news/business/economy/govt-to-launch-rs-4500-cr-national-supercomputing-mission-1112717.html (accessed on 29 January 2019).

In many countries, think tanks play an important role in developing norms and standards. Emerging think tank networks play a big role in knowledge dissemination, lobbying and advisory. This is true for instance in the case of cyberspace where most of the assets globally are held by private sectors. India is inadequately represented on global cyber fora. India's participation in the UN Group of Governmental Experts (GGE) on cybersecurity has been commendable but in the multi-stakeholder forum and Internet Governance Forum, it has been patchy and sporadic. We need a sharing think tank on science policy research which can engage with counterparts globally.

Technology has influenced the development of international law. Today, the world is concerned about norms in cyberspace. India must be more active in putting forward its own viewpoints and shaping the global debate in this arena. Similarly, development of autonomous weapon systems with autonomy in their critical functions, and use of artificial intelligence and other emerging technologies require a great deal of attention. India has once again been found wanting in this area.

Developed countries are devoting huge resources for the development of energy-efficient technologies to meet the challenge of climate change. Despite the fact that India has a major mission of climate change and some technologies have been developed, much more needs to be done. Similarly, major developments are taking place in the fields of materials, biotechnology and industrial systems. Missing out on these area can prove to be detrimental.

Development of defence technologies is an area of great importance. Unfortunately, despite the efforts of the Defence Research and Development Organisation (DRDO), India remains dependent upon imports of different equipment from other countries. Nearly 70 per cent of its needs are important despite the existence of a vast network of R&D and production units in the shape of DRDO and defence PSUs. Although DRDO has considerable expertise in defence R&D, its rules and procedures make it inflexible. Similar is the case with other defence PSUs. Flexibility in rules and work procedures is importance. A robust system of defence planning is needed. Innovation can happen only if the entire system of innovation starting from education and right up to the defence production is overhauled. India should aim to emerge as an exporter of defence items. Promoting defensible exports should become a part of India's foreign policy.

India has at present only four science counsellors in only four countries. This is too small in number when one considers the range and width of India's global S&T engagement. There is an urgent need to upgrade and expand India's S&T outreach programme. The number of science counsellors must be increased. India should participate in S&T shares across the world and also arrange similar fares in India. Collaboration with industry-developed countries should take the form of setting up S&T parks where innovation is combined with commercialization.

Achievements of Department of Science and Technology

India has an extensive S&T cooperation programme for which the nodal agency is the DST. According to the DST's Annual Report 2017–2018, presently India has bilateral S&T cooperation agreements with 83 countries with active cooperation with 44 countries. DST is responsible for (a) negotiating, concluding and implementing S&T agreements between India and other countries and (b) providing interventions on S&T aspects in international forums. It maintains coordination with several ministries and agencies like MEA, as well as other stakeholders including industry associations and academic institutions. It is the nodal agency for conducting bilateral, multilateral, regional S&T cooperation.

During the recent years, the cooperation has strengthened significantly with Australia, Canada, EU, France, Germany, Israel, Japan, Russia, the UK and the USA. Cooperation with African countries has also been strengthened through India–Africa S&T Initiative. The soft prowess of S&T has been leveraged to engage with several countries under India's Act East Policy and with some neighbouring countries. The Department currently supports three bi-national S&T centres which are independent entities established under intergovernmental bilateral agreements with France, the USA and Germany.[2]

The DST's key achievements in 2018–2019 were summarized by the Minister for S&T as follows[3]:

---

[2] Available at http://www.dst.gov.in/international-st-cooperation (accessed on 27 January 2019).

[3] Press Information Bureau, *Indian Science & Technology Takes Strides Towards Leadership Position during the Last Four Years*. Available at http://pib.nic.in/newsite/PrintRelease.aspx?relid=179849 (accessed on 7 June 2018).

- Translating basic research into technology development, technology transfer, innovation and commercialization of indigenous technology.
- Meeting the challenges in the areas of water, energy, health, environment, climate, agriculture and food.
- New missions in cyber-physical system, artificial intelligence, supercomputing, Deep Ocean, biopharmaceuticals and others, to become globally competitive.
- Connecting science to national priorities and needs of national missions such as Make in India, Startup India, Digital India, Swachh Bharat and Swasth Bharat.
- Building links with industry, education, etc.
- Strengthening international cooperation: India has become a partner in the LIGO project for gravitational wave detection; an associate member state of CERN.

The government has enhanced investment in science, technology and related areas. The budget of the DST was ₹19,764 crores in 2018–2019, an increase of 90 per cent. 'Similarly, there was an increase of 65% for the Department of Biotechnology; almost 43% increase for CSIR and 26% increase for Ministry of Earth Sciences.'[4]

Some more achievements listed by the ministry are as follows[5]:

- Transfer of over 800 technologies to the industry.
- Providing S&T solutions to other departments such as railways, heavy industry, urban development, defence, drinking water and sanitation, power, coal, and new and renewable energy, and Ministry of Petroleum and Natural Gas.
- S&T intervention in agriculture sector to improve crop productivity. The Ministry of Earth Sciences provides agro-meteorological advisories to 24 million farmers currently, which will be scaled up to 40 million by July 2018. More than 4 lakh fishermen are using information on potential fishing zones every day.
- Using newly acquired 6.8 petaflop supercomputing power, the Ministry of Earth Sciences has commissioned the Ensemble Weather Prediction system for providing block-level weather forecasts. This is conserved to be one of the best in the world. The timely weather has a positive economic impact of ₹50,000 crores to national GDP.

---
[4] Ibid.
[5] Ibid.

- A joint research by Council of Scientific & Industrial Research (CSIR), DBT and Indian Council of Agricultural Research (ICAR) has developed blight resistant improved Samba Mahsuri rice, which is now being cultivated in an area of 120,000 hectares in seven states.
- To reduce India's dependence on imports of chemical intermediaries and active pharmaceutical ingredient (API) needed for making medicine, the CSIR has initiated a project on mission mode.
- The investment in clean energy R&D has been doubled. India has announced the first International Clean Energy Incubator. CSIR has developed several technologies to increase the percentage of clean energy in the overall mix. These include solar power tree, novel hydroelectric cell, etc.
- As several areas in the country are facing acute shortage of water or poor quality of drinking water, the Ministry has launched several initiatives during the last four years to augment safe drinking water at affordable cost through appropriate S&T interventions developed indigenously.
- In order to boost the start-up ecosystem, government has increased the allocation by five times in the DST alone. The Ministry has supported more than 5,000 start-ups and 200 incubators. Apart from this, the Ministry has also launched a programme called Million Minds Augmenting National Aspiration and Knowledge (MANAK) to trigger innovation among schoolchildren from 6th to 10th standard.
- During the last four years, the Ministry has enhanced capacity-building of scientists, teachers, young researchers and attracting students to science streams. The Ministry supported around 11 lakh persons—right from school level to postdoctoral research. The Ministry has successfully attracted more than 600 eminent scientists of Indian origin from overseas to return to the country.

The NITI Aayog, a think tank of the government of India, unveiled a *Strategy for New India @ 75* which had a whole chapter on 'Technology and Innovation'. The document notes Indian achievements and observes that several leading global multinational companies have set up more than 1,100 R&D centres in India. Indian scientists are doing path-breaking work at the global level. India has developed cruise missiles like BrahMos, a range of missile and rocket systems, light combat aircraft and many other defence equipment. India now has credible achievements in the area of space technologies such as the development of Geosynchronous Satellite launch Vehicle (GSLV), a moon arbiter mission, Chandrayaan-1 and mars orbiter mission. India made a record of sorts by launching 104 satellites simultaneously. The government has also announced a manned mission to outer space to be completed by 2022. India is already the third largest country in the global ranking of new start-ups.[6]

However, the document also notes the constraints India faces, namely low R&D expenditure (only 0.7 of GDP as compared to 2% of GDP by China and 4.3% of GDP by Israel), low number of R&D professionals (218 per million population as compared to China's 1,113 and US 4,019); lack of career opportunities in basic sciences, delays in converting lab discoveries into products; low level of innovation by Indian industry; frequent violation of preferential market access rules by the government agencies which discourages indigenous industry and foreign bias in procurement of innovative technologies.[7]

From the aforementioned account given by the ministry, it would become clear that there is a fresh thinking in the government for using S&T for meeting the requirement for the nation. International cooperation in leading countries such as the USA has certainly helped. Some of the leading programmes which have shown good results are as follows:

- Defence Technology and Trade Initiative (DTTI), DRDO.
- India–US S&T cooperation began in the 1950s and currently has following programmes: Indo-US Science & Technology Forum (IUSSTF) Agreement, High Technology Cooperation Group (HTCG); Indo-US Strategic Partnership; NASA–ISRO Agreement/MoES NOAA Agreement; Indo-US Nuclear Agreement; Indo-US R&D Endowment Fund.
- Indo-German Sustainable Development Programme.
- India–Swedish partnership in the field of innovation.[8]
- Indo-French Centre for the Promotion of Advanced Research (IFCPAR/CEFIPRA).

---

[6] NITI Aayog, 'Technology and Innovation', in *Strategy for New India @ 75* (New Delhi: NITI Aayog, 2018), 17.

[7] Ibid, 17–18.

[8] Government of Sweden and Government of India, *Joint Declaration on Sweden–India Innovation Partnership for a Sustainable Future* (2018, 17 April). Available at https://www.government.se/497c4e/contentassets/177b03128a45 44038b546b890bfb7bf0/sweden_india_final_webb.pdf (accessed on 29 January 2019). The partnership covers areas such as smart cities and transportation including e-mobility, energy, smart grids, clean technologies; smart industry, digitalization, start-ups and IPR issues; new materials and advanced manufacturing; space and aeronautics; circular and bio-based economy including biomaterials; health and life sciences including biomedical devices.

- Indo-Japan S&T cooperation began in 1987 and now covers a wide range of areas including interdisciplinary ICT, biomedical sciences, material and nuclear sciences, etc.[9]
- Indo-Russian cooperation on S&T dates back to the Soviet times and has been renewed since then. The programme is implemented through a number of bilateral mechanism such as (a) Working Group on S&T, (b) Integrated Long Term Programme (ILTP) of cooperation in S&T, (c) Basic Science Cooperation Programme, (d) Inter-Academy Exchange Programme, (e) Indo-Russian S&T Centre, (f) inter-ministerial science, technology and innovation cooperation.[10]

These joint research programmes have the potential of strengthening basic research, crating IPR and transfer of technology. However, it will be some year before positive results will be visible.

India has also been at the forefront of sharing fruits of S&T with developing countries. It has set up a Pan-African e-network connecting all the African countries, implemented a telemedicine programme for Africa, set up a large number of information technologies centre of excellence in different countries and provided thousands of scholarship in scientific and technical areas to the students from developing countries. This has helped position India not only as leading donor country but also as a leader in S&T.

In a paper written by former secretary in the DST by Mr T. Ramasami and his colleagues, a number of suggestions were made how India can develop science diplomacy as a tool in foreign policy. The authors argued in favour of more science counsellor positions in missions abroad, a think tank mechanism for developing strategic relationships, creation of a mechanism for undertaking due diligence of technology partners, creation of technology fund for promotion of technology partnership, special packages for developing countries to help them strengthen their R&D institutions, an institutional mechanism for undertaking as assessment of

---

[9] Embassy of India, Science & Technology Wing, Tokyo, *Bilateral Cooperation in the Field of Science & Technology between India and Japan* (2019, January). Available at https://www.indembassy-tokyo.gov.in/st_cooperation.html (accessed on 29 January 2019).

[10] Embassy of India, Moscow, *Indo-Russian S&T Cooperation*. Available at https://indianembassy-moscow.gov.in/indo-russian-s-t-cooperation.php (accessed on 29 January 2019).

opportunities for S&T cooperation abroad.[11] These are eminent suggestions which need to be followed up.

The NITI Aayog's *Strategy for New India @ 75* document correctly notes that 'an empowered body is needed to steer holistically management of science in the country. Its scope will include science education and scientific research as well as coordinating and guiding various science initiatives'. It also identifies 'poor marketing skills and information dissemination' as major weaknesses of public-funded R&D bodies. It suggests several measures to improve technology commercialization including setting up of value-addition centre to improve technology readiness level (TRL) 4 to level 6/7, creation of national technology databank and sharp increase in the Atal Tinkering Labs to 5,000 by 2019 and 10,000 by 2020. With regard to foreign collaborations, it recommends discipline-wise foreign experts who can help Indian scientists to take basic research to new levels.[12]

These are eminent suggestions. Many of them require domestic effort. However, India can gain from experience of other countries as well. Here, foreign collaborations would help. Some additional suggestions how international collaboration can be leveraged are given as follows:

- All S&T cooperation MoUs should be linked with not only scientific goals but also national objectives.
- Like Singapore, China, Japan and many other countries, India should provide incentives to invite S&T experts in large numbers to its scientific and technological institutions to leapfrog in R&D and innovation.
- The institutional capacities for R&D collaborations should be enhanced. Indian institutions should be encouraged to look for strategic partnerships in the area of R&D. They should be permitted to buy R&D companies abroad if required.
- India should encourage export of scientific and technological products to other countries. Suitable incentives should be given. India should participate in more international S&T collaborations. Adequate resources should be provided for that.

---

[11] S. Relia, A. Mitra, and T. Ramasami, 'Science and Technology Perspective for India's Foreign Policy', *Indian Foreign Affairs Journal* 9, no. 2 (2014): 154–168.
[12] Ibid, no. 6: 18–19.

- Non-resident Indians (NRIs) to set up scientific and technological institutions. Suitable incentives should be given to them.
- Under the 'Make in India' programme, we should encourage companies to invest in India in hi-tech areas.
- All major programmes such as high-speed bullet trains and energy programme should be accompanied by the establishment of high-quality R&D institutions.
- India should ensure that its vast market is leveraged suitably for getting best technologies. The defence offset policy should be leveraged to encourage scientific R&D in India.
- S&T cooperation programme should also focus on enhancing the quality of our museum, school laboratory, Olympiad programme, student's exchanges, faculty's improvement, etc.
- India should set up S&T cooperation programme with the neighbouring countries in the areas of climate change, oceanography, agriculture, pharmaceuticals, etc.
- Mission-level programme should be set up in the area of artificial intelligence, robotics, machine learning, etc.
- India's human flight programme should be leveraged to encourage further R&D in space technology particularly in the universities. Universities should be involved in all hi-tech programmes.
- STEM education should be improved in the country.
- The pool of retired scientists should be used to improve S&T education. A scientist should not be retired. They can be harnessed as teacher, mentors, educators, motivators, etc.
- Indian industry should adopt industry 4.0 standards. A centre of excellence to promote this initiative needs to be at the earliest. Industry-academia, R&D projects should be identified. Foreign collaborations to promote this initiative should be pursued.

Conclusion

India cannot afford to miss the revolution in different fields of S&T. We will have to strengthen basic research, applied research as well as innovation. The three dimensions of S&T require different approaches. A holistic S&T policy which is integrated with foreign policy and national security objectives needs to be developed. At the same time, there is no getting away from the fact that India needs to enhance its gross expenditure on research & development (GERD) bringing it to at least 2 per cent of GDP. Development of human resources, improvement in the level of STEM education and strengthening of S&T infrastructure are crucial. While much of this has to be done through domestic initiatives, international collaborations can play an important role. Science diplomacy must emerge as an integral part of overall diplomacy. At the same time, India will have to devise ways and means to meet the competition from other countries as well as leading R&D companies. India is well placed to leverage science diplomacy for national objectives. In order to leverage S&T for national objective, a few recommendations can be made:

- Make a national policy on S&T which is integrated with foreign and national security objectives.
- Increase the number of science councillors from 4 to at least 20.
- Expose Indian diplomats to Indian achievements in S&T through training and refresher courses.

Indian Narrative through the Cold War Era
From Panchsheel to Détente

Vivek Prahladan

Introduction

An inevitability compelled by historical circumstances makes the international course clearer than the pressure of indulging in faithless foresight. Anticipating possible scenarios of historical changes does not immediately strike as an exercise in long-term risk management or appear as the assured foundation on which risks can be weighed. Forecasting historical shift might be faithless pursuit, but the favours of historical foresight outlast any other exercise of strategy. Relating past international opportunities and forthcoming ones requires conditioning of strategy to historical shifts. Indian geopolitical life has made it international profession to hold together through all its crisis with a method that concedes to the momentum of the international system as little as possible of its own national ideological momentum. India approaches the next historical shift in world politics with the desire to project its national momentum.

The Asian conflict system is making the rhomboid perimeter that holds India smaller with every passing year and has compelled New Delhi to posture as a grand wedge between the Eurasian and Indo-Pacific conflict system. In 1871, archaeologist and British engineer Alexander Cunningham wrote in his ancient geography of India *Geographica* about Greek polymath Eratosthenes and Strabo describing Indian subcontinent as a rhomboid or uneven quadrilateral. The triple partition of Indian subcontinent into India, Pakistan and East Pakistan (later Bangladesh) in 1947 after Britain vacated its golden colony displaced the natural consistency of this rhomboid geography. This triple partition eclipsed the natural geographical dividend that could have been bedrock of an Indian grand strategy that could in time replace the security scape of the British imperial system. British imperial system secured this perimeter by seeing Eurasia to East Asia as a single strategic crescent where survival meant pre-emptive intelligence on rival Russian, French and Dutch imperial system from Turkey, Persian Gulf, Central Asia, China, South East Asia and the Indian Ocean islands. Unlike China, the collapse of the imperial system in the Indian subcontinent left a strategic void both conceptually and in practice.

The critical dilemma of Indian foreign office is to balance its peace interests with its prosperity interests because shifts in the international system could mean that the arcs of peace and that of prosperity for India may not point in the same direction. In a recent speech at Davos 2018 Business Summit, PM Modi stated that '[trade] protectionism can be as dangerous as terrorism'. The international liberal order has provided Indian middle-class population access to global public goods. The international trade system has allowed Indian government to generate revenues to invest in public and strategic infrastructure and sustain economic growth. Eurasian diplomacy will compete with Indo-Pacific diplomacy in Indian Prime Minister's Office and Indian Ministry of External Affairs for influence over resources and prestige.

History of Asia and Great Power Containment

The Cold War map brought old nations with new histories to meet new nations with ancient histories. Even by 1960, the Cold War had not quite commissioned the subcontinent into its shadow death game. The subcontinent lay in the strategic wastelands of the doomsday machinery of the red star and the red stripes. The post-Second World War saw the USA and Soviet Union seeking a new balance of power and working out a place for the defeated powers, leaving the playing field open for erstwhile colonies to find national focus and identity. Controlled reconstruction and political control of post-war Germany and Japan through security treaties while keeping an eye on inner politics and strategic potential of these countries in check was the main task. The subcontinent had not yet shown traits of becoming a proxy theatre. Despite the domino theory, no communist threat had developed in the subcontinent. The criterion of gaining business class seats in the Cold War map was that there should be some possibility, even if a distant one, of the USA and USSR having a direct military confrontation. A threat of something spilling over beyond the diplomatic threshold into the pure military domain but the subcontinent showed no signs of being one. US State Department Memo from 1957 reads as follows: 'in Pakistan we [the US] had certainly gone much too far, the more so because attacks by the Soviet Union will not be made in these countries (of South Asia), nor would the US ever be likely to fight in India or in Pakistan' (FRUS Department 103, 1957).[1] Eisenhower was waiting and not watching. In National Security Council Meeting of 3 January 1957, US President commented on his conversations with Nehru and came away with the impression that 'Nehru did not want Russia running his country' (Department 1957). India was not yet a full-bodied 'Diplomatic State' that could have an impact on the Cold War this way or that. Eisenhower was sure that 'the area (South Asia) was simply too peripheral to our vital interests' (Department 1957). Détente politics from 1969 rearranged the foundations of distribution of power in Asia.

India, Détente and East Asia: Understanding Strategy as Power of Historical Expression

The intellectual legacy of Kissinger's détente politics of 1969–1971 carries itself on the principle that history gives depth to legitimacy; that historical expression assures a moral purpose to policy that can be held on to the moment of crisis and can be affirmed in the moment of strength. Détente politics carried an assurance that great powers would not act on their commanding positions through excesses, recognizing the historical force that legitimized new Asia's moral disposition to define its internationalism. Détente became symbolic of the impending sense in East Asia and among the great powers themselves that the international principles of the great powers were being left behind by a new historical principle, namely the rise of the new international East. Détente became a single definition of the problem-confronting Asia, yet for these states, there was no single definition of the resolution.

---

[1] FRUS, Vol. XIX, Document 103: Memorandum of Discussion at the 308th Meeting of the National Security Council, Washington, January 3 1957; https://history.state.gov/historicaldocuments/frus1955-57v19/d103

When the arc of détente waded into East Asia, its rules of engagement had to accommodate the historical process that leapt out first at Bandung in 1955 and by 1969 had turned into a distinct East Asian problem primarily because of the miring of America in Vietnam. Thus, what looked like an 'Asian Renaissance' in the making in 1955 that also included India's internationalism within this broader post-colonial geography, by the time of détente had become the beginnings of an 'East Asian Renaissance' with India increasingly being pushed into the periphery of this renaissance. Lee Kuan Yew understood that India needed to enter East Asia more directly as early as 1966 conveyed his views to India that India could define its interests in East Asia at a time when a power vacuum was on the verge of emerging in Asia from British withdrawal in Suez. India crooned itself into isolation by legitimizing its defensive multi-polarity based on indecisions and refusal to admit broader interests in Asia through expressions of Third World nationalism.

Lee Kuan's approach assumed that India was too large a country to refuse to identify regional aspirations, isolate itself and thereby giving China a measure of certainty in its internationalism that would allow it to expand its interest in Asia unopposed. Through the Cold War, Indian policy was content to have China contained within great power balancing that served not its interests but its anxiety about China hegemonizing East Asia. Soviet alliance lulled India into not having an East Asia policy since the alliance served to restrain if not contain China and it relied on great powers balancing each other's naval presence in Asia. Both these pillars of India's non-decisions on establishing interests in Asia collapsed with the end of the Cold War. It was only after the end of the Cold War, in the 1990s, that India could not rely on this vicarious satisfaction of its anxieties regarding Chinese influence in East Asia. It responded to the end of the Cold War by articulating the 'Look East' policy though it marked only the beginning of India translating its anxieties into identifying broader interests in Asia. The same question posed to India by Lee Kuan assumed greater historical weight at the time of détente when America sought to withdraw from Vietnam and a genuine chance lay in front of India to define interests in East Asia.

An 'Indian Renaissance' had to wait for the end of the Cold War, at the turn into the 21st century and only in the current era is Indian policy looking to integrate itself into a new East Asian order even as these East Asian states including Japan are looking for the next wave of prosperity and a second post-war Asian Renaissance that may include Indian interests at its core. However, even now India's long-term interests in East Asia remain tentatively articulated, reflected in denial of its membership on important East Asian forums. The American experience affected the prospects of the Soviet encroachment and posed the question to East Asian nation states as to how they might respond to the convergence of détente with their own post-colonial historical process. American grand strategy had no instruments to reconcile their heavy manoeuvrings to the vertical clash of history on the one hand, between Eurasia and Asia described by Lee Kuan Yew as conflict between 'the authoritarian bent of Confucian culture and the extreme individualism of Western liberalism' and, on the other, a horizontal clash of histories within Asian nation states themselves.[2] Much like the ancient Egyptians employed a weighing of the heart ceremony to determine whether the dead would enter the afterlife, East Asia was weighing the great power heart to decide the terms on which a tired America would withdraw from Vietnam. It was only natural that the 'Nixon Doctrine' had, as its core objective, to keep alive the power of the 'American spirit' that was mired in the East Asian archipelago while retaining the option to define the scope of this spirit as broadly as circumstances would permit. In other words, the 'content can be ascertained only by the interpretations provided by each side.[3] In 1971, at the State of the Union address, Nixon expressed this national ordeal as 'the dark night of the American spirit' and posed the American challenge in terms of how this spirit would respond to 'a quest for new greatness', one of redefining American purpose rather than a practical question of extricating American soldiers from Vietnam.[4] Invoking the archetype of the American spirit, Nixon knew that history was the metaphysics of the nation state. Détente became American commitment to introducing de-securitized Americanization as an ideological instrument in Asia of the sort laid out in W. W. Rostow's *The Stages of Economic Growth*.[5]

Working with preliminary on the broader scope of détente history, the chapter seeks to engage with Indian policy's inability through the Cold War process to define its interests for Asia, its callous assumption

---

[2] N. Gardels, *The Sage of Singapore* (2017, 6 June). Available at https://www.huffingtonpost.com/nathan-gardels/lee-kuan-yew-remembered_b_6920292.html (accessed on 25 November 2019).

[3] R. W. Stevenson, *The Rise and Fall of Detente* (London: Macmillan, 1985), 4.

[4] R. Nixon, *Annual Message to the Congress on the State of the Union* (1971, 22 January). Available at http://www.presidency.ucsb.edu/ws/?pid=3110 (accessed on 25 November 2019).

[5] K. Pyle, *Japan Rising: The Resurgence of Japanese Power and Purpose* (Williamstown, MA: 2007); K. B. Pyle, 'Japan and the United States: An Unnatural Intimacy (Review)', *The Journal of Japanese Studies* (2011): 377–395.

of détente marking a possible near to long-term decline of American purpose in East Asia, thereby weakening its necessity of anticipating the emergence of a robust 'hub and spoke security order' in East Asia based on revival of American alliances, its increasing isolation from the détente system in East Asia and inability to grasp the capacity of Asian archipelago states to respond coherently to the evolution of great power interactions through détente.[6] Indian Foreign Office overestimated the degree to which Japan's engagement in East Asia negatively impacted its own diplomatic scope for multilateralism in the 'great archipelago' that was East Asia and underestimated the degree to which Japan exercised freedom of manoeuvre within the San Francisco system. The chapter seeks an appreciation of Indian dilemma of how to negotiate the near simultaneous emergence of détente and its alliance with the Soviet Union and the reluctance of New Delhi to assume greater responsibility through this alliance in an Asian balance of power. Explanations for India's traditional inhibitions in seeing itself as part of the East Asian order in the political sense directs us to detailing the historical convergence of détente with the Indo-Soviet Alliance, India's shift away from expressing internationalism of decolonization nationalism to an increased invoking of a liberal political commitment concentrating on preserving the principle of sovereignty of nation state and Indian awakening to Indian Ocean diplomacy within an obscure assessment of the growing 'navalization' of the Cold War in the Asian archipelago. Reflecting on the correspondence between India and Japan's great power diplomacy in détente with the nature of their bilateral engagement that began earnestly with Prime Minister Nobusuke Kishi's visit to India in 1957, the chapter traces interactions between the newly minted Indo-Soviet alliance of 1971 to the sturdy US–Japan alliance of post-war vintage. Posing broader questions about great power approach to alliances, the chapter wades into a comparative perspective on Kissinger's assessment of US–Japan alliance and his sensitivity to implications of Indo-Soviet alliance on a coordinated great power détente posture, what Nixon described in his second inaugural address as a 'structure of peace'.[7]

---

[6] G. J. Ikenberry, 'American Hegemony and East Asian Order', *Australian Journal of International Affairs* 58, no. 3 (2010): 352–367.

[7] R. Nixon, *Second Inaugural Address of Richard Milhous Nixon* (1973, 20 January). Available at http://avalon.law.yale.edu/20th_century/nixon2.asp (accessed on 25 November 2019).

Eurasian Détente versus Asian Détente

While Eurasian containment grand strategy of Kennan was grounded in the flow of human history of the Western civilization that includes Russia, its technocratic extension into the great archipelago held no such historical mandate driven entirely by needs of absolute or grand assessments of security. Soviet Union's counter-containment patchwork suffered from equally grand assertions, though its support to decolonization nationalism in Asia–Africa had tactical grounding in history. The species of Eurasian-inspired continental style containment wouldn't breed within the 'great archipelago' ecosystem. 'Containment' as a strategy was thought of by strategists who acknowledged their lack of aptitude on the 'Far East'. Asia was on the periphery and peripheral Asia was even more distant as a subject for American strategy. George Kennan evaluated the Far East as 'a wholly different world [from Europe] not only geographically but also in thought and feeling, perhaps even in the nature of political reality'.[8] Notion of atomic security within the techno-strategic world of Paul Nitze made the problem of 'geo' within 'geopolitics' one of geographical range of deterrence and eclipsed the unresolved problem of history. Eurasian continental strategists had deferred the problem of having a strategy to understand geography of 'the Great Archipelago'. Eurasian order dug at the hearts of the continental strategists in a manner that East Asia didn't. Yet containment even within mainland Asia was not with contradictions from the start. This 'Asian containment' as a patchwork arrangement rather was evident when Pakistan began to declare itself anti-Communist simply to secure Western arms to challenge border status quo against India. Pakistan government calling itself anti-Communist was as much tragic humour as Bhutto canvassing elections in 1964 on Communist platform. Korean War was fought in the name of 'Containment in Asia' but even this did not turn it into an 'Asia Containment' strategy.

For the great powers, détente was a structure of suspicion, mutuality of ambition and a restoration of clarity in their historical processes while for post-colonial Asia a question of legitimizing the magnitude of historical grievances. At historical crossroads, Nixon had to come to terms to the fact that even if America no more saw evil on the far side of good, it still saw a whole lot of good in itself. This is reflected in Kissinger opening the Washington–Moscow hotline during the 1971

---

[8] F. Sempa, *George Kennan's Geopolitics of the Far East* (2015, 15 April). Available at https://thediplomat.com/2015/04/george-kennans-geopolitics-of-the-far-east/ (accessed on 25 November 2019).

Indian intervention in East Pakistan which splintered it from West Pakistan and established it as a newly independent state of Bangladesh and seeking Soviet cooperation in restraining Indian intentions. Détente meant that Kissinger had to settle for second-best as soon as the first option came under pressure from the Indo-Soviet alliance. However, it was President Nixon's appreciation of asserting American interests to an indivisible second-best option which was to preserve the integrity of West Pakistan, whereas Kissinger was determined to draw détente into preservation of his first preference, that is, to preserve the unity of West and East Pakistan, the domestic criticisms of the credibility of his backchannel diplomacy that caused Nixon to remark that 'we cannot have Henry having an emotional collapse'.[9] Kissinger's assessment of India had mellowed in the years where Nixon began to be drawn increasingly into the Watergate developments which made Kissinger 'increasingly responsible for articulating and conducting foreign policy', though his interest in Japan had remained relatively the same as it did in the early years of détente.[10] But this mellowing took place not without Kissinger carrying certain impressions from his intense involvement with entangling East–West diplomacy into the subcontinental affairs, the role of conventional forces in a short campaign geared to long-term political objectives. Vietnam War had damaged the credibility of conventional military as a political instrument, the success of the swift Indian campaign reminded the great powers of the continuing relevance of conventional strength in the gap that separated great balance of power and political evolution of decolonization nationalisms.

Japan and India in Asia

Immobility of political geography afflicted Japan and India Cold War and détente engagement. Japan's altered terms of engagement in the post-war era made India even more distant though not entirely absent in its liberal political imagination. At different ends of Cold War kinetics, India–Japan diplomatic encounters were marked by a distinct warmth matched by frankness. Although the tone of frankness was struck between Jawaharlal Nehru and Nobusuke Kishi in 1957, the

---

[9] R. Moss, *Nixon's Back Channel to Moscow: Confidential Diplomacy and Detente* (Lexington, KY: 2017), 135.

[10] Walter S. Poole, *The Decline of Detente: Elliot Richardson, James Schlesinger and Donald Rumsfeld 1973–1977* (Washington, DC: Historical Office, Office of the Secretary of Defense, 2015), vii.

chapter indicates India awakening to Japanese role in its strategic affairs in Asia only after the end of the Cold War.

To begin with, Japan was unsure about effectiveness of India's closer participation in Asian affairs. India, for its part, did not fully appreciate the ability of Japan to make independent choices despite the shadow of its leviathan alliance with the USA nor did it fully comprehend the ineffectiveness of its Asia–Africa appeal towards stirring Japan's interests. Bearings of this Asia–Africa diplomacy never transcended into tangible strategic impact through the quality of its power, its object of embedding decolonization nationalism into the international system trapped beneath the weight of its own concert. Neutrality without strength made little appeal to Japan that was historically accustomed to hard diplomatic volitions which then seeded its own internal transformations and destiny of its hard industries (manufacturing). However, Indian assessment on Asia revised under shadow of China's emerging nuclear and military menace parallel to a growing Indian realization of Japan's internationalism affecting scope of Indian interests in Asia. Japan, for its part, on question of strategy, pursued constant and deep observation of India's strategic potential. Possibilities of duality of finance and strategy in Japan's diplomatic approach were at times hard to reconcile for the Indian foreign office.

Asia and Nehru's World Historical Perspective

In the early years of Indian Independence (1947–1952), unsure of how the international system would evolve in the post-war era, Nehru raided the Commonwealth and the Asiatic tracks with equal ease without giving away which of these was a pursuit of passion and that of reason. In these early years, Nehru might be mistaken for a passionate 'Commonwealther' as easily as a reasoned 'Asiaphile'. India's first steps in international politics were through the Commonwealth Nations platform until Nehru strutted into the Asiatic homeland discourse on the back of his 'Panchsheel' principle. A more thorough assessment of Nehru's early reliance on the Commonwealth instrument and his hopes that it would form a foundation for India's nascent diplomacy has lost out to the overwhelming historical attention to Nehru's subsequent non-alignment neutrality movement that has painted and repainted Nehru as the conceited keeper of the Asian flame. As the momentum of decolonization unfolded, Nehru chose to draw deeper from the Asiatic diplomatic track. Nehru of the first decade of Indian Independence inherited the British 'Far East' tag for Japan that afforded him to take a distant or even conceptual view on Japan unburdened by urgent diplomatic exigencies.

In October 1950, Nehru wrote a note on 'Japanese Peace Treaty': 'Japan should not have an army and should be treated as a neutral country ... that peace must be based on an independent Japan'.[11] Simultaneously, a MEA note cites John Foster Dulles carrying out informal discussions with members of the Far Eastern Commission where India was represented through its Ambassador in Washington. Perhaps if the Cold War hadn't hard-boiled by the early 1950s, the international system may have witnessed a more consultative approach from the USA on Japan's integration into this system. Nehru's preference to square Indian diplomacy within the terms of the Commonwealth, especially on Japan, is further confirmed through his views on the 'wholly dissenting' judgement of Justice Pal (Indian Member) of the 'International Military Tribunal for the Far East'. Nehru and K. P. S. Menon (India's first Foreign Secretary 1948–1952) were considering the possibility of sending 'directives' to Justice Pal at this late juncture but they decided that it was too late to make this intervention. Justice Pal's views were described as 'extreme' and 'unfortunate' because Nehru had assumed that Justice Pal would go along with the views of the USA and the UK. Indeed, a note was intended for release to clarify that Justice Pal's views 'are not shared by the Government of India', though the final decision was not to release it.[12]

Another instance of Indian diplomacy on Japan furnishes additional substantiation that Nehru did not assess Japan beyond the terms of the 'Western-led' Commonwealth. In 1948, Soviet Ambassador Alexander Panyushkin began to convey Soviet approach of discerning Japan's economic needs from revival of 'war economy'. Soviet proposals on 'Level of economic life in Japan' were voted 10 to 1 against in the FEC meeting on 2 December 1948. India voted against the Soviet proposal. However, Nehru was not prepared for the onset of 'Asia containment' marked by increasing US unilateralism on Japan bypassing the Far Eastern Economic Commission (FEC) altogether. Indian interests in the Pacific made it unacceptable to Indian foreign office (MEA) that 'Japan was the sole responsibility of the US'.[13] Thus, 'Asia containment'

---

[11] National Archives of India, *Notes on China, Japan, Philippines and Malay Prepared for the Commonwealth Consultative Committee* (New Delhi: National Archives of India, 1950).

[12] Ministry of External Affairs, *Justice Pal's Judgement at the International Military Tribunal Tokyo* (New Delhi: NMML and NAL, 1949).

[13] National Archives of India, *ECAFE Resolution on the Contribution of the Japanese Economy to the Reconstruction and Development of the ECAFE Region* (New Delhi: National Archives of India, 1949).

in practice was beginning to do the opposite of what it conceptualized, driving a wedge between India and Japan as well as India and East Asia as early as 1948 since the containment principle did not harmonize the range of national interests within the 'great archipelago' that was conceptualized in terms of continental Eurasian containment. India as Far Eastern Economic Commission (FEC) member desired that the outcomes of the consultations process be structured in the future peace conference on Japan. India was critical of the rescinding the purge directive by Supreme Commander of the Allied Powers (SCAP) that had been decided upon in Washington. Withdrawing of the purge directive was seen by India as contradicting basic policy of the FEC. These views were conveyed by MEA to the Secretary of State for Commonwealth Relations. The Commonwealth Secretary acknowledged the arguments of the letter but added that 'many complex issues are involved and we should like to consult further with you'.[14] The disagreements between the two great powers in the FEC on Japan bears out Kathryn Weathersby argument cited by Melvyn Leffler on Stalin's Northeast Asian policy 'based on the assumption that Japan would rearm and again threaten the security of the USSR'.[15] Japan consultation at the FEC archivally verifies Leffler's 'complex interactions' of Soviet fears of Germany and Japan's military revival borne out of its Second World War experiences. This episode was the first break in Nehru's trust in the promise of the Commonwealth. Even at this stage (September 1948), Nehru agreed with His Majesty's Government (HMG) views that Japan's economic levels could not be artificially capped as suggested by in document FEC 242/32 yet it was sceptical of the ambitious economic revival suggested in Strike and Johnson Reports. MEA agreed with the Secretary that the USA should be persuaded to cap levels somewhere between the Strike–Johnson Report and the FEC 242/32. New Delhi informed Commonwealth Secretary that FEC may not withstand any more shocks from US unilateral decisions. On 28 September 1949, USSR had moved an amendment to FEC provisions to extend policy of 'Reduction of Japanese Industrial War Potential' (FEC 084/21) 'until adoption by the Far Eastern Commission of a decision on the level of economic life in Japan'.[16] The USA had opposed this amendment and countered that SCAP had eliminated specialized war-making industries in Japan. The USA wanted the provisions regarding the elimination of

---

[14] Ibid.

[15] M. P. Leffler, 'Bringing It Together: the Parts and the Whole', in *Reviewing the Cold War*, ed. O. A. Westad (London: Frank Cass, 2000), 43–63.

[16] National Archives of India, *ECAFE Resolution on the Contribution of the Japanese Economy to the Reconstruction and Development of the ECAFE Region.*

Japan's war-making industry to lapse as in its assessment they no longer served any purpose. India had no objections to the US view and had not supported the Soviet amendment proposal; however, US unilateralism had begun to strain Nehru's resolve in the inclusiveness of the Commonwealth Process. However, Nehruvian diplomacy retained faith in consultative credentials of HMG. Indian stance in the FEC steered the middle path that was willing to accommodate US interests through a genuine consultation process. In the longer run, this impacted US structural interests by further limiting its ability to patch together an 'Asia containment'.

By the time of his meeting with Nobusuke Kishi in 1957, Nehru had squared his Japan approach within an Asiatic arc and withdrew his entire international politics approach away from the Commonwealth-based diplomacy. However, Nehru's China policy shadow on Japan could have only further shrunk whatever space there was to engage each other. By 1960, Indian Embassy in Tokyo was reporting that Japanese television was already citing Indo-Tibetan border problems as example of Communist expansionism and China. Vijaya Lakshmi Pandit, Indian ambassador to Washington and sister of Nehru, made a private visit to Japan in 1954. Despite the private nature of the visit, she was received at Tokyo airport by the deputy prime minister, members of Diet and the British Ambassador Sir Esler Dening. Writing to Nehru, she wrote that 'the Gaimusho was most anxious for the Emperor to meet me' and the meeting did take place.[17] She gathered from some conversations that 'he [the Emperor] still feels he should have committed Harikiri' and noticed that 'a bad nervous twitch' had developed 'as a result of his deep humiliation at the unconditional surrender'.[18] It is vexing to understand the reasons that led her to write to conclude that 'India can play an important hand in strengthening Japan and helping her to assume a dignified place in the world'.[19] First, it is revealing that the report to Nehru in no way anticipates Japan's economic resurrection. Second, Nehru was unsure about the strategy to engage with Japan as he was unclear about its internal political developments. '[W]e should not put Japan in cold storage awaiting favorable internal developments ... It would seem ill-advised to leave the field open on all sides to America (just) because America is in control at present'.[20]

---

[17] National Archives of India, *Shrimati Pandit Report about Her Visit to Japan* (New Delhi: National Archives of India, 1955).
[18] Ibid.
[19] Ibid.
[20] Ibid.

By 1957, Japan's acknowledgement of establishing contact with India in order to explore its long-term capacity came at a time when the USA was still uncertain about how to stitch an Asian containment strategy even as Central Intelligence Agency (CIA) estimated in 1958 that 'within this alignment [with the US] ... Japan will be more assertive in pursuing its national interests'.[21] Prime Minister Kishi, a staunch anti-Communist, moved to make stronger links with Taiwan. Breaking off of relations by China in 1958 would have flagged off Indian subcontinent as a potential future resource whose patent goodwill towards Japan irrespective of its fundamental Cold War positions that did nothing to stir Japan's near-term interest. Indian economy was too weak to engage Japan commercially and the manner in which India defined its freedoms of inaction made it unviable as strategic asset yet Japan could not delay contact with India which might one day find itself on the wrong side of China. Kishi's policy implicitly anticipated political relations with India with considerable inbuilt potential for political engagement any time there would be a rift between India and China.

Indian foreign policy was placed at a more abstract footing from the domestic political issues that remained around internal socio-economic and post-colonial integration issues except for relations with Pakistan. This independence had its drawbacks as there was no political balance to Nehru's decolonization internationalism, whereas Japan's foreign policy had to have consensus within the ruling party and some elements outside of it but Nehru had no such limits. Nehru was afforded freedom of thought and practice on foreign relations within a democratic framework that would exceed the imagination of a despot. The exception on Pakistan policy of the Government of India linked to its performance in domestic politics remains to this day.

Second, how could Japan establish contact with India outside of the loaded decolonization framework, communicate its interests in India and yet accommodate India's interests and challenges as a newly independent country. Third, contrast between Nehru's high octane activist style public diplomacy and Kishi's 'low posture' diplomacy. Fourth, Japan's broader assessment of India would have to wait till India's specific interests in East Asia became clearer. At the same time, Nehru awaited domestic politics in Japan to settle down and perhaps hoped that socialists in Japan might get stronger. India couldn't find a way to

---

[21] CIA, *National Intelligence Estimate—Probable Developments in Japan's International Relations* (1958, 23 December). Available at https://www.cia.gov/library/readingroom/docs/CIA-RDP79R01012A011900010008–3.pdf (accessed on 25 November 2019).

get around the silent shadow of the US–Japan 'Treaty of Peace'. Fifth, Nehru's tendency to boost his Asiatic diplomacy through emphasis on China undermined the clean slate that the two countries could have had at the time. The differences in their interests in East Asia became apparent with their position of the Korean War and Taiwan.

Nehru was an enthusiastic supporter of Professional Regulation Commission (PRC) and its role in international councils. Japan entered into treaty with Kuomintang in April 1952 and had voted against China's admission into the UN. The 'Asia Containment' strategy of the USA, even though built around economistic instruments supporting Japan's integration with East Asian economy and not on explicit military principles, nevertheless drove a geopolitical wedge between the two that the two never quite overcame throughout the Cold War. Détente had a specific impact for Japan's drive to diversify its geopolitical interests in East Asia to include India. At last, Indian perception of US alliances in general was largely shaped by its experiences through frequent frontier escalation build-ups including wars in 1965 (Western Front) and 1971 (Eastern Front) with Pakistan. In 1954, President Eisenhower approved the arms supply arrangement with Pakistan and these were backed by reassurances to PM Nehru that the US arms were for defence against Communist attack. India's first serious approach towards Soviet Union came in October 1965, after the use of US arms by Pakistan in 1965 Indo-Pak war.[22]

Conclusion: India's Cold War Historical Experience and Possible Future Course of World Order

The new world historical era is synonymous with new Asian order, and India is inevitably one of the pillars of the new international Asian order that will be defined from within Asia for the first time in more than 500 years. Institutionalization, a common concern for India and China, would be a revolutionary conservative populist West from the Americas to Europe that would not let the international system remain benign collectively to India and China's economic and civilizational growth. While historically India and China have managed to sustain themselves as prosperous and thriving civilizations without significant contact with each other, a common threat to their prosperity from an inward-looking revisionary conservative anti-globalist West staring into an abyss of internal cultural wars between the populist left and

---

[22] V. Prahladan, *The Nation Declassified: India and the Cold War World* (New Delhi: Har Anand Publications, 2017).

the populist right would give them an opportunity to consider joint leverages and joint management of a new globalist Asia as the ideology of the 21st century. The essence of the long-term diplomatic situation facing India from Eurasia to the far side of the Pacific is how India will approach the question of institutionalization of the internal distribution of power in Asia, the integrity of this approach would hinge on its expression as an historical exercise, how would it structure its transition from being an inward-looking country from 1962 till about 10 years ago, its current phase of being in the middle of that transition to being an outward-looking country.

The Secretariat of the 21st century has a realistic chance of being headquartered in India within the next 20–30 years. What Samuel Huntington did not anticipate was a new globalist Asia that would extend its depth into Eurasia. For the first time, all of the major questions of world conflict are tied to core Indian interests and India's ability to have an international environment benign to its growth is likely to be affected by the approaches that the stakeholders apply to these diplomatic situations. Understanding approaches of world leaders who increasingly view themselves as revolutionary historical figures with mandate based on political populism requires grasping the intellectual foundations of the populism that brought them into office.

8

Rebalancing Foreign Policy and Non-traditional Security Issues

Uttam Kumar Sinha

Security Debate: A Historical Context

As a concept, security commands a great disciplinary power and that there is 'always something worth securing'.[1] From time immemorial, people have always alienated their fears to emperors and sovereign states in order to secure from the uncertainties. History has further shown that discourses on security are often competing against each other in order to gain legitimacy and to become 'the' discourse. Security, thus, has many interpretations with no overarching definition or broad consensus.

The non-state security or the non-traditional security as it is commonly referred to today is not entirely a new thinking.[2] It was given as much importance to territorial security by the founders of the

---

[1] Hugh Dyer, 'Environmental Security and International Relations: The Case for Enclosure', *Review of International Studies* 27 (2001): 441–450.

[2] Aspects of weather, terrain and environment change in both the Kautilyan precepts of power, place and time as well as Sun Tzu philosophy was understood from a very traditional security perspective.

United Nations.[3] The framers of the UN Charter strongly felt that the Second World War was largely a product of the social and economic pressures of the 1930s' Great Depression and, therefore, recognized that freedom from want is crucial to maintaining international peace and security.

During the Cold War, the bipolarity of the international system meant that states were preoccupied with the traditional notions of 'defending' national interest and, therefore, they ignored the necessity to 'redefine' national security based on existential threats. Explaining this, Arnold Wolfers in his 1952 seminal work *National Security as an Ambiguous Symbol* writes:

> In a very vague and general way national interest does suggest a direction of policy which can be distinguished from several others which may present themselves as alternatives. It indicates that policy is designed to promote demands which are ascribed to the nation rather than to individuals, sub-national groups or mankind as a whole. It emphasises that the policy subordinates other interests to those of the nation. But beyond this, it has very little meaning.[4]

Arnold did not explicitly define the term security in military terms; nevertheless, implicitly national security is exclusively related to the state security or, in other words, with the traditional notion of security.

In the 'dominant centre, less-dominant periphery'[5] matrix of the Cold War, security was based primarily on the 'realist' framework

---

[3] At the San Francisco Conference (April–June 1945), the US Secretary of State, Edward R. Stettinius identified two fundamental components of human security:

> The battle of peace has to be fought on two fronts. The first front is the security front, where victory spells freedom from fear. The second is the economic and social front, where victory means freedom from want. Only victory on both fronts can assure the world of an enduring peace ... No provisions that can be written into the Charter will enable the Security Council to make the world secure from war if men and women have no security in their homes and their jobs.

Cited in UNDP, *Human Development Report 1994: New Dimensions of Human Security* (New York, NY: United Nations Development Programme, 1994), 3.

[4] Arnold Wolfers, '"National Security" as an Ambiguous Symbol', *Political Science Quarterly* 67, no. 4 (1952): 481.

[5] James Der Derian, 'The Value of Security: Hobbes, Marx, Nietzsche, and Boudrillard', in *The Political Subject of Violence*, ed. David Campbell and Michael

of defence and military with little space for alternative interpretation. Soon after the end of the Cold War, the bipolarity diffused and the realist-dominated security gave way to an international system impacted by varied political, economic, national and environmental issues—described as 'decentred security'.[6] As a result, the discourse and queries on security underwent a profound change from being primarily state-centric to a 'reinvention of security in terms other than military'.[7]

In the immediate post-Cold War times of peace-dividends, institution-building and new approaches to resolving conflict, the spotlight fell on environmental issues. The UN Security Council Resolution (January 1992), in a new favourable international system, acknowledged that

> The absence of war and military conflicts amongst states does not in itself ensure international peace and security. The non-military sources of instability in the economic, social, humanitarian and ecological fields have become threats to peace and security. The United Nations membership as a whole needs to give the highest priority to the solution of these matters.[8]

Environmental issues, so to speak, became 'located in a security logic'.[9]

What made environmental problems a case so compelling as to brush aside state-centric proprietorship of security? First, since environmental problems cut across borders, it challenges the dominant security themes of 'territoriality' and 'impermeability'.[10] Considering environmental issues as one of five different interacting sectors of security—military, political, economic, societal and environmental—corresponds to the fact that the state is being challenged by a new set of intertwined

---

Dillon (Oxford: Basil Blackwell, 1987), 94. Also, see James Der Derian, 'On Diplomacy: A Genealogy of Western Diplomacy'.

[6] Ibid, 95.

[7] Barry Buzan, Ole Waever, and Jaap de Wilde, *Security: A New Framework for Analysis* (London: Lynne Riener Publishers, 1998), 210.

[8] Available at https://www.upi.com/Archives/1992/01/31/The-following-is-the-text-of-the-Security-Council/3433696834000/ (accessed on 25 November 2019).

[9] Jef Huysmans in Robert Miles and Dietrich Thranhardt, eds., *Migration and European Integration. The Dynamics of Inclusion and Exclusion* (London: Pinter Publishers, 1995), 54.

[10] John Herz, *International Politics in the Atomic Age* (New York, NY: Columbia University Press, 1959), 76.

problems.[11] Second, in the traditional security understanding, the protection of territorial integrity is primarily based on the threat from an enemy 'other'. In the case of the environment, the threat comes from the imbalances in the ecosystem, policies of the state, the attitude of people and the mindset of corporations. Third, in the traditional security approach, actor participation and contribution to enhancing the understanding of security is limited, whereas mapping environmental threats and seeking remedies to prevent it requires a broad-based participation.

From the points of view of both policy and practice, the Human Development Report (1994)[12] became a defining document that not only presented a holistic approach to human security linked to human development but also emphasized the need for broader concepts of security. In terms of concept and content, it drew inspiration from the Commission on Global Governance (1992) which outlined ways in which the international community might cooperate to further the agenda of global security. Despite the questioning on the policy relevance of the idea or the criticism on it being conceptually overstretched and not having analytical traction, the Human Development Report reset the question on what needs to be secured both from an intellectual perspective and from a practical approach. The Foreword of the Report says:

> Behind the blaring headlines of the world's many conflicts and emergencies, there lies a silent crisis—a crisis of underdevelopment, of global poverty, of ever-mounting population pressures, of thoughtless degradation of environment. This is not a crisis that will respond to emergency relief. Or to fitful policy interventions. It requires a long, quiet process of sustainable human development.[13]

The Report did not romanticize that the state will disappear but expanded security 'horizontally' beyond the military to include other interlinked issues such as the environment, economy, culture, gender and health. More importantly, it expanded 'vertically', questioning

---

[11] Barry Buzan, *People, States and Fear* (London: Harvester Wheatsheaf, 1991), 17.

[12] Members of the UNDP team included an Indian, Saraswathi Menon, and a Bangladeshi, Selim Jahan. The panel of consultants included Meghnad Desai and Sudhir Anand. Mahbub ul Haq, the Pakistani development economist, conceptualized the report and later wrote an acclaimed book *Reflections on Human Development* (Oxford: Oxford University Press, 1995).

[13] UNDP, *Human Development Report 1994*, iii.

the state-centric views and suggesting that security might have other referent subjects. The expansion was both upwards to embrace regional and global identities and downwards to society and to the individual. The Report noted: 'The threats to human security are no longer just personal or local or national. They are becoming global: with drugs, AIDS, terrorism, pollution, nuclear proliferation. Global poverty and environmental problems respect no national border. Their grim consequences travel the world.'[14]

In a changed international context, a renewed search for international order and cooperation contributed to the 'humanization of security and the development–security linkage'.[15] A series of UNDP documents can be highlighted during the decade including *Integrating Human Rights with Sustainable Human Development* (1998) and the *Human Development Report* (2000). Further, a number of important reports highlighting the need for holistic security came about. The UN *Millennium Declaration* (2000) emphasized on good governance, access to education and health care noting, 'Freedom from want, freedom from fear and the freedom of future generations to inherit a healthy natural environment—these are the interrelated building blocks of human—and therefore national security'.[16] The *Responsibility to Protect* (2001) unequivocally stressed on the security of people '… their physical safety, their economic and social well-being, respect for their dignity and worth as human beings'.[17] The World Bank, *World Development Report* (2000/1) worked out a strategy for alleviating poverty through empowerment, security and opportunity.[18] Building on all these reports and documents, the Commission on Human Security, in 2003, presented its report *Human Security Now* to raise public consciousness and to develop the concept as an operational tool for policy formulation and implementation.[19]

---

[14] Ibid., 2.

[15] Neil MacFarlane and Yuen Foong Khong, *Human Security and the UN: A Critical History* (Bloomington, IN: Indiana University Press, 2006), 63.

[16] United Nations, *UN Millennium Declaration* (2000). Available at http://undocs.org/A/RES/55/2 (accessed on 25 November 2019).

[17] International Commission on Intervention and State Sovereignty, *The Responsibility to Protect* (2001). Available at http://responsibilitytoprotect.org/ICISS%20Report.pdf (accessed on 25 November 2019).

[18] Available at https://siteresources.worldbank.org/INTPOVERTY/Resources/WDR/approutl.pdf (accessed on 25 November 2019).

[19] Available at https://reliefweb.int/sites/reliefweb.int/files/resources/91BAEEDBA50C6907C1256D19006A9353-chs-security-may03.pdf (accessed on 25 November 2019).

New Age Security

Security in the 21st century has manifold meanings and as a concept has become increasingly institutionalized.[20] The realist minimal understanding and the liberal maximal notion of security continue to present tensions in both the understanding and the approaches in dealing with security. While traditional security paradigms such as great power rivalries, force capability, great power status and threat perception continue, domestic factors and non-military sources of instability through the weakening of the social fabrics continuously challenge the state-centric approach to security.

That said, traditionalists continue to argue that attempts to broaden and deepen the scope of security beyond its traditional scope make it intellectually incoherent and practically difficult. This constituency remains influential in policymaking and resultantly debates over 'alternative understandings' and 'rethinking security' reveal an unfortunate tendency to foreclose arguments in understanding the complexities of contemporary security and a clearer assessment of their relevance.

Beyond the conceptual debate on security, there is now an acceptance that the global security landscape has significantly changed with the emergence of new threats, particularly the widespread effects of climate change and its impact on food, water and energy resources, which in turn has a spiralling effect on the economy of nations, migration and outbreak of pandemic diseases that cut across political boundaries. Other threats such as transnational crime, regional and global financial crises are equally debilitating with repercussions on national, regional and global security. Given the non-military threats potential to exacerbate existing tensions and deepen the fault lines, these threats can dangerously transform to being territorial and military. Hence, a blurring of the lines between what constitutes traditional security issues, as represented by military concepts, and those that are non-military by definition, which challenge the very survival and well-being of people, is taking place.

Today, non-traditional security issues are therefore being perceived to be as critical to national and global security and are being accorded increasing prominence in policy formulation, within the strategic and

---

[20] Ewing John Jackson, 'Traditional and Non Traditional Security: Exploring Practical and Conceptual Challenges', in *Non-Traditional Security Challenges in Asia*, ed. Shebonti Ray Dadwal and Uttam Sinha (London: Routledge, 2015), 30.

academic community as well as business and international organizations. They are often transnational in scope, defy unilateral remedies and require comprehensive political, economic and social responses.

Broadening Security: How Helpful or Useful?

It is also now fashionable to view security as being all-inclusive and as a basket full of everything. This is neither helpful nor is it useful. To give it policy coherence, the comprehensive nature of security needs to be bereft of 'individual idiosyncrasies and non-human element'[21] or the optimization of security in which the scope of security should be 'delimited in terms of causal factors for which human groups/communities are responsible'.[22] If that be the case, then a need to develop a continuum in which differentiating between security issues based on the application of hard power or those less so and those which are not would be important.

Not all concerns are threats and it would be a dangerous proposition to search for threat in every issue. An enlarged security definition would always remain discomfiting and suggestion of a 'security audit'[23] to signify the relevance of issues and where to draw the line is a useful methodology. Prioritizing or categorizing issues either as a zero-sum or as a non-zero-sum challenge is a practical way to shape responses.[24] Therefore, a proper assessment and evaluation is required not only from the security practitioners' perspective but also in drawing in a collective knowledge from the academic and strategic community as well as the media and civil society. A compartmentalized approach to threats that are multidimensional and complex can only lead to a weak and wobbly response mechanism. Many would argue that the distinction is not so much about what constitutes traditional and non-traditional security threats as it is about finding new approaches in dealing with new set of challenges that are clearly far more interlinked and transgressing national boundaries.

---

[21] T. K. Oommen, *Understanding Security: A New Perspective* (New Delhi: Macmillan India, 2006), 7.
[22] Ibid, 8.
[23] Kanti Bajpai, Human Security: Concept and Measurement (Kroc Institute Occasional Paper No. 19, Notre Dame, IN: University of Notre Dame, August 2000), 57.
[24] Shivshankar Menon's speech at the 14th Asian Security Conference on Non-Traditional Security Issues (14 February 2012). Available at https://idsa.in/keyspeeches/ShivshankarMenon_14ASC (accessed on 25 November 2019).

In an important sense, the understanding of comprehensive security, which has Asian resonance and pedigree,[25] facilitates the acceptance of non-traditional security. On the contrary, human security because of its emphasis on justice and emancipation tends to draw hesitation. However, the purpose of this chapter is to look at security as a continuum and not as a binary with an aim to make security effective as well as more cost-effective for foreign policy.

The chapter hereon identifies some of the important non-traditional issues for India in the regional context. Because non-traditional issues are interlinked and interconnected, searching for 'security optimality' is crucial. While doing so, it does not undermine the role of state or the importance of national security but reframes the role of state in providing security and development. The non-traditional issues identified such as climate change and the food–energy–water nexus along with connectivity and infrastructure development are challenges both within and between nations and often originate from growing socio-economic deprivation and disparities. These are essentially non-zero-sum challenges and therefore the cost of non-cooperation in terms of ecological, social and economic costs can be high. Further, creating interdisciplinary evidences and communicating evidence-based information to policymakers play an important role particularly in the sustainable management of the natural resources. The importance of transparency and information-sharing, institution-building and an emphasis on governance rather than governmentalization bring in new perspectives in dealing with the non-traditional security issues in the neighbourhood.

The Neighbourhood

Intersperse of religious and linguistic groups across national boundaries in South Asia presents an intimate intertwining of the external and the internal security issues. India's stature in the region apart its size and economic and military prowess also comes from its pluralistic social fabric. In the neighbourhood, all states have a state/national religion except India and all except Sri Lanka and India have one official language. India's pluralism gives it the strength to transcend ideological barriers. The *sab ka saath sab ka vikas* [alternative perspective on unity

---

[25] Amitav Acharya, Human Security: East versus West (RSIS Working Paper No. 17, September 2001). Available at https://dr.ntu.edu.sg/bitstream/handle/10220/4416/RSIS-WORKPAPER_25.pdf?sequence=1&isAllowed=y (accessed on 25 November 2019).

with inclusive growth] of the incumbent NDA government, while rooted domestically, has a regional span. The neighbourhood is the least economically integrated region in the world. Intra-regional trade is low and investment even lower. Resultantly, the region is poorly connected to global economy. Yet the region is one of the most dynamic and has enormous potential. In the last four years, emphasis on regional governance, region-building and institutionalism has been actively pursued by India vis-a-vis its neighbours as a strategic necessity. Several sub-regional emphasis like the Bangladesh, Bhutan, India, Nepal (BBIN), the Bay of Bengal Initiative for Multi-Sectoral Technical and Economic Cooperation (BIMSTEC) and the Indian-Ocean Rim Association (IORA) are feeding into the effort to boost regional cooperation and create infrastructure for the public good, in other words, leveraging mutual strengths. These initiatives are not in isolation but connected to each other. The BBIN links the eastern part of South Asia, while BIMSTEC connects South and South East Asia. The BBIN is a regrouping of the earlier trilateral mechanisms within the SAARC, for example, the Nepal, India and Bangladesh (NIB) trilateral on the development of the Ganga basin and Bangladesh, India and Bhutan (BIB) on the hydropower development on the Brahmaputra.

The regional institutional push is complemented with the 'credible first responder' approach that reflects India's capabilities and willingness to contribute resources to prevent and mitigate regional crisis in the both Indian Ocean region and the land mass subcontinent with particular attention to natural disasters by supporting neighbouring countries in relief operations. In 2015, India responded within 6 hours to the massive earthquake in Nepal by sending in the national disaster response force and in the next few days contributed 520 tonnes of relief material to the people of Nepal. In 2017, in response to Cyclone Mora, India was first to respond to the devastating floods in Sri Lanka and Bangladesh. This new regionalism is a functional integration that overlay political divisions by spreading a network of activities and agencies, and seems to blur distinction between the national and regional, the political and non-political.[26]

Of all the non-traditional issues, climate change is possibly the greatest challenge to state and society. Over the last decade, with substantial evidences, climate change is no longer a matter of dispute but a hard reality that encompasses issues such as energy, economics,

---

[26] David Mitrany, historian and political theorist, in his acclaimed work *A Working Peace System* (1943) presents his thoughts about the voluntary cooperation of nations to create institutions with common interests.

health, food production and other existential issues that affect daily activities. Besides, the vulnerability to disasters from both natural and man-made activities has increased considerably—earthquakes and forest fires, tsunamis, oil spills, droughts and floods. These disasters cause devastation to both human life and infrastructure and have a ruinous impact on the economies of nations.

With increasing population, rapid urbanization, deterioration of natural ecosystems and ever-greater concentration of people, capital assets and economic activity in natural hazard-prone areas, the risk of disaster losses is rising. More than 90 per cent of disasters in India are related to hydro-meteorological phenomenon such as floods, droughts and cyclones.[27] In the next 10 years, a large proportion of the world's infrastructure will be built in India and it is expected that India will double its energy output, increase the length of national highways by 50 per cent and increase the length of metro lines by six times.[28] All of this infrastructure will be exposed to hydro-meteorological hazards. The United Nations Office for Disaster Risk Reduction (UNISDR) Global Assessment Report 2015 pegged India's expected Annual Average Losses (AAL) from disasters at $10 billion per year. Of these, the AAL for floods account for 70 per cent of the total expected losses.[29] While infrastructure projects are designed for a long life cycle, climate- and weather-related hazards will almost certainly impact the durability. According to the Economic Survey (2017–2018), the current infrastructure gap in India stands at $526 billion and approximate $1 trillion will be needed to make existing and future infrastructure in India climate resilient.[30]

Given the vulnerability of South Asian states to climate change impact, it is important for India to partner with its neighbouring countries to build a coalition of disaster-resilient infrastructure. In 2016, Prime Minister Narendra Modi announced that India will work with partner countries and stakeholders to build a coalition for promoting disaster-resilient infrastructure. Since 2017, India along with the UNISDR has been working on the development of such a coalition with an emphasis on infrastructure finance development, operation and maintenance as well as reconstruction and recovery

---

[27] Kamal Kishore, Disaster Risk Management in Changing Climate: Reflections from India (A Think Piece for IDSA–PRIO Event on Climate Mitigation and Adaptation: Key Strategies, Bonn, 17 November 2017).
[28] Ibid.
[29] Ibid.
[30] Aparajit Pandey and Ritwik Sharma, 'Our Infrastructure Must Become Climate Resilient', *Hindustan Times* (New Delhi, 30 August 2018).

of key infrastructure sectors after disasters.[31] Climate resilience policy and disaster risk reduction clearly needs to be incorporated in larger strategic planning and overall development and progress. This also aligns with the Sustainable Development Goal 9 to 'build resilient infrastructure, promote inclusive and sustainable industrialization and foster innovation'.

Need for Climate Diplomacy

There are enough evidences to suggest that climate change is an existential threat to humanity, and developing countries are particularly vulnerable to its impact. Mitigating climate-related impacts can help in regional stability and conflict prevention. But with varied stakeholders and their competing interests, international climate negotiations invariably end in deadlocks and incompatible political outcomes. The Intergovernmental Panel on Climate Change (IPCC) report in 2018 strongly suggested a sharp reduction in global carbon emissions by 30–50 per cent by 2030 to avert catastrophic climate change. The international system has yet to develop a profound politico-climate consciousness and unable to unshackle the messiness of politics, culture and economics. Given the current situation concerning challenges to food, energy and water supply in the medium and long-term as a result of climate change, diplomacy in the regional context has an important role to play.

The ADB forecasts that the costs of climate change and adaptation in South Asia for the six countries—Bangladesh, Bhutan, India, the Maldives, Nepal and Sri Lanka—will see an average economic loss of around 1.8 per cent of their collective annual gross domestic product (GDP) by 2050, rising sharply to 8.8 per cent by 2100 in the current fossil fuel-intensive path.[32] Understanding the causal dynamics of climate change is essential for rationally managing the risks, especially in cases where adaptation is needed rather than simple mitigation. 'Conflict constellations' can occur, for example, climate change can accelerate natural disasters, degrade freshwater resources and reduce food production, which in turn can induce migrations. Such situations can lead to political crises and diplomatic deadlocks particularly if the

---

[31] UNISDR, *India Seeks Coalition on Resilient Infrastructure*. Available at https://www.unisdr.org/archive/56630 (accessed on 25 November 2019).

[32] Asian Development Bank, *Assessing the Costs of Climate Change and Adaptation in South Asia* (2014). Available at https://www.adb.org/sites/default/files/publication/42811/assessing-costs-climate-change-and-adaptation-south-asia.pdf (accessed on 25 November 2019).

affected states are fragile and unstable. Both in terms of the political boundaries and geographical cohesiveness, such a scenario is not improbable in South Asia.

Himalaya: Hot Spot of Climate Change

The Hindu Kush Himalayan (HKH) mountain system,[33] running across five South Asian countries plus Afghanistan, China and Myanmar, is one of the world's most fragile and hazard-prone region. Temperature rises faster at higher elevations which means a global temperature increase of 1.5°C could rise to 2.1°C in the HKH. Unabated warming is eroding the glacier-covered peaks with projected reductions in pre-monsoon river flows and changes in the monsoon, which will 'throw urban water systems and food and energy production off kilter'.[34]

India's area included in the HKH region has a population of 86.21 million (2017) that includes 11 mountain states and the districts of Darjeeling and Kalimpong in West Bengal. By adding the mountain population of Bangladesh (Chittagong district, 1.78 m), Bhutan (0.78 m), Nepal (28.75 m) and Pakistan (51.47 m), a total of 169 million people with diverse cultures, languages, religions and traditional knowledge are dependent on the HKH ecosystem services to sustain their livelihood.[35] As the largest area of permanent ice cover outside the North and South Pole and home to four global biodiversity, the HKH becomes an existential zone where decisions on investment and economic development has to be carefully assessed and administered. Adaptation alone cannot be a way for preventing crisis such as flood and drought, migration and future change in water availability of the major river basins in the HKH. It needs to be bolstered by analytical capacity, improving the information base and early warning system, conduction

---

[33] The mountain system is referred to as Hindu Kush Himalaya (HKH), coined by Kathmandu-based International Centre for Integrated Mountain Development (ICIMOD).

[34] ICIMOD, *Landmark Study: Two-Degree Temperature Rise Could Melt Half of Glaciers in Hindu Kush Himalaya Region, Destabilizing Asia's Rivers* (Press Release). Available at http://www.icimod.org/?q=33860&fbclid=IwAR05CoZPKfweL_K_3 kBsZ4_7OH_2i4KLki5ECtKlZtVyUjxK6ofYjNM2mD0 (accessed on 25 November 2019). Also see, Philippus Wester, Arabinda Mishra, Aditi Mukherji, and Arun Bhakta Shrestha, *The Hindu Kush Himalaya Assessment: Mountains, Climate Change, Sustainability and People* (ICIMOD report; Basel: Springer, 2019).

[35] The 11 mountain states are Assam, Uttarakhand, Himachal Pradesh, Manipur, Jammu and Kashmir, Meghalaya, Mizoram, Nagaland, Sikkim, Tripura and Arunachal Pradesh (Ibid, 3–4).

of integrated climate risk assessment and improving communication between government and non-government institutions.

India can take leadership role in framing a new climate security mechanism in the region. Some of India's recent initiatives have been noteworthy, for example, in setting up the International Solar Alliance (ISA) and anchoring the first summit in New Delhi in 2018. The ISA is not only an expression of India's global outreach to fight climate change through cost-effective renewable energy but equally a positioning of its global power status that is benign, rule-based and creates opportunities for wider diplomatic engagement on crucial development issues. Similarly, India has taken a strong lead in reaffirming its commitment to the cause of disaster risk reduction by hosting for the second time the Asian Ministerial meeting in 2016.

Since the Himalaya is now popularly known as the Third Pole,[36] a strong case has been argued for introducing research and science cooperation and building the necessary trust that will enable the establishment of an intergovernmental cooperation in the Himalaya similar to the Arctic Council, which to recall had brought former adversaries of the Cold War to cooperate and share scientific information on snow, water, ice and permafrost. Such a regime, with India's regional leadership, could become the basis of informed diplomatic and political cooperation in the Himalaya.[37]

Bringing in science, an underutilized tool in diplomacy, into the conversation in South Asian relations adds to the collaborative framework on climate change, weather forecasting, land monitoring, efficient resource mapping and quick response to natural disasters. The launch of the South Asia Satellite (GSAT-9) in 2017 is seen as India's technology largesse to the people in the region. As Prime Minister Modi noted, 'With its position high in the sky, this symbol of South Asian cooperation would meet the aspirations of economic progress of more than 1.5 billion people in our region and extend our close links into outer space'.[38] In 2018, the prime minister set up the International Rice

---

[36] Ólafur Ragnar Grímsson, the president of Iceland, has spoken extensively on the Arctic and the Himalaya regions. See http://english.forseti.is/media/PDF/2015_02_05_Butanraeda.pdf (accessed on 25 November 2019). Shailesh Nayak, former Secretary Ministry of Earth Science, Government of India, also spoke of a Himalayan Scientific Forum at the IDSA BIMSTEC Track 1.5 Security Dialogue Forum (22 September 2017).

[37] Ibid.

[38] D. S. Madhumathi, 'India Launches Satellite to Help South Asian Nations', *The Hindu* (2017, 5 May). Available at https://www.thehindu.com/sci-tech/

Research Institute South Asia Regional Centre in Varanasi as a hub for South–South collaboration on rice research that would develop high nutritional value rice with low sugar content and grow on less water. This brings in an important understanding of the interconnection between science and technology, and society. Any knowledge produced or innovation created needs to be distributed effectively within the geographical clusters which share natural and social characteristics. By 2030, the government aims to place India among the top 3 countries globally in science and technology. To realize this vision, the Union Budget increased its allocation in these areas by 7.5 per cent in 2018–2019 to ₹65,741 crore.[39]

India has an unrivalled youth demography in which half of the country's population of 1.3 billion people is under 25 years of age. This aspirational youth growing up in the post-1991 liberalization of the Indian economy period brings in an important view about the role of the youth bulge in the economic development and changing technology. But with poor quality of education and low rate of female participation, the dividend can be a loss leading to societal friction and unrest. Reforming the higher educational sector along with vocational education and emphasizing on skill development at a time when programmes are designed to facilitate investment, foster innovation and build manufacturing hubs is crucial for India's stability and progress.

The Riverine Neighbourhood

India and its neighbouring countries share one common trait (among several others)—high level of dependence of a large part of the population and economy on agriculture. Other relevant common traits are inadequate focus on water use efficiency in all the sectors of the economy, rising manufacturing base that demands more water resources and increasing urbanization that leads to rising water requirements in urban areas. With the NDA government's plan to raise manufacturing levels in India (also as a way to increase jobs), demand for water from the industry will only rise in the coming years and decades. Industries such as food processing, organic chemicals, thermal and solar energy, steel and mining, and fertilizers are large users of water and these are critical to the Indian economy. The waterscape is set for tougher negotiations

---

science/india-launches-south-asia-satellite/article18391277.ece (accessed on 25 November 2019).

[39] Budget speech by Arun Jaitley (1 February 2018). Available at https://www.indiabudget.gov.in/ub2018–19/bs/bs.pdf (accessed on 25 November 2019).

over the shared water resources among the countries of South Asia and hydro-diplomacy will be a key enabler for regional cooperation, with opportunities for dialogue, consultation and data-sharing both between and within states.

Transboundary rivers link their riparian in a complex network of environmental, economic and security interdependencies. Cooperation among the riparians in the region is well below its potential with competing claims for water. By all accounts, water will remain deeply political. Often water agreements are not always about water. History and hegemony play an important role in understanding the strategic interaction among riparian states and in the contextual framework under what circumstances politics interfere with cooperation or whether sharing of water acts as a neutralizing factor in difficult political situations.

While the possibility of future tension over water cannot be ruled out, evidences suggest that there are always avenues for benefit-sharing. For example, India's National Waterways Act, 2016, which declared 111 rivers for navigation as a cheaper form of transport can also be extended to benefit trade with the neighbouring countries. Bangladesh has been in the process of developing large number of waterways, some of them to connect with those in India to facilitate transboundary navigation. Nepal has agreed to develop inland waterways for cargo movement within the framework of trade and transit arrangement with India and Bhutan is waiting in anticipation to be connected to the seaports via the waterways. The transboundary navigation projects could result in greater and faster economic growth but also importantly lead to wider cooperation on water among the South Asian countries. For example, water storage in the upper reaches of the rivers could provide the multiple benefits such as adequate water flows for navigation, better flood management, lower pollution levels and greater climate change adaptation and spur higher water use efficiency across all sectors.

Treaties/arrangements on water sharing have persisted between countries in South Asia in spite of political difficulties. Some of these treaties, for example, the Indus Waters Treaty, signed in 1960, are under severe hydrological stress and might require reformulation or even a new text. But any resetting cannot be attempted unilaterally as it might lead to other political spillover. Restructuring the treaties based on new hydrological knowledge, the impact of climate change and new engineering dam designs has to come through dialogue and discussion involving wider stakeholder participation. In the short term, however, while not disregarding the water treaties, India can initiate a multi-basin approach to water management.

China will present a new set of hydrodynamics in the region and none of the South Asian countries, more so India, can escape the reality of China as an upper and powerful hydrological neighbour. There is, of course, a Joint Expert Level Mechanism between India and China, and an MoU on hydrological and flood data-sharing that needs to be reinforced. Any linear thinking based on fear psychosis that China will intentionally harm India on the Brahmaputra is reductionism. There are concerns but that need best to be dealt with downstream actions. India can build a lower riparian basin coalition on the Brahmaputra with Bangladesh and Bhutan to tackle both the bane of floods and the boon of navigation. There is about 1,800 km of potential waterways and navigation in the north-east along with viability to build more water storages to exert prior rights with China. International law, international institutions such as the UN or third party mediation cannot be relied upon, and therefore, India must overcome the challenges of a water stress future domestically, bilaterally and or by developing a multi-basin approach. For long, water allocation decisions have rested with the hydraulic engineers but with water becoming more a social problem the decisions now cannot rest entirely with the 'technocratic-bureaucratic-official-state'.

Conclusion

Differentiating between military and non-military security is becoming difficult and probably not necessary. One can continue the debate whether the issues, as discussed in the chapter, are security issues or not but they certainly seem to be critical drivers to regional diplomacy. Specific terrains and natural frontiers define many of the non-traditional issues today. The internal dynamics and extraneous factors are orienting a new set of diplomatic approaches. The traditional contours of territorial-based diplomatic engagement in South Asia are moving beyond 'protected peace' to 'functional peace' taking into account the well-being of the people. The sociopolitical context and development dynamics cannot be kept out of any national security debates. In conclusion, the chapter calls for foreign policy to be pluralistic, in the strong sense of valuing and integrating different intellectual approaches and methods and to rise above the orthodoxy and be informed by voices and conversations beyond the traditional and insular policy communities.

The Economic Dimension of India's Foreign Policy

Prasenjit K. Basu

Throughout history, India's influence on the world has been closely linked to the size and importance of its economy. In the year of Christ's birth, India accounted for 32.9 per cent of the world's economy (comfortably larger than any other civilizational entity), and India's was still the world's largest economy in the year 1700—when India accounted for 24.4 per cent of world's GDP, still slightly ahead of China's 22.8 per cent. Naturally, India's cultural influence pervaded Asia (which, in turn, was the centre of world civilization during the first millennium of the 'Christian Era', for want of another phrase).

This Indic influence radiated east, west, north and south. Around the time of Christ's birth, just as Sanskrit was dying out in India proper, that language acted as a binding force for Southeast Asia, creating new Indic civilizations in Java, Sumatra, Bali, Cambodia, Siam, the Malay Peninsula, Burma and Vietnam (Champa). Remnants of those influences are still visible in the royal practices of Thailand and Cambodia, and in the popular culture and literature of Indonesia. Tantric and Buddhist practices travelled north from Bengal to Tibet, thence to Mongolia and Manchuria, and further east to Korea and Japan. The Mongol (Yuan) dynasty created the nation we now call China—after the Mongols had fully adopted Buddhism, deeply imbued with Sanskrit influence—and the Manchu (Qing) were able to re-establish Buddhist control over China after a brief Confucian interregnum (Ming).

In the West, India's civilizational links to Persia (pre-Islamic Iran) were reflected in close linguistic ties that created the Indo-Persian language family, which includes Farsi, Dari, Pashto, Tajik and Kurdish. The linguistic link to Western languages—German, English, Dutch, French, Italian—also developed through migration and trade. Although those links were lost in the mists of time, particularly with the onset of Islam and Christianity—which created their own religion-based networks that eclipsed the older civilizational links—the linguistic link to Europe gives India important cultural and civilizational entrée into the Western world that Sinitic civilizations lack.

The Islamic and European conquests of India, respectively, caused a gradual and a precipitous decline in óur share of world income and wealth. Between 1700 and 1990, India suffered the severest decline in its share of world's GDP that any surviving nation or civilization has ever suffered—falling from 24.4 per cent in 1700 to 3.1 per cent in 1990. The rapid shrinkage in our economic importance caused a near-automatic contraction in our influence on the world. Despite demography—at least one in every seven humans has always been an Indian—our ability to influence the course of world history remained negligible in the 20th century, having been steadily eroded during the long period of Islamic and European domination of India.

While India's economic rebound over the past three decades has created important opportunities to advance our foreign policy goals, the economic gap between India and China remains large, constraining our ability to act independently in our region and around the world. Through most of history, our northern neighbours were Nepal and Tibet—both heavily influenced by Indic civilization, just as our neighbours to the east (Burma and Thailand), south (Lanka) and west (Persia and Afghanistan) were. Trade also provided deep-seated links to Africa, reinforced by a common colonial experience. The erasure of an independent Tibet has had catastrophic consequences that we must seek to reverse if our long-term economic viability is to be restored. With the restoration of our trading links across the globe, and economically reinvigorated by a declining dependency ratio over the next quarter-century (while Japan, China, Korea and Thailand suffer rising dependency ratios), we are positioned to see India's economic importance grow rapidly—bolstering India's global importance.

The Eclipse Caused by the British Interregnum and Its Enduring Drag

Sedentary civilizations such as India's (or China's) were subject to periodic raids throughout history. India's economy was temporarily weakened by invasions such as those of the Greeks, Huns, Scythians, Mongols, Afghans (Ghazni and Ghori) and Turks (mainly from Central Asia). Most of these proved to be temporary setbacks, as the value of India proved a magnet for the invaders, leading most to settle down and adapt to Indian ways. The Muslim invaders similarly settled into India but brought a millenarian faith that clashed with India's tolerant Indic traditions, weakening India's civilizational fabric.

Unlike previous invaders who had adapted to the Indic way of life, the Muslims sought to convert Indians to their faith—largely succeeding in the subcontinent's north-west and north-east over the course of nearly a millennium. Across the Gangetic plain, the destructive trail of the early Muslim invaders (and later fanatical rulers such as Aurangzeb) wiped out the civilizational heritage of North India's temples, palaces, arts, music and festivals, obliging the Sanatani faiths—'Hinduism', Buddhism, Jainism and Sikhism—to shed their collective and public forms of worship and celebration, and to turn inwards. As the practice of faith became increasingly secretive and private, the will for collective action was fundamentally emasculated, and a slavish mentality of publicly kowtowing to the rulers' whims became part of the national fabric.

India's knowledge base in mathematics, astronomy and medicine was carried Westwards and helped invigorate the nomadic Arab and Turkic peoples, vastly enriching their civilization through both the loot and the knowledge of India. The destruction of India's great universities (Taxila, Vikramshila, Nalanda)—which had been the global trailblazers of knowledge until the 10th–12th century CE—was a debilitating blow to India's civilizational advance. But after the first two centuries of loot, the Muslim invaders chose to settle in India, and the relative importance of India as the world's largest economy endured.

Britain's economic impact on India began long before the East India Company (EIC) actually gained its foothold in the vast Mughal province of Bengal in 1757. During the previous 150 years, the British EIC (and its French, Dutch and Portuguese rivals) had established a vital trading presence across India, plugging into the vast trading networks that Indians had always had across the Indian Ocean (into Southeast Asia) and the Arabian Sea (into Persia and the Arabian peninsula). In 1708,

Daniel Defoe wrote about how cloth from India (made of colourful cotton and muslin) had improved English lives by replacing the sweaty and scratch-inducing roughness of wool: 'it crept into our houses, our closets, our bedchambers. Curtains, cushions, chairs, and at last beds themselves were nothing but Calicoes or Indian stuffs'.

Elihu Yale (British governor of Madras, 1687–1692) made enough of a fortune from his tenure in India to invest it in a college that bore his name in New Haven (Connecticut), eventually becoming one of the world's great universities. One of his successors (Madras governor from 1698 to 1709), Thomas Pitt was named 'Diamond Pitt' because of his glittering collection of precious stones from India, some of which he used to buy several 'rotten boroughs' in the House of Commons, which his descendants, William Pitt the Elder and Younger, used as the springboards to create England's greatest political dynasty of the 18th century. The loot remitted from India by the likes of Yale and Pitt paved the path to the enriching of England, and the financing of its industrial revolution.

Although India was still the world's largest economy in 1700, per capita income in parts of Europe—England, Spain, Portugal, the Netherlands (the earliest colonizers)—was beginning to edge well ahead of India. The dirty little secret of the First Industrial Revolution was that Britain imposed a complete ban on imports of Indian cloth in 1701, over 50 years prior to the start of its Industrial Revolution (1760). While the technological innovations of the spinning jenny, etc., played an important role in bolstering productivity in textile manufacturing, Britain still needed an import duty of 81 per cent as late as 1820 (six decades after the onset of the Industrial Revolution) for Lancashire's textiles to compete with India's (primarily Bengal's). By the 1820s, however, the growth of Lancashire's textile industry was spawning other innovations that led to the steam engine, the steel industry and telegraphs, all of which vastly widened the gap in per capita incomes between an increasingly prosperous Britain and the emasculated civilization it ruled in India.

Britain consciously sought to keep India from acquiring the wherewithal to industrialize. Colonial policy was skewed severely against Indians: until 1850, India had one of the world's largest shipbuilding industries, and Indian ships dominated shipping across the Indian Ocean, but discriminatory policy killed the Indian capacity to build ships, and eventually the great shipping fleets around India's seas came to be dominated by British lines. Indian entrepreneurs were the early investors in industries such as tea, jute and collieries, but the active hostility of the colonial state (and growing support from it for White-owned businesses) wiped out most Indian industry by the end of the 19th century, confining Indian enterprise primarily to trading and local finance.

Education (in English) was confined to a minuscule minority of the urban elite, while education in Indian (vernacular) languages withered and waned. At the start of the 20th century, less than a tenth of Indians were able to read any language, and less than 1 per cent of Indian spoke or understood English—and yet that was the language of governance (in the previous era—1550–1800—Farsi was the language of governance, and that too was spoken mainly by the Muslim elites and a small proportion of Sanatanis, likely no more than 5%, including some Brahmins and most Kayasthas, the latter comprising those who learnt enough of Farsi to become accountants and civil servants in the Muslim courts). Of the Indian elites that spoke English, the vast majority were educated in the liberal arts, very few in engineering or other technical skills.

It required the Swadeshi movement in opposition to the first partition of Bengal (1905) to stimulate the establishment of electrical and mechanical engineering schools at the Banaras Hindu University (BHU) established by Madan Mohan Malaviya in 1916. That pioneering initiative was built upon by Nalini Sarkar and Bidhan Roy in creating a world-class Indian Institute of Technology (IIT) in Kharagpur, followed soon after by Kanpur—and several years later with the IIMs at Calcutta and Ahmedabad. While this addressed the lacuna of technical and managerial expertise, the economy couldn't grow fast enough to absorb their graduates in the first three decades, and the IITs and IIMs instead became a subsidized source of expertise for the West—only now (in the past two decades) being redirected partially towards helping India.

Another upshot of being colonized was that India's traditional textile industry was largely destroyed. When a modern one emerged (especially after each world war, and particularly the second), India under Nehru made the cardinal policy error of overvaluing the rupee and imposing import protection on virtually all industry, which had the practical effect of destroying the export potential of the infant textile and garment industries in the 1950s (ironically, the first industry minister, Syama Prasad Mukherjee, had quite sensibly sought to encourage the whole swathe of textile industries, but he resigned in April 1950). The impact of British rule had caused India's share of world's GDP to decline from 24.4 per cent in 1700 to 4.5 per cent by 1950.

Political independence, however, did not suffice to stem India's relative economic decline. India's share of world's GDP continued to decline further until 1980, when it bottomed out at 3.1 per cent—remaining at that level until 1990. While India sought, during this period of continuing economic decline, to use the Non-Aligned Movement (NAM) as a means of playing the two superpowers off against each other—and use the weight of NAM to offset India's economic feebleness—India's economic re-emergence (i.e., its rising share of world's GDP, as India's GDP keeps growing faster than the world average for the next 25 years at least) will steadily make India's voice more meaningful in world councils. India's share of world's GDP is now 4.2 per cent but has risen steadily in the past 28 years. Unless very grave policy errors are made, India's share of world's GDP will rise steadily until at least 2045 (to 15% or more) and India's position in the world league table of per capita income should move past the middle, from being in the bottom third currently. By virtue of its growing economic importance, India's voice in world affairs will begin to count far more than it has in the first 75 years of independent modern India.

The Rebirth of a Globally Connected India; Leveraging Off Indian Multinational Corporations

The reopening of the Indian economy via the far-reaching reforms undertaken by P. V. Narasimha Rao's government in 1991 placed India onto a sustainably faster growth track. By capitalizing on India's comparative advantage—which turned out to be in computer software and skill-intensive manufacturing—the economy has avoided a recession for the past three decades (and the balance-of-payments crises that caused those recessions in each of the previous four decades). Since the liberalized economy was exporting more, it was able to import more of both capital goods (to fuel future growth) and consumer goods (to widen domestic consumer choices and bolster competition and, hence, productivity in these sectors).

India's exports of goods and services have increased more than 25-fold in the past 30 years. The ASEAN economies (led by Singapore) and China sought to induce multinational corporations (MNCs), to invest in export-oriented manufacturing, and thus became important cogs in the global supply chain. Unlike them, however, India's exports are mainly manufactured by Indian companies. The disadvantage of this approach is that India's exporters are far less plugged into the global supply chain. But the advantage is that India retains the brand equity, related royalties and profits from the exports these companies generate—akin to the outcome in Japan, South Korea and (to a large extent) Taiwan. And another major long-term advantage is that the Indian companies themselves have become MNCs, acquiring a global or regional presence that makes them potential vehicles to advance India's national interests.

Indian MNCs such as the Tata group (TCS with its global software presence, Tata Motors with Jaguar Land Rover, Tata Steel with Corus and its fledgling ThyssenKrupp partnership, Tata Global Beverages with Tetley) and ArcelorMittal (the world's largest steel producer, created and owned by an Indian citizen and run almost entirely by Indians, albeit only now acquiring a presence in India), the software exporters Infosys, Wipro and HCL, pharmaceutical exporters such as Dr. Reddy's, Cipla, Sun Pharma, Lupin and Biocon, and Vedanta (among the top 5 metal producers in the world, with a presence across India, Africa, Asia, Australia and Europe), Mahindra (a global player in tractors, and an emerging one in SUVs), Hero, Kirloskar, Adani, AV Birla Group and Reliance (Mukesh Ambani) need to be closely embedded into the foreign policymaking process.

As exporters, manufacturers overseas and corporates with a presence in foreign markets, their interests will not always align with those of India as a nation. But a formalized process of dialogue needs to exist, so that mutual interests can be aligned—India acting to advance its corporates' interests abroad, and the corporates staying cognizant of advancing India's.

As a globalized economy, India's economic influence emanates from its *exports of goods and services, the size of its domestic market* (which makes it attractive to import into India or to manufacture in India to supply that market, and eventually export some of that output too), *its role as a recipient of foreign direct investment (FDI), its potential to acquire assets overseas, a source of technical expertise among its diaspora* (students, temporary residents and emigrants), *a recipient of technology inflows and a source of students with their youthful vigour and entrepreneurship and as a destination for portfolio investors to make long-term returns* and (eventually) raise capital.

The three decades of globalization have increased India's influence in all these dimensions, but only in services-exports is India's presence significant enough to make a genuinely global difference. Services-exports encompass software, shared-service and business process outsourcing (BPO) by Indian companies, as well as the large presence of Indians (mainly PIO/OCIs and a sprinkling of Indian citizens) in California's Silicon Valley, where Indians have started about a third of all new companies over the past two decades and retain a very substantial presence in private equity (PE) and venture capital (VC) financing (where between 30% and 40% are Indians, albeit mainly OCIs). Even in services-exports, India's role is essential but replaceable. Indian companies have not made the transition to create branded software products (such as Facebook, Twitter, Instagram) or even apps that are globally significant.

Related to the software, VC, PE presence in globalized cities is India's diasporic brain deposits in the academic realms there. Indians are much better represented in business school faculties across the world than any other national diaspora, but the presence among social science or international relations faculties is more modest. In particular, however, the vast majority of Indian academics outside the business school space (and even some of the latter) are of the extreme left persuasion—varying degrees of Marxist, and hence of little use to India. We need to consider a concerted effort to deepen the Indic influence over social science and humanities faculties, by enrolling Indian business groups and wealthy families to endow academic chairs that are more positively inclined towards India, and oriented towards furthering India's interests in the world (this is a long game, as it will have to begin with altering the mix of the Nehruvian–Marxist establishment across the social sciences in India itself).

China, despite being a bit player in software services, has developed its own versions of Amazon, Facebook, Twitter, WhatsApp, etc., in Alibaba, Baidu, Tencent, WeChat, which make China self-sufficient in the Internet economy. This being the case, India will perforce be the world's largest market for Facebook, Amazon, Twitter, Instagram and other major branded applications. Regulating the nature of their access to India will be an important determining factor in either developing Indian competitors to them or leveraging these platforms to create an Indian ecosystem of apps and other software that adds value to customers' experience. Developing successfully in either direction can help make India a powerful force in the Internet economy, in turn enabling India's foreign policy to leverage off that web-based power/reach. As the largest market for the global software giants, India must enrol them as allies in furthering India's global interests. Consumer-goods sellers, producers of consumer-electronics and cars in India are others who are investing in India's success, and need to become formal allies of India in their home markets (e.g., Suzuki and Honda already are in Japan, LG and Hyundai are to some extent in Korea; but the likes of GE, Texas

Instruments, Unilever, BP, ABB, Siemens, Procter & Gamble need to do more to advance India's cause in the USA, the UK, Germany, Sweden, etc.; they will want to do more once their Indian operations begin to make a material difference to their global bottom line).

By virtue of having the lowest cost data access in the world (India's average data costs are 1/34th of the non-India global average, 1/25th the cost in the UK and 1/48th the cost in the USA!), India has the potential to rapidly develop an Internet-based ecosystem of apps, start-up leaders ('unicorns') and services that could—if properly harnessed—catapult India into a position of leadership in web-based services and applications within the next decade. When that happens, India will have substantially greater leverage in trade and foreign policy discussions. For now, however, the low cost of data constitutes merely a *potential* source of great possibilities in the future.

Since India's export strategy depends more on Indian companies leading the export sector, rather than MNCs doing so (as in China and Singapore), India has traditionally received substantially lower levels of FDI (especially when compared with China). However, there has been a quantum jump in FDI inflows into India over the past decade—and especially the past half-decade. Annual FDI inflows averaged US$33.63 billion in the first four fiscal years of the NDA2 (Narendra Modi) government, up sharply from the US$18.19 billion averaged during the previous four years (the final 4 years of UPA2). But even the NDA2 levels of FDI amounted to just 1.5 per cent of India's GDP. Until FY 2006–2007, India was receiving less than US$10 billion of FDI inflows annually. The quantum jump in FDI inflows over the past decade has created a substantial stock of international companies with a stake in India. They provide the wherewithal to develop an India Lobby among the major business chambers in the USA, the UK, Japan, Germany, France, etc., that can become the first line of defence against any 'India-bashing' policies that a future administration may develop (for instance, the Trump administration's decision to drop Generalized System of Preferences (GSP) privileges for Indian exports). Japan, Germany and China have very substantial lobbies within American chambers of commerce, comprising US companies with substantial exposure to those economies (through large stocks of FDI into those economies and/or a need to ensure access to the US market for products produced by them in China/Japan/Germany).

India's great economic failure has been in globally competitive manufacturing, apart from pharmaceuticals, metals processing (including steel), some engineering goods, automobile components and specific labour-intensive niches such as gems and jewellery, tea, jute and (less successfully in) garments and textiles. The Modi government's 'Make in India' initiative has begun to make some difference in essential new areas such as defence production (which could have significant spillover technological benefits when successful), and incipient steps in the electronics/semiconductor/component space that China has come to dominate over the past two decades (but will gradually vacate over the next decade as its working-age population shrinks). There is enormous untapped potential for India in these areas. Indians' vital role in the PE and VC financing spaces creates an obvious opportunity for greater synergies—including a governmental facilitative role in linking financiers to opportunities in India.

The Modi government has begun to tap into India's diasporic networks to create a space for Indic culture (yoga, language, dance, music, film) across the world. Getting Muslim majority countries such as the UAE to allow prominent Hindu temples, the world to adopt an International Yoga Day and emphasizing India's movie, dance, song and art on all foreign tours have helped spread India's soft power across the world. Even during the periods of Muslim and British rule, India's art and culture survived in the many kingdoms that maintained relative autonomy (even if they were politically subservient to the hegemonic power), and the modern Indian state did well to nurture and develop Bharatanatyam, Odissi, Kathak, Kathakali, Kuchipudi, Manipuri and Bengali dance forms, as well as the Hindustani and Carnatic musical traditions—which now can be the bridge to the art forms of the rest of Asia that were heavily influenced by the Indic past. Tagore (still loved in China, Korea, Turkey and elsewhere as an Asian literary trailblazer) can also help deepen cultural linkages across Asia. Linguistic and cultural links to the rest of Asia remain a relatively untapped area—although this gap has been steadily bridged in the Look East era of diplomacy launched since the 1990s.

The Size versus Proximity Challenge in the International Pecking Order

At market exchange rates, India is now the world's fifth largest economy (behind the USA, China, Japan and Germany). That India's GDP was no larger than Britain or France's until 2018 (despite the fact that India's population was nearly 20 times the size of each of those country's) is a sobering reminder that the average Indian is still abjectly poor (i.e., our ranking in per capita income remains dismal, still in the bottom third of the world). Given India's demographics (with the dependency ratio declining for another quarter-century), the economy should continue to be among the world's fastest-growing over the next two decades. This will ensure that India will be at least the third largest (and possibly the second largest) economy in the world by 2030 (especially if China's bubble of industrial and real estate capacity bursts, causing a severe disruption to its financial system).

However, as an international trader, India's impact on the world remains puny compared with China's today. India was only the 19th largest exporter of goods in the world in 2017 (18th if Hong Kong is excluded), and likely to have risen to 16th in 2018. China, the largest, exports about seven times as much as India does annually. However, India was the 11th largest importer of goods in the world in 2017—and likely to have risen to 9th place among the world's importers in 2018. China (the second largest importer) still imports four times as much as India does annually. Correspondingly, India's influence on the world is thereby much lower than China's; despite the widespread non-tariff barriers that it imposes on imports, China is the world's second largest importer (behind only the USA), and hence remains a far more important market for the rest of the world. As India's economy grows faster than the world's average, its imports will perforce rise faster than the rest of the world—and hence rise up the league table of world importers, likely to the top 4 within the next decade. By that point, its importance as a market for the world's exports will become significant enough for India's voice on trade issues to matter significantly.

As an exporter of services, India was the world's 7th largest country in 2017 (marginally behind Japan), but is likely to have risen to 6th (marginally behind China) in 2018. The USA accounts for nearly four times India's annual services exports. This is an area where India's comparative advantage has been manifest over the past two decades, but there is still considerable scope for growth, including gains in market share at the expense of the top 5 (the USA, the UK, Germany, France and China).

Although India had been the largest trading nation on earth for much of recorded history, its role as a trader has ebbed in the past two centuries and is still at the early stages of being revived. Modern India's neglect of its immediate neighbours to the east was the most striking feature of the 1950–1990 period—partly arising from India's tilt towards the Soviet Union during the period, and much of East Asia's alignment with the USA (including China after 1971). The neglect of East Asian ties has been partially redressed in the past quarter-century, but India continues to trail China's deep involvement in the region. As a result, China (and its allies such as Cambodia) succeeded in ensuring that ASEAN created institutions that excluded India initially ('ASEAN+3' included Japan, China and South Korea, for instance, but excluded India).

The flow of Indian labour to West Asia (Oman, the UAE, Qatar—in all of which, Indians account for 20–25% of the population—and Saudi Arabia) and India's dependence on oil imports from Iraq and Iran ensured close trade ties with that region, including substantial exports to and remittances from those countries. Until the Modi administration, however, India did little to leverage these deep commercial ties with West Asia into a foreign policy advantage: Saudi Arabia and the UAE, for instance, remained Pakistan's key financiers (including as allies in the creation of the Taliban), although India had far more trade with them (the UAE in particular). This has changed somewhat during the Modi years, with the crown princes of UAE and Saudi Arabia ('MBZ' and 'MBS', respectively) seeking to modernize their approach to global issues—and reduce their attempts to spread the extremist Wahhabi/Salafi ideology across the world. While the initial attempts at tighter engagement are bearing fruit, concerted pressure (alongside the USA and Israel, among others) needs to be applied to bring about greater change.

The substantial presence of Indian businesses in East, South and West Africa has ensured that India's trade links with Africa persisted through the second half of the 20th century—despite anti-Indian policies in some countries (Kenya, Tanzania), culminating in the expulsion of all Indians from Uganda by Idi Amin in August 1972. Uganda's Museveni has, in the past two decades, sought to expiate for Amin's sins, inviting Indians to return. Africans' recent experience with China's neocolonialism has revived the continent's interest in engaging more closely with India as an alternative pole of investment, technological collaboration and trade. After a near-tripling of trade with Africa in the past 12 years, India is now sub-Saharan Africa's second-largest trading partner (having surpassed the USA and Japan over that period). Services trade is also rising rapidly but remains an area of huge untapped potential.

The BRICS grouping holds valuable possibilities—both economic and strategic—for India. While there is a great danger of the group being hijacked by China, India has South Africa and Brazil (especially under Bolsonaro) as vital partners in balancing China, while Russia's embrace of China too remains wary—and its long-standing ties to India retain residual but fading strength. Despite the strong trading ties that existed with the Soviet Union (albeit based on barter and a fragile currency arrangement), India's commercial ties with the successor states—Russia, the Central Asian republics and the Caucasus nations—remain tenuous. Indian businessmen have been engaged in that region, and India has strong military ties to Tajikistan, but there is ample scope to create mutually beneficial trading relations with a region with which India has historic ties. South Africa, Brazil, Russia (and its Eurasian economic union partners) all have economies that are complementary to India—exporting minerals and importing manufactures and services. India needs to explore ways of deepening economic ties with Brazil, South Africa and Russia that involve exchanging Indian software/services and manufacturing (both labour- and skill-intensive) for minerals. Rosneft's purchase of Essar Oil presents a good beginning; other opportunities for two-way flows of capital need to be explored.

Proximity ensures that China is currently the largest source of imports and the third largest country market for India's exports, though it is a distant third for the latter, far behind the USA (which accounts for 16% of India's exports) and the UAE. If the EU is taken together, it accounted for 18 per cent of India's exports in 2018 (although the departure of the UK will reduce that to 15%). Importantly, India has a much more diversified basket of trading partners than most of East Asia (which is extremely dependent on China as a market). Asia as a whole accounts for nearly half of India's exports, but Bangladesh (2.7%) and Nepal (2.3%) also figure among the top 10 export destinations (8th and 10th, respectively). SAARC gets a bad press primarily because of the dysfunctional India–Pakistan relationship; the other members of SAARC are vital markets for India's exports—and India is the most important source of their imports (including Afghanistan, which gets more than half its imports from India).

India has a ludicrous imbalance in its trade with China, with a bilateral deficit of US$57.3 billion in 2018 (imports from China of US$73.7 billion and exports to China of merely US$16.4 billion). Most of India's other bilateral trade deficits are with the Organization of the Petroleum Exporting Countries (OPEC) economies of Saudi Arabia (US$22.9 billion), Iraq (US$21.2 billion), Iran (US$11.3 billion), Qatar ($8.9 billion) and Nigeria ($8.4 billion), and other commodity exporters such as Indonesia ($11.2 billion) and Australia ($10.4 billion). Proximity has been a massive bilateral trading advantage for China thus far, as indeed it has been for Australia and Indonesia. India needs to develop country-specific strategies to boost exports to these three economies—and particularly reduce the trade deficit with China (an adversarial power), by ensuring that non-tariff barriers are removed and China's subsidized exports are countered with adequate domestic relief for Indian competitors.

The USA and EU remain vital markets for Indian exports. Given their size—and still nearly unlimited potential for increased market share in those markets (where India's market share is about a tenth of China's)—they need to remain the focus of India's commercial diplomacy. India has a bilateral trade surplus of US$19 billion with the USA, and large surpluses with the Netherlands ($5 billion), the UK ($2.7 billion) and over $2.5–3.5 billion each with Spain and Turkey, so broadening the India–EU trade agreement has to be a focus, and institutionalizing the trading arrangements with the USA need to be prioritized. As a rising power that the USA wishes to align with, India needs to find ways to encourage US consumer goods and retailing companies to source on a massive scale from India—replacing China as their main supply source, especially as China's labour and other costs rise rapidly.

India's other large bilateral surpluses are with Bangladesh (US$7.9 billion), Nepal (US$6.9 billion) and Sri Lanka (US$3.3 billion). These neighbours will remain crucially dependent on net imports from India, but we need to work with them to deepen their economic vitality (particularly for Sri Lanka and Nepal, which are otherwise being enticed into China's imperial embrace). India also has a bilateral trade surplus with OPEC member UAE ($2.2 billion), suggestive of substantial Indian exports that are routed via Dubai to Pakistan. Chabahar port will help deepen India's economic engagement with Afghanistan (a country that obtains 56% of its annual imports from India), but should also be used to add greater balance to the trading relationship with Iran.

Proximity remains the reason for some of India's largest bilateral trade surpluses (Bangladesh, Nepal, Sri Lanka, UAE, Kenya)—and its largest bilateral trade deficit (with China). The enormous trade imbalance with China needs to be urgently redressed, with anti-dumping duties needing to be used aggressively, and infant industry protection being considered for an array of industries in which India has a comparative advantage (textiles, garments, shoes, toys, processed food, steel, aluminium, chemicals and especially electronics) in order to nurture the growth of a healthy manufacturing sector that can gradually fill much of the space currently occupied by China in the global economy. Proximity to Africa gives India advantages that need to be built upon, especially given Africa's growing distaste for Chinese imperialism. Export and import insurance need to be stepped up to allow the threefold increase in India's exports to Africa over the past 12 years to persist or quicken over the period ahead.

But commercial diplomacy must still focus primarily on enabling India's exporters to gain market share in the world's two largest markets, the USA and EU (plus the UK post-Brexit). Since India's share of US imports is still only about a tenth of China's, and its share of EU imports about an eighth of China's, there is limitless potential for India's exports to those two markets to grow. The USA sees India as a key strategic partner, but India must now look to add real depth to that strategic relationship by identifying areas of economic engagement (particularly manufacturing for export) where India can effectively replace the US dependence on China. While the EU will be more difficult to crack using a strategic argument, India has enough commercial allies in the EU (the Netherlands, Germany, France and Spain) and those just outside (the UK, Turkey) to build a strong case for India to be the EU's long-term partner to replace an increasingly high-cost (and strategically unreliable) China.

Economic Alliances in the Remaking of a Dynamic Indian Economy

Japanese and South Korean companies have been vitally important investors in India—with Suzuki (Maruti) and Hyundai dominating the domestic car market (and also accounting for the bulk of car exports), motorcycles dominated by Japanese brands (Honda, Kawasaki, Yamaha) but facing increasing Indian competition (Hero, Bajaj, TVS), and consumer electronics brands such as Sony, Panasonic, LG and Samsung also having a significant presence. In turn, Indian companies have acquired key Korean brands—including Tata's purchase of Daewoo's truck manufacturing business, and Mahindra's acquisition of SsangYong Motor—and used them to acquire technology and enter third-country markets. The Japanese purchase of Ranbaxy was an unhappy transaction, but also established a crucial India–Japan commercial link. India's computer software sector has a rapidly growing presence in both Japan and Korea.

Given the strategic dimensions of China's Belt and Road Initiative (BRI), and China's persistent hostility to India, it would be sensible to strengthen commercial links with other Asian economies that have surplus capital and the need for growing markets. Japan is the most natural partner for India: Japan's demographics perfectly complements India's, and Japan's formerly world beating companies can reinvigorate themselves for the long term via a deeper partnership with India—entailing manufacturing in India for both export and domestic sale, technological collaboration that capitalizes on India's engineering expertise and genuine partnerships in infrastructure building such as

Delhi-Mumbai Industrial Corridor Project (DMICDC) and various highspeed rail projects. Japan's strategic affinity for India is clear too, with the Quad providing a natural arena for naval and air-force cooperation in the Indo-Pacific.

South Korea is a slightly more complex partner, given its ambivalent approach to North Korea (especially under the 'liberals' led by current President Moon Jae-in, and predecessors Roh Moo-hyun and Kim Daejung) and hence to China. The conservative legatees of Park Chung-hee are likely to be more amenable to closer strategic ties with India, while the liberals are wont to try appeasing China in order to enable a reduction in inter-Korean hostility. Xi Jinping saying to President Trump that 'Korea used to be part of China' (during their first summit at Mar-a-Lago in April 2017) had a chilling effect across Korea. But South Korea under Moon has continued to place its bets squarely on a rapprochement with North Korea. India has some opportunities there too, given that commercial ties to the DPRK are not entirely absent. But the main area of focus in India–Korean ties has to be on inducing a deeper engagement with South Korean chaebols (Hyundai, Samsung, LG and SK) in technology, infrastructure and especially in telecommunications (5G) and the Internet. That about a tenth of South Korea's population claims descent from an Indian princess from Ayodhya (Queen Suriratna, or Heo Hwang-ok, who married King Suro of the Geumgwan Gaya kingdom of Korea in 48 AD) is an additional emotive factor that can contribute to deeper ties. Moon Jae-in has a 'southern strategy' aimed at reducing Korea's economic dependence on China (especially after the threats and boycotts Korean chaebols faced following the deployment of Terminal High Altitude Area Defense (THAAD) missiles by South Korea in 2017). This should dovetail perfectly with moving more manufacturing (of consumer electronics and semiconductors) to India, especially as Korean chaebols face increasing competitive pressure from China.

India's approach to BRI has been correctly sceptical, as it is clearly a Chinese imperial initiative, aimed at making 'partner' countries subservient to China's capital and technology. Even the labour used in BRI projects is almost entirely from China, so there are few benefits for the local economy. Sri Lanka and Pakistan's experience (as well as Kenya's) suggests that China's aim in BRI projects is to force the partner country to take on excessive debt and then oblige it to do a debt–equity swap that results in Chinese ownership of large assets and land in the 'partner' country—correctly labelled 'neocolonialism' by Malaysia's PM Mahathir. While staying completely away from BRI, India has done well to participate in the Asian Infrastructure Investment Bank (AIIB) and the New Development Bank (sponsored by the BRICS). Although headquartered in China, both AIIB and NDB have institutionalized ownership structures (with India as the second largest shareholder), and are thus akin to the ADB and World Bank—except with a larger Indian say in decisions, though China has the bigger say (BRI, by contrast, is a Chinese imperial project, where ownership is 100% Chinese). The AIIB, NDB, World Bank and ADB represent a wider ecosystem of development lending that India can and must effectively utilize.

Oil exporting allies such as Iran, Iraq and Oman—and with suitable modifications, the UAE, Bahrain and Qatar—can be important sources of capital flows. While 'petrodollars' were previously recycled mainly via London's Eurodollar market, these OPEC nations are increasingly looking to diversify their investments, including through their well-established sovereign wealth funds (the most successful of which is the Abu Dhabi Investment Authority, managing close to US$1 trillion). They are all increasingly paying attention to India for its stable and positive returns on investment. Singapore's GIC and Temasek too are important sources of capital inflows that need to be tapped. India needs a long-term strategy for oil and mineral supply, so developing a mutually beneficial relationship with mineral exporters is crucial.

For historic reasons, British banks (HSBC and Standard Chartered) have a substantial presence in the Indian market, although both British-owned banks are more closely tied to (and dependent on) China than the Indian market. The US commercial banks (Citibank and JP Morgan) have a substantial presence in India too, but the investment banks (Goldman Sachs, Morgan Stanley, BoAML) do much less in India than in China and Indonesia. Among the Europeans, Deutsche Bank has shrunk since Anshu Jain's departure as CEO, while Credit Suisse (CS) and UBS have a strong presence in India. In expanding free trade agreements with the USA and the EU, India should demand reciprocal market access for Indian banks. HDFC, Kotak Mahindra, SBI and ICICI Bank have the wherewithal to acquire more of a global distribution capacity that will enable them to compete as international banks. London, in a post-Brexit Britain, would be an obvious financial centre where India's banks should look to establish themselves by acquiring assets (for instance, HDFC Bank or Kotak Mahindra buying Deutsche's international operations, or acquiring Standard Chartered outside China; current valuations make these real possibilities). Thus far, Britain has wooed China, but the core Brexiters led by PM Boris Johnson are more enamoured of the link to India—which we should explore fully, especially in the financial sector. Given that ArcelorMittal and Tata are among Britain's largest employers, the missing element is a major Indian presence in the city to complement the industrial and culinary dominance.

Strategic Importance of Manufacturing: Leveraging our Software Advantage

China is the world's largest manufacturer of almost every kind of manufactured product, accounting for more than half of all global output of steel, aluminium and cement, and more than a third of all global output of chemicals and automobiles. It is also the largest single producer of the world's electronics products (with a 9% share)—albeit as part of an Asian supply chain, which ensures that China has large bilateral trade deficits with Taiwan and South Korea.

China currently produces about eight times as much steel as the second largest producer (India) and nearly nine times as much cement as India (which is the second largest producer of cement too, producing nearly three times as much annually as the third largest producer, the USA). Contrary to perceptions, India already has the fifth largest industrial output in the world (barely one-seventh the size of China, but now only about a third smaller than fourth placed Germany, with the USA and Japan ahead). India is the fifth largest oil refiner (after the USA, China, Russia and Japan), automobile manufacturer (after China, the USA, Japan and Germany) and aluminium producer (following China, Russia, Canada and the UAE), the sixth largest zinc producer, ninth largest chemicals manufacturer and tenth largest pharmaceuticals exporter in the world.

One obvious consequence of India's industrial output being larger than those of Britain, France, Italy and Canada is that *India should long ago have been invited to join the Group of Seven (originally billed as the 'club of the world's largest industrialized democracies')*. India should be the fourth member of the G7; there is no legitimate basis on which India can be excluded now, and it is time that the case is made properly for India to be included.

But the two areas of manufacturing where India has lagged behind are at the opposite extremes—labour-intensive textiles, garments, shoes, toys and processed food; and technology-intensive electronics. No nation has ever successfully industrialized without first mastering labour-intensive manufacturing. Britain, the USA, Germany, Japan, South Korea, Taiwan, Singapore and China all began with labour-intensive manufacturing—which absorbs the masses of unemployed and underemployed, and transforms their lives by creating a disciplined and industrious workforce that can later be deployed in newer industries. India's failure to benefit from the dismantling of the multi-fibre arrangement (MFA) of quotas which regulated the textile/garment trade under GATT (until 1994, with 10 years to its full dismantling) owed primarily to the rigidities in India's labour market.

The mild reforms undertaken by Rajasthan and several other states in 2014–2015 only slightly altered the picture. Large-scale and significant labour market liberalization is needed if India is to see the needed boom in labour-intensive manufacturing. The second Modi administration's determination to streamline India's labour laws into four simplified new labour codes is a positive signal, but the opportunity needs to be seized to make India's labour market genuinely flexible. Merely simplifying existing labour laws, with modest changes (such as flexibility on hiring apprentices, and allowing companies with 300 workers—up from the previous limit of 100—to fire workers without seeking government permission) will do little to fundamentally reform the labour market, and encourage vastly more employment in labour-intensive manufacturing. Textile, garments, toys and electronics manufacturing all require vast scale (tens of thousands of workers in each factory), and imposing an artificial limit of 300 workers is counterproductive and irrational.

China's rising wages will perforce result in massive relocation of all these industries; currently, only Vietnam, Bangladesh and (to a limited degree) Indonesia are gaining from this relocation. India is perfectly poised to be a big winner, but only if the labour market is significantly liberalized. Clothes, shoes, toys and food are the essential products that all humans consume, so the size of the market for these is huge (and grows with the human population). Electronics is the essence of the technology industries of today and tomorrow. As the examples of each wave of 'flying geese' in Asia's industrialization have shown, these labour-intensive industries cannot be successfully automated, so the opportunity for growth remains enormous for India in this area.

India provides a panoply of protections for labour in the 'organized' sector (which accounts for less than 10% of industrial employment) while providing no support to the vast majority in the unorganized sector. A via media needs to be struck. The February 2019 interim budget provided an incentive for the unorganized sector worker to self-declare by starting a generous pension scheme. Counting the unorganized sector worker is the first step towards rational reform. A truly liberalized labour market would involve reduced protections for the organized sector (to ensure more employability in the organized sector), and a modest and steady increase in protections for workers (including the pension scheme, and eventual inclusion in the provident fund arrangements) for the unorganized sector worker. The latter needs to be done gradually in order not to destroy the implicit flexibility that currently exists in the unorganized sector's labour market. But a rationalization of the whole labour market (by reducing the excessive protections of the organized sector—which deter employment—while increasing those for unorganized labour) is crucial to accelerate industrial output, by employing the vast labour surpluses of the underemployed and unemployed that India still has.

There are some promising developments in electronics manufacturing in India over the recent years, with a quantum leap in smartphone production, and Taiwanese OEM/ODM manufacturers such as Foxconn (Hon Hai) and Wistron steadily expanding their investments in India. Taiwanese companies have hitherto used China and Vietnam as their main manufacturing/processing bases. But given some smoothening of crinkles in the GST system and further liberalization of the labour market, India is likely to see a quantum jump in electronics manufacturing. The potential for growth of the Indian domestic market is one attraction, but producing in India for export to the world ought to be even more attractive. Deepening ties with Taiwan, South Korea and Japan—the three key technology leaders in process technologies in electronics—will provide the basis for a truly transformative move in Indian manufacturing.

The July 2019 budget extended investment-linked incentives (under Section 35AD of the Income Tax Act) to semiconductor, wafer fab, electric vehicle, solar photovoltaic cell and lithium-ion battery manufacturers to set up large-scale manufacturing units in India. The GST rate for electric vehicles was cut to 5 per cent and other incentives were provided to purchasers of electric vehicles. These are worthwhile steps to induce manufacturers of these high-technology products (currently dominated by China, Taiwan and South Korea) to move some of their manufacturing to India. In the electric vehicle and solar technology complex, however, China has a very substantial lead—and eroding that even slightly will require a more determined policy effort.

Over time, success in industries such as steel, cars, trucks and chemicals should also translate to more success with capital-intensive manufacturing of ships and aircraft. India's focus on private sector participation in defence-related manufacturing is essential from a foreign policy standpoint. The US Defense Advanced Research Projects Agency (DARPA) is an excellent prototype of collaboration between government researchers, academics and the private sector in creating not only defence-related products but also many positive spin-offs (such as the Internet, and graphical user interface [GUI], which were both invented by DARPA). China has also taken massive strides in defence production, though it is far from being at the frontiers of global technology. Having a diversified and employment-intensive manufacturing sector is the key to creating a vibrant ecosystem that will eventually spawn a successful defence-related manufacturing base. They go hand in hand.

Overall, the continued vibrancy of the Indian economy is crucial to enhance India's voice in global affairs. Once India is the third largest economy in the world, it will automatically have a place on the global high table. But in the interim, it is important to use a variety of strategies—as a middle power that is living in the economic shadow of an aggressive northern neighbour—to multiply India's existing economic endowment with smart strategies, enhanced engagement with the world and continued diversification of the economy to make it ever more attractive for other nations to want to partner us in our upward journey.

Domestic Drivers of India's Neighbourhood Policy

Ashok Behuria

India's neighbourhood policy is more than a mere subset of its foreign policy. Ever since Indian Independence, the neighbourhood has always received prime attention of the leadership. This has been quite visible in the selection of seasoned diplomats to represent India in the neighbouring countries and the economic as well as the political capital that India spends to maintain friendly relations with each of the countries in the face of challenges of legacy issues and fear of its dominance as the preponderant country in the region. The current government's 'Neighbourhood First' policy is a natural outgrowth of the policy advocated by previous governments towards India's neighbours.

Given the historical and geo-cultural linkages that bind India to its neighbours, it is natural to find India sharing overlapping ethnic, linguistic and cultural space with most of them. One can aver, most countries have bits of India in their midst as much as India has bits of them in its entrails, which tend to add complexities to India's bilateral relations with each one of them by heightening their suspicion of extension of Indian influence at one level and acting as inerasable links that can promote mutual trust and understanding at another. It is also inevitable that constituencies within India, given such overlaps, will have cross-border ties which may impact internal politics in both countries and affect interstate relations. In this context, it is useful to first get an overview of India's foreign policy, isolate the domestic drivers of India's foreign, as well as neighbourhood policy, and analyse their impact on India's bilateral relations with its neighbours.

Overview of India's Foreign Policy Matrix

It is pertinent here to start with a brief overview of India's foreign policy and situate India's neighbourhood policy within its ideological and philosophical settings. The literature that emerges from annual reports, joint statements and various publications by the Indian Ministry of External Affairs (MEA) would identify the fundamental principles of India's foreign policy as 'respect for state sovereignty, peaceful settlement of disputes, the use of force as a last resort, and opposition to all attempts to reorder societies from outside with military force'.

The official literature says that 'India's foreign policy, rooted in the national ethos, supports the processes of national development and transformation through the furtherance of the country's national interests'. It seeks to ensure India's 'security', promote its 'socio-economic development', maintain 'strategic autonomy' and work towards 'a more just global order'.[1] It also says that 'India aspires for a peaceful and secure periphery, expanding ties with its extended neighbourhood, cordial and balanced relations with major powers and mutually beneficial partnerships with developing countries'.[2]

In recent years, there is an official claim that India has tried increasingly 'to occupy a new role in the world, as a confident, articulate, rising power, willing to claim its place on the global high table and able to discharge its responsibilities'. 'No longer content to merely react

---

[1] Ministry of External Affairs, Government of India, *Annual Report 2012–2013*. Available at http://mea.gov.in/Uploads/PublicationDocs/21385_Annual_Report_2012–2013_English.pdf (accessed on 27 November 2019).

[2] India's foreign policy according to official proclamation also has a strong multilateral dimension with the country working closely with partners in international bodies and fora to tackle global challenges of today such as terrorism, climate change, sustainable development, energy and food security and cyber and space security. India seeks reform of international institutions to reflect the global reality of the present-day world and to ensure an appropriate role for India.

to international developments', it has 'frequently acted to shape and even initiate them', especially 'on issues ranging from global governance reform, climate change, multilateral trade negotiations, internet governance & cyber-security, and trans-national terrorism'.[3] The latest annual report of the MEA reiterates the main thrust of India's 'pragmatic and outcome-oriented foreign policy' which aims at 'achieving the key goals of ensuring national security and upholding territorial integrity, attaining national economic transformation, and addressing regional and global issues'.[4] A brief overview of the current Indian Prime Minister Narendra Modi's speeches would also suggest that India has an unwavering commitment to work with the international community 'to help shape a peaceful, prosperous and sustainable world in this century'.

The objectives of Indian foreign policy have been identified by Prime Minister Modi through his speeches, as: 'supporting India's economic transformation', 'seeking a peaceful and stable neighbourhood' and 'fulfilling [India's] international responsibilities to steering a more stable, sustainable and secure future for the world'.[5] There are three elements to this new vision of Indian foreign policy spelt out by the prime minister which reinvigorate India's engagement with the wider world: (a) a 'geopolitical framework for addressing India's immediate and long-term strategic challenges in a world of shifting power balances and unpredictable changes', (b) India's 'economic rise and transformation of the lives of ordinary Indians are closely linked to the external world' and (c) the cultural dimension of India's external policy, 'not just in terms of elevating India's soft power to a global phenomenon but also delving deep into India's civilisation and culture to frame an Indian discourse on global issues'.[6] The National Democratic Alliance (NDA) government led by the Bharatiya Janata Party (BJP) has also tried to bring about symbolic changes in the core of India's stated foreign policy principles. *Panchsheel* (five principles) that

---

[3] Ministry of External Affairs, Government of India, *Annual Report 2015–2016*. Available at http://mea.gov.in/Uploads/PublicationDocs/29521_MEA_ANNUAL_REPORT_2016_17_new.pdf (accessed on 27 November 2019).

[4] Ministry of External Affairs, Government of India, *Annual Report 2017–2018*. Available at http://mea.gov.in/Uploads/PublicationDocs/29788_MEA-AR-2017-18-03-02-2018.pdf (accessed on 27 November 2019).

[5] Narendra Modi, *Select Speeches on Foreign Policy, 2014–2015* (New Delhi: Ministry of External Affairs, 2016). Available at http://mea.gov.in/PM_SpeechBook_2014-25/?page=14 (accessed on 27 November 2019).

[6] Ibid.

formed the essence of Indian approach to the wider world so far has been quietly overtaken by a newly coined principle, *Panchamrit* (five nectars)—dignity, dialogue, security, shared prosperity and culture, guided by three C's—culture, commerce and connectivity. The former was rather proclamatory and ideological wedded to universal values; the latter is aspirational, rooted in local culture and values. BJP, the dominant party in the NDA, having a majority by itself in the legislature, has attempted to use 'religious and cultural resources—primarily Hinduism—unapologetically as elements of [India's] soft-power on the international stage'.[7]

While enunciating the broader strands of India's foreign policy by the Indian leadership over the years, there is an acknowledgement that the 'immediate neighbourhood remains the area of greatest attention and emphasis ... under an articulated policy of "Neighbourhood First"'. That India takes its neighbourhood seriously can be gleaned from a statement by the Indian Prime Minister Modi that the future he would dream for India would be the future he would dream for India's neighbours. The present discussion takes off from here.

Domestic Drivers of Indian Foreign Policy

The first-ever scholarly study on domestic roots of India's foreign policy was undertaken by A. Appadorai in 1981.[8] He had isolated five elements influencing India's foreign policy decision-making. They are: tradition and history, democracy, the demands for economic development, the pluralistic nature of the society and leadership (then Nehru's charismatic personality). He concluded that the record of parliament in influencing foreign policy decision-making was very poor. He studied Indian federalism in action and held that successful 'implementation of foreign affairs [would require] the willing cooperation of the states'. He referred specifically to the specific interests of the provinces inhibiting the ability of the government to make agreements with India's neighbours and advised Indian government to fulfil its contract obligations with neighbouring countries such as Sri Lanka and Bangladesh.

---

[7] Atul Mishra and Jason Miklian, 'The Evolving Domestic Drivers of Indian Foreign Policy', Report (Oslo: Norwegian Peacebuilding Resource Centre, 2016), 1–8.

[8] Angadipuram Appadorai, *Domestic Roots of India's Foreign Policy, 1947–1972* (New Delhi: Oxford University Press, 1981).

Other studies by Andersen,[9] Varghese,[10] Mohan,[11] and Mishra and Miklian[12] focus on the role of domestic factors on the making of Indian foreign policy. Andersen begins by quoting Appadorai that it is natural for Indian foreign policy to be 'influenced by domestic concerns, institutions, and the political elites that articulate demands' at the internal level. He draws attention to the fact that India does not have any institutions 'to mobilise internal popular support for specific foreign policy positions' and foreign policy decision-making was limited to very few at the top, even if the nature of influence exercised by the leadership differed from person to person managing the top decision-making positions.

Andersen argues that even if Nehru had an unassailable sway over India's external affairs and mostly had his way with framing of India's policy towards the wider world, he had to take decisions under pressure on some occasions during the fag end of his political career/life. At times he was a victim of the ideological consensus that he had himself engendered in a bid to define the broad contours of India's foreign policy. Even Nehru had to revoke his decision to permit Voice of America to transmit to China from Indian soil when his own party men opposed his move on the ground that it would violate India's principled advocacy of non-alignment as a cornerstone of its foreign policy.

Nehru was followed by others who sought to retain their control over the way decisions would be made in the realm of foreign policy. Even if domestic concerns often defined Indian leadership's approach to foreign economic policies, Andersen finds Indian business concerns at times influencing decisions taken during the late 1960s to devalue Indian rupee and invite foreign investment. Indian government's return to conservative decision-making in the economic arena also had much to do with domestic resentment occasioned by short-term negative impact of devaluation. The other important area where domestic impact is unmissable is India's approach to the region because of 'ethnic, religious, and geographic linkages between India and its South

---

[9] Walter Andersen, 'The Domestic Roots of Indian Foreign Policy', *Asian Affairs* 10, no. 3 (1983): 45–53.

[10] G. Varghese, 'Domestic Politics of India's Foreign Policy Decision-Making', in *New Directions in Indian Foreign Policy*, ed. A. Mattoo and H. Jacob (New Delhi: Manohar, 2013).

[11] C. Raja Mohan, *Modi's World: Expanding India's Sphere of Influence* (New Delhi: HarperCollins, 2015).

[12] Atul Mishra and Jason Miklian, 'The Evolving Domestic Drivers of Indian Foreign Policy'.

Asian neighbours'. To justify his proposition, he cites the influence of state government of Tamil Nadu on Mrs Gandhi's approach towards Sri Lanka and that of the mass migration from East Pakistan into Indian state of West Bengal leading to India–Pakistan war of 1971. He goes on to identify the linkages between India's approach to Pakistan and Muslim states of West Asia and presence of a large Muslim minority in India. The overlapping water resources as a factor in India's relations with Bangladesh have also been discussed by him. He would argue that the potential for foreign exploitation of internal tension in India is another area that influences India's foreign policy considerations. He points to the dominant role played by the Prime Minister's Office (PMO) at the cost of the MEA during the rule of Mrs Gandhi, which was also true when her son Rajiv Gandhi served as the prime minister following her assassination in 1984. He is of the opinion that coalition governments would be more vulnerable to pressure from domestic constituencies than single-party majority governments.

Mishra and Miklian expand the argument and hold that it is not fully correct to argue that foreign policy decision-making is only a top-down exercise and the focus remains only on 'New Delhi-centred variables' consisting of the prime minister himself, the PMO, the ruling party, 'the ministries involved in foreign policy issues, the political elite, and opinion-making individuals and institutions' and ignore 'the immense influence that domestic forces have on India's foreign affairs and concepts of the "national interest"'.[13] To justify their argument, they would cite the examples of unsuccessful yet significant domestic pressures in the wake of Indo-US nuclear deal in 2005–2006, the successful opposition of Paschim Banga (then West Bengal) leadership to Teesta river water sharing deal attempted by the central government in 2012, and Indian decision to honour pressures from Tamil Nadu to censure Sri Lanka at United Nations Human Rights Council (UNHRC) and later boycott Commonwealth Heads of Government's meeting in Colombo.

They would also argue that the structure of government—the dual power centre, during the rule of the United Progressive Alliance (UPA), coalition led by Congress Party (2004–2014), as well as the rupture in consensus over foreign policy—weakened the hands of the central government and emboldened domestic constituents to shape India's foreign policy. This period also witnessed the rise of a federalist impulse leading to arguments that India needed to federalize its foreign policy and accord legitimate importance to border states while framing its

---

[13] Ibid, 2.

policies towards the neighbours. Before assuming prime ministership, Modi, as chief minister of Gujrat, had vigorously advocated greater role for states in foreign policy decision-making.

In the earlier discussion, it is assumed that domestic factors do impinge on Indian foreign policy and more so in India's approach towards its immediate neighbours. While the argument in favour of natural influence of domestic politics on foreign policy can apply to every state, in the specific case of India in the South Asian neighbourhood, it is too obvious to be missed. India is a country sharing either land or maritime borders with almost all its neighbours and with all except four provinces not sharing either land borders with neighbouring states or international waters. It has an unmistakable centrality in the region, with cross-border geo-cultural contiguity that engenders complex webs of relationships across state-national boundaries, some of which are not yet settled. Therefore, India gets drawn into the vortex of internal power politics of its neighbours, against its desire and often without machination, forcing it to take policy measures to protect its interests and ensure regional peace. Against this backdrop, the next sections deal with domestic drivers shaping India's neighbourhood policy.

Neighbourhood Policy: Tracing the Domestic Roots

In 2012, there was an attempt by scholars in Institute for Defence Studies and Analyses (IDSA) to critically analyse India's neighbourhood policy. The scholars began by asking the question: 'Does India have a neighbourhood policy?'[14] It was found that if at all there was a policy towards neighbourhood, it remained fuzzy and under-articulated. The scholars published a research article wherein they isolated some elements of an unarticulated policy and suggested that

> India must effectively communicate its vision of regional integration to its neighbours, enable them to participate profitably in its growing economy, spell out its 'non-negotiables' in matters concerning its security and national interest, maintain linkages at the highest political level, open multiple tracks of communication and take a leadership position in multilateral forums like SAARC and BIMSTEC to bring peace and prosperity to the region through greater cooperation in diverse areas. This, they concluded, would 'prove effective in improving its relations with its neighbours'.

---

[14] Ashok K. Behuria, Smruti S. Pattanaik, and Arvind Gupta, 'Does India Have a Neighbourhood Policy?' *Strategic Analysis* 36, no. 2 (2012): 229–246.

This article claimed that the essential elements of India's approach to neighbourhood included the following, which were interrelated:

- Concern for security takes precedence over economic interest in India's neighbourhood policy.
- India has never attempted to impose any political ideology on any of its neighbours. It has studiedly avoided any attempt to transport its version of secularism or democracy to these countries.
- There is an open denial of Indian intent to have a 'sphere of influence' at the official level, but India has reflexively shown its anxiety about extra regional powers seeking to increase their strategic footprints in the region. India has all along sought to retain its pre-eminence in the region. This has been interpreted by neighbours as 'hegemonic' leading to mutual distrust which impacts India's policy towards them.
- India has, over the years, provided non-reciprocal and unilateral concessions to its neighbours (with an exception to Pakistan perhaps), which became the core of Gujral Doctrine in the mid-1990s and this has been followed in practice ever since.
- Pakistan has remained a major foreign policy challenge for India in the neighbourhood, and India has been particularly concerned about Sino-Pakistan strategic linkages as well as growing Chinese influence in the neighbourhood.

As can be gleaned from the earlier discussion pertaining to India's approach to its neighbourhood, India considers that it is natural and legitimate to retain its preponderant influence in the region and considers any challenge to its pre-eminence as a strategic threat affecting its 'security', which is the fundamental aim of its foreign policy. India's unannounced efforts to emerge as a net security provider and shaper of regional future are encouraged by the quiet acceptance of India-centric security architecture of the region by almost all the neighbours with the sole exception perhaps of Pakistan. It is also true that while the neighbours concede India its pre-eminence, in the conduct of India's neighbourhood policy, India often encounters resistance of varying degrees from most of its neighbours who interpret Indian policies as hegemonic,[15] and hence detrimental to their long-term strategic interests, leading them to fashion out countervailing strategies that weaken India's influence in practice. It is therefore important here to ask as to why India exerts such natural influence across the regional geopolitical

---

[15] Fatima Raza, Fahad Khan, and M. Taimur, 'Indian Foreign Policy: Chaos Theory and Perception Management', *Strategic Studies* 37, no. 4 (2017).

space, on the one hand, and why it induces a sense of fear and anxiety in its neighbours on the other. It is here that the domestic drivers of India's neighbourhood policy may provide some useful lead.

The search for domestic drivers of India's neighbourhood policy should be undertaken in the context set out earlier. While it is true that politics anywhere is related to politics everywhere and domestic–foreign policy linkage has been discussed widely around the world in different geopolitical contexts, it is necessary to bring in the Indian experience here.

This brings us to the discussion on domestic drivers of India's neighbourhood policy today. Why has domestic politics assumed more salience in Indian approach to neighbourhood over the years and what are the main drivers?

As we all know, India is a plural country—state-nation comprising many nations, cultures, communities and interest groups. It is still a state-nation in the making. It is a country of continental proportions. As stated earlier, from ethno-cultural perspective, it has a bit of all the neighbouring states within itself. Leaving out four states, all other states of India have either territorial or maritime frontiers with countries in the immediate and extended neighbourhood. There are historical, cultural and geographical contiguities which have led to close people-to-people interactions across territorial frontiers which are mostly porous and easily penetrable. Therefore, ethno-cultural contiguity remains a major determinant of Indian approach to neighbouring states. Foreign policy decision-makers in India have found it difficult to ignore this reality of cross-cutting affinities characterizing relationship between the people of India and people of various neighbouring states.

The cases in point are the Tamils of Tamil Nadu having ethnic linkages with the Tamils of Sri Lanka, the linguistic affinity between the people of Paschima Banga and Bangladesh as well as the two Punjabs in India and Pakistan, the linkages between the northern states and the people of Nepal in the Terai region known as Madhesis, the overall religious and cultural linkages of Hindus with the non-Madheshi population, and the linkages between communities in the north east and their ethnic cousins across the border in Myanmar and last but not the least the large Muslim population in India and their co-religionists in Pakistan, Bangladesh and extended neighbourhood in Western and Central Asia.

Because of these linkages, India has been drawn into internal political matrices in the neighbourhood against its wishes. The cases in point are

Indian interventions in Bangladesh (then East Pakistan in 1971) and Sri Lanka (in 1986–1987). Interestingly, in some cases, like in the cases of Nepal and Sri Lanka, the neighbouring states have felt deeply insecure about these linkages and resorted to policies that have, at times, forced coercive policy behaviour from Indian policymakers. Indian decision to close down India–Nepal border in March 1989 showed Nepalese vulnerability to Indian pressures in the face of Nepalese government's decision to establish security arrangements ignoring Indian concerns. However, India's alleged unofficial blockade in September 2015 indicated Indian sensitivity to the interests of the Madhesis inhabiting southern Terai region of Nepal which has deep ethnic linkages with border states of Indian states in the north.

The case of Tamil ethnic problem in Sri Lanka continuing to influence India–Sri Lanka relations in spite of the elimination of LTTE is also another case in point here. Indian government's position on protection of ethnic demands made by Sri Lankan Tamils through a mutually acceptable power-sharing arrangement hardly conceals the central government's compulsions to factor in domestic sympathies, especially in the southern state of Tamil Nadu while framing its policy towards Sri Lanka. That it is misinterpreted as unnecessary interference by Sri Lankans has been noted by policymakers and analysts in India; nevertheless, in the era of coalition politics, factoring the sensitivity of political parties in a major province in the south has traditionally become more expedient and regarded more morally acceptable to the ruling parties/coalition in New Delhi, than mollycoddling an obstinate majority community in a neighbouring country.

The case of camaraderie being exhibited by Punjabi-speaking elite on both sides of India–Pakistan border in recent years is yet another demonstration of an overlapping linguistic community cutting across international borders with shared history and culture reinforcing central government's approach in India to develop positive engagement with even a neighbouring country regarded as importunately hostile to its interest. In times of disharmony between states, however, such ethnic sympathies may also serve as a point of concern for New Delhi when the neighbouring state seeks to leverage such ties for strategic reasons. It is not surprising that Pakistan's bid to reap sympathies of Punjabi-speaking Sikh community by extending its support for opening up Kartarpur corridor facilitating visa-free travel for pilgrims from India to the Sikh shrine of Gurdwara Darbar Sahib Kartarpur (in Punjab, Pakistan) in 2018 was received with concern by some strategic analysts in India. Officially, India has supported the move even in the face of grave acts of terrorism sponsored by Pakistan in Kashmir in recent months, for fear of provoking sentiments of the Sikhs in India, some would argue. A section of population in Punjab advocating reconciliation with Pakistan in an atmosphere of pervasive tension following Pulwama terror attack and operation Balakot in February 2019 has drawn the ire of the ruling dispensation, without, of course, affecting engagement on the Kartarpur corridor issue. It goes without saying that possibilities of positively harnessing such sympathies in normal times to improve ties remain.

The federal government at the centre has, of late, tried to fashion a policy of active engagement with its own federating units to overcome such limitations. However, in view of the growing assertion of regional and local parties and governments and growing ideological polarization in Indian politics, the central government is unlikely to successfully implement its policies vis-à-vis neighbours in future. The inability of the central government, both UPA and NDA, to resolve the Teesta river water sharing issue with Bangladesh because of resistance from the government of Paschima Banga illustrates this point. Moreover, the failure of Indian government to convince Tamil Nadu government over the Tamil fishermen issue is another such example. This is not to deny that in the past, there were instances of central leadership ignoring local sentiments (as in the case of signing away the 285-acre Kachchatheevu islands to Sri Lanka by Mrs Gandhi in 1974) and pursuing a policy aimed at improving bilateral relationship.

All this shows that there is a lack of consensus between the central and provincial leaderships and governments on how to approach individual countries in the neighbourhood on specific issues, while there could be a larger agreement on the necessity of forging better relationship between the countries. Apart from ethno-cultural and linguistic factors, religious and communal factors have also influenced Indian approach to some of the neighbouring countries. Pakistan's bid to project itself as a guardian and protector of the Muslim community of India and the stiff reaction of the Muslims to such a formulation has widened the gulf between Pakistan and India. Similarly, despite the presence of a vocal constituency within the ruling establishment today advocating military engagement in Afghanistan, Indian government has avoided taking such risk because of its concerns about possible negative reaction from the large Muslim population to any such efforts.

Despite all this, there may be a domestic consensus guiding Indian government's overall policy towards its neighbours purely from the standpoint of Indian security. In the case of Pakistan and its policy of subversion and terrorism in Kashmir, there is such consensus driving the government's policy towards Pakistan. In some cases, the government's bid to engage Pakistan has been thwarted by strong reaction against such policy.

An assertive media whipping up sentiments to the contrary has often discouraged the government from transforming the nature of engagement between India and its neighbours. This is most evident in the case of India's policy towards Pakistan. The new-age Indian media has emerged as a major stakeholder in the business of building narratives on India's long-term strategic interests and requirements not always necessarily toeing the official line. The business community in India presents itself as another important constituency influencing India's foreign and neighbourhood policies. Regarded as pragmatic and liberal, this community has transcended ideological barriers and conditioned the approach of the central government for proactive engagement with neighbours even when there is an evident lack of political will to do so. As Mishra and Milkian would argue, 'The effect of corporate lobbying in New Delhi on both elections and policymaking is ... deeply understudied, but anecdotal evidence suggests that both national and multinational firms have a greater degree of access to and influence over Indian foreign policy than ever before.'

As it has been discussed in the chapter so far, it is natural to find domestic factors driving India's foreign and neighbourhood policies, the more so in the case of the latter. The states of India, bordering neighbouring states, have influenced/and will continue to influence government's policy towards the neighbourhood, although the responsibility for defining larger policy prerogative, as well as policy priorities, remains with the central government. Even the current government with its clear and strong popular mandate has not been able to withstand this pressure from the periphery. The domestic drivers will continue to influence and impact India's neighbourhood policies in the days to come. It devolves on the leadership to frame its foreign and neighbourhood policies in an innovative manner, keeping in mind the positive utility of the domestic factors that inevitably impinge on their decision-making, rather than regarding them as policy inhibitors. A proactive engagement with constituencies using domestic factors as a constraint on foreign policymaking, through well-crafted institutional arrangements, is in order here.

Intelligence and Foreign Policy
India and the World in 2050

Vikram Sood

Introduction

Foreign policy initiatives, defence preparedness, along with accurate and timely intelligence about external threats and challenges, technological prowess, economic growth that invites foreign investment and promotes trade would be some of the main means for the preservation and enhancement of a country's national interests abroad. This chapter discusses mainly the challenges to intelligence operations working in tandem with foreign policy goals in the years ahead assuming other aspects of geopolitics would have been discussed in detail in other chapters.

For the world of intelligence, the situations of 1990 and 2020 (almost here) have been remarkably different and the world of 2050 will be even more different in many ways. Cold bipolarity lasted until 1990 and there was some kind of certainty and predictability in that. The end of the Cold War has led to an endless global churn and perhaps by 2050 global power equations will have altered with the US profile comparatively lower and that of China much higher. This may or may not mean that bipolarity will return as, conceivably by then there will be other powers, India included, who would matter in these equations. Asia and Africa will largely remain troubled with their endemic problems, unending terrorism and major powers competing for access to markets and resources as well as seeking strategic dominance and control.

In India, we began to change slowly in the 1990s, taking pride in our slowness and taking comfort in our ancient civilization while unsure about having to give up socialist populism in favour of global pragmatism. China, on the other hand, changed much faster in the aftermath of the horrendous genocides that Mao had carried out in his lifetime. Undeterred by niceties of democracy and human rights, the Chinese were single-minded in their endeavours and they seemed to work on the global scene. Change in India has become discernibly faster in the last five years as there is now a realization that India cannot afford to miss the current Technology-Information Revolution because failure to do so will knock us back into perpetual dark ages. Climate change and its natural and geopolitical repercussions, the nuclear bomb and weapon of mass destructions (WMDs) along with the scourge of global terrorism will continue to be the main unconventional threats to security. The changes that are upon us will cover all aspects of human life but the one factor that will matter most will be the rapid changes in technology. Those who did not remain ahead of the curve will lose out. There will be no comeback performances.

We are living in an era of exploding aspirations, individual ambitions and societal expectations. In the midst of traditional threats, there will be new threats, new concepts of warfare and new arenas of war. The current technology blitzkrieg will gather speed exponentially and it is difficult to predict where we will be in 2050. It will change our lives in many unforeseen ways. All these will change the meaning of security, which will include threats to water-starved nations, climatic changes, biological and chemical warfare in the hands of terrorists, apart from WMDs that nations possess. A radical Islamist ideology that is willing to use any means to attain its goals will be the most clearly visible global threat. Events like Pulwama and Colombo will continue to happen. Wars will be increasingly high tech fought either bloodlessly or with miniature weaponry.

For India specifically, there is little likelihood that Pakistan will voluntarily scale down its hostility towards India. It will retain its paranoid policies towards India. Yet that country will not be an existentialist threat to India but will remain a constant nuisance until, by some miracle, its army understands that its peace dividend can be higher than the war dividend and it can continue to retain policy and resource supremacy in Pakistan.

China and India will become the two largest powers in Asia, with two of the largest armies that are nuclear equipped and largest populations with a long un-demarcated boundary. India will not be in the same league in terms of power and reach as China but a power to reckon with globally. Thus, there will be inevitable competition, sometimes cooperation perhaps confrontation but hopefully no conflict. The relationship is expected to remain stable in a formal way but not close in any partnership. India will continue to seek a balance with offshore powers without destabilizing its relationship with the resident emerging superpower.

India will be a 3 trillion dollar economy later this year, and expected to attain 5 trillion by 2024 and a 10 trillion dollar economy by 2032. We shall truly be on the global scene with its attendant problems of rising abilities, interests and expanded definitions of national interests and security. Attempts will be made to pull us down in the competition for resources, markets, influence and domination. India will need to assert itself more strongly and visibly if it seeks to protect and enhance its global interests. This will require a combination of traditional diplomacy that adapts to the new age, similarly sharpened intelligence systems that remain relevant for handling the new threats and effective state-of-the-art defence systems catering to the nation's new needs and new responsibilities. The need for accurate external intelligence analysis, pure espionage and covert operations closely synchronized with foreign policy would be the ideal situation. Intelligence activity is an unending business, and peace and tranquillity should not reduce the effort. Thus, to stay ahead of the competition, there would have to be a first-rate external intelligence mechanism, manned by men and women of appropriate skills for the mid-21st century. Preparations for this need to begin now bearing in mind what may lie ahead and that such systems cannot be created or refurbished during crises but in times of peace with time in hand.

What the Future Would Look Like?

In the West, especially in the USA, there has been an upsurge in intelligence activity as the USA battles to secure itself in the new global war in the new Internet world and information overload delivered at immense speed. Faced with this overload, intelligence activity has been outsourced in a major fashion, particularly in the USA. Instead of just being a military-industrial complex, it is also an intelligence-industry complex where major corporate players in technology are now active associates of the CIA, NSA and the Pentagon in intelligence activities at home and abroad. Some others provide the muscle power. Their charter includes covert operations and interrogations of suspects. Privatization of espionage and authorized privatization of violence will change societies in ways that will realize only later when the power of these groups may exceed those of the state, especially in weaker or smaller states.

Intelligence collection and analysis in the US intelligence is now aided by private industrial and technology houses such as Boeing, IBM and SAIC. All information or data generated globally by phone calls, credit card receipts, social networks, GPS tracks, cell phone geolocation, Internet searches, Amazon book purchases, Internet money transfers, in all languages, is gathered and stored. It is like a giant vacuum cleaner sucking in everything that comes its way. Mountains of data measured in peta and exabytes have been stored and hopefully processed into usable intelligence. In the 21st century, intelligence collection is far more complicated, urgent and often has to be in real time.

Intelligence leaks of the largest ever number of diplomatic and defence documents by Bradley Manning to Julian Assange of WikiLeaks in 2010 created global furore and embarrassment. Edward Snowden and PRISM followed headline news in 2013 because of the sheer volume, geographical spread and range of subjects of surveillance activities of the American intelligence system. The extent of US intelligence surveillance activity, including the joint Anglo-American Project PRISM, was the best known secret in the intelligence world. Total 97 billion pieces of information were collected from all over the world in March 2013, for instance, and that frightened many and visibly annoyed others. There was also disbelief that this massive surveillance had been taking place in the great open American society.

With the miniaturization of technology to nanotechnology, we are looking at entirely new ways by which the Big State can keep watch on citizens, all movements, speech, action and possibly even thought so that all coverage is automatic, instant and all-pervasive. Add to this the artificial intelligence that would be faster than human intelligence, and Big Brother will know us by our barcodes. Nowhere has this been employed so extensively for counter-intelligence purposes than in China.

Pakistani anti-Indian and jihadi organizations will continue to use the Internet, social media and other sites for their psy-war and intelligence operations. These and a host of similar other accounts and sites are the kind that Indian intelligence would be watching instead of blocking sites such as Jihad Watch considered to be a counter-jihad movement and especially after the experience of Tahrir Square. Social media activities are useful to the dissident, the lawbreaker and for the law enforcer as well as the intelligence agent. Surveillance of social media by intelligence organizations is to be expected.

The trend now is towards intelligent and miniaturized weapons systems with precise missions that are network centric, capable of swift decision and superior performance in all echelons with fewer casualties. Even today, an average US infantryman is probably equipped with the lethality and staying power of a company. Experts estimate that seven such infantrymen have enough weaponry, munitions and staying power to battle off a battalion. The unmanned aerial vehicle of tomorrow will be the size of bumblebees; there has been research in the USA to develop devices that are smaller than birds and called 'smart dust' which are complex sensor systems not much bigger than a pinhead. Millions of such devices could be dropped in enemy territory to provide detailed surveillance and ultimately support offensive war missions. Smarter weapons that 'think' designed as precise missions to maximize damage and minimize own casualties is the trend. Latest indications are that US military scientists have, in fact, invented Covert Autonomous Disposable Aircraft (CICADA), a drone that could fit in the palm of a hand and eventually cost as little as US$250. Nano-weapons would render present unwieldy weapons as out of date and 'smart weapons' would replace the present dumb missiles and other smart weapons.

Robotic armies and battalions would make military interventions more tempting. Missiles will be designed to fly at hypersonic speeds. Imagine the impact on terrorism and military operations this could have globally. This is the shape of threats that will emerge later in the century. All this will impact on intelligence collection and operations in the future.

By the end of 2030 or 2040, cyber warfare will move centre stage where information control of one's own communication systems and disrupting the enemy's communication, command and control will be the first determinant of military success. The Chinese have been watching these US military developments very closely to see how wars of the future will be conducted. We are still trundling along, unable to decide which artillery gun to buy, leave alone manufacturing one ourselves. We need to pay attention to high-tech research before our armed forces become military dinosaurs—quaint but ineffective. Google estimates that by 2020, the entire world will be online. If the enemy is able to cripple these systems, there would be unimaginable chaos with the country caught in a digital gridlock unless there is a credible backup. Intelligence agencies have to be prepared for the worst.

Hackers are a fast-growing category of global criminal activity which gets linked to the world of terrorists. This is now a highly organized and professional global activity. Hackers work in syndicates as they steal computer identities, commit credit card and other banking and financial frauds. According to research by Verizon Business Services in 2013, in the case of 62 per cent of these illegal intrusions, it took two months to detect. The Verizon study also revealed that in about 75 per cent of the cases, the defences of an average computer system are breached within minutes of the attempt. In about 15 per cent of the cases, it can take as much as a few hours. Hackers can have unfettered access to private data systems for months and months, and able to steal everything from passwords to work projects.

This technological revolution has altered not only the targets of intelligence operations but even the processes of collection of intelligence. Human sources will remain the link between the real and the virtual world but will also remain the core of classical intelligence. This is unlikely to change in its essential nature but adaptation to the new world and new ways of doing things has to be fast. Inevitably, the surveillance of these new methods of communication will be increasingly technology intensive, intrusive and expensive. This would only mean that the debate between the needs of security and principles of privacy would never be satisfactorily solved.

There are many players in the field today—the fanatics, the criminals, the drug traffickers and the human traffickers. This problem will not go away easily, soon or completely. It is the use of modern technology by the terrorist that has led the counterterrorist to evolve expensive, all-pervasive surveillance and counterterrorist techniques in ways that leave the espionage and counter-espionage activities of the Cold War years far behind.

The buzzword today is globalization, including in the business of terrorism. Armed groups have linked up internationally, financially and otherwise, have been able to operate across borders with Pakistani jihadis doing service in Chechnya and Kosovo, or Uzbek insurgents taking shelter in Pakistan. The extensive use of the Internet by terrorists has prompted counterterrorist experts to refer to the Internet as a 'terrorist university'—as this enabled terrorists to learn new techniques, acquire new lethal skills, clandestine communications and launch cyberattacks. Africa and Asia, and to lesser extent, Europe, will remain the preferred destinations of demobilized jihadis. The USA is the main enemy on the ISIS list but so far, America has made itself relatively secure inside a gigantic electronic bubble.

Modern terrorism thrives not on just ideology or politics. The main driver is money and the new economy of terror and international crime has been calculated some years ago to be worth US$1.5 trillion (and growing), which is big enough to upset Western hegemony. All the illegal businesses of arms and narcotics trading, oil and diamonds smuggling, charitable organizations that front for illegal businesses and the black money operations form part of this burgeoning business. Terror has other reasons to thrive. There are vested interests that seek the wages of terrorism and terrorist war.

In today's world of deregulated finance, terrorists have taken full advantage of systems to penetrate legitimate international financial institutions and establish regular business houses. Islamic banks and other charities have helped fund movements, sometimes without the knowledge of the managers of these institutions that the source and destination of the funds is not what has been declared. Both Hamas and the Palestine Liberation Organization (PLO) were flush with funds with Arafat's secret treasury estimated to be worth US$700 million to 2 billion. The world has not seen financial terrorism something that would send the dollar into a spin.

All the illegal businesses of arms and narcotics trading, oil and diamonds smuggling, charitable organizations that front for illegal businesses and the black money operations form part of this burgeoning business. Terror has other reasons to thrive.

The Nightmare of the Intelligence Services

Some national threats may change but traditional threats from traditional adversaries will continue—be they conventional, subconventional or from WMDs. The meaning of security is now larger to include resource security, market and investment security and cybersecurity. Future wars are unlikely to engage massive armies locked in prolonged battle for real estate. Attacks could now come by stealth, masterminded by some computer whiz kid along with some science graduate, and the targets will be our ways of life. The radical Islamist terrorist of the day wishes to use 21st-century tools to push us all back to the 7th century. If states hope to fight a highly unconventional war only with conventional weapons or tactics and succeed, then they are being unduly optimistic. Intelligence and security agencies will have to continue to watch and counter this much larger threat.

Unless the state learns to be flexible and agile, and unless there is full scope cooperation internally and internationally, batting terror, for instance, will always be an uphill struggle. Ultimately, pursuit of national interests externally through a dynamic foreign policy assisted by an effective intelligence agency will determine a nation's standing in international relations and secret intelligence agencies become an expression of the nation's subconscious. Pakistan's ISI, the Soviet Union's KGB, the American CIA and Mossad are some of these perfect examples. Egypt's subconscious was reflected in its Mukhabarat or that of Iran in the Shah's SAVAK.

An Indian government of the future, with its heightened international role and commitments at home and abroad, will need an intelligence set-up that can deliver these requirements. Smart intelligence will remain an essential ingredient for preservation and enhancement of national interests.

What kind of an intelligence organization would thus be needed either to protect our interests, prevent others from upstaging us or, if required, reversing the trend among our rivals in say 2050. If not, what needs to be done so that we are not found wanting in 2050? In doing so, we have to evolve our own systems and not just copy other systems.

Whatever technology an Indian intelligence agency may acquire for future use, skilled human resources will be the main factor determining accurate intelligence. Reforms would be needed. Reforms in India have had two characteristics. These have either concentrated on providing mostly better career opportunities within the existing cadres and creation of new agencies. In-house reviews that deal merely with career enhancements are inadequate. On the other hand, any intelligence reform should endeavour to build the strengths of the organizations. Unfortunately, most governments all over seek solutions that affect their tenures. Reforms have to be more fundamental and far deeper, done in the fullness of time; have to be long term based on periodic re-evaluations and not when a crisis has begun to loom. In India, reforms have been episodic, usually following a debacle and not based on periodic threat assessments.

Government needs to plan efficacy of intelligence in the future, say 2050. Having assessed the state of the world, threats and challenges at that time, government needs to determine today the kind of human capabilities required 30 years from now and the intelligence agency remains relevant delivers the required intelligence. The world of espionage, like the rest of the world, has also moved from the easier paced 20th century to the data-driven hi-tech 21st century. The value of skilled analysis will be different in an information age where there is information overload that is freely available in a flash of a second, algorithms will provide some of the answers and communications through secret messenger online services and make surveillance a particular art.

A good deal will have to change; even analysis work for it may not be possible to draw accurate and far-reaching analysis when the data keep changing rapidly. Consumers and producers will probably have to be satisfied with an intelligence product that conveys a sense of the intelligence rather than complete accuracy. Intelligence reforms have to be futuristic extending beyond simply creating promotion opportunities or determining deputation quotas. This is something which has to be done by the strategic and intelligence community including the armed forces, or if the threat is economic or technological (cyber, for instance) along with other appropriate experts.

The human component of such an intelligence agency would remain relevant even as technology makes greater inroads into intelligence collection and operations, especially for India. The civil service apparatus in India, a universal truth, tends to be conservative, more interested in preserving its supremacy and control, often strengthened in the name of reforms. An intelligence organization must continue to get the appropriate kind of human material to form the core on a long-term basis. Intelligence as an activity has to be made more attractive, not just in terms of career progression but also in the content of the job.

It needs to be examined whether the secretariat system as it works with the Government of India where promotions are linked to promotions in the IAS are really suitable in organizations such as the RAW. Intelligence agencies do not compete with the rest of the civil service for posts and promotions; all their promotions are within the organization and determined by their performance in the sphere of work. These are not in competition with the rest of the bureaucracy. This linkage and equivalence should be delinked and intelligence officers seek their own career progression independent of the civil service career paths. At the same time, too many bureaucrats in an intelligence organization could end up making the organization a victim of what Robert Gates once famously advised his CIA Chief William Casey when he said that the CIA was 'a case of advanced bureaucratic arteriosclerosis' where the arteries are clogged with careerist bureaucrats who have lost the spark. This is the danger of an intelligence that is manned solely by career civil servants, some of whom have joined the organization as an escape from uncomfortable state cadres or political inconvenience. An intelligence agency cannot be a haven for refugees nor for birds of passage.

The manner in which a young person is recruited, trained and honed for later use in the field or at the desk will remain the most crucial determinant of the final intelligence product or operation. The main requirement for an external intelligence agency will be human expertise in large numbers and equipped with necessary and extremely varied skills or trained to meet the needs and operating in hostile surroundings. The business of writing an intelligence report collected from disparate sources requires specialized skills. A report may have to be backed by area, language and subject expertise—an expertise that is built over a long time. Only this gives an intelligence officer the ability to analyse and assess. Operational intelligence requires different expertise and aptitudes. An intelligence agency must continue to have covert and psy-war capabilities, which have long gestation, cannot be empirically measured but have to be consistently pursued and continuously honed.

A modern intelligence agency responsible for the analysis of the reports before their dissemination to the consumers would need an abundance of graduates and well-qualified analysts. A modern intelligence agency responsible for the analysis of the reports before their dissemination to the consumers would need an abundance of graduates and well-qualified analysts. The need would be for regional experts, subject experts and those with domain knowledge, special skills in cipher and cyber, a huge army of language experts. This would mean not just those who specialize in their language but analysts and operatives would also need to be fluent in more than one language.

The existing practice of relying on the usual chain of first borrowing personnel from among those who have qualified the UPSC entrance examination has its severe limitations that will become more acute with the passage of time. The practice of recruiting officers on deputation and then trying them out for a few years is unsatisfactory and works against the principle for long-term experience in any field of intelligence. There are some inherent limitations in this system in vogue since the beginning but now increasingly archaic. Recruitments to any senior government vacancies have been through the UPSC or the State Public Service Commissions. These are elimination contests where candidates are considered eligible for the entrance examination on their educational qualifications—graduation at the minimum. The final selection is based on marks where the test is essentially for knowledge and not aptitude or other skills. Moreover, the civil services are no longer the best source for recruitment to an external intelligence organization. Regardless of his/her length of service, such a person would need to acquire operational and language skills, area and issue expertise and, in some cases, the ability to handle interrogations, hostage negotiation; other would need economic and financial expertise, military, science and technology, cyber and cryptanalysis.

Normally, an officer borrowed from another service would be at least around 25–27 years old but often older. Readjustment for such persons will become increasingly difficult in the new age. He or she will not come equipped with the new skills which then have to be imbibed. The two-year probation that is the norm for the civil services is not enough for intelligence personnel. It takes 5–10 years to train a young recruit into an intelligence officer before he can be let out into the big arena; there is no overnight expertise. By this time, he or she is 35 years old. So this person returns to his parent service that means RAW must start afresh having lost a person with about 10 years' experience. This person also takes away with him all the secret ways of functioning and a lot else about the organization and this is neither healthy nor desirable. Revolving doors are not suitable for an intelligence organization barring the odd subject/area expert working on a specified project.

There is good logic to adopting the practice in other countries about recruitment. The CIA, SIS and Mossad recruit form colleges and universities. The idea is to catch them young and then mould them; the later they join, the more fixed they are in their attitudes and become risk-averse. These organizations use websites and the social media to advertise, compete on the campus with other recruiters, organize simulated discussions, create mock analytical situations all designed to gauge suitability and attitudes. Recruitment for the future will have to be at a younger age, soon after school, so that he or she can be moulded early, before attitudes and mindsets firm up or the recruit is just too old to take chances in the field. Thus, a young recruit accepted when he or she is 18 or 19 years old is available to the organization for full service of more than 35–38 years after three years of training.

A three-year 'graduation' course at a residential intelligence academy run more or less on the patterns of a military training establishment that imparts the required theoretical knowledge and practical skills in various aspects of intelligence work is necessary. This would be the training academy—a kind of would-be spymasters university. These institutes could work on the pattern of the defence academies that we have in

India but naturally on a much smaller scale. The faculty would comprise those with tremendous field experience. Here, they would impart analytical skills because report writing is an undervalued skill, develop an eye for details, memory skills, communication and surveillance techniques, skills to improvise as situations demand, besides creating intense physical and mental toughening; as is agent handling, especially when dealing with the tough, nasty or slippery ones. Hostage negotiations, language mastery, surviving interrogation would also be art of the curriculum as also area and issue expertise. Such long training courses have the great advantage of helping recruits bond and empathize with each other. It gives a sense of belonging. The present system of short-term shotgun courses to small disparate groups is hardly conducive to building an abiding organizational culture so very essential to secret agencies. It is essential for new recruits to be assigned for attachments with the armed forces and some paramilitary organizations. An attachment with the foreign office is extremely necessary.

There is more to intelligence work than just analysis and dissemination of intelligence. The methods of collection will change with technological changes. Technical prowess is expanding in some countries much more than in India. One could say that we are still to make the grade in this big league of cyber and crypto superpowers—the USA, Russia, China, France and the UK, plus Israel. Technology has made data collection easier and the mobile phone is perhaps the best means to have owner of that phone under surveillance. At the same time, operating in the real world with cover stories and multiple identities is now increasingly difficult with facial recognition software, biometric identity cards, passports and visas. Intelligence collection has become much more difficult in advanced countries than it was 20 years ago. The old system of operating under diplomatic cover will have to be substantially augmented through privatization of intelligence collection. This has begun to happen in a systematic way in the West, especially the USA, China and Russia.

Countries like India will need both—technological prowess that matches the best and skilled human resources to tackle the traditional threats. It is only when intelligence organizations acquire appropriate human skills that they can hope to produce intelligence that is well tuned to foreign policy goals and national interests. We still have time.

PART B

Relationships

India's Relations with the Great Powers

Rajiv Sikri

Introduction

When Prime Minister Narendra Modi came to power in 2014, he envisaged India as a 'leading' power, not merely a 'balancer' or a 'swing' state. He surprised many by embarking on a very active foreign policy, visiting countries that had been ignored for many years by his predecessors, besides taking bold initiatives in many directions, including India's immediate neighbours as well as the USA and China. It has been his government's belief that India could, and must, make difficult choices and take risks in its foreign policy. There have been many notable successes in India's foreign policy over the last five years. India is no doubt an important regional and global player. On many issues, its voice is heard with respect and often heeded. However, the realities of international power politics and India's own constraints and weaknesses have brought home the realization that it is perhaps too early and premature for India to think of itself as a 'leading' power, on par with the other global powers.

For now, India is only a potential 'leading' power. It can, over time, actually become a leading power if it leverages the many factors that work in India's favour. India's strengths include its size and pivotal geographical location in the heart of Asia; a growing and youthful population that is in contrast to the demographic trends in most other countries or regions that are present or potential poles of influence and power in the world; a reasonably strong scientific and technological base; an open society; a diversified economy with a promising rate of economic growth; deeply embedded democratic traditions and the rule of law that provide resilience and some insurance against social and political instability and various elements of India's 'soft power'.

However, all these advantages are subject to important caveats. The demographic dividend could become a liability unless people are healthy and well educated, which implies that India must give more focused attention and allocate more resources to the health and education sectors. In the science and technology domain, both the quality and extent of research and the innovation in Indian institutions are grossly inadequate. Caste-based reservation policies, which seem to have become a permanent feature because of political compulsions, undermine meritocracy. In any case, public service no longer attracts the most talented people into public service to serve as military officers, civil servants, doctors, teachers, scientists and technologists. On the economic front, while India is no doubt making steady progress, poverty is still widespread, and economic growth remains uneven, with sharp regional disparities and many sections of the population excluded or marginalized. This in turn has given rise to growing Left-wing extremism and violence across large parts of India. Sadly, democratic traditions have weakened. Not only has political polarization sharpened but there is also a growing credibility gap between the masses and the ruling elite. India's institutions are under strain, be it the legislature, the judiciary, regulatory bodies or investigating agencies. The police and the bureaucracy are generally viewed as unresponsive and corrupt. Other weaknesses that need to be overcome include inadequate infrastructure, unplanned urban growth, poor sanitation, paucity of indigenous energy resources, looming freshwater shortages and alarming environmental and ecological degradation. The road ahead is indeed long and tortuous.

There are many other constraints, both internal and external, that inhibit the rise of India to true great power status. To start with, India itself is a reluctant power. In contrast to existing great powers (such as the USA, Russia and China), India remains hesitant to use force to achieve its diplomatic goals and shies away from sending its troops abroad on military missions except under a UN umbrella. Its resort to coercive diplomacy is infrequent with mixed results. India's generally soft approach to interstate relations emanates from India's ethos, traditions and history. This was brought out starkly by a recent statement of the chief of army staff that India would not like to engage in offensive hybrid warfare against Pakistan, even though Pakistan is actively engaged in such tactics against India. Never having had hegemonic aspirations, India has always had a moral and ethical element in its foreign policy, reflected in moralistic posturing, emphasis on South–South cooperation and anti-colonial activism.

But even if India were to shed its pacifist tendencies, many other hurdles remain on the path to great power status. India does not have the power and shield of permanent membership of the UN Security Council. Nor is it recognized as a nuclear power under the Non-Proliferation Treaty. India's social, religious and cultural diversity and its fractured polity make India vulnerable to external machinations that seek to keep India weak and divided. On the other hand, its high dependence on imported defence technologies and equipment limits India's freedom of manoeuver. Despite a huge gap in the size, resources and capabilities of India and its South Asian neighbours, India has been unable to establish an unquestioned sphere of influence in South Asia. It is true that great powers too have difficult relations vis-à-vis their smaller neighbours and often cannot get their way, primarily because the latter have the support of other great powers. The difference in India's case is that India lacks the power to create corresponding pressures on other great powers in their neighbourhood or otherwise hurt their global interests. Finally, India should also bear in mind that its ambitions for great power status will meet stiff resistance from the established great powers.

China

China's spectacular rise over the last couple of decades has created problems and dilemmas for all countries, but none perhaps faces the triple challenge that India does. India has to deal with China as a global player, as an aggressive regional power-seeking hegemony in Asia and as a neighbour having a long and unsettled border with India. Following Deng Xiaoping's dictum, for long China 'hid its capabilities and bided its time', but now it is brazen about its ambitions to be the world's leading power. Its economic growth has been unprecedented. It is the world's largest trading country that is tightly interwoven into global supply chains. It has huge amounts of money to invest overseas, which it is systematically and ruthlessly doing in a blatantly exploitative manner through its strategic Belt and Road Initiative. China has made breathtaking advancements in developing indigenous military and civilian technologies, including in many cutting-edge and frontier areas such as artificial intelligence, robotics, cyberspace, solar power and electric vehicles. It uses its power as a permanent member of the UN Security Council and as a recognized nuclear weapons state under the Nuclear Non-Proliferation Treaty to gain impunity for its actions, as well as to give shelter to and thereby gain influence in smaller countries, including Pakistan.

China is a long-term, and most serious security challenge for India. China is steadily and unremittingly encroaching on India's security space and strategic backyard. China's 'all-weather' friendship with Pakistan, which goes back many decades, has now made Pakistan a de facto client state of China. China's grip on Pakistan has steadily tightened. The China–Pakistan Economic Corridor is the flagship project of the Belt and Road Initiative. Pakistan's parlous economic situation has ensnared it into China's debt trap and its unremitting hostility towards India has pushed it into a virtual military alliance with China. Increasingly worrisome is China's growing reach and influence in India's other South Asian neighbours such as Nepal, Bhutan, Sri Lanka, the Maldives, Bangladesh, Myanmar and Afghanistan. China's presence in the Indian Ocean has sharply increased, with a base in Djibouti, another coming up in Gwadar and potential bases in Sri Lanka, the Maldives and Myanmar. It also has a presence in Mauritius and Seychelles. China's activism in Africa is well known, as is its growing economic clout in the Central Asian countries. Despite much sound and fury, no one has been able to prevent China's de facto control of the South China Sea. This gives it two significant advantages of concern to India—one, China secures its back as it expands into the Indian Ocean; two, it gives China a potential maritime counter-choke point on the energy, trade and naval sea lines of communication between the Western Pacific and the Indian Oceans.

At the bilateral level, India's principal concern is the unsettled border. Historically, there never was an India–China border, only an India–Tibet border. It was only after China occupied Tibet in 1950 that the two countries became neighbours. In the decade or so following the Chinese takeover of Tibet, China's foremost concern relating to India was the security of Tibet, over which China's hold was tenuous. India's position mattered because Tibet is culturally much closer to India than to China and at that time the principal access to Tibet from the outside world, including China itself, was via India. In the 1950s, most of the conversations between Indian and Chinese leaders centred on Tibet. Chinese suspicions about Indian intentions became much more acute with the flight of the Dalai Lama to India in 1959. Relations dipped sharply after the 1962 border war. Even though China's grip on Tibet has become firmer, the Chinese have a nagging worry about India's position on Tibet. After having accepted Tibet as a part of the People's Republic of China, India has stopped reiterating that position in official statements over the last decade or so. India also continues to host the Dalai Lama, who is demonized by the Chinese, as well as the so-called Tibetan government-in-exile. It is principally because of the assistance and facilities provided to the Tibetan refugee population in India by the Indian government that Tibetan culture, language and traditions have been preserved, and there is global awareness of a so-called 'Tibetan question'. How this problem will resolve itself in a post-Dalai Lama situation remains unclear. Apart from the political aspects of the Tibetan question, there is a potential India–China conflict over water, arising out of unsatisfactory and unreliable data-sharing arrangements on river water flows, construction of dams on the Tsangpo river, creation of artificial dams and lakes that have the potential to create havoc downstream in India, not to speak of the nightmare scenario of possible diversion to the north of rivers rising in Tibet. There is a lurking danger that, if not handled carefully and sagaciously, the Tibetan question could derail the entire India–China relationship.

Without a resolution of the Tibet question to China's satisfaction, it is unlikely that China would agree to a border settlement with India. Unfortunately, a resolution of the Tibetan question is a necessary, but not a sufficient, condition for a border settlement. Even if Tibet is out the way, many other hurdles remain. For one, a clear settlement is probably ruled out since the public positions of the two sides are so far apart that it would be politically very difficult for either side to make compromises or adjustments without inviting the charge of a sell-out. For another, it doesn't suit China to have an early border settlement. Thus, China is dragging its feet on even a clarification of the Line of Actual Control, probably because it feels that a degree of controlled tension, short of actual conflict, along the border, serves its interests. The face-offs at Depsang (2013), Chumur (2014) and Doklam (2017) bear this out. An unsettled border prevents India from diverting more attention and resources to ensure its faster economic growth that could narrow the gap between India and China. That does not suit China, which is not prepared to give India any kind of parity with China, even in Asia, much less globally. China's global ambitions depend on its ability to dominate Asia, where India is the principal obstacle. On the economic side, simply because of its size, resources and economic trajectory, India is the only Asian country that can potentially match China. From a politico-strategic perspective, India is a neighbour to China's troubled and restive regions of Tibet and Xinjiang. While China considers these its 'core interests', for India too developments here affect India's vital interests as these are the only territories under China's control that directly about India's frontiers. China's control of Tibet enables it to exert pressure on Nepal and Bhutan, and its control of Xinjiang provides vital overland access to Pakistan-occupied Kashmir and Pakistan. Although this is a far-fetched scenario, China remains wary of India stirring trouble in these regions.

Based on past experiences and current trends, one can expect China to always try to keep India down, hemmed in and unable to break out of the South Asia *Lakshman rekha* that China has drawn for India. The illusion of a bhai–bhai relationship went out of the window a half century ago. Can there be even peaceful coexistence? That depends on China. China's strategic alliance with Pakistan is a major obstacle in overcoming the trust deficit between India and China. The heart of the problem is that China has never regarded India as an equal, nor will India accept an inferior status in a China-led hierarchical Asian and world order. This situation is unlikely to change. India's decision to openly reject China's Belt and Road Initiative, Xi Jinping's signature project that has been endorsed by the Chinese Communist Party and legislature, was an unambiguous public declaration of its unwillingness to be part of a Sino-centric world. With Xi likely to remain in power indefinitely, there is a looming clash between India's and China's respective 'core interests'.

All these factors go towards making the India–China relationship an essentially competitive one. True, there is limited cooperation between the two countries on some global issues such as climate change, the importance of an equitable multilateral trading system and the reform of international institutions. Both India and China are members of the Shanghai Cooperation Organisation, the Russia–India–China dialogue framework and BRICS. But these are not enough to overcome the mutual tension and mistrust arising out of geo-strategic competition and differences on tackling Pakistan-supported terrorism, as brought out by the Chinese reaction to the Pulwama terrorist attack in February 2019. To this must be added the worries generated by the alarming bilateral trade imbalance in favour of China, principally arising out of large-scale imports of power and telecommunications equipment, mobile phones, rare earths and active pharmaceutical ingredients.

India needs a well-thought-out strategy to deal with the serious challenge posed by China. Given the current overall power gap between the two countries, prudence dictates a cautious tactical approach in the near term that serves to lower tensions and mistrust. In the long term, however, the outlook for India–China relations remains pessimistic, notwithstanding the improved rhetoric and optics following the 2018 Wuhan Summit. Short of a fundamental and credible change in China's mindset, India and China will remain strategic competitors. Thus, India must have the will to compete with China. Unless Indians have the self-belief that India has been in the past, and can become in the future, the equal of China, the contest is lost. India has to highlight its own relative advantages, not overestimate China's strengths, and exploit China's weaknesses. It did this admirably during the Doklam stand-off, when it kept its cool and successfully resisted China's coercive tactics and propaganda. China's preferred strategy is to defeat the enemy by psychological warfare, without actually risking fighting a war, whose outcome would be uncertain and the fallout unpredictable, even dangerous. This doesn't mean that India should ignore the imperative of military deterrence. It has to continue to build up its infrastructure and military deployment in the border areas, develop the Andaman and Nicobar Islands as a full-fledged base, extend the range of its missiles and upgrade its naval and air force assets. A long-term strategy must strike at the roots of China's spectacular rise, namely its economy. China's economic growth, which is critical for China's internal social and political stability, remains export-dependent, though less so than before. Given the ongoing US–China strategic rivalry and an increasingly wary Europe, India's growing market will become more important for China. India has to restrict this access—by diversifying its imports, curbing Chinese investment in sensitive areas, using both tariff and non-tariff barriers against imports from China, not giving China market economy status, influencing India public opinion to curb their appetite for Chinese products and preventing China from using India's neighbours to access the Indian market. India should also see how it could complicate life for China in China's neighbourhood in Central and East Asia.

The United States of America

Even with all these measures, India would find it extremely challenging to tackle the growing challenge from China on its own. India will need the support of powerful friends and supporters. Although the global balance of power is shifting away from the West, and Asia's weight and importance are rapidly growing, the USA is still the only true superpower. Many factors go towards making it so. It has unsurpassed global military capabilities and dominance; remains the leading global centre of innovation and high technology; dominates cyberspace; has a huge consumer market; controls the global financial system and takes full advantage of the status of the USD as the virtual global reserve currency and as the currency for oil pricing. Its soft power complements and magnifies its hard military and economic power. Even though its power has probably reached a plateau, and it no longer enjoys the global dominance it did in the second half of the 20th century, the USA has comprehensive power that is markedly superior to that of any other power. It displays a willingness to use force and other strong-arm tactics vis-à-vis the rest of the world to achieve its politico-strategic objectives. It has not wavered from its long-term goal to remain the unquestioned global hegemonic power.

India has never had any problem in accepting the primacy of the USA in international affairs. From the early days of its Independence, it sought good relations with the USA, and looked to it to assist India in its nation-building. However, relations during the 20th century were fraught with suspicion and mistrust at the state level. The principal reason was that the USA viewed India through the lens of its Cold War rivalry with the Soviet Union. India's complex and messy democracy and assertive non-alignment tended to irritate and frustrate US policymakers. On the Indian side, the US military alliance with Pakistan and its hostile attitude towards India on vital and sensitive issues such as Kashmir, Goa (1961), Bangladesh (1971) and Sikkim (1975) prejudiced India against the USA. It was only after India became a nuclear weapon power in 1998 that the USA began to view India seriously. Over the last two decades, leaders on both sides have worked steadily to overcome the 'hesitations of history' and take forward this relationship, which has steadily evolved into a strategic partnership. Democracy and an open society, free market economy and the English language provide a congenial and strong structural framework for the relationship. The convergence of such fundamental values makes both sides comfortable in dealing with the other, under both Republican and Democratic Administrations in the USA. Fortunately, there is bipartisan support in the US Congress for closer ties with India. In India too, barring the Communists, there is a general political consensus on the desirability of having closer relations with the USA. Extensive and growing people-to-people links, be it businessmen, investors, students, professionals or tourists, are a key driver of this relationship. The affluent and well-connected Indian American community has played a great role in nurturing India–US ties. With more and more Indian Americans now active in US public life and corporate America, India has influential friends who play an important role in India's image building in the USA and act as a bridge between the two countries. Their role has increased in the last five years as the Modi government has made a special effort to reach out to Indians settled in the USA to make them active partners in India's development plans and progress.

Today, there is a broad strategic convergence between India and the USA. This assumes many forms—close and frequent political consultations; regular and frequent exchange of visits including at the highest levels; overlapping interests in the Indo-Pacific; a constructive and helpful US policy towards South Asia; a narrowing of differences in other areas such as the Persian Gulf and Afghanistan; intelligence sharing and practical cooperation on tackling terrorism; growing defence cooperation involving extensive joint military, naval and air force exercises, military exchanges and large-scale purchases of US military equipment; and easier access to US civil and military high technology. With shared concerns about the rise of an assertive China that is flexing its muscles and pursuing aggressive policies in the Western Pacific and the Indian Ocean, the USA and India are closely cooperating with Japan within a robust and well-established high-level trilateral framework. There are also incipient moves of the three countries to gradually move towards quadrilateral cooperation with Australia, though the so-called 'Quad' is so far limited to a non-provocative dialogue among senior diplomats and naval officers of the four countries. While there are many disruptive and unpredictable elements in President Trump's policies, the increased US pressure on Pakistan to deliver on terrorism and on China on the economic front certainly meets India's long-term interests. The USA helped India to become a member of technology denial regimes such as the Missile Technology Control Regime, the Wassenaar Arrangement (dual use items) and the Australia Group (chemical and biological weapons). Contrary to the position only a few years ago, the USA is now more enthusiastic about India joining the Nuclear Suppliers Group. It is also formally supportive of India's permanent membership of the UN Security Council, but this should be viewed as mere lip service, unless the USA takes more concrete steps, such as supporting a resolution to get India into the UN Security Council.

At the same time, bilateral relations are also beset with tensions and frictions in many areas. On the political side, the main issues of concern are the sanctions that the USA has imposed on Iran and Russia that, under US law, also affect third countries such as India doing business with these two countries, especially in sensitive areas such as defence and oil. To these must be added the recent US threats to punish countries that are buying oil from Venezuela, which is a significant exporter of oil to India. Fortunately, India has withstood US pressure, at least for now. It has managed to persuade the USA that it cannot, and will not, break off military cooperation with Russia that involves transfer of high-end equipment and technologies. As for Iran, neither is it feasible for India to bring down its oil imports from Iran to zero, nor will India desist from going ahead with the Chabahar project that is a critical element of ensuring India's access to Afghanistan and Central Asia. President Trump's 'America First' policy and the US trade deficit with India have led to differences on trade-related issues that threaten to escalate into disputes. The USA has filed cases against India in the WTO on India's export subsidies, raised tariffs on selected Indian exports and initiated moves to deny GSP privileges to India. US companies also have concerns vis-à-vis India on intellectual property rights, e-commerce and data localization. Indians working in high-technology sectors in the USA have been hit hard by restrictive US immigration policies that curb grant of H-1B and H-4 visas. India has threatened to raise tariffs on selected US exports, but has desisted from actually doing so.

Realistically, one should recognize that the current phase of an overall ascendant India–US relationship is unlikely to be permanent. A true strategic partnership requires more equal terms and greater mutual respect than exists at present. Thus, there will always be limits to the India–US partnership. Even the long-term allies of the USA now openly question US reliability. There's another point to be kept in mind. If India continues to grow even at the current rate, over the next couple of decades or so, it will become a formidable economic power with an economy the size of America's, possibly even bigger. In that case, were India to pose any kind of serious economic, technological or strategic challenge to its domination, the USA can be expected to take steps to cut India down to size. In this connection, the current US attitude towards China is instructive. After all, the USA facilitated China's rise in the expectation that China would become a responsible stakeholder in the US-led world order. Things haven't turned out quite as the USA expected, since China is now trying to establish its own Sino-centric world order. Second, India will have to factor in the periodic fickleness, inconsistency and unreliability of US foreign policy. Aberrations in US foreign policy can be expected under idiosyncratic and transactional leaders such as President Trump, who lacks a long-term vision and is uninformed, only mildly interested in, and often derisory about India. Currently, there is a drift in India–US relations as there is neither any personal chemistry between President Trump and Prime Minister Modi, nor any high-level interest in the Trump Administration to push for greater engagement with India. Based on its past experiences, India also remains wary of the USA and China striking a deal that would be to India's disadvantage. At least twice over the last two decades, once under President Clinton, again under President Obama, the USA and China took some initial steps to work out a common position on South Asia. Such moves cannot be ruled out in the future.

On the other hand, India should be alert to take advantage of windows of opportunity whenever possible to further its national interests. Both sides will have to bear in mind a few realities. Given the present global power balance, India must have a benign, not a hostile, USA in order to have a conducive external atmosphere for its growth. It would be even better if the USA were to actively support India's rise in order to check China, without expecting that India would align its foreign policy to that of the USA. One can be reasonably confident of US support, provided India is content to be a power at a rung lower than that of the USA. In addition, India should be careful not to needlessly annoy the USA where India's vital interests are not threatened. Similarly, the USA too should realize that for now and in the foreseeable future, India is willing to live with the USA, but not China, as top dog, and that it is not in the interest of the USA to gratuitously alienate a rising India.

Russia

Apart from the USA and China, Russia is the third great power whose policies and actions have a global impact. Although its clout and importance are much reduced compared to Soviet times, Russia should not be underestimated. A dispirited and flailing country in the 1990s, contemptuously condemned to irrelevance by the West, Russia has regained much of its self-confidence under President Putin's rule. Russia once again has the mindset and behaviour of a great power. It has regained ground in its strategic neighbourhood (Ukraine, Crimea, Georgia, Transdniestria, South Ossetia, Abkhazia), become a key player in regions further afield such as the Middle East (Syria and Iran in particular) and is actively involved in the search for a solution to the Afghan imbroglio. Russia's huge territory and rich natural resources are valuable assets. Europe remains heavily dependent on Russian gas. Not to be ignored is Russia's control of large sections of the Arctic, a region of growing economic and geopolitical importance. Russia's military, nuclear and space capabilities remain formidable, including some unique state-of-the-art military technologies such as the S-400 anti-missile system. The USA is painfully aware that Russia is the only country that poses a credible military threat to the USA. That is probably why the US establishment continues to target Russia, even though it is China that poses a more serious long-term economic and strategic threat.

For decades, the political, diplomatic, security and economic support that Russia (in its Soviet incarnation) gave India made it a valued and trusted strategic partner. With changing times, the foreign policy priorities of both countries have understandably changed. For Russia, India no longer has the importance it did during the Cold War era. Similarly, Russian support to India on political issues does not have the same value that it did in Soviet times. While both seem to have downgraded the relationship to a secondary rung, there remains a long-term strategic convergence of interests. Both countries want a multi-polar world, not a US–China global duopoly. It is true that Russia has come closer to China as it tries to fend off US pressure. China is extremely important for Russia for trade, inward investment and tourism. It's an important market for Russia's oil and gas at a time when Europe is consciously trying to reduce its energy dependence on Russia. However, the current Russia–China bonhomie is only tactical. Apart from its historical memory of conflicts with China, Russia has its own long-term vision of its place in the world and will never want to be permanently in China's shadow. It has no illusions about China and is aware that too strong a China would pose a threat to Russia's position in Eurasia and the Far East. This brings out the importance of India, whose weight in world affairs is rising. Russia would not like to see a weakened India under China's hegemony. It has always tried to maintain good relations with both countries and would not like to have to make a choice. That is why it is for better India–China relations. Russia was the initiator of the Russia–India–China trilateral dialogue, and pushed for India's entry into the Shanghai Cooperation Organisation to balance China's dominance in that body. The three countries are members of BRICS. All these structures would weaken if Russia were not to maintain some equidistance in India–China disputes and conflicts. Nor would Russia like to push India closer to the USA and the West, or see any strengthening of the Quad. From India's perspective, a good relationship with Russia is important as it would be unwise to put all its eggs in the US basket, as well as to ensure that Russia doesn't drift too close to China and, increasingly now, Pakistan.

Russia and India have been reliable friends for many decades. Neither country wants to jeopardize this time-tested relationship, particularly as the unfolding global scenario remains uncertain and troubling. For two decades now, India and Russia have made it a point to have an annual summit-level dialogue, for many years, a unique structure in India's foreign policy. However, unlike in Soviet times, the India–Russia relationship is now a more equal one, since Russia is no longer a superpower and India has graduated from being merely a large developing country. The two countries do not have any serious clash of interests. There is reciprocal support and understanding for each other's priorities and policies in their respective strategic neighbourhoods—South Asia in the case of India, and the former Soviet Union in the case of Russia. Pragmatism, not ideology or sentimentalism, is now the guiding principle in relations between India and Russia. The defence partnership is vital for both countries. Although it has diversified its defence purchases, India is, and for a long time will remain, heavily dependent on Russia for critical military equipment, supplies and spares. Russia is still the only country willing to supply high-technology equipment unavailable from other sources, including nuclear submarines and an aircraft carrier. For Russia too, the large Indian market is very valuable for Russia's own defence industry. The problem is that the India–Russia partnership is overly dependent on defence cooperation. Realizing that this is not a healthy situation, both sides are now making a conscious effort to reduce the salience of defence ties in bilateral relations. With synergies arising out of the fact that India is an energy-deficient country and Russia an energy-surplus one, energy is a promising new area of cooperation. Russia is the only country that has set up nuclear power plants in India (and more are envisaged). There are Indian investments in the upstream oil and gas sector in Russia and Russian investments in the downstream oil sector in India.

So far, it has proved impossible to overcome a fundamental weakness, namely that neither Russia nor India has a strong domestic constituency driving the relationship. There are no meaningful people-to-people linkages between India and Russia. Without broad public support, it becomes difficult to provide a sound foundation and long-term stability to India–Russia ties. Trade and economic relations have not taken off meaningfully, and the prospects remain bleak. Mutual perceptions do not conform to contemporary realities. Ironically, close relations during the Soviet era have become unwanted baggage. The new generation of Russia's ruling elite has an outdated view of India that is stuck in the time warp of mid-20th century India. There is little understanding of the much richer, self-confident and savvier India of the 21st century. A similar situation prevails on the Indian side. It is not enough that there is an across-the-board political consensus in India on the importance of relations with Russia. The Indian elite's thinking and lifestyle is heavily oriented towards the West. Both countries need to do much more to change this narrative. India has to build contacts with the entire spectrum of stakeholders and interest groups in the political, economic, military and other spheres throughout Russia. Similarly, Russia will have to learn how to deal with new centres of power and influence in India.

Conclusion

Even though achieving great power status remains a distant goal, India will continue to pursue strategic autonomy in foreign policy. India's size, achievements, sense of self-worth and the fact that it is too big and prickly to accept the security umbrella of any country (not that any country has offered it) means that India will have to chart an independent course among the great powers to protect its national interests. It will have to pick and choose the possible areas of cooperation with the great powers while ensuring that its choices do not impose on it unnecessary burdens or painful penalties. There is no getting away from making choices, at times difficult ones, but these will have to be calibrated to minimize risks and avoid a negative fallout for India.

India is faced with a key strategic choice: does India want to be co-opted into the existing international structures that have been fashioned by and are dominated by the West in general and the USA in particular, or does India see itself as a rival 'pole'? Should it strive to play an independent role in the world or be content to remain a second-rung player? India can become a major world power in the 21st century only on its own strength and political will, not because others want it to. In international affairs, no state has been known to cede its power willingly to another. Power is always taken, never given. India can become more powerful only if it becomes stronger and existing great powers relatively weaker. A prolonged struggle over redistribution of power is under way in all the major international organizations such as the UN, the WTO and the IMF. India has to try to muscle its way to a more advantageous position in all these organizations. India should also draw lessons from its fruitless attempts to join the Nuclear Suppliers Group and to become a permanent member of the UN Security Council. Clearly, India is not yet strong enough to break into the ranks of the most exclusive clubs in the world, but is it strong willed enough to resist admission as an associate member with permanently fewer rights and privileges?

The Modi government does envisage an eventual true great power status for India. Whether this policy can, and will, be sustained in the long term remains to be seen. For the next decade or two, it will have to manoeuvre skilfully among the existing great powers. India would do well to heed former British Prime Minister Lord Palmerston's adage that nations have no permanent friends or enemies, only permanent interests. If India hopes to achieve great power status by centenary of India's Independence, it is the next decade that will be critical for India to put in place policies, both domestic and foreign, that enable it to achieve this goal. This is the challenge before India.

India's Relations with Its SAARC Neighbours

Satish Chandra

India's relations with its SAARC neighbours have seen many ups and downs barring Pakistan and Bhutan. With the former, they have always been very bad and with the latter always very good.

The volatility in India's relations with each of its SAARC neighbours, notwithstanding their multifaceted links, is to an extent attributable to the huge power differential between them. This has often bred unnecessary fears and suspicions among them, which in the absence of frequent high-level exchanges have tended to create trust deficits and adversely colour relations. These negativities have been reinforced by perceptions, some real and some imagined, of Indian arrogance and interference.

Another factor making for volatility in India's relations with its SAARC neighbours is that most of them are at best fragile democracies plagued by severe governance deficits which often have a spillover impact on India. For instance, the governance deficit in Nepal led to the Maoist insurgency and more recently to Madhesi discontent; in Afghanistan it led to warlordism, the rise of the Taliban and drug trafficking; in Bangladesh it fostered illegal migration, gun running and Islamic fundamentalism; in Pakistan it bred terrorism and the radicalization of society and in Sri Lanka it led to Tamil separatism. All these have impinged adversely on India.

India's relations with these countries have also been bedevilled with issues common to neighbours the world over such as differences over borders, both land and maritime, water sharing, connectivity, illegal migration, smuggling, drug-trafficking and terrorism. The close cultural, linguistic, ethnic and religious affinities between the populace in Indian states and that across the border, far from being a bridge, have on occasion become a source of friction on account of the near inevitable Indian interventions on behalf of the latter when mistreated and denied their rights by the ruling elite.

India's relations with neighbours have also often taken a hit due to their insensitivity to its core interests. Most have used the China card against India and some have gone so far as to use terrorism against it and promote separatism.

India has been much more sinned against than it has sinned in terms of its outreach to its neighbours. While it caused angst in Nepal for its efforts in support of democratization or of the Madhesi cause and in Sri Lanka for pressing for the legitimate rights of the Tamils never did it encourage secessionism in its neighbours barring the special circumstances under which it supported the breakaway of Bangladesh from Pakistan. India has, furthermore, been highly supportive of its neighbours as a source of economic and development assistance, as a first responder to natural disasters, and in helping foil coup bids. In its quest for better ties, it has not shied away from making major concessions such as concluding the extraordinarily generous Indus Waters Treaty with Pakistan in 1960 or in ceding Kachchatheevu to Sri Lanka in 1974.

It has been argued that good relations with neighbours are essential for a country's rise and that India should, therefore, do more to create a harmonious South Asia. This line of argumentation is flawed as many countries such as Britain, France and China, despite tensions with neighbours, have gone on to become great powers.[1] There is, of course, some merit in examining what India should do for a better relationship with its neighbours as a harmonious neighbourhood is more conducive to a country's rise than a fractious one. This is all the more pertinent at a time when the Chinese footprint is on the increase in these countries.

---

[1] Kanwal Sibal, *India and the South Asian Neighbourhood*. Available at https://www.vifindia.org/article/2012/november/19/india-and-the-south-asian-neighbourhood (accessed on 28 November 2019).

As we enter 2020, it would be fair to suggest that India's ties with Afghanistan, Bangladesh, Bhutan and the Maldives are excellent, those with Sri Lanka are good, those with Nepal are prickly and those with Pakistan are hostile.

An effort has been made in the succeeding paragraphs to provide an overview of the aforesaid relationships, evaluate the prospects and suggest what India could do to best promote its interests.

Afghanistan

Post-Independent India and Afghanistan have enjoyed excellent ties barring the nearly 10-year interlude of the Rabbani and Taliban regimes (1992–2001).

With the advent of the Karzai regime in December 2001 and later the Ashraf Ghani government in 2014, India–Afghan relations once again reverted to their customary warmth. India's re-engagement with Afghanistan though largely driven by the traditional friendship between the two countries was also influenced by the democratic and pluralistic nature of the Afghan governments and the need to ensure that the country does not once again become a nursery of terror. In these circumstances, despite changes of government in both countries, India has been deeply involved in capacity building in Afghanistan in virtually every sphere as well as the development of its infrastructure. Towards this end, it has to date pledged $3 billion for economic assistance to Afghanistan becoming the largest regional donor and the 5th largest donor globally.[2]

Since Indian economic cooperation programmes in Afghanistan are demand-driven and not conditioned on any quid pro quo, they have earned enormous goodwill and accordingly India's popularity in Afghanistan far exceeds that of any other country. Despite a draw down in international aid to Afghanistan since 2014, the Indian commitment to help it remains undiminished.

An important milestone in the upward march of India–Afghan ties was the 2011 Strategic Partnership Agreement which provides a comprehensive framework for cooperation. It, inter alia, envisages Indian assistance to help rebuild Afghanistan's infrastructure and institutions,

---

[2] Rani D. Mullen, *India in Afghanistan: Understanding Development Assistance by Emerging Donors to Conflict-Affected Countries* (Williamsburg, VA: College of William & Mary; Washington, DC: Stimson Center, August 2017).

technical assistance to rebuild indigenous Afghan capacity in diverse fields, investment in Afghanistan's natural resources, duty-free access to the Indian market for Afghanistan's exports, etc. It also includes a peace and security component which among other things not only envisages 'close political cooperation' between the two countries but also the 'training, equipping and capacity building programmes' of Afghan forces by India.[3]

Future Prospects and Options

The future of India–Afghan ties is uncertain as the fate of the National Unity Government (NUG) hangs in the balance and the Taliban return to power seems increasingly likely. This is mainly due to the eroding legitimacy of the NUG coupled with the declining level of US commitment to Afghanistan which has fostered a rapidly deteriorating security situation. President Ghani acknowledged as much in January 2018 when he stated that Afghanistan was 'under siege' and that the army would not last more than six months without the US support. It is estimated that the Taliban control as many as 50 districts, 120 are contested and the balance of over 200 are under government control.[4]

The Taliban smell victory as borne out by their refusal to engage in direct talks with the NUG. It enjoys Pakistan's backing, Chinese and Russian financial support and virtually all countries are dealing with them and are prepared to see them in power.

The US 'desperate to end the war' has had three rounds of talks with the Taliban in Qatar, has not included it in its list of foreign terrorist organizations[5] and has failed to persuade it to talk to the Ghani regime. Indeed, at the recently concluded talks with the Taliban towards the end of January 2019, the USA agreed to the former's demand for a US military withdrawal from Afghanistan in return for a pledge that it would not allow international terrorists to operate from the country. The Taliban did not, however, agree to enter into talks with the Ghani government which it regards as illegitimate. One can expect the US–Taliban dialogue process to continue towards facilitating the US exit from Afghanistan in the coming months which will jeopardize the Afghan presidential elections scheduled for July 2019. Regrettably, the dialogue process with the

---

[3] Available at mea.gov.in/bilateral-documents.htm?dtl/5383/ (accessed on 28 November 2019).
[4] Ibid.
[5] Brahma Chellaney, 'Pakistan's Double Game Stymies Afghan Peace', *Hindustan Times* (25 October 2018).

Taliban is unlikely to be Afghan led, Afghan owned or Afghan controlled as had been promised by the USA and hoped for by the international community. The principal players in this process will, of course, be the US and the Pakistan backed Taliban. The just held Moscow conference at which the Taliban participated in a dialogue with some opposition Afghan participants is no more than a side show.

In these circumstances, a Taliban dispensation in Afghanistan appears to be on the cards and in this eventuality a civil war cannot be ruled out as the non-Pashtun elements may not be willing to accept it.

India's influence in regard to Afghanistan has always been marginal. While India cannot be a spoiler, its presence at the Moscow Format talks is recognition of the fact that it is a widely accepted development partner. Some have advocated that India should consider defending its interests in Afghanistan with boots on the ground. This would be a grave mistake not only because the success of such a move cannot be assured but also because it would impose an onerous financial, military and diplomatic burden. The best that India can do is to continue to support the existing dispensation in Afghanistan with economic, technical and limited military support. There is no call to get into joint projects in Afghanistan with China or with any other country as it will not add value to what we do and will dilute the benefits that accrue to us.

Additionally, we need to deepen contacts with all sections in Afghanistan including elements of the erstwhile Northern Alliance, many of whom feel neglected, and the Pashtuns, among whom our standing is not as good as it should be. In this process, we should also discreetly reach out to the Taliban because once in power national interests will inevitably lead them to view us more favourably unless we treat them as untouchables.

Finally, India should disavow the Durand Line. Every Afghan regime would welcome such a move which will facilitate the process of enabling India and Afghanistan working together on Pakistan-related issues within the framework of the Strategic Partnership Agreement.

Bhutan

India–Bhutan relations have been governed by the Treaty of Friendship concluded in August 1949 and updated in March 2007. The 1949 Treaty, inter alia, provided for India's non-interference in Bhutan's internal affairs, the latter being 'guided' by the former's advice in regard to its external relations, free trade between the two countries, 'equal justice' for each other's nationals residing in the other country, etc. The 1949 Treaty was updated in 2007 essentially to face the new realities of Bhutan not requiring any hand holding in the management of its foreign policy. Accordingly, the 2007 Treaty, while reiterating many provisions of the 1949 Treaty, on foreign policy-related issues simply states that the two countries 'shall cooperate closely with each other on issues relating to their national interests. Neither Government shall allow the use of its territory for activities harmful to the national security and interest of the other.'

Nehru's landmark visit to Bhutan in 1958, the first ever by a head of government to that country, was a catalytic factor in forging closer India–Bhutan ties. It influenced the latter to gradually give up its self-imposed isolation and embark on a process of planned development with India's full support. China's takeover of Tibet in 1950 coupled with its claims on Bhutan was also an important factor in causing it to look to India for support. Similarly, China's build-up in Tibet impelled India to strengthen ties with Bhutan because of the latter's strategic location overlooking its vulnerable chicken's neck area.

With India's support, Bhutan became a member of several regional and international organizations. Bhutan, in turn, has not only been generally supportive of India at regional and international fora but also sensitive to the latter's security concerns. Thus, in 2004, it expelled the ULFA insurgents operating from its soil against India. Similarly, Bhutan did not accept China's offer for a settlement of their border differences entailing forfeiture by the latter of its territorial claims in northern Bhutan in exchange for concessions by the former in the Doklam region which overlooks the chicken neck's area. It was, therefore, only natural for India to stand up for Bhutan during the Chinese intrusions in this area in mid-2017.

India–Bhutan relations, characterized by mutual trust and understanding, have matured over the years and have been sustained by frequent high level visits. Prime Minister Modi made it a point to ensure that Bhutan was the first country he visited after assuming office in 2014.

Economic cooperation is an important element in India–Bhutan bilateral relations. India is Bhutan's largest development and trading partner. Planned development began in Bhutan in 1961 and the first two Five-Year Plans were entirely financed by India. Its contribution to Bhutan's development plans has gone up from ₹107 million in the first plan to about ₹50,000 million for the just completed 11th Plan (2013–2018).[6]

While India's involvement in Bhutan's development is multifaceted, one of the most important areas of economic cooperation is the hydropower sector which provides a reliable source of inexpensive and clean electricity to India and generates substantial export earnings for Bhutan providing more than 40 per cent of its domestic revenues and constituting 25 per cent of its GDP.[7]

India–Bhutan bilateral trade is transacted in their respective currencies and in 2016 stood at ₹8,723 crore with total imports being ₹5,528.5 crore (82% of Bhutan's total imports) and exports recorded as ₹3,205.2 crore including electricity (90% of Bhutan's total exports).[8]

Future Prospects and Options

The current exemplary India–Bhutan ties have a bright future. This is all the more so as the newly elected prime minister of Bhutan, Dr Tshering, had a very successful state visit to India in December 2018 during which he along with Prime Minister Modi pledged to take the bilateral partnership to 'newer heights'. Specifically, agreement was reached on tariff for export of surplus power to India from Bhutan's Mangde Chhu project, the commitment to develop 10,000 MW of hydropower generating capacity in Bhutan was reiterated, and India increased its five-year economic assistance programmed for Bhutan from ₹50,000 million to ₹65,000 million.

The China factor could, however, rock the boat. Enticed by China's spectacular rise, there is always the possibility that Bhutan may consider permitting it to open an embassy in Thimpu, enhancing bilateral economic ties, or even accepting the border settlement deal offered by it. India, therefore, needs to sensitize Bhutan to the dangers of cosying up to China and provide appropriate incentives to it to desist from so doing. This exercise must, however, be undertaken with finesse so that we do rub Bhutan the wrong way.

---

[6] Joint Press Statement on the State Visit of Prime Minister of Bhutan to India (28 December 2018). Available at: https://www.mea.gov.in/bilateral-documents.htm?dtl/30853/Joint+Press+Statement+on+the+State+Visit+of+Prime+Minister+of+Bhutan+to+India+December+28+2018.

[7] Ministry of External Affairs, India Bhutan Relations September 2017. Available at: http://www.mea.gov.in/Portal/ForeignRelation/Bhutan_September_2017_en.pdf.

[8] Ibid.

In order to sustain the current excellent ties with Bhutan, India must maintain frequent contacts at all levels particularly with the monarchy as the King is universally revered. Another important power centre to be cultivated is the 25-member National Council which is mandated to review matters related to 'security, sovereignty and the interest of the country'. While maintaining links with all parties, we must not be perceived to be taking sides.

As Bhutan's younger generation lacks the connect that their elders had with India, this gap should be bridged through imaginative outreach efforts.

Since India's economic cooperation programmes provide a critical underpinning to the bilateral relationship, they must be enhanced and restructured to fit in with the priorities of the new government with a tilt towards areas such as agriculture, education and health.[9] In keeping with Bhutan's sensitivities, the development projects undertaken by us must be environment-friendly. In order to address concerns in Bhutan that much of their external public debt is owed to India, some of our development credits, particularly for hydroelectric projects, may be converted to outright grants.

Finally, as regards Doklam, we should reach out to all parties in the Haa district as their position on the issue is likely to be important in taking a final call on China's offer of a border settlement deal. India would also do well to create awareness of the value of this region to Bhutan because of its rich pasture land.[10]

India–Bangladesh Relations

Despite the huge sacrifices made by India for the liberation of Bangladesh in 1971, relations between the two for much of the latter's history have been uneasy. This is mainly because for most of its existence, Bangladesh has been governed by pro-Pakistan elements averse to good ties with India.

Bangladesh has always been deeply polarized between those at the forefront for the liberation struggle, as represented by the Awami League with its more secular and India-friendly outlook, and those opposing it many of whom had their sympathies with Pakistan and enjoyed radical Islamic support.

---

[9] Shubhajit Roy, 'New PM, New Challenges' *Indian Express* (29 October 2018).
[10] Ibid.

Following the liberation struggle until August 1975 when Sheikh Mujibur Rahman was at the helm of affairs, India–Bangladesh relations were cordial. From his assassination right until the advent of Sheikh Hasina's to power in 1996, India–Bangladesh ties were strained. During this period, Bangladesh sought to internationalize the Farakka issue, boundary-related disputes raised their ugly head, border clashes occurred between the BSF and the Bangladesh Rangers, Bangladesh took offence at India's efforts at fencing the border and worst of all Bangladesh accorded sanctuary and support to secessionist elements from the north-east.

With the advent of the Awami League government under Sheikh Hasina in 1996, there was an upturn in bilateral ties and it was possible to conclude a 30-year Farakka Agreement which put paid to the bickering on the sharing of the Ganga waters. However, most of the issues which bedevilled the relationship could not be addressed in Sheikh Hasina's first term in office and with Khaleda Zia's return to power, India–Bangladesh relations once again deteriorated.

With Sheikh Hasina's assumption of office, once again as prime minister in January 2009, her path-breaking visit to India in February 2010 and Dr Manmohan Singh's visit to Bangladesh in September 2011, India–Bangladesh relations have been on an upward trajectory. A further fillip was given to this process by Prime Minister Modi's visit to Bangladesh in 2015 and Sheikh Hasina's visit to India in 2017.

The qualitative improvement in ties was triggered by the Awami League government's readiness to meet India's security concerns without seeking any quid pro quo, its secular outlook and an openness to explore wide-ranging cooperation with India. While in the past Bangladesh had provided sanctuary and support to anti-Indian elements particularly from the north-east, the Sheikh Hasina government not only put a stop to this but handed over scores of ULFA leaders such as Rajkhowa and Anup Chetia who had taken to operating against India from Bangladesh. It was also on the same page as India in dealing with Islamic terrorist elements and shed the earlier inhibitions about engaging in mutually beneficial bilateral economic and connectivity-related cooperative projects. In these circumstances, both the UPA and NDA governments enthusiastically worked to radically upgrade India–Bangladesh ties which today are at an all-time high.

The contentious land and maritime boundaries have been settled, thereby eliminating a major cause of tension.

There are over 50 bilateral institutional mechanisms between the two countries to service cooperation in diverse areas ranging from economic assistance to border management, from trade and commerce to defence, from power and energy to transport and connectivity, and from science and technology to defence.[11]

India has extended three Lines of Credits since 2010 to Bangladesh amounting to US$8 billion making it the largest recipient of such funds from the former to date.[12] Bilateral trade has grown more than sixfold from 2001–2002 to 2016–2017[13] and since 2011 India has been providing Bangladesh duty-free and quota-free access to imports from the former on all tariff lines except tobacco and alcohol.[14]

Future Prospects

With Sheikh Hasina's re-election to office for the third consecutive term in December 2018, the current excellent India–Bangladesh ties are on course for further consolidation. Much still, however, remains to be done in order to make this upturn in ties irreversible particularly in the context of the overtures being made to Bangladesh by China.

Since water is a highly emotive issue in Bangladesh, one of the most important steps India could take is to work out water-sharing arrangements on some of the rivers flowing from India to Bangladesh starting with the Teesta. We should also agree to provide financial support for the Ganges Barrage at the earliest.

Since the registration of Indian citizens in Assam has caused much concern in Bangladesh, we need to reassure the latter that the issue of illicit Bangladeshi migrants in India will not be allowed to come in the way of bilateral ties and that they would be allowed to stay in India on the basis of work permits.

India also needs to take a more proactive stance on the Rohingya issue. Specifically, while continuing to provide relief support in this regard to Bangladesh it should seek to encourage Myanmar to create conditions for their return.

---

[11] Ministry of External Affairs, India Bangladesh Relations September 2017. Available at: https://mea.gov.in/Portal/ForeignRelation/Bangladesh_September_2017_en.pdf

[12] Ibid.

[13] High Commission of India, Dhaka, India Bangladesh Exports and Imports. Available at: https://www.hcidhaka.gov.in

[14] Ministry of External Affairs, India Bangladesh Relations September 2017. Available at: https://mea.gov.in/Portal/ForeignRelation/Bangladesh_September_2017_en.pdf

Finally, we need to vastly increase transportation, power and telecommunication connectivity between the two countries with a view to enhance their interdependency so that their ties become immune to the vagaries of regime change. Interdependencies can be further enhanced manifold through joint management of river basins for irrigation, flood control, power generation and transportation. Such basin-wide joint management of rivers can, where appropriate, be extended to other regional countries notably Nepal, Bhutan and China.

India–Maldives Relations

India was among the first countries to recognize the Maldives after its independence in 1965 and the relationship flowered in the succeeding decades. Apart from being a leading development partner, India came to the help of the Maldives whenever required whether it was to foil the November 1988 coup bid or to provide relief in the aftermath of the 2004 tsunami.

India–Maldives ties were excellent until the advent of the Waheed and Yameen presidencies in 2012 and 2013 when they touched rock bottom.

Both Waheed and Yameen displayed pronounced pro-China and anti-India tilts and deeply resented the latter's calls to abide by constitutional norms. Waheed cancelled the GMR contract granted by his predecessor in 2010 for upgrading and running of Male International Airport, sought to induct China into SAARC and lauded it for non-interference 'unlike other influential countries'.

Yameen endorsed China's Maritime Silk Route project, awarded a waft of infrastructure projects to China, permitted three Chinese warships to dock at Male in 2017, signed a free trade agreement with China and effectuated constitutional amendments designed to enable China to acquire land in the Maldives on long-term lease. Simultaneously, India was asked to withdraw the two helicopters gifted by it to the Maldives along with the locally stationed IAF personnel and work permits were denied to its Indian nationals.

Under Yameen, authoritarianism was taken to a new level. Judicial independence and freedom of the press were severely constrained. Anyone who spoke up was victimized including former allies. Religious fundamentalism was allowed to increase and scores joined ISIS.

India's expression of concern at the arrest and manhandling of Nasheed in February 2015 on unfounded terrorism charges and its pleas for a resolution of differences within the constitutional framework were disliked by the Yameen government. The ensuing tension led to the cancellation of Modi's visit to the Maldives scheduled for March 2015.

Relations between the two countries touched an all-time low when India called on the Maldives to abide by its Supreme Court ruling of 1 February 2018 to free the nine political prisoners including former president Nasheed, Jumhooree party leader Qasim and Adhaalath party leader Abdulla, reinstate the 12 MPs who had been stripped of their positions and convene the new session of parliament on 5 February 2018. Yameen responded, inter alia, by declaring a state of emergency, arresting the chief justice and strong arming the Supreme Court to reverse its ruling. These flagrantly unconstitutional moves impelled India to express its deep dismay and concern,[15] and, in turn prompted China's state-run *Global Times* to warn that 'If India one-sidedly sends troops to the Maldives, China will take action to stop New Delhi [sic]'.[16]

While Gayoom and Nasheed had also cultivated China, they remained sensitive to India's security concerns which both Waheed and Yameen blatantly disregarded.

Happily, the 23 September 2018 Presidential elections despite rigging by the Yameen regime[17] resulted in a resounding victory for the sole opposition candidate, Ibrahim Mohamed Solih who, riding on solid multiparty support, secured 58.4 per cent of the votes cast and assumed office on 17 November 2018 at the head of a coalition government. Solih's success against all odds is an impressive example of people power in the Maldives which saw a huge voter turnout of over 89 per cent.

India's leadership needs to be commended for having desisted from the use of force against the Yameen government, despite severe provocations, and from taking any steps which could hurt the common Maldivian. Accordingly, India never became an election issue and this worked in Solih's favour.

Future Prospects

With Solih having taken over as president on 17 November 2018, India–Maldives ties are on course to revert to their earlier excellence.

---

[15] S. Chandrasekharan, 'Maldives on the Boil—Yameen Declares Emergency to Avoid Court Orders' (2018). Available at http://www.southasiaanalysis.org/node/2261 (accessed on 28 November 2019).

[16] Available at www.firstpost.com/india/maldives-crisis-india-must-intervene-militarily-if-abdulla-yameen-rebuffs-peaceful-mediation-masterly-inactivity-will-embolden-china-4361929.html (accessed on 28 November 2019).

[17] *The Economist*, 'Stuffing the Ballot Boxes' (20 September 2018).

Modi's visit to the Maldives, as the sole head of government, for Solih's inauguration and the latter's return visit the following month have completely repaired the relationship. This is reflected in the fact that during Solih's India visit, he 'reaffirmed his government's "India-First Policy," and commitment to working together closely with India'.[18] The joint statement issued on the occasion further asserts that both leaders recognizing that the security interests of their countries are interlinked 'reiterated their assurance of being mindful of each other's concerns and aspirations for the stability of the region and not allowing their respective territories to be used for any activity inimical to the other' and 'agreed to strengthen cooperation to enhance maritime security in the Indian Ocean Region through coordinated patrolling and aerial surveillance, exchange of information and capacity building'.[19]

During the visit, India, inter alia, pledged a $1.4 billion economic support package as well as 'all possible support' to the Maldives in its socio-economic development inclusive of vastly increased help in capacity building, better connectivity, visa facilitation, etc.

Though China's investments and projects in the country will be under the scanner, its presence in the country is a reality and its influence cannot be wished away because of its economic capabilities. Moreover, the stability of Solih's rainbow coalition government remains to be seen.

India should remain focused on rebuilding ties with the Maldives through economic cooperation programmes, strengthening people-to-people links, enhancing political cooperation particularly in areas dear to the Maldives like climate change, and developing a closer security and defence relationship. In juxtaposition to China, it must stand out as a benevolent power anxious to help create a more prosperous, secure and democratic Maldives at peace with itself. In the process, it should engage in capacity building in the Maldives in diverse areas including particularly the judiciary, bureaucracy, police, media and security agencies as this would help in achieving the shared objective of building a moderate and liberal country governed in accordance with democratic constitutional norms.

---

[18] Joint Statement on the occasion of State Visit of the President of the Republic of Maldives to India (17 December 2018). Available at mea.gov.in/bilateral-documents.htm?dtl/30765/joint+statement+on+the+occasion+of+state+visit+of+the+president+of+the+republic+of+maldives+to+india+december+17+2018 (accessed on 9 December 2019).

[19] Ibid.

India–Nepal Relations

The common threat perception arising from China's annexation of Tibet induced India and Nepal to conclude a Treaty of Peace and Friendship in July 1950. It along with its side letter provided for 'everlasting peace and friendship' between the two countries that neither country would tolerate any threat to the security of the other by a foreign aggressor, each country would accord 'national treatment' to the other's nationals in participation in any developmental activity, each country would, on a reciprocal basis, grant to the nationals of the other the same privileges in the matter of residence, ownership of property, participation in trade and commerce, movement and privileges of a similar nature and that arms imports would be effected by Nepal only with India's assistance and agreement.

India has significantly influenced Nepal's constitutional development. Its intervention helped restore the monarchy to power under King Tribhuvan in 1951 and rid the country of the century-old corrupt and autocratic Rana oligarchy rule, establish multiparty democracy under a constitutional monarch in 1990 and facilitate agreement between the Maoists and the seven-party alliance which culminated in the abolition of the monarchy and creation of the Federal Republic of Nepal in 2008.

Guided largely by local democratic aspirations, it was usually ahead of the curve and its advice often rubbed the ruling establishment the wrong way. This largely explains Nepal's unhappiness with India and propensity to whip up anti-India sentiment, its tilt to China and its dissatisfaction with the Treaty of Friendship.

Relations between the Federal Republic of Nepal and India have been as volatile as under earlier dispensations. While this is partly due to the bitter party rivalries in Nepal, which from May 2008 to date saw as many as 11 changes of incumbency in the Prime Minister's Office,[20] it is mainly due to India's repeated interventions with the leadership on behalf of the long neglected Madhesis, Tharus and Janjatis to take on board their demands in the new Constitution. Nepal's ruling hill elite, cutting across party lines, which was reluctant to make any concessions to the denizens of the Terai did not take kindly to this. Such Nepalese hypersensitivity to well-meaning Indian suggestions has been the bane of the bilateral relationship.

---

[20] Available at https://en.wikipedia.org/wiki/List_of_Prime_Ministers_of_Nepal (accessed on 28 November 2019).

The issue blew up with the Madhesis launching a four-month blockade which caused great economic disruption. Many Nepalese squarely blamed India for it. India bashing grew exponentially. Relations between India and Nepal touched a new low with Prime Minister Oli recalling and dismissing the Nepalese Ambassador to India in 2016 for conniving with India to 'topple' his government and abruptly cancelling the visit to India of President Bidhya Devi Bhandari.

Through 2018, much effort was expended by both countries to normalize relations including exchange of prime ministerial visits and announcement of projects. That all is not well in the relationship was apparent, however, from Nepal's announcement in September 2018 that it would merely send observers and not participate in the India-hosted BIMSTEC military exercises. Moreover, earlier in the year, Prime Minister Oli in an interview to the *South China Morning Post* indicated that he wanted to deepen ties with China and review the special provisions pertaining to India–Nepal ties including Indian recruitment of Nepalese soldiers.[21]

Nepal's tilt against India is surprising given the many benefits that have accrued to it through the India connect. More than 551 large, intermediate and small-scale projects at an estimated cost of NPR 76 billion have been implemented in diverse spheres across Nepal under Indian financial support since 1951. For the April 2015 earthquake alone, India was the largest donor with pledged assistance of $1 billion. India accounts for over two-thirds of Nepal's merchandise trade, about one-third of trade in services, 46 per cent of foreign direct investments and a significant share of inward remittance on account of pensioners and workers. There are about 125,000 pensioners in Nepal mainly from the army who are in receipt of about ₹3,000 crores annually.[22]

Future Prospects

Clearly, the 2015 blockade delivered a body blow to the bilateral relationship and addressing the prevailing anti-Indian sentiment is a primary challenge for India.[23] This has been accompanied by increased

---

[21] Extracted from article by S. Chandrasekharan, 'Nepal: Use the China Card for Getting More Leverage with India—K. P. Oli-Update No. 360' (Note No. 796, South Asia Analysis Group, 2018).

[22] Ministry of External Affairs, *India–Nepal Relations* (New Delhi: Ministry of External Affairs).

[23] Rohit Karki and Lekhnath Paudel, 'Challenges to the Revision of the Nepal–India 1950 Peace and Friendship Treaty', *Strategic Analysis* 39, no. 4. (2015, July–August).

Chinese popularity with many in Nepal wanting a 'much closer relationship with China at the cost of traditional ties with India'.[24] In these circumstances, India may consider the following moves:

- Press for re-negotiation of the Treaty of Friendship which is unpopular in Nepal and which is not observed by the latter for the most part. While conceding requests for deletion of clauses pertaining to restrictions on Nepal's import of arms, employment of foreigners, etc., India should insist on observance of strict reciprocity on grant of 'national treatment' and on issues such as employment, residence and movement. If Nepal does not agree to reciprocity, India should suggest scrapping of this provision in totality. Nepal must be made to appreciate that walking out of a special relationship will entail costs.
- Porosity of the Nepal–India border should be reduced through better policing as closer Sino-Nepal ties will effectively make it India's first line of defence and not the Himalayas. Accordingly, the border disputes currently afflicting as many as 21 of the 26 districts of Nepal adjoining India must be resolved expeditiously.[25] While we should not shut down all movement across our borders, we should ensure that it is properly regulated.
- Ban on recruitment of Nepalese soldiers to the Indian Army should not be resisted. This is of no consequence to us and will only redound adversely on the Nepalese government.
- India must avoid any competitive economic outreach to Nepal in order to prevent it from coming closer to China. Nepal will soon realize the travails of a suffocating Chinese embrace. When it does so, it will do the running to meet us half way.
- Indian economic cooperation programmes in Nepal may be continued at a modest level directed mainly at capacity building and such infrastructure projects that we are comfortable with in areas of connectivity and hydropower generation. These programmes should not ignore the Madhesis.
- India's soft power should be used to project its non-threatening ethos. Contacts must be maintained with all sections. Special efforts should be made to cultivate the Madhesis and ex-servicemen who have a natural India connect.

---

[24] Krishna V. Rajan, 'Nepal Today: Bad Politics Trumps Good Economics' *Indian Foreign Affairs Journal* 11, no. 2. (2016, April–June).

[25] Rohit Karki and Lekhnath Paudel, 'Challenges to the Revision of the Nepal–India 1950 Peace and Friendship Treaty'.

- The two plus one dialogue format for South Asian countries floated by China should be flatly rejected. This is ploy to undermine India's role in South Asia to the benefit of China.
- India should not agree to guarantee hydropower offtake generated by Chinese constructed plants in Nepal. Import of power if required may be undertaken purely commercial terms.

India–Pakistan Relations

India–Pakistan relations have been troubled since inception mainly because of the latter's visceral antipathy towards the former.

The origins of this antipathy are rooted in Pakistan's failure to evolve a sense of identity. Lacking any unifying sense of identity, Pakistan cultivated anti-Indianism as a glue to keep itself together. This animus manifests itself in Pakistan's quest for parity with India which being unattainable on account of the latter's vastly greater comprehensive national power further accentuates its animosity. Hatred for India is at such a pitch that Pakistan has taken to adopting policies detrimental to its own well-being as they also hurt India. This explains why Pakistan has sought to make up for its power differential with India by pursuing a policy of militarization to the neglect of development, creating an infrastructure of terrorism for use against India and entering into opportunistic linkages with disparate foreign players irrespective of ideology.

The situation has been exacerbated by the fact that for much of its history Pakistan has been governed by the military—either directly or by remote. In order to keep themselves in power and democracy at bay successive, Pakistani military regimes have had a vested interest in promoting the idea of an Indian bogey. They have done so by propagating many blatant falsehoods about India such as that it wants to undo Pakistan, that it has hegemonic designs on Pakistan and that it is averse to good ties with Pakistan. The fact that many Indian leaders from Nehru onwards have asserted that India wishes Pakistan well, that all the India–Pakistan wars were initiated by latter and that India has sincerely sought to improve ties has not dispelled these falsehoods which enjoy wide currency in Pakistan. Some notable Indian moves for improved ties with Pakistan are the conclusion of the highly generous Indus Waters Treaty in 1960, the return of nearly 5,400 square miles of Pakistani territory captured during the 1971 conflict, the unilateral accord of most-favoured-nation (MFN) treatment to Pakistan and its facilitation of the release of the over 90,000 prisoners of war (PoWs) held under the joint India–Bangladesh command.

Accordingly, an adversarial mindset against India has been ingrained into Pakistan's psyche. Kashmir is merely an excuse for the troubled relationship. Were it to be somehow resolved, other issues would be found to poison relations.

Pakistan's inimical mindset towards India finds expression in a host of activities designed to enervate the latter by promoting secessionism in Kashmir and Punjab, provoking communal tensions, exporting terrorism and pumping in fake currency and drugs. Clearly, it is this mindset which is at the root of the rocky India–Pakistan relationship and not the differences between the two countries.

The policies of India and Pakistan towards each other have shown remarkable consistency. While Pakistan has always sought to undermine India, the former has shown little inclination, barring in 1971, to impose costs on the former.

Such pusillanimity has only emboldened Pakistan in its endeavours against India. Accordingly, India would be better served by adopting a sustained approach designed to impose costs on Pakistan for its adventurist policies.

The case for persisting with India's existing policies towards Pakistan rests on specious arguments. It is, for instance, made out that as a neighbour India has no option but to mend fences with Pakistan. This line of argumentation is intrinsically flawed as it takes two to mend fences and given Pakistan's anti-Indian mindset no amount of accommodation by India will lead to an amelioration in the relationship.

The contention that dialogue redounds to India's benefit as it will strengthen democratic forces in Pakistan vis-à-vis the military has little value as the perceptions of the former on India mirror those of the latter.

The argument that policies designed to impose costs on Pakistan may trigger a nuclear conflict is ill-founded as India has an effective nuclear deterrent which secures it from any nuclear attack.

The imposition of costs on Pakistan for its inimical moves against India demands pursuit of a suite of sustained and concerted policies such as:

- A campaign calling for imposition of sanctions against Pakistan for its export of terrorism. To carry conviction, it should be accompanied by an act of Parliament declaring Pakistan as a terrorist state, recalling our high commissioner, downsizing our mission in

Pakistan, abandoning any high-level dialogue or entering into any confidence-building measure (CBM) with it.
- Maximization of the use of the Indus waters as permitted under the Indus Waters Treaty followed by a suspension of its operation by recourse to Article 62 of the Vienna Convention on the Law of Treaties permitting the same if there is a fundamental change in the circumstances. Pakistan's use of terrorism against India constitutes a fundamental change in the circumstances in which the Treaty was signed.
- Exploitation of Pakistan's fault lines in Baluchistan, Khyber Pakhtunkhwa and Sindh.
- Covert action and focused strikes against terrorist elements and their supporters in Pakistan.
- Withdrawal from Turkmenistan–Afghanistan–Pakistan–India (TAPI) pipeline and of unilateral accord of most favoured nation (MFN) status to Pakistan. Undercutting Pakistani exports and ensuring that the EU does not continue to provide duty-free access to its textile products to which we had acceded.
- Disavowing the Durand Line.

India–Sri Lanka Relations

India–Sri Lanka relations were more or less on even keel from Independence onwards through the 1970s. This was largely due to India's highly accommodative stance reflected in its acceptance of Sri Lanka's dalliance with China, taking back 600,000 plantation Tamils and ceding Kachchatheevu to Sri Lanka.

The rising Tamil-Sinhala ethnic tensions from the late 1970s culminating in the anti-Tamil programme of July 1983 and the consequent civil war in Sri Lanka resulting in the migration of 150,000 Tamils to India led to a serious deterioration in India–Sri Lanka ties. This was exacerbated by the pro-West tilt of the Jayewardene government. Indeed, by 1986, not only the USA and Israel but also Pakistan were providing training, intelligence and arms to Sri Lanka.[26] Despite these provocations, India remained committed to the integrity of Sri Lanka as borne out by the India–Sri Lanka Accord of 1987 which was designed to restore harmony by disarming the LTTE and providing a modicum of autonomy to the Tamils as later encapsulated in the 13th Amendment. The Accord, under the aegis of which the Indian Peace Keeping Force

---

[26] Neil Devotta, 'When Individuals, States, and Systems Collide: India's Foreign Policy towards Sri Lanka', in *India's Foreign Policy*, ed. Sumit Ganguly.

(IPKF) operated, was also tailored to curb foreign military presence in Sri Lanka.

With the Accord attracting widespread Sinhala opprobrium and with the Premadasa government helping the LTTE to resist disarmament and calling for the IPKF's withdrawal, India had little option but to comply. This move 'saved the LTTE from annihilation'[27] and thereby caused much suffering in Sri Lanka by prolonging the civil war by nearly two decades.

The IPKF imbroglio and Rajiv Gandhi's assassination in May 1991 made India wary of any direct engagement in Sri Lanka's ethnic problem. With the intensification of the civil war following Rajapaksa's assumption of power, India's decision to limit its assistance to the Sri Lankan government to non-lethal supplies laid the field open to other powers like China and Pakistan to do so and thereby further strengthen their links with Sri Lanka at its cost.

The LTTE's military defeat in May 2009 only marginally reduced the salience of the ethnic issue in India–Sri Lanka ties as the former continued to press for meaningful autonomy for the Sri Lankan Tamils which neither the Rajapaksa nor the Sirisena regimes, despite initial favourable indications, delivered upon. Sri Lanka's obduracy on this account compelled India, much to the former's distaste, to vote in favour of the UN Human Rights Council resolutions critical of Sri Lanka in 2012 and 2013.

India's repeated support to Sri Lanka in respect of both man-made and natural disasters has not prevented increasingly closer ties between the latter and China. Sino-Sri Lanka relations were upgraded in May 2013 into a strategic partnership and the latter came out in enthusiastic support of the Belt and Road Initiative. China's involvement in Sri Lanka is wide ranging. Expectations of a dilution in ties between the two with the advent of the NUG in 2015 have been belied.

The Modi government, while maintaining India's traditional stand on the ethnic issue and pressing for the implementation of the 13th Amendment, has gone the extra mile in trying to improve ties with Sri Lanka through stepped-up economic cooperation particularly after the establishment of the NUG. These endeavours bore fruit but with the break-up of this government consequent upon the Sirisena–Rajapaksa tie-up, fresh uncertainties have once again clouded India–Sri Lanka ties.

---

[27] Hariharan, *India and Sri Lanka's Internal Conflict: Q&A* (2018, 26 May). Available at: www.southasiaanalysis.org

Future Prospects

Sri Lanka–India ties may currently be termed as good. Further improvement is likely to be difficult due to four major impediments, notably the China factor, a deep-rooted anti-Indian mindset, the ethnic issue and the fishermen problem.

China's increasing influence in Sri Lanka is inevitable as the former's support to the latter on the ethnic issue is unequivocal, as it is seen as a balancing force vis-a-vis India, and as it is major source of developmental funding. All that India can do is to sensitize Sri Lanka to the dangers of its China dalliance and hope that it will see reason.

The anti-India mindset in Sri Lanka constitutes the strongest impediment to smooth bilateral ties. It colours many of Sri Lanka's actions such as the reluctance to sign the Comprehensive Economic Partnership Agreement or award major projects to India, and a propensity to see Indian moves to destabilize the government where none exist. Changing such a mindset will require a multi-pronged approach entailing extreme tact in our dealings, projecting that we regard a stable, united and inclusive Sri Lanka as a source of strength to India, maximizing people-to-people contacts as a bridge builder and ensuring good relations with the entire spectrum of the Sri Lankan leadership.

India's handling of the ethnic issue has earned it the ire of both the Sinhalese and the Tamils. India must convince Sri Lanka that it has no intention of imposing solutions and that its call for grant of autonomy to the Tamils through dialogue is only in Sri Lanka's best interests. It should also do much more to cultivate the Sinhala community.

Indian fishing activity in Sri Lankan territorial waters is illegal and an unnecessary irritant. Indian fishermen must be weaned off from such activity and induced instead to undertake deep sea fishing.

Conclusion

Though India enjoys deep historical, cultural and linguistic links with each of its neighbours, it cannot have a one-size-fits-all policy for them. Its policy towards each has to be tailored to that country's evolving political dynamics and circumstances as well as its approach to India. There are, of course, many commonalities which confront India in its neighbourhood such as a knowledge deficit about neighbours, China's increasing footprint, negativity about India, long festering bilateral issues and serious governance deficits leading to instability and even regime change.

A sine qua non for a successful neighbourhood policy is in-depth knowledge about each neighbour. Our woeful inadequacy in this regard must be made up urgently. This can be done by creating a number of think tanks which are exclusively devoted to studying each of our neighbours.

Given its deep pockets, China's increasing influence in the region is an inevitability. Since resource constraints make it difficult for India to successfully compete with China on capital-intensive projects, its focus should instead be on areas below the latter's radar which are not capital-intensive and where we excel such as capacity-building, small and medium enterprises, health, education and agriculture. Where Chinese activities pose a strategic challenge, we should make known our concerns unequivocally.

Nothing can be done about the prevailing anti-Indian sentiment among our neighbours to the extent that it is due to the big country–small country syndrome. However, there are many other factors which have led to anti-Indianism such as arrogance, both at the personal and national level, which often manifests itself in imposed rather than jointly arrived at outcomes, inability to deliver on promises in a timely fashion and a tendency to let down friends. Remedial action coupled with carefully crafted policies designed to align our moves with popular aspirations will help in mitigating anti-Indian sentiments to some extent. Frequent and informal ministerial level exchanges will also be useful in not only increasing bonhomie but also in dispelling unnecessary misunderstandings. It would also help if special attention is given to appropriate media projection in the neighbouring countries about India and its policies calculated to dispel false propaganda about it.

The early resolution of long-festering issues with many of our neighbours would go a long way in creating a much better relationship with them. The timely delivery on promises made can be facilitated by the creation of an inter-ministerial committee for neighbourhood projects and by improving our institutional mechanisms.

A radical and urgent upgradation of the existing substandard infrastructure in our border areas is essential not only to improve the quality of life of our border population but also to instil a sense of respect for India among its neighbours.

The insulation of India's neighbourhood ties from the vagaries of regime change calls for the creation of interdependencies in diverse areas such as transportation, power transmission, river basin management, etc. Where feasible, this could include countries such as Nepal, Bhutan and Bangladesh bilaterally or on a regional basis. Multilateral projects are, however, not the modality of choice as their progression is hostage to the whims and fancies of the most reluctant partner. SAARC's failure due to Pakistan's recalcitrance and BIMSTEC's example are cases in point.

Additionally, people-to-people links are an important instrument for forging stronger ties and should be increased exponentially by providing visa on arrival for those from neighbouring countries, providing greater access to our medical, technical and education facilities, and by promoting greater cultural, sporting, religious, etc., exchanges. These are areas in which we enjoy an unmatched advantage vis-a-vis any other country because of our geographical propinquity and shared multifaceted linkages.

Finally, we must have complete clarity about our policy towards each neighbour and a commitment to pursue it in a sustained fashion. Specifically, we need to be clear as to what we are prepared to do for each neighbour in terms of support and resolution of differences, what we expect from it and how far we are prepared to go to ensure that it lives up to our expectations. India's policies in this regard have varied over the decades. At one end of the spectrum while the Rajiv Gandhi government was prepared to impose economic sanctions on Nepal and sign the India–Sri Lanka Peace Accord to disarm the LTTE, promote minority rights and curb Sri Lanka's foreign military links, the Gujral government came out with the doctrine of non-reciprocal munificence in good faith and trust to all its smaller neighbours barring Pakistan. Neither succeeded.

The need of the hour is a specifically tailored policy for each country. The Modi government has attempted this. It has been more focused on our neighbours than most earlier governments with Modi being the only Indian prime minister to have visited all our SAARC neighbours, inclusive of Afghanistan, some twice or more. It has been far more supportive of neighbouring governments in terms of economic cooperation programmes and more tolerant of the increasing external influences in the neighbourhood, whether Chinese or Western, than most previous regimes. When red lines have been crossed, as in the Maldives or in Nepal, it has shown great restraint and not taken any punitive steps with mixed results: in the former, this approach facilitated a regime change favourable to India but in the latter it has not induced the government to mend its ways. With Pakistan, much like most previous governments, it extended a hand of friendship only to be rebuffed. Unlike them, it adopted a posture of no dialogue but did not take it to its logical conclusion of imposing costs on Pakistan for its export of terror to India as a result of which we continue to suffer.

14

Political Economy of India's International Relations
A New Path for Sustained Strategic Interlinkages

Arun K. Singh

Global economic and political relations are in flux. In this context, this chapter seeks to examine the possible advantage to India from looking at economic, political and strategic relations with the USA in an integrated manner.

The USA Is Changing Rules It Created

The USA is seeking to not live by and change the rules it had worked to create, especially since 1990, to link economies globally to the advantage of its companies. It has stymied work at the WTO by not approving appointments to appellate bodies. It has unilaterally sought to terminate North American Free Trade Agreement (NAFTA) with Mexico and Canada, negotiated during the Clinton Administration. It has coerced Mexico and Canada to agree to a replacement with higher local content requirements, environmental and labour standards (new agreement is pending US Congressional approval). President Trump walked out of the Trans-Pacific Partnership (TPP), negotiated during the Obama Administration. It was then aimed at excluding China, and strategically linking other major economies in the Pacific region, to deal with the consequences of an economically and militarily rising China. Projected aim of TPP was to 'shape the environment' around the rise of China, so as to influence its policy choices and actions.

The new US approach has been imposed by President Trump, responding to his electoral compulsion of a support base that saw itself as losing from the economic globalization process, which otherwise benefitted the US economy in macro terms, and its top percentile elites. Today, nearly 40 per cent of income and wealth in the USA is attributed to top 1 per cent of the population. On the other hand, 40 per cent of the population, in the middle class, saw its employment opportunities, especially in manufacturing, health and education indicators and longevity, suffer during the post-1990 globalization.

Europe Thwarted by Brexit and Internal Divisions

Europe is experiencing its own flux. Brexit has put a brake on the hitherto gradually but inexorably expanding membership of the EU. Mess in the Brexit process, and sharply divided opinion in the UK among people, parties and constituent entities such as Scotland and Northern Ireland, have highlighted the potential disruptions, and different losers and gainers from severing of growing links and harmonization of norms and standards.

Within Continental Europe too, there is a drift.

Germany, after its unification in 1990, had emerged as the largest economy, and leader in intra-European processes. Its voice has now been subdued by domestic weakening of the hitherto tallest European leader, Angela Merkel, by rise of the right-wing and anti-immigrant sentiment. Across many countries in Europe (Italy, Austria, Hungary, Netherlands, Poland), right-wing and anti-immigrant parties have come to power or gained in political traction. For now, the ever-present simmering sectional opposition to strengthen European integration has come to the fore, even though additional exits are not presently expected after the divisive experience of Brexit.

France, under President Macron, was initially seen as picking up the gauntlet from a weakened Germany. Macron was seen as the standard bearer of a values and rules-based order, as well as globalization and European integration, faced with the challenge from anti-globalization US under Trump. His standing has been weakened by the sustained and periodically violent 'Yellow Vest' protests, articulating concerns and demands similar to the core Trump supporters in the USA.

European processes have normally advanced based on what has been described as the Franco-German tandem. These two countries reflect different political and economic cultures, with France being generally more social democratic and welfare oriented; they also embody differences between Northern and Southern Europe, with France symbolizing the aspirations of Portugal, Spain, Italy, Greece, etc. This tandem is not delivering for now, a problem which intensified post the 2008 Global Financial Crisis, with French economy slowing down considerably during the tenure of President Hollande. Early expectations of revival of meaningful coordination under a new, more right-wing French president, were subsequently belied, and as France is now coping with the Yellow Vest opposition to economic and social policies.

Europe is divided too in approach to Russia and China.

Russia's move into Crimea, and its perceived support to armed opposition elements in Eastern Ukraine, led to US and European sanctions. However, in France, Italy, Greece and several other countries, there is support for normalizing with Russia, even as many of the front-line Central European (Poland) and Scandinavian ones (Sweden) remain opposed. Germany continues work on a new gas pipeline from Russia, bypassing Ukraine, even in face of strident criticism from President Trump.

The EU was not able to come up with a consensus position critical of China, because of Greece blocking it, after China rejected the international tribunal's ruling on South China Sea. This was attributed to Chinese loans to, and investments in, Greece, including controlling stake in the port of Piraeus. Despite concern from leading EU member countries, such as France and Germany, China had created a grouping of 16+1, comprising China and 16 countries from Central and Eastern Europe. France and Germany were excluded. Greece has just joined the group, making it 17+1. Italy recently became the first G7 country to sign up to the Chinese BRI. Central and Eastern European countries see potential economic opportunity in enhanced connectivity and do not want to be left out of any Chinese investment plan in the region. There is opportunity for China because there is no clear direction and leadership coming from within Europe, and messaging from the USA under Trump is deriding the value of Europe, alliances and US economic and strategic commitments to the region. During President Xi's visit to France in March 2019, Macron also invited German Chancellor Merkel and EU President Juncker to try and project a united European approach. The fact that he felt the need to do this reflected Chinese inroads and recognition of Chinese influence and reach. In his comments, Macron called upon Xi to 'respect European unity'!

Expanding Chinese Influence

Chinese GDP now is five times and military expenditure at least four times that of India. Its interlinkages with US, European, Russian, Japanese, Australian, ASEAN, African and Latin American economies, through trade and investments, are far deeper than India's. For many countries, it has now emerged as the largest trading partner.

To some extent, the economic and ensuing political and military rise of China has been facilitated by the USA, West and Russia, in search of economic and strategic gains.

The USA had done its initial outreach to Communist China in 1971 to sharpen the Sino-Soviet split and to turn the global balance of power to its advantage. When China initiated its economic reforms in 1979, under Deng Xiaoping, US and European firms rushed in to get a foothold in the largely untapped market. Opportunities for lowered cost exports from China generated benefits for the Western consumer, profits for the Western companies, jobs and access to new technologies for the Chinese. Western approach was to 'integrate China into the international mainstream', integrate Chinese economy with that of the West and get China to accept and live by the West-set rules of the international political and economic order.

Initial concerns in the USA suggesting that their expectations were being thwarted appeared during the George W. Bush Administration. US and European companies began to speak of restricted market access and forced technology transfers by the Chinese. The Obama Administration, in its first phase, spoke of 'strategic reassurance to China', that its rise would be accommodated in a non-confrontational manner, and mindful of its interests. This later led to 'pivot' and then 'rebalance' to Asia, suggesting that the USA needed to do more to push back on Chinese economic, technological and political forays. This new messaging and articulation was not followed through effectively in implementation because the USA remained preoccupied in Europe because of new tensions with Russia, and in West Asia because of the Arab Spring and destabilization of several governments.

President Trump adopted a more strident approach to China, driven by the compulsions of his winning electoral strategy in 2016. He imposed enhanced tariffs on more than $250 billion of Chinese products, including steel and aluminium, and has threatened to widen the scope. Intense negotiations followed on issues of market access, intellectual property rights, forced technology transfers, cyber theft, etc. There is some expectation that a new agreement may be worked out, leading to a visit to the USA by Chinese president, but negotiations and Trump's assessments of progress remain volatile, and threats of additional tariffs repeatedly held out. At the same time, recognizing the technological challenge from China, the USA has strengthened provisions of Committee on Foreign Investment in the USA (CFIUS) to prevent Chinese takeover of sensitive and critical new generation technologies in the USA. It is also advocating with its allies and partners to not allow Chinese Huawei to be the provider of 5G technology and infrastructure, citing security concerns. It has threatened to restrict intelligence sharing with the UK if it allows Huawei to participate in 5G even in 'non-core' areas. Access of Chinese students and scholars to US universities in sensitive areas of S&T research is being curtailed.

Europe has by and large let the USA take the lead on strategic issues related to China, and itself focus essentially on the trade and economic relationship. There has been competition among European countries, including Germany, France and the UK to be in the lead in terms of being preferred partners for China. Leaders from these countries have made repeated visits to China. The UK tried to be the centre in Europe for renminbi transactions. European leaders have been reluctant to meet with Dalai Lama, fearing Chinese economic retribution. Norway was left to fend for itself in face of Chinese economic 'sanctions' following award of Nobel Peace Prize to one of its dissidents. However, on BRI, leading European countries have stayed away from endorsing, citing lack of transparency and debt unsustainability practices. Germany has introduced enhanced scrutiny for Chinese investments and blocked several high-technology acquisitions. On the margins of Europe, Turkey was threatened with economic measures when it criticized recent Chinese practices in Xinjiang.

BRI is the latest and most ambitious effort by China to expand its reach and influence, building upon its new economic size, surplus capital and manufacturing capacity and technological heft including in digital, 5G, artificial intelligence, etc. Referring to the second BRF (Belt and Road Forum), held in China in April this year, the Chinese Ambassador to India, Luo Zhaohui, wrote in *Hindustan Times* on 6 May 2019 that forty leaders, including heads of State and Government and heads of international organizations, attended the round-table summit. More than 6,000 foreign guests from 150 countries and 92 international organizations were present at the forum. Over 100 multilateral and bilateral cooperation documents were signed between China and relevant countries and international organizations. A list of 283 concrete deliverables was put together. Chinese and foreign enterprises reached cooperation agreements worth more than 64 billion US dollars in total.

Chinese comments also indicated a projection that they were adapting to criticism and negative reactions in many of the recipient countries. There was a promise to enhance transparency and look at debt sustainability issues. According to the ambassador, in his keynote at the Summit, Chinese President Xi spoke of 'extensive consultation, joint contribution and shared benefits with partner countries', and that 'China will follow international rules and standards widely supported by all parties and respect the laws and regulations of each country'. How much of this is observed or implemented in practice remains to be seen.

Russia is today compelled to work more with China, on account of difficulties in its relations with the USA and Europe, and Western sanctions. It has built an energy partnership through pipeline linkages. It also supplied weapons and defence technologies to China, when the USA and Europe refrained from doing so. In the longer term, however, Russia would certainly have concerns with the growing Chinese presence in Central Asia and in its Siberian region.

China's potential for influence today also derives from the fact that in many countries that are strategic adversaries, including the USA, Japan, Australia and in Europe, and potentially Russia, it is the largest or among the largest economic partners.

India's International Political–Economic Interests

India will, thus, need to pursue its strategic interests keeping its economic and political interlinkages and convergence in view, as well as the ongoing flux and reshaping of the international order.

For long, it was perceived that the Indian economy was autarkic, isolated from global norms and trends, and essentially driven by domestic demand. Now, however, nearly 50 per cent of our GDP is generated by the external sector. External financial and investment flows, technology partnerships and infusions, and trade are important parameters as the economy strives to meet the growing aspirations.

The USA

If one were to look at comprehensive national interest: political, economic, strategic, impact on people, etc., clearly the US relationship would be among the most vital. It is our largest trading partner, with overall trade in goods and services being around $140 billion. The IT sector is critical to further technology development, contributes nearly 8 per cent of our GDP and significant portion of it is exported to the USA. The USA is among the largest sources of foreign direct investment (FDI) to India, accounting for around $28 billion, including flows through the Mauritius and Singapore routes. With around 4 million persons of Indian origin, the USA is the largest single country with the presence of Indian origin diaspora. One out of seven patients in the USA is seen by an Indian origin doctor. Total 40 per cent of hotel rooms in the USA are estimated to be owned or managed by Indian origin entrepreneurs, accounting for nearly $13 billion of revenue and contributing significantly to taxes and social security. In the 2016 and 2018 elections, 5 Indian Americans were elected to US Congress, while till then historically only 3 had ever been similarly elected. Nearly 200,000 Indian students study in US universities, enhancing future opportunities for themselves and creating networks for further economic interlinkages between India and the USA.

Starting from scratch in 2008, the USA has contracted to supply $18 billion of defence equipment to India, and the two countries are exploring its deepening through the Defence Trade and Technology Initiative (DTTI). The USA and India carry out a large number of bilateral, trilateral and multilateral military exercises with each other for various services. They also signed Logistics Exchange Memorandum of Agreement (LEMOA) in 2016 and Communications Compatibility and Security Agreement (COMCASA) in 2018. These could enable increased interoperability. Reportedly, text of Industrial Security Agreement (ISA) has been finalized, which could enable Indian companies to become part of global supply chain of US defence manufacturing companies. There is also readiness now to begin negotiations on Basic Exchange and Cooperation Agreement (BECA) which would enable sharing of geo-spatial information.

The USA has also provided unique support to India to meet its strategic objectives. India's ability to now access the international market for uranium and civil nuclear power in general was possible on account of US decision to allow such cooperation bilaterally and pursue India-specific exemptions at International Atomic Energy Agency (IAEA) and Nuclear Suppliers Group (NSG). The USA has also successfully supported India's membership in multilateral export control regimes such as Missile Technology Control Regime (MTCR), Australia Group and Wassenaar Arrangement and made effort (thwarted by China) to pilot India's membership of NSG. These have enabled India to access higher levels of technology. The USA has also declared India a major defence partner in 2016 and articulated in principle support in 2010 for India's permanent membership in UN Security Council.

In the aftermath of the 14 February Pakistan-based Jaish-e-Mohammed organized terrorist strike in Pulwama, US position had perhaps been internationally the most supportive. Following a conversation with India's National Security Advisor, the US National Security Advisor Bolton supported India's right to self-defence. After India's 26 February strike in Balakot on a Jaish terrorist training camp, US Secretary of State Pompeo described it as a 'counterterrorism' action, in language similar to India's. The USA, along with the UK and France, successfully pushed subsequently for listing of Masood Azhar as a global terrorist at the UN, eventually getting China to withdraw its 'technical' objection.

Europe

Europe would closely follow the USA in terms of India's multidimensional interlinkages. Overall India–EU goods trade is larger than with the USA, but a close second if services trade is also included. The UK has a large, around 1.5 million, Indian origin diaspora. India–France trade, at $10 billion, is below that with the UK at $15 billion, and Germany at $20 billion. But France has been a long-standing partner for India in strategic areas such as civil nuclear, space and defence. France had also been supportive of India after Pulwama, and in the UN listing of Masood Azhar.

Relations with European countries would need to be followed in a differentiated manner. India's economic relations with Germany are the strongest, but Germany does not take a lead in global political issues or strategic issues related to Asia. It takes a lead in intra-European issues or Europe-focused security issues such as with Ukraine and Russia.

The UK has traditionally been supportive of Pakistan on India–Pakistan issues, and not as forthcoming as we would expect on India-focused terrorism or separatism issues.

France has issued a joint statement with India on the Indian Ocean (it has an exclusive economic zone of 9 million sq. km in the Indian Ocean and Pacific), has signed a logistics support agreement and carried out major military exercises including the naval exercise Varuna. The latest edition in May this year included their aircraft carrier and was conducted both near Indian coast and near Djibouti where both France and China have bases. France has also invited India (along with South Africa, Australia and Chile) to the next G7 summit being held in Biarritz in August. Aside from a recognition of the strong bilateral relationship with India, it is also an assertion of its enhanced focus on the Indo-Pacific (the non-G7 invitees are from the Indian Ocean and Pacific regions).

Russia

Russia has been a traditional partner of India since the 1950s. It enabled India to withstand US and UK pressure in UN Security Council on Kashmir. Khrushchev visited Srinagar, during his visit to India in 1955, and declared Soviet position as recognizing J&K as an integral part of India. Indo-Soviet Treaty of Peace, Friendship and Cooperation of 1971 impacted the international situation around the emergence of Bangladesh. Defence supplies from the Soviet Union were provided at prices and levels of technology not available from elsewhere. Currently, around 60 per cent of India's defence inventory is reported to be of Russian origin. Assistance was also provided to development of heavy industry in India. Rupee–rouble trade provided special access for Indian products in the Soviet market.

However, the economic linkage with Russia, civilian technology flows and people-to-people links pale in comparison to those with the USA, Canada, Europe, Australia, West Asia and Africa. Exception to this has been Indian investment in energy in Sakhalin and Russian investment in Essar in India.

Russia's growing dependence on China will circumscribe it on India–China issues. Partly at China's prodding, and partly seeing India's deepening links with the USA and Europe, Russia has been opening out to Pakistan, supplying helicopters, doing military exercises and less than fully supportive of India on India–Pakistan issues. After the Pulwama-related developments, Russia, while expressing solidarity with India on terrorism in general, called for de-escalation and said it was ready to strengthen counterterrorism cooperation with both

India and Pakistan. Unlike the USA and France, it made no reference to cross-border terrorism.

China

China is India's largest trading partner in goods. However, the trade is heavily skewed in China's favour. India has concerns on market access issues. China also has a strong and growing presence in India in power, telecom and digital. Huawei is making a bid to be part of 5G roll-out.

An adversarial relationship with China is likely to endure for some time to come. The border remains unresolved, and China's positions have hardened. China has supported Pakistan politically and through military supplies. On Masood Azhar, it coordinated its position with Pakistan. It has blocked India's membership of NSG, suggesting parallel consideration for Pakistan. Its growing naval presence in Indian Ocean, base in Djibouti and potentially in Gwadar (Pakistan), growing economic presence and asset acquisitions in India's neighbourhood, particularly in Sri Lanka, Nepal and the Maldives are cause of concern.

Jury is still out on whether China's trade and economic interlinkage with India in some sectors will give leverage in the relationship to China or to India. It has also been observed that China treats India with more care when it sees its strengthening links with others, particularly the USA and Europe.

Other Regions

Several other regions are economically and strategically important for India.

West Asia is the source of more than 70 per cent of India's energy imports, hosts an Indian origin diaspora of around 8 million and accounts for $40 billion of annual remittances. Efforts over the past few years to consolidate relations with Saudi Arabia and UAE in particular will contribute to India's energy security. Saudi Arabia and UAE national oil companies are now investing in a petrochemical complex in Maharashtra, and in our oil reserve facility. Their sovereign wealth funds are looking for investment opportunity in India. Enhanced economic linkages with India will lessen their earlier tendency to lean towards Pakistan on India–Pakistan issues. They also find the India relationship stabilizing as the USA withdraws from its global footprint, and to balance the increasing Chinese presence. Iran, similarly, is important for transit to Afghanistan, Central Asia, Caucasus and Russia, but the energy partnership is complicated for now because of US sanctions requiring that such imports be reduced to zero. Chabahar port being developed partly by India, in Iran, has potential to assist significantly for transit.

ASEAN, with a total population of 600 million, $70 billion of trade with India, strong India origin population in Myanmar, Malaysia, Thailand and Singapore, historical cultural links with Laos, Cambodia and Indonesia, strategic convergence with Vietnam, lies strategically astride the Indo-Pacific. This region, transit for a large part of global energy supplies and trade, has now emerged as a focus in Indian strategic planning. With the USA, a Joint Strategic Vision for the region was declared in 2015. Malabar series of naval exercises are carried out regularly with the USA and Japan. Quadrilateral meetings are now being held regularly with addition of Australia.

Africa has traditionally received attention in Indian efforts because of commonality in struggle against colonialism, diaspora presence in Eastern and Southern Africa and potential for new economic linkages. Africa, with a combined population size and GDP similar to India, is now emerging as a growth area.

Latin America with a population of more than 650 million, GDP of around $7 trillion, proximity to the North American market and similarity with US time zone also provides opportunity.

There is growing Chinese presence in Africa and Latin America. Countries are looking for opportunities to balance and hedge. The USA, Japan, France, among others, are exploring partnerships with India in these continents.

Suggestion for a Comprehensive Approach to the US Relationship

Post-Second World War, Europe revived its economy through US supported Marshall Plan and enhanced access for its products and to its technology. Japan, South Korea, Taiwan, ASEAN, at various stages, benefitted from becoming part of the global value chain.

International political–economic relations are today in flux. New US trade requirements and tariffs are disrupting existing supply chains.

Many companies shifted production from China to Vietnam and elsewhere. New opportunities are being sought by them.

New trade and investment patterns will be determined by absorption of new technologies, such as 5G, Big Data and artificial intelligence. Trade, investment, security, international relations would need to be looked at in an integrated manner to seize new opportunity and maximize gains. The free, open and democratic system in India offers to many a more acceptable alternative to the Chinese model.

There is a structure for coordinated thinking in India on strategic issues through the mechanism of the National Security Council and National Security Advisor, bringing together foreign and defence policies and intelligence.

More coordinated policy and decision-making is required, bringing together strategies in industry, commerce and finance on one side, and foreign, defence and national security strategy on the other.

Relations with the USA have seen periodic challenges because issues are often seen in silos. The problem exists on both sides, despite US recognizing in its National Security Strategy document of December 2017 that 'economic security is national security'.

In 2012–2013, there was intense negativity in some US business associations and Congress, because of India's policy introduced to encourage localization in telecom production and long-standing differences on intellectual property rights particularly in the pharmaceutical sector. A few US companies were able to use their clout in US Congress, because of funding support for election campaigns, to pursue their specific and narrow agendas, unmindful of the wider impact. Some used their access to the administration, for instance, in the dairy sector, to push for market access in terms that could generate adverse social and political reaction in India. Some in the administration, especially in the Office of the United States Trade Representative (USTR), unable to achieve their targets, opposed a strategic view to the India economic relationship, arguing against advocacy for India's membership in Asia-Pacific Economic Cooperation (APEC). They also pushed for a narrow approach in pursuing case against India at the WTO on our solar panel manufacturing plans, ignoring the broader relationship and India's thrust towards expanding renewable in the energy mix. President Trump's decision to levy tariffs on steel and aluminium imports from India ostensibly on national security grounds (a measure essentially aimed at China and to appease his support base), flies in the face of a declared strategic partnership. Similar is the case with the notification to Congress to withdraw generalized system of preferences (GSP) benefits for Indian products.

Similarly, India has approached its differences and negotiations with the USA on economic issues without necessarily factoring in the overall relationship, and future trends in technology and supply chains. Transactional compromises are often missing, strengthening those in the USA who advocate against India citing our alleged intransigence. India is also seen as obstructive in multilateral trade negotiations.

Undoubtedly, there are some exceptions. India's recent decisions to repeatedly postpone levy of retaliatory tariffs for the steel and aluminium tariffs reflect a factoring in of the overall relationship. Similarly, reported US decision to postpone action on GSP withdrawal, till after the general elections in India and formation of post-election government, suggests a sensitivity to India's political compulsions.

As India's Ambassador to the USA, I had occasion to visit Silicon Valley several times. I could see first-hand the mainstream presence of Indian-origin tech workers, companies and start-ups in the US global leadership in digital technology. We have to only look at the CEOs of leading US companies such as Microsoft, Google and Adobe to get a visible example of such linkage. Reportedly, one-third of start-ups in Silicon Valley by foreign-born persons are those by persons of Indian origin. There is great potential, therefore, for strengthening links in this sector, and its future evolution, between the two countries to mutual advantage.

Opportunities would also arise in the new areas of focus such as data and artificial intelligence. A balance would need to be struck between advantages in terms of profit and technology generation from localization and from being part of value chains. Recent announcement of Mastercard to invest an additional $1 billion in India for a data centre, innovation and start-ups is indication of potential.

The USA and India can also gain from joint third country projects. They have already identified some cooperation in a few countries in Africa and in Afghanistan. There will be opportunities in the Indo-Pacific. Speaking at the Indo-Pacific Business Forum of the US Chamber of Commerce on 30 July 2018, US Secretary of State Pompeo announced new US plans for promoting digital connectivity, cybersecurity partnership, Asia EDGE (Enhancing Development and Growth through Energy), Infrastructure Transaction and Assistance Network, pledging seed money and planning to also tap the US BUILD Act fund of

$60 billion. This US effort is clearly aimed at responding to the Chinese BRI challenge. India's Act East policy should find some convergence in the US effort.

Another recognized lacuna in Indian international efforts has been implementation, particularly of economic and connectivity projects, leading to long delays and cost overruns, affecting India's credibility as a partner, and comparing unfavourably with China in this aspect. Mechanisms for this would also need to be re-evaluated, as India seeks better impact and more effective third country projects with partners. The Asia Africa Growth Corridor project, with Japan, in some Asian and African countries is another example.

Even while there would be advantage to both US and India in taking a comprehensive, and not silos based, approach to the relationship, it will not be easy or smooth. Sectional and narrow corporate interests often drive US policy. The USA also expects its own domestic politics and compulsions-based decisions to be accepted by others, especially when it is helpful in other contexts. Reports in the media suggested that Secretary Pompeo told India's external affairs minister, during their phone call on 27 April 2019, that the USA expected India to be more cooperative on implementation of Iran sanctions since it had been very helpful in the context of Pulwama and its aftermath. Since the USA remains the dominant global political and economic power, its unilateral decisions have impact and consequences on all, and it has capacity to pressurize for its views and decisions to be accommodated or at least addressed in some way. Other countries do not have the same capacity or the same obviously coercive approach, although China has also applied or threatened selective trade and economic measures bilaterally to show displeasure with a particular country's approach related to Dalai Lama, Tibet, Xinjiang, Taiwan or Chinese dissidents.

Despite this, an integrated and comprehensive approach to the relationship will enable India to build additional constituencies of support and leverage. This is the more effective way, as Israel has shown by its example in dealing with US politics. Recently, 25 Congressmen wrote to President Trump asking him to delay decision on GSP withdrawal. The India Caucus is the largest single country caucus in both the House of Representatives and the Senate. There is broad bipartisan support at the moment for the India relationship. A significant number of Congressmen and Senators turned up to meet the Indian prime minister and to greet the audience when he addressed nearly 20,000 strong Indian origin community gathering in New York in 2014 and in San Jose in 2015. Several prominent US business groups and CEOs split off from the US–India Business Council (USIBC) to form US–India Strategic Partnership Forum (USISPF) when the former came under pressure from its parent the US Chamber of Commerce to be transactional and critical rather than strategic in its approach to the trade and investment relationship with India. In 2016, India was able to lobby US Congress to block the Obama Administration decision to supply additional F-16 aircraft to Pakistan.

Of course, as India may seek a comprehensive approach to the US relationship, same would apply to its other relationships in South Asia, Europe, West Asia, Africa, Latin America, with Russia, Japan, China, ASEAN, etc. The overall determinant of balance of cost and advantage would need to determine policy choices as we navigate a multi-polar world in flux with shifting weights.

Dealing with the Rising China

Sujit Dutta

Managing a stable relationship with China has been among the most challenging tasks in India's foreign policy ever since the founding of the People's Republic of China by the Communist Party in 1949. As the diplomatic relations between India and China enter the 70th year, this basic reality has not changed. Large territorial claims and occupation by China along the contested Himalayan border region, as well as constant tactical shifts in Chinese posture towards India, have led to deep mistrust of its strategic intentions. Repeated tensions over the territorial dispute, Chinese unwillingness to reach a fair-boundary settlement, deep encroachments across the Line of Actual Control (LAC) at different times as a way of exerting pressure, military build-up and alliance formation with Pakistan mean sustaining stability, cooperative ties and peace are a constant struggle. As China's power rises, the challenges too consistently increase. Growing Chinese economic and military presence in the Indian Ocean and in India's continental periphery are creating new challenges that need response if India's security is to be ensured. The geopolitical scope of India–China security and diplomatic interaction is widening. India needs a comprehensive new strategy and not mere ad hoc responses.

Relations with China, of course, have witnessed a degree of uneasy calm since the informal Modi–Xi summit in Wuhan in April 2018.

Officially the agreement to maintain peaceful and cooperative ties has been described optimistically as a 'reset' and is seen as a crucial step in mitigating the tensions that had built up ever since the assertive and conceited phase in Chinese foreign policy was initiated in the final years of Hu Jintao and through the Xi Jinping regimes—2009 onwards. The summit was seen by many as having turned the two countries away from the path of military escalation and tensions towards a modicum of stability and deeper engagement. India opened its doors further to Chinese imports after the summit even as China lowered some of the multiple barriers that it has placed on entry of Indian goods.

The process, however, has already received a setback as a result of China taking the matter of the abrogation by the India of Article 370 of the Constitution applicable to Jammu and Kashmir—a matter that is entirely within India's domestic jurisdiction—for an informal discussion at the UN Security Council on behalf of Pakistan in August 2019. The move followed only a few days after the External Affairs Minister of India S. Jaishankar was in Beijing to prepare for the proposed Second India–China informal summit and had already told the Chinese Foreign Minister Wang Yi that abrogation of Article 370 was an internal administrative matter and did not involve change in external orientation in India's Ladakh. The Chinese envoy at UN, however, impudently called India's action 'dangerous', 'unilateral' and 'not valid' and claimed it violated the 'peace and tranquillity' between the two countries and affected China's sovereignty.[1] This, of course, had an effect on the atmospherics leading up to the second summit and raises doubts about Xi's sincerity.

There were, of course, very good reasons for scepticism about where the Wuhan process was headed even before the latest Chinese interference in India's domestic affairs. There were serious doubts whether it would lead to any meaningful step towards the settlement of existing disputes, especially the territorial issue, or was it going to be yet another round of talks—this time at the highest level—with little impact on resolution of the crucial territorial dispute and finding a stable modus vivendi. For analogy, just recall the informal and formal talks over 6 years (1954–1960) between Prime Ministers Jawaharlal Nehru and Zhou Enlai that failed to resolve the growing differences over the boundary, Tibet and global issues. The process visibly collapsed as the Chinese forces first began to occupy large segments of Indian Territory and

---

[1] Press Trust of India, 'With No Outcome or Press Statement, UNSC Meet on Kashmir Deals Blow to Pakistan,' Report from New York, *Business Standard* (17 August 2019).

then attacked across the borders in 1962. In the post-Mao period, in four decades of intensive diplomatic talks that began in 1981, very little progress has been made to resolve the territorial dispute. China has simply dragged on the process. In the hope of giving the highest level political backing to the process in 2003, the two countries agreed to raise the level of talks from that of Foreign Secretaries to National Security Advisor–Vice Premier. In 22 rounds of talks till date between the two 'special representatives', the only achievement has been the Agreement on Political Parameters to settle the territorial dispute signed in 2005. But China set it aside soon after signing it. The Chinese Foreign Minister Jiang Jieshi himself questioned India's interpretation of its terms and China has not facilitated any progress on its implementation in the past 14 years. Instead, increasingly confident that its power is rising, China adopted an assertive stance on the Dalai Lama's presence and role in India, stepped up its claims on Arunachal, began visa denials to Indians from Arunachal and issued stapled visas to visitors from Jammu and Kashmir in order to please Pakistan. The entire 2009–2018 decade was tense as result of repeated Chinese violation of the LAC and diplomatic high-handedness.

Second, agreements with China are often tentative, in terms of both interpretation of its terms and implementation, dependent on the dynamics of both bilateral and global balance of power. Its current relatively moderate approach towards India is a direct result of two perceptions—one, India's assertive stance at Doklam indicating that it's not going to be pushed over by coercion, bullying and occupation of Bhutanese territory and risky escalation is to be avoided at this stage; two, a rapidly deteriorating relationship with the USA that increasingly resembles a New Cold War necessitates a modified regional stance. Such a stance may not last long and cannot be taken for granted. China, for example, has signed four major Confidence-Building Measures (CBM) documents with India—in 1993, 1996, 2005 and 2012 that prohibit deep intrusions across the Line of Actual Control (LAC). Yet the People's Liberation Army (PLA) was not restrained or deterred by these vital agreements from repeated deep encroachments, just as the 1954 *Panchsheel* Agreement, with 'mutual non-aggression' and respect for 'sovereignty' as its key principles, did not prevent it from invading India in 1962 in pursuit of its vast territorial claims and to 'teach India a lesson', as Deng Xiaoping bragged in Tokyo in 1979, drawing parallels with China's invasion of Vietnam that year.

Finally, China's assertive nationalism and geopolitical thinking also drives it towards tensions and disputes with neighbours unless they accept Beijing's principal demands. The extreme nationalism that drives China's foreign policy rests on the belief that it must incessantly accumulate power in order to protect its expanding 'core' interests and prevent domination by rival powers, such as the USA. Nationalism and a self-serving nationalist historiography also help sustain the Communist Party in power and legitimizes its authoritarian rule. Similarly, China's geopolitical and security thinking propels it to exercise strong influence and control over its non-Han periphery so that the core Han area can be secured. This has led China to claim and occupy Tibet, Xinjiang and Inner Mongolia, and thereafter try and exercise influence over the new set of states that now border China, including the trans-Himalayan states that constitute India's security periphery. Its large territorial claims on Indian border territories and provinces—Ladakh and Arunachal Pradesh—flow from its occupation of Tibet and Xinjiang, and are perceived as their security buffers. The neighbouring states, therefore, incessantly face the risk of Chinese pressure and coercive diplomacy if they are not seen as 'friendly'. Its diplomacy, trade, loans, military exports and ties are all aimed at achieving a subdued and controlled neighbourhood.

The deep intrusions of the PLA in the Ladakh sector in the 2013–2016 period and in Doklam in 2017 were examples of its high-handed 'assertive' policy against India and Bhutan—the two continental neighbours with whom it has not been able to resolve its borders so far. Similarly, China's territorial expansion in the maritime East Asia has already led to tensions with the USA, Japan, Vietnam and the Philippines. China's expanding power, coercive policies and growing sphere of influence are fundamentally changing the Asian security order, its institutions and its economic dynamics. Its impact on India's security now goes well beyond the Himalayan frontiers. Its deepening alliance with Pakistan, port- and base-building efforts in the small states around India and in the Indian Ocean, and its growing naval presence in the Indian Ocean mean India's security space and its diplomatic influence are being increasingly constricted and threatened. Going by China's statements and practice so far, Xi Jinping is unlikely to have made any commitment at Wuhan that would compromise China's expanding role, or its mercantile and military goals in the Indo-Pacific or continental Asia.

Faced with the expanding geopolitical ambitions—both on the Eurasian and on Indo-Pacific maritime domains—of an increasingly assertive and powerful China, India is, therefore, destined to face multiple challenges and threats. To cope with them and ensure a peaceful environment for its growth and development, India needs a grand strategy with three parallel and interrelated strands. First, it needs to evolve an engagement strategy with China that is based not on unilateral concessions but on reciprocity and mutual gain. Second, it requires to rapidly enhance its comprehensive power—economic, technological, military so that it can safeguard its interests. Third, it needs to forge strong comprehensive ties with its principal strategic partners—the USA, Japan, Russia, France. While India and China have found ways to avoid intense rivalry and war since 1962, China's assertive stance and expansionism have been a constant cause for serious concern. The prospects for stable relationship with China in the coming months and years in the context of Xi Jinping's 'China Dream' are at best uncertain and rest on what measures India takes internally and externally to ensure that a balance of power with China is maintained. The understanding reached at Wuhan and Mahabalipuram, and China's current relatively less abrasive tone is a tactical move to gain time so that it can focus on the growing dispute with the USA. India too must see it as such, speed up the development of its comprehensive power and make crucial foreign policy adjustments that will strengthen balance of power in Asia.

China's rising power and expanding geopolitical ambitions both on the Eurasian continental Indo-Pacific maritime domains are casting a long shadow on peace and stability in Asia, with a wide impact on India's security and foreign policy independence.

Xi's New Era

Soon after Xi was appointed the general secretary of the Communist Party of China (CPC) in November 2012, he declared China's intentions to step up efforts to become a modern, advanced and 'fully developed' nation by 2049 with a world-class military. This was the essence of his much publicized 'China Dream'. He also set a series of targets to be attained—an advanced industrial nation by 2025 under the Made in China programme launched in 2015 and a leading nation in technology by 2035, complete military modernization by 2020 and military mechanization and informationization by 2035. In 2013, he announced his grand vision of economic connectivity across Eurasia, Africa and the Indian Ocean overlap with large-scale and generously funded infrastructural projects. A series of Chinese-sponsored organizations and mechanisms have the potential to challenge and constrain American and European predominance in important international institutions and policy areas also constrain India. In his first summit with US President Obama in June 2013, Xi proposed the new concept as the basis for the future conduct of the bilateral relationship. According to State Councillor Yang Jiechi, the 'new type of great power relationship' will be defined by three essential features: the first is 'non-conflict and non-confrontation'; the second is 'mutual respect' of each other's different political systems and core interests and the third is 'win-win cooperation'.[2]

'Peaceful Rise' to 'Striving for Achievement'

Since the beginning of the post-Mao modernization, Chinese leaders on the whole have been conscious that the success of its ambitious reforms, modernization and rise as a great power require a peaceful and stable external environment. It led to the enunciation of the guiding policy of 'peace and development' under Deng Xiaoping's leadership, 'peaceful periphery' and 'harmonious world' under Jiang Zemin and 'peaceful rise/peaceful development' under Hu Jintao. In keeping with this guideline, the major priority of Chinese foreign policy from the early 1990s was to consolidate its territoriality and resolve outstanding territorial disputes on both land and sea, and to pacify external concerns of the perceived threat from a rising China. Accordingly, 'hiding one's capabilities and biding one's time' (taoguang yanghui) articulated by Deng Xiaoping became a defining guiding principle for Chinese diplomacy, especially under Xi's predecessor, President Hu Jintao. Under the 'peaceful development' phase, China substantially improved its relationship with the outside world, especially with countries in East Asia through its active diplomatic engagement, expanding trade and economic ties and increasing involvement in regional institutions.[3]

---

[2] Yang Jiechi, 'Implementing the Chinese Dream', *National Interest* (10 September 2013). Available at http://nationalinterest.org/commentary/implementing-the-chinese-dream-9026 (accessed on 29 November 2019).

[3] Jian Zhang, 'China's New Foreign Policy under Xi Jinping: Towards "Peaceful Rise 2.0?"', *Global Change, Peace & Security* 27, no. 1 (2015): 5–19. doi:10.1080/14781158.2015.993958. Also see David Shambaugh, 'China Engages Asia: Reshaping the Regional Order', *International Security* 29, no. 3 (winter 2004–2005): 64–99. On 'Peaceful Rise' see: Zheng Bijian, 'China's "Peaceful Rise" to Great-Power Status', *Foreign Affairs* 84, no. 5 (September/October 2005): 18–24. And also, Information Office of the State Council, 'China's Peaceful Development Road', *China Daily* (22 December 2005). Available at http://www.chinadaily.com.cn/english/doc/2005-12/22/content_505678.htm (accessed on 29 November 2019); Information Office of the State Council, 'China's Peaceful Development', *Xinhua News* (6 September 2011). Available at http://news.xinhuanet.com/english2010/china/2011-09/06/c_131102329.htm (accessed on 29 November 2019).

This consensus began to undergo a basic revision around 2009–2010 and especially after Xi became the new general secretary of the CPC and thereafter president of China. This is most clearly reflected in Xi's speech to the 3rd Politburo study session on China's peaceful development policy in January 2013. He told the gathering, 'We will keep walking on the peaceful development road, but we must not forsake our legitimate rights and interests, must not sacrifice core national interests'. On this basis, he further warned that 'no countries should expect us [China] to make a deal on our own core interests' and 'no countries should expect us [China] to swallow the bitter fruit that undermines our sovereignty, security, and development interests'.[4]

Scholar Jian Zhang captures the essence of this significance in China's approach:

> While protecting national interests is a default foreign policy objective of all countries, including China, Xi's statement was the first time that the Chinese leadership linked the issue to China's peaceful development policy in such a striking manner. The statements showed that protecting China's core national interests was given equal and even greater importance than 'peaceful development' as the fundamental principle of China's foreign policy. To a certain extent, Xi's statements imply that China would not sacrifice its core national interests, however defined, for the sake of maintaining peace.[5]

In keeping with his vision, in his address to the People's Liberation Army's (PLA) delegation to the National People's Congress in early 2014, Xi called for the Chinese military to accelerate its efforts of military modernization and improve its capabilities of fighting and winning wars, stating that 'we long for peace dearly, but at any time and

---

[4] Xi Jinping *zai zhonggong zhongyang zhengzhiju di san ci jiti xuexi shi qiangdiao genghao tongchou guonei guoji liangge daju, hangshi zou heping fazhan daolu de jichu* [Xi Jinping stressed at the 3rd study session of the politburo the need for coordinating domestic and international strategic situation, building a solid foundation for walking on the peaceful development road], *People's Daily* (30 January 2013); cited in Jian Zhang, 'China's New Foreign Policy under Xi Jinping'. For an intellectual justification of the new line, see Yan Xuetong, 'From Keeping a Low Profile to Striving for Achievement', *Chinese Journal of International Politics* 7, no. 2 (2014): 153–184.

The transition towards the new policy line is anticipated and analysed in Bonnie S. Glaser and Evan S. Medeiros, 'The Changing Ecology of Foreign Policy-Making in China: The Ascension and Demise of the Theory of "Peaceful Rise"', *China Quarterly* 190 (2007): 291–310.

[5] Jian Zhang, 'China's New Foreign Policy under Xi Jinping'; Xi Jinping', op, cit.

under any circumstances, we will not give up defending our legitimate national interests and rights, and will not sacrifice our core national interests'.[6]

Great Power Status and Core Interests

The major goal in Xi Jinping's China Dream is to assert China's status as a great power equal to the USA. This was first articulated by Hu Jintao in his summit with President Obama in 2010, when he proposed 'a special type of great power relations' between the USA and China in which each would recognize and respect the other's 'core interests'. The new period was, therefore, seen as an era of opportunity for China in which the strategic environment was favourable for seizing the moment, pursuing its 'core' interests aggressively and to discard the restraint Deng had called for during its rise. China had risen, Xi argued, and others agreed. The peaceful rise discourse has been replaced by a great power discourse of status, claims and assertion of power and intent. The Communist Party's hard-line newspaper *Global Times* bluntly made the point that China's comprehensive national power has reached a point where it is time 'to actively get something done'.

Xi made special great power relations a focus of his diplomacy with the USA, raising it several times with Obama for his endorsement, including at their summit in 2013. The proposal has not been accepted by either Obama or Trump. The high strategic and diplomatic costs of such an acceptance obviously have prevented Washington from going down that path. It would have potentially involved, for example, acquiescence to China's territorial occupation of the South China Sea islets and base building, its forcible takeover of Taiwan. That is what China expects from other states as well—big and small—status recognition as a great power and respect for its subjectively defined 'core interests', even if this violates the 'core interests' of others, such as Vietnam and the Philippines in the South China Sea, or India in Jammu and Kashmir and Arunachal Pradesh. Xi's attempt to replicate a new relationship with the USA that entailed recognition of each other's sovereignty claims, spheres of influence and duopoly, would have significantly advanced China's strategic interests. It would have gradually marginalized the

---

[6] Xi Jinping *qiangdiao qiangjun yu hanwei 'hexin liyi'* [Xi Jinping emphasizes building up a strong military and protecting 'core interests'], BBC Chinese net (2014). Available at http://www.bbc.co.uk/zhongwen/simp/china/2014/03/140312_xi_jinping_core_interests (accessed on 4 December 2019), cited in Jian Zhang, 'China's New Foreign Policy under Xi Jinping'.

USA in Asia since it involved acceptance of Chinese large territorial claims in East and South China Seas and its domination of its sea lines of communications (SLOCs) within what it calls the 'first islands chain' or the near seas. Such an arrangement would have immediately undermined the existing balance of power and threatened the security and sovereignty of Japan, South East Asian states and India. The ongoing face-off with the USA on trade, technology and security issues indicates that Xi is not willing to abandon his goal of attaining predominance in East Asia and increasingly globally. As an astute observer of China's rise comments:

> The true bearing of its great aspirations is increasingly clear: to fulfil them, China must become the most powerful country in Asia by far, and attain the power to deter other protagonists by force. The chance that its peaceful rise will continue is therefore small. Either China's growth will run into trouble or it will become harder to maintain the peace.[7]

China's vision clearly is at odds with the multi-polar vision of India, Japan, Russia, France and other major states, such as Brazil and Germany. The fact that China has systematically opposed the inclusion of India and Japan as permanent members of the UN Security Council is a good indicator that China does not want such multi-polarity that raises the status of those it perceives as potential rivals. China has instead focused on building alternative global and regional institutions where its policies would have a sway. These include the Shanghai Cooperation Organisation, the Asian Infrastructure Investment Bank, the BRICS New Development Bank—in all of which India is a member.

One Belt and One Road

The centrepiece of China's global economic outreach under Xi is his 'One Belt, One Road' (OBOR) initiative announced in 2013, and renamed as the Belt and Road Initiative (BRI) for the international audience to make it appear benign. It brings together and provides strategic direction to Chinese state-owned companies engaged in road, railway, port and digital communication building across China's Eurasian continental periphery and the sea lanes across the Indo-Pacific leading up to Europe and Africa. It is a grand plan to intertwine its near and outer

---

[7] Jonathan Holsag, 'The Smart Revisionist', *Survival: Global Politics and Strategy*, p. 56: 95–116. doi:10.1080/00396338.2014.962802. Also see, Oriana Mastro, 'Why Chinese Assertiveness Is Here to Stay', *The Washington Quarterly* (2015 Winter).

periphery of states with the Chinese economy and thereby bring them under Beijing's political and military influence. At the centre of OBOR is the infrastructure building financed by China in developing Asia, Africa, Latin America as well as East and South Europe. The projects facilitate Chinese exports and jobs through a system of tied loans to countries that are desperate for development finance but are unable to secure it from the World Bank, Asian Development Bank (ADB) and international banks because of their strict conditionalities. China imposes no such apparent conditions. It is a deal in which China uses its large foreign reserves to advance loans at commercial rates through its state-owned development banks such as to fund infrastructure or power projects to be constructed by Chinese firms which then import construction material and manpower for undertaking the projects. According to Xi, investments in BRI could go up to a staggering 1 trillion dollars. Some 900 projects are currently under way under the BRI with 80 per cent of the contracts awarded to Chinese enterprises.

BRI is, therefore, a key geo-strategic project in building up parallel structures. The primary goal is to create novel Eurasian transport and trade infrastructures. The second step would be removing barriers to free trade. The Maritime Silk Road initiative serves the diversification of Chinese trade routes and an expansion of China's geo-strategic power. Alongside security concerns in the neighbouring regions, South East, South and Central Asia, energy interests, the opening of new markets and lower transportation costs in foreign trade with Europe all play a role for China. Some of the BRI projects may not be economically viable and others face high political risks. They have been criticized for those reasons by some Chinese bankers and academics. Xi, however, does not see them in purely economic terms, but as strategic assets with long-term pay-offs. If the countries are unable to pay back, the projects and other collaterals such as ports, mines, oil and gas fields, power stations, telecommunications, agricultural land, would come under Chinese control, as in the infamous case of the Chinese built Hambantota port in Sri Lanka. China's growing economic role would mean the Renminbi would become an alternative currency in these countries. The railway gauges, 5G networks and satellite navigation systems would be standardized along Chinese requirements by its companies, creating long-term dependence for equipment, management, know-how and expertise from China.

Port building is the focus of China's 'Maritime Silk Road' component of BRI. Chinese companies currently manage and operate over 70 terminals and ports along the maritime trade routes across the world. Some of these, such as Gwadar in Pakistan, have been regularly visited by the PLA Navy and are interested in a base facility near it. It already has access to the Karachi port. The PLA has grand plans to protect China's sea lines through which its 4.5 trillion-dollar trade flows. It needs access to ports such as Hambantota, Gwadar, Kyaukpyu in Myanmar and others in the vast Indo-Pacific region. The PLA has also acquired its first overseas base in Djibouti in the Indian Ocean. The Chinese military's expanding role and reach are intrinsically interconnected with the vision of BRI. China has now begun to move rapidly towards the next generation of projects focusing on the digital economy, telecommunications, 5G, operation of stock markets and satellite earth stations.

India has opposed the BRI for not being transparent in its terms and conditions, for not respecting sovereignty of other states and for creating dependencies and driving recipient countries into debt. The China–Pakistan Economic Corridor (CPEC), a flagship project under BRI, violates its sovereignty as it traverses through Pakistan's illegally occupied part of Jammu and Kashmir. CPEC is among the most important segments of the BRI, connecting China's land-locked western region to the Indian Ocean and the oil resources of West Asia. China has promised to invest over 60 billion dollars in building rail and road corridors, high-speed digital networks, satellite navigations systems, industrial zones and cities. How a financially strapped Pakistan would finance its large loan repayments to China is now an open question, and many of the projects have been cancelled or stalled. But one clear effect of CPEC has been to make Pakistan a dependent state of China with significant part of its economy, and therefore its foreign policy, under Chinese influence. The BRI's reach into Pakistan, Sri Lanka, Nepal, Myanmar and the Maldives—all developing and fragile states that border India—has large economic, political and strategic implications. The ports built by Chinese state-controlled corporations in the Indian Ocean (in Sri Lanka, Burma, Bangladesh and Pakistan) could serve as important transport hubs. It raises the costs of maintaining India's vital security interests and positive influence in the region. A new and robust approach for regional integration, partnership and security amidst dramatically rising Chinese influence is clearly necessary.

Military Build-Up

China's 2019 Defence White Paper released on 24 July claims that '[a] strong military of China is a staunch force for world peace, stability, and the building of a community with a shared future for mankind.'

Shorn of this public posture, what stands out is the rapid build-up and reorganization of the PLA undertaken since Xi's rise to power, with the Navy, Air Force and Rocket Forces receiving prominence. It is easily one of the most important peacetime military modernizations undertaken by any country since the end of the Cold War and is reminiscent of the German militarization of the 1920s and 1930s. With three decades of high-speed military build-up, China has emerged as the second largest military power in the world, overtaking Russia, Japan, France, Britain and India. According to SIPRI, China's military expenditure increased by 396 per cent in the period 1995–2015, as compared to only 87 per cent by India. It also has the world's fastest growing navy among all the major powers. The 2015 Chinese Defence White Paper had already indicated a major shift in strategic thinking from land to sea and China's changing maritime goals. It said: 'The traditional mentality that land outweighs sea must be abandoned, and great importance has to be attached to managing the seas and oceans and protecting maritime rights and interests.' The Chinese navy, it stated, should protect 'the security of sea lanes of communication and overseas interests'. Its steady military seizure of South China Sea islets from Vietnam and the Philippines since Xi rose to power in 2012 and the high-speed construction of an air and naval base on occupied islets has sent shock waves through East Asia, catching the USA off guard.

The 2019 White Paper states: 'One of the missions of China's armed forces is to effectively protect the security and legitimate rights and interests of overseas Chinese people, organizations and institutions.' In keeping with this expanding overseas interest, in August 2017, it acquired PLA's first overseas military base, the 'PLA Djibouti Support Base' at a crucial location in the Indian Ocean trade route. The White Paper states that additional 'overseas logistical facilities' are being developed. Chinese state-owned firms are, for example, constructing or managing 'dual use' ports—to which both China's ships and naval vessels have access—across the Indo-Pacific, Africa and the Mediterranean and Europe. The 2019 White Paper noted that the PLAN

> in line with the strategic requirements of near seas defense and far seas protection … is speeding up the transition of its tasks from defense on the near seas to protection missions on the far seas, and improving its capabilities for strategic deterrence and counterattack, maritime maneuver operations, maritime joint operations, comprehensive defense, and integrated support, so as to build a strong and modernized naval force.

The Indian Naval Chief Admiral Karambir Singh has expressed his concern regarding China's rapid construction of a blue-water navy. He said:

> Lot of resources have been shifted from other arms to the PLA Navy, obviously in line with their intention to become a global power. We have to watch it carefully and see how we can respond within our budget and the constraints that we have.

'We require long-term fiscal support to build a Navy; that is the only way we can plan. And, this has been my constant refrain.'[8] But that won't be easy. India's defence expenditure at $43 billion in 2019–2020 was one-fourth that of China's. Much of this would go for pay and allowances, with little left for modernization, including that of the Navy.

China's military expenditure has grown faster than its GDP for many years. In 2019, it was raised by 7.5 per cent to $177.61 billion, which is several times higher than that of Russia, Japan, France, Britain and India. Years of high military spending powered by high economic growth are starting to manifest themselves in new defence technologies. Beijing has made visible strides in its aviation, naval, cyber and missile defence capabilities. The 2019 White Paper stated that 'the national security issues facing China encompass far more subjects, extend over a greater range, and cover a longer time span than at any time in the country's history'. These include four 'critical domains' and corresponding forces: 'seas and oceans, outer space, cyberspace, and nuclear ....'

Whether it be making territorial claims in the South China Sea or opening up its first overseas military base in Djibouti, China is starting to exert military influence in its near abroad and beyond. With its mounting global economic interests, China is likely to increasingly rely on military force to safeguard those interests. In the words of an expert on the Chinese military:

> In key areas of its latest Defense White Paper, as well as in key domains, we are witnessing an increasingly assertive China increasingly determined to forcefully pursue its own interests on its own terms. Observers should look elsewhere for the latest insights on the specifics of PLA development, but no one should miss the ambition, assertiveness, and resolve permeating this official policy document. Real and consequential actions will follow from these sometimes

---

[8] See the *Times of India* (25 July 2019).

vague but often forceful statements. Prepare for trouble ahead: we have been warned.[9]

China is expanding its power and influence on a grand scale across land and sea, marrying its economic and military interests just as the European imperial powers had done in the 19th century and the USA did in the 20th century. Globalization has a distinct geopolitical meaning for Xi's China. However, for the first time in four decades, China does not enjoy a cozy relationship with the USA. In fact, the relationship has soured over trade, technology, steady territorial expansion and robust military build-up that the USA now sees a security threat.

Dilemmas in India's Approach

Indian analysis of relations with China and the security challenges China poses has for long been focused on the territorial dispute, tensions along the Himalayan frontier, the Sino-Pak alliance and the need for engagement to keep differences from boiling over. While India must continue to monitor these key security concerns since they remain alive and relevant, such a limited approach to China no longer suffices to deal with the realities of its growing regional and global security impact. While India has so far consciously avoided being drawn into a strategic rivalry or arms race with China, a quiet and limited strategic competition has always existed ever since China occupied Tibet in 1950–1951 and began to threaten India's security. Yet till China began its globalization, the geopolitical scope of the strategic competition was limited to the Himalayan frontier and coping with many adverse effects of China–Pakistan alliance.

The scope of that competition, however, has expanded into the wider Indian neighbourhood, the maritime domain of the Indian Ocean, and the economic and digital domains over the past decade. China continues to rapidly modernize its military in its quest to become a great power and build a world-class military that can fight and win wars, it is investing in strategic corridors that connect its inland provinces to the Indian Ocean, setting up military bases and builds large naval forces to protect its trade and investments. All this has been taking place in peacetime well before its relations began to deteriorate with the USA.

---

[9] Andrew S Erickson, 'China's Defense White Paper Means Only One Thing: Trouble Ahead', *National Interest* (29 July 2019).

India's post-Cold War détente with China was constructed on mutually agreed commitment to peaceful coexistence, engagement, normalizing political ties, military CBMs and that force would not be used to settle existing disputes. India did not fully accept Deng's formula of 'setting aside differences and focusing on common areas of interest' and wanted a two-track approach—engagement and parallel talks to resolve the territorial dispute. In this period, trade ties have grown manifold, four CBM agreements are in place to ensure differences do not escalate and military conflict does not occur (1993, 1996, 2005 and 2012), several rounds of Foreign Secretary-level talks to resolve the territorial dispute were upgraded to Special Representative or Vice Minister–NSA-level talks in 2003 during the Vajpayee–Hu Jintao summit. Even after 22 rounds of SR level talks, the goal of resolving the territorial dispute or even the clarification of the Line of Actual Control (LAC) has not been attained. The Chinese did not want to exchange the maps of the Western and Eastern sectors after the Central sector maps were exchanged in 1999. The LAC, therefore, remained prone to intrusions as it was understood differently in several key areas by the two sides. The PLA's deep intrusions in Ladakh, between 2013 and 2016, were a logical outcome of Xi's assertive stance.

The resultant 'engagement'-dominated relationship has suffered from several weaknesses. One, the parallel track of dispute resolution has been systematically stymied by the Chinese side, and instead of the two-track approach it has become a one-track approach preferred by the Chinese and as originally desired by Deng. Two, the economic side of the engagement has been entirely unequal and one-sided year after year, with India opening its markets for Chinese imports and China keeping its markets closed behind a wall of opaque restrictions. Even as trade climbed to $95 billion in 2018–2019, China's trade surplus rose to over $55 billion. Three, China's economic, technological and military power has grown rapidly in this three-decade period without an adequate Indian response. Deep power asymmetries have a direct impact on bargaining and negotiations on all bilateral issues and most crucially territorial negotiations. Its persistence has derailed prospects of a stable relationship. Finally, as China's power has grown, its trade, investment, communications, military ties have expanded all around India both on land and sea. The 'string of pearls'—originally an American conception about China building a series of naval outposts/bases in the Indian Ocean and around India to secure its trade, resource supplies, maritime and strategic interests is already in an advanced stage of being realized.

The internal and external balancing that is essential for ensuring equal relations did not get the policy attention of the Indian political and foreign policy elite from the very beginning of post-Independence diplomacy and had disastrous consequences. It was not put in place even in the new post-Cold War strategic context as India began its fresh engagement with China. The leverages to strengthen India's bargaining strength across a host of issue remained neglected. In such a context, stable relations could not emerge. In fact, over the past three decades, the Chinese have blown cold and hot depending on the global strategic balance and its ties with the USA. Whenever ties with the USA have been tenuous—as in 1989–1992 post-Tiananmen period, or the Trump push back phase that began in 2018—Beijing has courted India, softened its stance and talked about cooperation and peace. When ties with the USA have been favourable, China has hardened its position. Following the 1998 Indian nuclear tests, as India's relations with the US deteriorated over sanctions, China arrogantly demanded India to give up its nuclear option and stalled high-level diplomatic talks for over a year. The talks resumed in 1999 after Indo-US nuclear talks began. Ties significantly improved over the next few years and in 2005 the Agreement on the Political Parameters and Guiding Principles for Settling the Boundary Question as well as new CBM agreements were signed. Relations significantly became turbulent and difficult through the 2009–2018 period as China's power rapidly grew and an assertive foreign policy was launched. It abrasively protested Indian leaders' visits to Arunachal Pradesh and the Dalai Lama's visit to the Buddhist monastery in Tawang, and the PLA deeply encroached across the LAC in Depsang and Chumur in Ladakh. A similar PLA encroachment in Doklam, in Bhutan near the India–Bhutan–Tibet tri-junction led to a military stand-off with the Indian Army that lasted 72 days. Similarly, it relented on listing Hafiz Sayeed as a global terrorist at the United Nations—after singularly stalling it for a decade—under pressure from all other leading powers and wide support for India's position.

The following can therefore be concluded:

- High-level political and diplomatic dialogues have characterized India–China engagement since External Affairs Minister Vajpayee's visit to China and his meeting with Deng Xiaoping in February 1979. The Modi–Xi informal dialogue continued that engagement. There has been overall peace. Yet, little progress has been made to resolve the boundary question. Uncertainty and strategic competition are discernible.
- China continues to claim large populated areas such as the entire province of Arunachal Pradesh, calling the territory that it has never

controlled or administered in history as 'South Tibet', and provocatively giving new Chinese names to some of the areas.
- It is engaged in strategic alliance building with Pakistan and has given complete support to the regime at a time when the Pakistani military was orchestrating some of the most serious terror attacks against India by the Lashkar-e-Taiba and Jaish-e-Mohammed any of which could have escalated to a war. It continues
- It is engaged in port building in Gwadar and a military base is planned, port building in Hambantota with potential Chinese naval access, island buying in the Maldives with potential base facilities, the port construction in Kyaukpiu, Myanmar in the Bay of Bengal and expanding the presence of the PLA Navy in the Indian Ocean. These steps are rapidly changing the security environment and are a cause for concern.
- It repeatedly obstructed attempts by India and others at the UN to blacklist the Jaish-e-Mohammed and its terrorist leader Masood Azhar, and continues to prevent India's entry into the Nuclear Suppliers Group even after the Wuhan summit.
- Its grand plan 'One Belt One Road' aims to construct trade routes across the Eurasian land mass and in the Indo-Pacific and redirect them towards the Chinese heartland. OBOR is also leading to a series of Chinese dependencies such as Pakistan, Tajikistan, Cambodia and Laos, with wide economic, political and strategic ramifications. It has driven Sri Lanka, the Maldives and Pakistan into unsustainable debt.
- It has constructed a military base at the entrance of the Indian Ocean and on militarily seized islets of the South China Sea and plans to send its aircraft carriers under construction regularly into the Indian Ocean.
- It attempted to internationalize India's abrogation of Article 370, and entirely internal matter, at the behest of Pakistan in August 2019. Although the move failed and the UNSC only met informally and did not issue any statement on the matter, the Chinese provocative action and interference cast a shadow on the Modi–Xi talks in October 2019. An authoritarian state that regularly violates human rights in the mainland, Tibet, Xinjiang and Hong Kong, ironically, raised the issue of human rights in Jammu and Kashmir.

The Wuhan Reset

The informal summit at Wuhan between Prime Minister Modi and Chinese President Xi Jinping in April 2018 was received positively by the people in India. It had become necessary to de-escalate the tensions that had steadily climbed as a result of China's assertive military posture and diplomacy in Xi's first term as China's president that resulted in a series of military confrontations along the Himalayan border region that began in 2013 and reached their peak at Doklam in the India–Bhutan–China un-demarcated tri-junction at the Sikkim border in June 2017. Assessing the Summit, Prime Minister Modi told an international gathering at Singapore in June 2018:

> In April, a two-day informal summit with President Xi helped to cement our understanding that strong and stable relations between our two nations are an important factor for global peace and progress. I firmly believe that Asia and the world will have a better future when India and China work together in trust and confidence, sensitive to each other's interests.[10]

A leading Chinese expert on the Indian Ocean region and on China's strategy in the region, Cuiping Zhu argues that India must accept the reality of China's rise. India cannot keep China outside the sub-continent. Instead, it should turn China's economic strength into its own advantage. India needs to abandon the idea of rejecting Chinese investment, and leverage China's economic strength to accelerate India's economic growth. Delhi should also stop complaining about China's large-scale investment projects in its neighbouring states such as Pakistan, Sri Lanka and Myanmar. Zhu also claims that India could pursue a partnership with China to undermine US hegemony in the Indian Ocean. Such an assumption indicates a deeply flawed understanding that Chinese elites have of India. India is not against China's development and rise but is deeply concerned about the path and tenor that 'rise' has taken, and the hegemonic and coercive effects of Xi's China dream. As David Brewster rightly observes: 'The argument that India should accept the material benefits from China in some sort of nominally equal (but actually 'big brother') relationship in South Asia and the Indian Ocean fails to understand that India could never accept such as status in its own neighbourhood.'[11]

Based on the experience so far, would it be prudent to believe that in the coming years India and China 'can jointly work towards global peace'? Indeed, the very idea of what constitutes 'global peace' is

---

[10] See Prime Minister Narendra Modi's Keynote Address at the Shangri-La Dialogue, Singapore (1 June 2018).

[11] David Brewster, 'Book Review of Cuiping Zhu: India's Ocean: Can China and India Coexist?' *Journal of the Indian Ocean Region* (2018): 2. doi:10.1080/19480881.2018.1473088

understood very differently by India and China. As maritime affairs scholar James Holmes candidly observes:

> Totalitarians excel at defending the indefensible through euphemism. The more candid among them confess that diplomacy is warfare through alternative means. This is ground truth.... Sure, Beijing is sincere about its love for peace. But it defines peace as others' submitting meekly to the (Communist) Party's demands, however unjust or unlawful.[12]

There is a fundamental tension between China's profession and desire for a peaceful security environment and its 'peaceful rise' theory flowing from its focus on modernization and globalization on the one hand, and the Communist regime's nationalist, irredentist and expansive agenda rooted in the imagined imperial domain of the Qing dynasty and Xi's vision of global power. Just as the rapid growth through globalization and 'peaceful development' is seen as crucial for China's modernization and rise, the pursuit of its growing 'core' national interest agenda is seen crucial for the legitimacy of the Communist Party's rule and its nationalist credentials. Restoration of sovereignty over the so-called lost territories appears to have become the CPC instrument for mobilizing the cadres, the growing middle class and the elites, even though much of the historiography of such claims is singularly unidimensional and self-serving, and widely disruptive.

Conclusion

It is difficult to argue that India–China relations will be significantly determined by what is agreed at Wuhan or its follow-up summit in Mahabalipuram. It won't. Instead it will be determined by whether Xi Jinping is able to get away by using mercantilism and coercive power as his principle instruments to dominate Asia, including India. If he is able, then the chances that he will reach a compromise with India to resolve problems and restrain China's claims, ambitions and neocolonial instruments would be minimal. Alternatively, he can be restrained—first by his own party seniors who can see the dangers that Xi Jinping's assertive policies, bravado and a new Cold War poses for China; second, by the pushback against China's policies that the USA has initiated, and finally, by India building its capabilities to balance

---

[12] James Holmes, 'Don't Believe China's Commitment to Peace and Stability', *National Interest* (7 August 2019).

China. While there are reports about some in the Chinese political and intellectual hierarchy not being too happy with Xi's policies and postures that have led to a confrontation with the USA, it is difficult to see at this point any open revolt against or criticism of Xi.

India has for too long stuck to the mantra of 'strategic autonomy' while waving its good intentions and soft power. But 'autonomy' whose essence is an independent foreign policy cannot be ensured without strong investments in scientific research, economic and military power. China's rising power has already constricted India's space for diplomatic manoeuvre in South and South East Asia where China is building the BRI corridors and port/naval outposts. India needs to step up its economic, trade and military profile. It requires a more assertive policy towards China based on strict reciprocity, a more equal economic relationship and deepening strategic and techno-economic ties with its leading partners—the USA, Japan, Russia and France. In Asia, India would have to step up its economic and other ties with South Korea, Vietnam, Indonesia, Taiwan and Mongolia—states that are concerned about China's expansive territorial and security policies and want India to play a more significant role in sustaining peace in Asia. China's rise under Xi is casting long shadow over the Asian order and turbulent times lie ahead.

Japan and India
Partners in Progress

Deepa Gopalan Wadhwa

In the turbulent churn of geopolitics and strategic alignments in the world today, the India–Japan relationship stands apart as an exemplar of stability. The relationship has evolved in under two short decades, from a benign status to a 'Special Strategic and Global Partnership', marked by annual prime ministerial-level summit meetings which underscore the importance attached by both sides to sustaining and deepening the relationship. The steadily widening areas of cooperation and dialogue are an acknowledgement of the symbiotic need of both countries to work together for bilateral benefit and shared strategic objectives.

On the bilateral front, there are clear structural complementarities between the economies and demographics of the two countries, bound ideologically as democracies, with similar threat perceptions in their sub-regions and shared aspirations for a greater role in world affairs. On the strategic front, the pluridimensionality of the thrust areas, as well as the rapid pace of progress of the engagement, has made the relationship one of the most closely watched in the Indo-Pacific region dealing with the rise of China which seeks to alter not only the balance of power but also rules of international engagement through its military and economic heft. The belief is that the India–Japan relationship could offer an alternate option for advancing peace and prosperity within an open, transparent, rule-based regional order.

For an understanding of how the relationship between India and Japan, which form book ends of continental Asia, reached this point of congruence, we need to delve a bit into recent history, elaborate the elements of the often-cited transformative potential and convergences, and study priority areas of cooperation which could help realize the respective ambitions of both countries.

History

There is a broad-based positive perception of each other at the popular level in both countries deriving from relatively lesser known cultural and historical ties which exist despite the distant geographies. There are many strands of common heritage which bind the two and await greater discovery, such as the journey of Buddhism from India, how Hindu gods stand alongside Shinto and Buddhist deities in the Japanese pantheon, the Indian connection of the phonetic Hiragana script and religious practices and beliefs on which values systems came to be based.

Empirical evidence of historical contacts date, for most part, from the era of European mercantilism from which vestiges of traded commodities such as copper from Japan, and textiles and spices from India validate the indirect contacts between the two civilizations. These contacts took on a more direct form post the Meiji Restoration of 1868, and the subsequent Japanese outreach to European and colonial powers in Asia, such as the British in India. The last decade of the 19th century witnessed an increase in contacts due to direct shipping links which also carried luminaries such as Sir Jamsetji Tata and Swami Vivekananda to the shores and experiences of Japan.

The foundation of modern-day perceptions of each other was laid in the early decades of the 20th century, which was a period of historic twists and turns in our respective national destinies. As Indians felt emboldened to assert their demand for independence from the British, Japan was experiencing a period of unprecedented industrialization and expeditionary militarism, which ended for the latter in devastation and humiliating defeat in the Second World War. Those years saw Indian nationalist leaders such as Rash Behari Bose and Netaji Subhas Chandra Bose operate from Japan as fugitives from British India and draw the Japanese political establishment into the struggle for Indian Independence. In the narrative of some of the right wing in Japan, the failed INA–Japanese Imphal campaign of 1944, paradoxically, accelerated the withdrawal of the British from India.

The point of highlighting these early contacts between India and Japan is that they are little known, and the widespread perception is that the current bilateral relationship is almost entirely a consequence of the realignments post the Cold War and India's own economic and political choices by which we set aside old suspicions and improved relations with the USA and other Western powers, including Japan, as a close ally of the USA. While the reality is that the first decade and a half after the end of the Second World War for Japan and Indian Independence was a period high on symbolism and special gestures between the two countries to mark the beginnings of a new relationship marked by warmth and friendship. In April 1947, Prime Minister (PM) Nehru welcomed Japan to the Asian Relations Conference despite it still being under foreign occupation of the Allied Powers. In 1951, he decided against participating in the San Francisco Peace Conference because he considered the process as imposing limits on Japan's sovereignty, and India separately signed a peace treaty with Japan establishing relations in 1952. This was soon followed by exchanges of visits between the PMs of the two countries in 1957. PM Shinzo Abe's grandfather's, Nobusuke Kishi, visit resulted in India becoming the first recipient of Japanese yen loans in 1958. Visits by President Rajendra Prasad and Crown Prince Akihito followed in 1958 and 1960. Japanese official development assistance (ODA) provided the ballast for the relationship in the years to follow when the institution of the Cold War placed the two countries in opposing camps and the relationship which had started off so well plateaued to one of benign status.

Reset in Relations

India–Japan relations underwent a qualitative change at the dawn of the 21st century. The preceding two years were the nadir of the relationship with Japan's harsh reaction to our 1998 nuclear tests, when they took a harsher line than other Western powers, withdrawing ODA and even reaching out to Pakistan to dissuade them from testing with the bait of helping them raise the Kashmir issue in multilateral fora! The change in relations was led by PM Yoshiro Mori who believed that a reset in relations was required and undertook a visit to India in August 2000, during which the India–Japan Global Partnership was launched. In taking the initiative, he was no doubt conscious of growing closeness in India–US relations, as well as foreseeing the threats from the rising economic and military might of China. PM Atal Bihari Vajpayee reciprocated with a visit the following year for the 50th anniversary of the establishment of diplomatic relations.

These visits in quick succession prepared the ground for an examination of the growing bilateral congruence and the converging regional and global interests of the two countries. There is no doubt that considerations such as India's growing economic clout and lure of its market, and Japan's financial and technological strengths were part of the calculus. The visit of PM Junichiro Koizumi in April 2005, at the invitation of the UPA leadership, set in motion the establishment of a comprehensive, multi-layered, architecture of exchanges which continues to expand in form and substance. During the following year, the relationship was broadened to a 'Strategic and Global Partnership' with annualized prime ministerial meetings, which India hitherto only had only with Russia, and Japan with no other country. The rapid and purposeful ratcheting of engagement within a few, short years, made it one of the foremost successes of our foreign policy.

Political Convergence

In analysing the drivers of the relationship, one needs to start with convergences in the political sphere, which continue to be relevant. While the reset had its beginnings during the NDA under PM Atal Bihari Vajpayee, the successor government of the UPA continued to strengthen and elevate the relationship to an even higher plane with defence and security dimensions, recognizing the growing strategic relevance of the relationship in the light of changes taking place in the region. Thus, it was no surprise that PM Modi, who had visited Japan twice as chief minister of Gujarat, decided on Japan as his first official bilateral visit, outside South Asia, after the NDA victory in the 2014 polls. The changes in governments in Japan from the Liberal Democratic Party lead coalition to the Democratic Party Japan in 2009 had also seen a seamless continuum in the relationship which is a pointer to bipartisan support across political parties in both countries to strong India–Japan ties. The absence of any baggage of history or territorial disputes and a mutual commitment to democracy and its attendant institutions and values are other factors which anchor the relationship.

Similar sentiments have encouraged Japan, once firmly ensconced in the Western Group in multilateral institutions, and India, a leading player in developing country groupings such as G77 and NAM, to recognize the changing priorities of global discourse and see the merit in working together in areas such as UN Security Council reforms, counterterrorism, cybersecurity and climate change.

The perception of the special nature of the bilateral relationship in a world beset with ever-changing equations has percolated down to remarkable goodwill for each other at the popular level. This is manifest in growing contacts between parliamentarians, political personalities and think tanks, prodded no doubt, by good relations between the formal establishments. The realization of the mutuality of interests is also no longer confined to national capitals as can be seen by growing of exchanges between Indian states and Japanese prefectures and partnership agreements signed between Gujarat–Hyogo, Andhra Pradesh–Toyama, Maharashtra–Wakayama, Kerala–Sanin region, Fukuoka–Delhi, Tamil Nadu–Kanagawa and Karnataka–Mie.

Strategic Convergence

What has caught international attention is the growing strategic convergence between the two countries. In the new phase of our relationship, the focus is not only on the bilateral but, as the moniker strategic and Global Partnership denotes, also on converging interests and the desire of both to take on regional and global responsibilities. Bilaterally, strategic convergence has been manifest in the growing defence and security relationship, the agreement on cooperation in the peaceful uses of nuclear energy, MOU on space research with dialogues on cooperation in outer space, counterterrorism and cybersecurity. Japan has also supported India's full accession to international arms' export control regimes, including the Nuclear Suppliers Group.

Starting from the negligible due to Japan's self-imposed restraints, defence cooperation has taken off since the 2005 PM Koizumi–Manmohan Singh's summit, followed by the visit of then *Raksha Mantri* [Defence Minister] Pranab Mukherjee in 2006, during which a menu of bilateral dialogues, contacts and visits led by the defence ministers themselves was established. This was followed by an MOU on cooperation between Coast Guards and a Joint Declaration on Security Cooperation during the PM's Summit of 2008—the second such declaration signed by Japan outside the US alliance. The year 2009 saw the adoption of an action plan to advance security cooperation, which went beyond bilateral ties to provide a blueprint for regional strategic cooperation covering information exchange and policy coordination of security issues in the Asia-Pacific region, and in 2014 a Memorandum on Defence Cooperation and Exchanges was signed during PM Modi's visit. Other agreements marking the deepening of defence exchanges signed in recent years have been Agreement concerning the Transfer of Defence Equipment and Technology signed in 2015 following Japan's lifting of restrictions on arms export in 2014, and Agreement concerning Security Measures for the Protection of Classified Military Information (2015). During the most recent Summit of October 2018, an Implementing Arrangement for Deeper Cooperation between the Indian Navy and the Japan Maritime Self-Defense Force (JMSDF) was signed to cover maritime security cooperation through exchanges on maritime domain awareness and mutual logistics support in the Indo-Pacific region, and the start of negotiations for an Acquisition and Cross-Servicing Agreement (ACSA) was announced. Quite clearly, these will significantly upgrade strategic collaboration between the two countries, going beyond intent to tangible action.

In the area of defence acquisitions, the Joint Working Group on Defence Equipment and Technology set up in 2014 continues to meet but progress in cooperation has been slow due to a variety of reasons including Japan's own internal reservations which are a holdover from the past. Thus, while the negotiations on the ShinMaywa US-2 amphibious aircraft are still on, little progress seems to have been made. A recent development is an agreement between the Defence Research and Development Organisation (DRDO) and Acquisition, Technology & Logistics Agency (ATLA) of Japan to cooperate in research in robotics and unmanned ground vehicles (UGV).

Since 2006, besides annual defence minister level talks, exchanges have been established between the ministries of defence and all other wings of the military, with established regularity of bilateral visits. These include the newly upgraded ministerial level (2+2) dialogue of foreign and defence ministers, the Defence Policy Dialogue, the National Security Adviser's Dialogue and staff talks across the three services and the Coast Guards. There are also now joint exercises between all three services as well as the Coast Guards. Naval exercises include passage exercises (PASSEX), bilateral exercises called Bilateral Maritime Exercise between Japan and India (JIMEX) held in 2012 and again in 2018, and giving a strong signal, Japan was invited as a regular participant in the Indo-US Malabar exercises which is deemed a show of strength in the Indo-Pacific region.

The first counterterrorism exercise, called Dharma Guardian, between the Japan Ground Self-Defense Forces (JGSDF) and the Indian Army was held in Mizoram in November 2018. This is a significant step in an area where it had taken some time for Japan to understand India's sensitivities and concerns. Japan sought to seek deeper dialogue and exchange of intelligence following a terrorist attack targeting Japanese nationals in Algeria in 2013, and the killing of a couple by the ISIS. The convergence of perception on terrorism as a global security threat has led to cooperation in the area of counterterrorism and in greater responsiveness on the Japanese side to the problem of cross-border terrorism emanating from Pakistan. This is reflected in the language of annual Joint Statements issued since the prime ministerial summit of 2014 which for the first time mentioned the need to bring perpetrators of the 2008 Mumbai attack to justice. This was followed by calling for the elimination of terrorist-safe havens and infrastructure in 2015 and the naming of Pakistan for the first time in 2016 post the Uri attack. The 2017 and 2018 joint statements have followed the precedent of the BRICS summit and called for strengthened cooperation and named terrorist organizations including the Jaish-e-Mohammed and Lashkar-e-Toiba, in addition to the Al-Qaeda and ISIS. Both PM Shinzo Abe and Foreign Minister Taro Kono were prompt in condemning the killing of CRPF personnel at Pulwama on 14 February 2019, and though not mentioning Pakistan or the JEM, reiterated commitment to combat terrorism in cooperation with India.

Japan's shift from its traditional balanced position on India–Pakistan issues could be a consequence of our growing ties but also its own increasing vulnerability to terrorist attacks. At the same time, the conundrum is that it had supported the US-led coalition's efforts in Afghanistan and viewed Pakistan as a front-line state in that context in the fight against terrorism, continuing to aid and support efforts to stabilize Pakistan's economic and political situation, no doubt at the behest of the USA.

In the context of cooperation in the Indo-Pacific, PM Modi has called the India–Japan relationship a cornerstone of India's Act East policy as the two countries seek to align their initiatives in the area and agree on principles which govern their interests and objectives in the region, such as the centrality of the ASEAN, inclusivity (a recent addition, post PM Modi's speech at the Shangri-La Dialogue in June 2018), need for a rule-based order that respects sovereignty and territorial integrity and ensures freedom of navigation and unimpeded commerce, respect of international law and peaceful resolution of disputes. The unstated target is clear. The stated objective is to enhance maritime security cooperation in the region, improve connectivity in the wider Indo-Pacific and strengthen cooperation with ASEAN countries.

There is, thus, emerging congruence of perceptions on regional threats such as the challenge to the balance of power due to the rise of Chinese military assertiveness, its maritime and naval over reach and projection of economic power through the BRI; the dangers of an unstable regime in North Korea with nuclear and missile capabilities; traditional and non-traditional threats to the freedom of navigation and trade in the Indian Ocean, key to the economic security of both nations; the importance of peace and prosperity in the ASEAN which is central to India's Act East policy and Japan's Free and Open Indo-Pacific vision. The regional security environment, therefore, has become a significant factor in the convergence of strategic ties between India and Japan promoting cooperation to safeguard sea lanes and maritime domain awareness.

Recognition of China's growing coercive economic power and the leverage it exerts on smaller countries has resulted in the desire for greater cooperation between the two countries in developing infrastructure connectivity and capacity-building initiatives in the expanded Indo-Pacific region, including Africa. A beginning has been made with projects identified in Sri Lanka for the development of LNG-related infrastructure; Myanmar on collaboration in housing, education and electrification projects in the Rakhine state; and cooperation in road and rail reconstruction in Bangladesh. Both countries have spelt out the principles underlying their cooperation, highlighting that they will offer an option which steers clear of the pitfalls of the BRI by responsible debt financing practices and respecting the development priorities of the recipient states. In the context of Africa, it is thought that common objectives can be achieved best through industry-lead collaborations, and the 13th PM level summit in October 2018, agreed to work for the establishment of an India–Japan business platform to develop industrial corridors and industry networks in the region.

Other expressions of the strategic convergence have been dialogues involving third countries such as the US–India–Japan dialogue at the ministerial level and the Indonesia–India–Australia dialogue at the official level. There has been the revival in November 2017 of the concept of the security diamond, through the Quadrilateral Security Dialogue involving the USA and Australia, which has its origins in PM Abe's idea of bringing democracies of the region together to discuss strategic security issues. In the three meetings held so far, the group has identified humanitarian assistance and disaster relief (HADR), energy security, connectivity and cybersecurity as areas of collaboration. At the last meeting in November 2018, however, the participating countries issued separate statements calling for cooperation for a free, open and prosperous Indo-Pacific but avoiding an overt anti-China stance which is understandable given their respective bilateral engagements with China. Japan, for example, has worked hard to normalize relations with China and during PM Abe's bilateral visit in October 2018, after a hiatus of 7 years, pledged to 'actively participate' in the BRI and work together on infrastructure projects in third countries, to the surprise of many.

Economic Convergences

Economic engagement is a key dynamic of the growing India–Japan partnership and has in recent years moved towards some limited realization of potential. Japan has emerged as the third largest investor in India in terms of foreign direct investment (FDI) with a cumulative investment of US$27.28 billion since 2000 and the largest ODA partner, supporting transformative projects, especially in key areas of infrastructure and transportation. On the trade front, a free trade agreement (FTA) called the comprehensive economic partnership agreement (CEPA) was signed in 2011 but has not lived up to expectation with bilateral trade slumping from a modest high of US$18.32 in 2011–2012 to US$15.71 in 2017–2018.

Any discussion on India–Japan economic cooperation calls for a reiteration of the logic of economic convergence between the two based on several self-evident complementarities. Some of these are: (a) demography—Japan's greying and declining population and India's youthful profile with over 50 per cent of the population below 25 years sets off India's abundance of human capital with Japan's growing labour scarcity. In this lies also an area of identified cooperation, namely the focus on skill development of India's labour force to meet the needs of both countries; (b) India's large and growing domestic market and its rapid pace of urbanization which calls for large investments in infrastructure and manufacturing should be attractive for Japanese industry seeking foreign markets; (c) India as a capital-stretched but resource-rich industrializing country with low labour costs and Japan as a capital surplus and high technology-driven country should be able to ideally combine to produce knowledge-intensive capital goods for the world market. An example of this is the success story of the automotive sector; (d) India's strengths in IT software and Japan's excellence in hardware could produce a distinctive collaborative model integrating India's expertise and engineering skills and Japanese enterprise and technology.

India moved in 2014 to the top of the list of favoured countries for investments in the medium term in the Japan Bank for International

Cooperation (JBIC) annual surveys of overseas business operations by Japanese manufacturing companies, overtaking China for 3 years, coinciding with the downturn of Japan–China relations after the Senkaku stand-off. While China has regained its position in the past two years, India has continued to retain a higher rating than countries such as Vietnam, Thailand and Indonesia. Despite these favourable ratings, India continues to get but a small fraction of Japan's total FDI, lagging consistently behind China and the ASEAN, which have been the favoured destinations as Japan seeks partners for the labour-intensive parts of their global supply chains.

Thus, despite complementarities, CEPA and the special strategic relationship, and though Japanese companies are seen to be moving production abroad, looking for expanding markets and lower manufacturing costs including wages, Japanese FDI in India has been small compared to its total outward FDI. The figures for FY 2015–2016 were US$2.61 billion, FY 2016–2017, US$4.7 billion and 2017–2018, a mere US$1.2 billion, with most going to the automobile sector. The number of Japanese companies in India has, however, shown steady growth and stood at 1,441 in October 2018, with manufacturing firms accounting for more than half.

This raises the question whether despite the improvement in India's rating in ease of doing business, there still is a perception gap among Japanese companies. This could be because India is a relative newcomer in the context of economic engagement with Japan, as compared to the ASEAN countries and China, and a lack of familiarity, as also an information deficit is keeping more Japanese companies, especially SMEs, from investing in India. Efforts are being made to change this. A Japan Investment Promotion Partnership was launched at the first Modi–Abe Summit of 2014, which targeted a doubling of FDI and the number of Japanese companies by 2019, with PM Abe expressing the intent to raise Yen 3.5 trillion of private and public investment for India in 5 years. At the Summit in 2015, based on the success of the Japanese industrial park in Neemrana in Rajasthan which had shown that Japanese companies prefer to establish in clusters in ecosystems designed for their special needs with developed infrastructure and operational platforms, 12 potential sites for Japan Industrial Townships (JITs) were identified, out of which 6 are reported to be operational as of end 2018.

In addition to FDI, there had been growing portfolio investments in India as the stock markets offered Japanese institutional fund managers, including pension funds, mutual funds and insurance companies' favourable returns. Japanese foreign institutional investor (FII) investments in Indian stocks and bonds were estimated at $13 billion at the end of June 2017 starting with data available from 2012. Fund managers felt India was the only country among major emerging markets with high growth rates and yields, and a large-sized economy with political stability. However, according to a Nikkei report of December 2018, high oil prices, a low rupee value, the Infrastructure Leasing & Financial Services Limited (IL&FS) debacle, and stock market volatility have affected inflows into India-focused stock funds which are at a 5 year low.

A new area of potential and growth has been Japanese interest in the India start-up ecosystem with investments by Japanese private equity and venture capital funds growing from around US$2 billion in 2015 to US$5.9 billion in 2017. And while the number was relatively subdued in 2018 at US$2.1, the decline is not seen as a slowdown but overshadowed by two mega deals in 2017 of investments into Flipkart of US$2.5 billion and US$1.4 billion into Paytm. The number of deals per year has remained high with 32 in 2018, and the sectors diverse as in e-commerce, automotive, real estate, biotech, media, transport, etc. While led by SoftBank, which is one of the biggest investors in Indian start-ups so far, with investments in Ola, Paytm and Oyo, other Japanese VCs and industrial houses have also secured investments into Indian start-ups. A Japan India Startup Hub has been established in Bangalore in May 2018, following on a decision taken at the 2017 PM's Summit to serve as a platform for facilitating mutual investments.

India and Japan signed one of the most comprehensive FTAs India has with any country, which entered into force in 2011, covering agreed measures on liberalization of trade in goods and services, and cooperation in related areas such as IPRs, trade facilitation, rules of origin and movement of natural persons. Despite this, bilateral trade saw a steady decline from a peak of US$18 billion in 2013–2014, in itself an insignificant figure given the size of the economies of the two countries. India accounts for less than 1.7 per cent of the total trade of Japan, and Japan 2.5 per cent of India's. This is an area which requires special efforts including trade diversification. A study of the CEPA done by the research information system (RIS) concluded that India needed to increase competitiveness, strengthen compliance and standards, and enhance export-related infrastructure and capacities.

Again, CEPA has not helped in India getting a fair share of the IT and IT-enabled services market in japan even though Japan is the second largest market after the USA. Total 80 per cent of our software exports are directed to the USA and Europe with barely a 2 per cent share of the Japanese market. While only 10 per cent of Japan's IT industry is offshored, China receives 50 per cent of that share.

An area of economic cooperation in which progress is laudable is ODA-related projects implemented by the Japan International Cooperation Agency (JICA). India has, since 2004–2005, become the largest recipient of Japanese soft loans, grants and projects addressing national areas of priority such as infrastructure expansion, modernization of ports, road and rail transportation, energy supply and efficiency, building of industrial nodes and corridors, sustainable agriculture and forestry, environmental degradation, and social sectors such as health, sanitation and human resource development. Examples of these are the Western Dedicated Freight Corridor, the Delhi–Mumbai Industrial Corridor (DMIC), covering 6 states and 7 new smart cities, the Chennai Bengaluru Industrial Corridor (CBIC), metro systems in several cities across the country, the iconic Mumbai–Ahmedabad High-Speed Rail Project and projects for the development of the Northeast, including improving connectivity to the ASEAN and Bangladesh. As is evident, the canvas is very wide and these projects can plug India's vast infrastructure needs and also provide opportunities for Japanese consultancies, investments, products and technical know-how fostering a greater interdependence between our economies.

The Way Ahead

Annual PM-level summitry is a unique mechanism between the two countries which provides the opportunity and impetus to review and record progress in agreed areas of collaboration and identify new areas given the clear political will to deepen cooperation. Of the areas identified for cooperation, some have greater salience as thrust areas for the future to ensure a meaningful and sustained engagement beneficial to both countries. These are as follows:

- Defence and security cooperation is at the core of the India–Japan strategic partnership and must remain an area of focus. The areas of cooperation stand identified as expanding the scope and complexity of bilateral and trilateral military exercises aimed, inter alia, to enhance interoperability and anti-submarine warfare capabilities; trade, co-development and co-production of defence equipment and technologies; cooperative research in areas such as UGVs and robotics; exchange of information in maritime domain awareness as per the implementing arrangement signed in October 2018, and to fast-track negotiations of the Acquisition and Cross-Servicing Agreement (ACSA) which will facilitate mutual sharing of logistics and access to each other's naval bases.

- Japanese involvement in the development of our Northeast under the aegis of the India–Japan Act East Forum established in 2017 based on Japan's historical ties with the region and its strategic location as a bridgehead to the ASEAN, important to both India's Act East policy and Japan's Free and Open Indo-Pacific vision. Japan has been the trusted foreign partner of choice for the development of this politically sensitive region for projects related to infrastructure upgradation, power generation, environmental sustainability and human resource development and has evinced interest in projects related to enhancing connectivity with the neighbouring countries of Bangladesh, Myanmar and Thailand where it has undertaken complementing projects.
- Cooperating in undertaking projects in third countries in the Indo-Pacific for strategic benefit has been on the speaking agenda of both countries for some time now. This has taken concrete form through projects identified at the last Summit in October 2018 in Sri Lanka, Myanmar and Bangladesh. There are also ongoing consultations to build a cancer hospital in Kenya which will be the first trilateral development cooperation project in Africa. Both India and Japan have jointly enunciated the principles underlying such cooperation and the successful completion of these projects in time will determine the future of such strategic collaboration.
- In the Internet of things (IoT) and 5G era, India and Japan have strengths seen as complementary and partnering in digital technologies and S&T could be advantageous to both. While a beginning has been made with initiatives such as the start-up hub in Bangalore which seeks to connect Indian start-ups with front-line technologies and large Japanese companies, Japan and India signed an umbrella agreement in October 2018 seeking further collaboration and joint research in IoT, AI, Big Data Analytics, robotics, next generation communication networks, electronics systems and design, cybersecurity, etc. This is an area of promise which could help both countries in their quest for globally competitive manufacturing and seeking innovative solutions for societal challenges and use in modern urban infrastructure intended for smart cities.

India and Japan have also upgraded science and technology (S&T) exchanges identifying areas of common interest in life and material sciences, agricultural sciences, energy efficiency and storage, alternate sources of energy, such as research in methane hydrates, robotics and the peaceful uses of outer space, among others. The use of the mechanism of joint laboratories, already in place for research in biomedicine and information and communication technology

(ICT), and significantly ramping up student and academic exchanges between identified institutions, are clearly the way forward to synergize our capabilities for productive outcomes.

- Japan can be a leading partner in India's skill development programmes to harness our youthful demography. After a Memorandum of Cooperation signed in 2016 on the promotion of manufacturing skills, 8 major Japanese companies have established Japan Institutes of Manufacturing (JIMs) to teach Japanese-style manufacturing processes and methods, and 2 Japanese Endowed Courses (JECs) have been started in selected colleges to train middle management engineers. Both these initiatives contribute to the 'Skill India' and 'Make in India' programmes and need to be expanded in scope and scale. Japanese companies investing in manufacturing industry in India should be asked to focus on skill development as part of their corporate social responsibility (CSR), perhaps adopting existing Industrial Training Institutes (ITIs), to help create an employable workforce. Young Indians beginning to be sent to Japan under the Technical Intern Training Programme (TITP) which will provide on-the-job training for 3–5 years and the promise of jobs is another area of cooperation which needs to be expanded and will be of mutual benefit to both countries.

The partnership between India and Japan in the 21st century is based on compelling mutuality of interests. Both PMs Abe and Modi speak of the 'unparalleled potential' of the relationship. The structures are in place, the areas have been identified and cooperation is deepening. What is required now is to focus on fulfiling the expectations of the potential.

India–Russia Ties
Exploring Convergences and Divergences

Ajai Malhotra

With the end of the Cold War, the USA emerged as the pre-eminent world power, possessing a global reach in defence, financial and economic terms. The Russian state that succeeded the Soviet Union in 1991 initially imparted a pro-USA tilt to its foreign policy. That would not have been taxing for India, except that Russian Foreign Minister Kozyrev focused almost exclusively on partnering with the West. As a result, India–Russia ties initially languished.

A major directional shift in Russian foreign policy took place in early 1996 with Kozyrev's replacement as foreign minister by Yevgeny Primakov. Pursuing Russia's interests with greater determination, Primakov implemented a tougher foreign policy line towards the West and firmly opposed North Atlantic Treaty Organization's (NATO) eastward expansion into the ex-Soviet space excluding the Baltic Republics. He also encouraged closer Russian ties with major Asian countries such as India and China, and India–Russia relations soon reverted to an even keel. Primakov was elevated as prime minister of Russia in September 1998 and his visit to India from 21 to 22 December 1998 was the first official visit by a P5 Head of State/Government to India subsequent to its May 1998 nuclear tests. Responding to a media query during that visit, Primakov spoke of the need for a 'strategic triangle' of Russia, India and China to 'ensure regional peace and stability'. His words grabbed world headlines, voiced as they were at a stage when the USA, Japan and others had imposed unilateral sanctions on India as a consequence of its 1998 nuclear tests.

Following Vladimir Putin's election as president of Russia in 2000, he visited India in October of that year and signed with Prime Minister A. B. Vajpayee the Declaration on Strategic Partnership, making Russia the first strategic partner of India and reflecting the conviction on both sides of the need to build a multi-polar global structure. It also institutionalized the practice of annual, stand-alone bilateral summits, with the expectation that their regular convening at the highest level would benefit ties. India–Russia summits have since been held annually, without exception, with the 20th such Summit to be convened in late 2019. A decade later, to qualitatively distinguish the India–Russia strategic partnership from others subsequently entered into by both countries, the term describing it was jointly elevated in 2010 to 'special and privileged strategic partnership'.

Underlying the goodwill between India and Russia is the reality that neither perceives a security threat from the other. Indeed, each sees benefit for itself in the increased political and economic strength of the other. At the political level, a unique consensus, cutting across political party lines in both India and Russia, recognizes the importance of warm and friendly linkages between us. A strong, secure and prosperous Russia, fulfilling its international responsibilities, meets India's interests and vice versa.

India's ties with Russia have for many decades been characterized by close cooperation in strategic and sensitive fields, such as defence, nuclear energy, oil and gas, space, and science and technology. Despite efforts to diversify its economy and reduce reliance on oil and gas revenues, Russia's range of internationally competitive and tradeable products remains limited. Indeed, the three main branches of the Russian economy with serious business potential—oil and gas, defence and nuclear energy—are all ones in which India and Russia already cooperate closely.

Still, India–Russia bilateral trade has remained below expectations. After crossing a modest peak of US$11 billion in 2012, it has since been stuck in the US$7 billion–US$10.7 billion range, with two-way trade in services of just over US$1 billion annually. However, bilateral trade data captures only part of the picture of India–Russia commercial and economic interaction. If one also looks at two-way investments, the picture changes substantially and offers hope of meeting the target of $50 billion two-way investment by 2025 set at the 2018 Annual Bilateral Summit.

Thus, India is the world's fastest growing energy market, while Russia is a major oil and gas producer and exporter, making us natural partners. India's cumulative oil and gas investment in Russia presently exceeds US$15 billion. Moreover, easily the most oil that India annually extracts from its investments in foreign oil and gas fields is from Russia. However, since most of the older Indian refineries are not designed for processing Russian crudes, they are disposed of rather than shipped to India and, thus, do not show up in our trade figures.

In the other direction, Rosneft and its partners purchased Essar Oil (since renamed Nayara Energy) in 2017, paying US$12.9 billion for India's second largest private sector oil refinery at Vadinar, the attached port and power plant, and fuel stations across India. As a result, total Russian investments in India exceed US$18 billion. Rosneft will also supply 10 million tonnes of crude annually for a decade out of Venezuela for processing at Vadinar. Nayara Energy operates India's largest private sector fuel retail network (5,000+ operational stations and 2,800+ under commissioning) and is investing further $850 million to set up a petrochemical plant by 2022. Separately, as per a 2012 agreement, in June 2018 Russian company Gazprom has started delivering 2.5 million tonnes of liquefied natural gas (LNG) annually to GAIL for the next 20+ years. The deal has an estimated cumulative value of US$25 billion.

Turning to India–Russia cooperation in nuclear energy, two 1,000 MW nuclear power units at Kudankulam are operational, the third and fourth units are under construction, while negotiations on the fifth and sixth units are under way. Six more 1,000 MW nuclear power units are to be built at a coastal site in Andhra Pradesh. Increased localization of manufacture of nuclear equipment in India, for its both 1,000 MW units and the Rooppur NPP in Bangladesh, is also under way.

Bilateral space cooperation has been under way since the launch in 1975 of India's first satellite, Aryabhata. Russia will train the crew for India's Gaganyaan mission, which will send an Indian astronaut into space in 2022.

India–Russia defence cooperation, an important component of our ties for nearly six decades, also largely bypasses our trade statistics. Access to sensitive Russian technologies and materials has enhanced

India's security, while Russian enterprises have benefited from having India as a reliable partner. India manufactures Russian weapon systems such as SU-30MKI fighters and T-90S tanks and our defence ties, are gradually transforming from a buyer–seller relationship to one involving joint design, research, development and production of advanced weapon platforms. The BrahMos supersonic cruise missile is a world-class weapon and a practical example of 'Make in India' cooperation with Russia. Intergovernmental agreements have been signed for procuring five S-400 air defence systems and purchase/construction of four more Project 1135.6 stealth frigates. A joint venture for manufacturing Ka-226T light utility helicopters in India has also been finalized. In the context of persistent complaints by India of product support deficiencies, Russia has offered to locate manufacturing facilities for its defence components and spares in India.

Alongside purchases from Russia, India has tapped diverse sources buying, for example, the Anglo-French Jaguar, French Mirage 2000 and Rafale, Swedish Bofors 155 mm artillery, Israeli Spike missiles, Czech Tatra trucks, Swiss Pilatus PC-7 trainers and US P-8I Orion maritime reconnaissance planes and C-17 Globemaster military transports. While India must reduce its huge dependence on imported defence items, in many instances it still has no choice except to buy cost-effective quality weaponry from abroad. Of late, the USA and Israel have joined Russia as important defence partners for India; still, despite India's increased options, Russia will remain a key defence partner for India for the next quarter century.

Russian diamonds, imported largely via Belgium and Israel, are cut and polished in India and then overwhelmingly exported to the USA. As a result, they are not reflected in India–Russia trade data, but surface as a major Indian export to the USA. Direct delivery of purchases from Russia will lower transaction costs for Indian diamond merchants and add heft to our trade figures.

Supply of competitively priced medicines by Indian pharmaceutical companies helps rein in medicine prices in Russia, whose market is dominated by pharma multinationals. To benefit from Russia's 'Pharma 2020' strategy, some Indian pharma companies have invested in pharma production in Russia; this too dampens the scope for Indian pharma exports to Russia.

Western sanctions on Russia have generated opportunities for exporting Indian food products. Indian companies have long exported frozen seafood to quality-conscious Japanese and American consumers and can comfortably meet stringent Russian manufacturing and packaging conditions. Indian agro and milk products also have good Russian prospects. Attractive import items for Indian companies from Russia include chemicals, paper, timber and fertilizers. IT and IT-enabled services are sectors with good cooperation prospects.

Recognizing India's growth potential, Russian private companies are also investing in it. Russian billionaire Yuri Milner, through his firm DST Global and his personal investment company, Apoletto Asia, has for many years been a major investor in online start-up businesses in India, such as Flipkart, Ola, Practo, Grofers, Swiggy, Udaan and Craftsvilla.

Multifaceted India–Russia scientific and technological cooperation has traditionally been close and continues to make good headway. Interest in Indian films, dance, music yoga, and Ayurveda, as well as two-way tourist flows, continues to grow.

Overall, boosting India–Russia cooperation must also incorporate elements such as (a) vigorously implementing the multi-modal International North–South Transport Corridor, first proposed by Russia in 1993, which would drastically improve connectivity, reducing transit time by 40 per cent and costs by 30 per cent for moving containers from Mumbai via Bandar Abbas to Russia and onwards to Western Europe or Central Asia; (b) more actively pursuing Comprehensive Economic Cooperation Agreement between India and the Eurasian Economic Union, though given the bureaucracies involved negotiations will likely take at least half a decade more; (c) expanding a payments settlement system in national currencies; (d) improving banking arrangements; (e) further simplifying and speeding up procedures for issuing Russian tourist and business visas; (f) Russia effectively implementing a single window customs clearance procedure; (g) active outreach by Indian and Russian businesses to Russia's regions and India's states, respectively; (h) promoting wider interaction among our businessmen and entrepreneurs and (i) projecting the latest capabilities and achievements of both countries so that old mindsets are left behind.

India, Russia and a Polycentric World

Turning to the foreign policy front, both India and Russia favour a polycentric world and have a converging outlook on principles governing international relations. Their participation in groupings such as RIC and BRICS also broadly reflects such a desire. However, they diverge in the direction and evolution they would like the current world situation to take in order to enhance polycentricity. The roots of this divergence lie in the fact that India regards China as its primary strategic rival, even as both Russia and China separately visualize the USA as their main strategic competitor.

Russia would like a diminution in US global dominance leading to a more evenly balanced world. This is even more so now, with Western sanctions directed against it, and given its serious concern over the threat of NATO's further eastward expansion. Russia also regards US foreign and security policies as harmful to its vital interests, viewing its encouragement of freedom and democracy, for example, as a selective attempt to undermine countries that the USA acknowledges may challenge it in the future. Indeed, criticism by the USA of the unsatisfactory situation in Russia with regard to freedom of expression, democratic rights, rule of law and lesbian, gay, bisexual, and transgender (LGBTQ) rights has often raised bilateral tensions.

In contrast, while India welcomes a more democratic and inclusive world order with multiple power centres, its effort is primarily focused on enhancing its own global standing, rather than reducing that of the USA. As a deep-rooted democracy, India does not feel particularly threatened by efforts by the USA to promote freedom or democratic values worldwide. Indeed, India is a member of the Community of Democracies and a major contributor to the UN Democracy Fund.

On financial matters, the positions of India and Russia converge in desiring a greater say in the international financial system of which the USA is the primary custodian. This is especially so as regards decision-making at international financial institutions.

Russia would also like to see the dominance of the USD undercut, more so as Western sanctions target its access to international money markets. In contrast, India's modest aim is to maintain a modicum of stability in the exchange rate between the Indian Rupee vis-à-vis the USD.

In recent years, India's relations with the USA have witnessed a growing convergence of interests. The USA views India's rise positively, especially given the challenge to its own dominance posed by China. It is also natural that India be interested in partnering more closely with the USA, whose pre-eminence is likely to remain intact till the middle of the 21st century. President Obama endorsed USA–India relations as the 'defining partnership' of the 21st century and India's broad-based ties with the USA have consolidated further under President Trump, especially in certain sensitive directions. An India–US Defence and Security Partnership was finalized in 2005; India was designated a Major Defense Partner in 2016; India received Strategic Trade Authorisation-1 status in 2018 and efforts are presently under way to make India a Major Non-NATO Ally.

As regards Russia, its preferred choice has long been partnership with Europe, rather than Asia. It feels peeved that, despite the end of the Cold War, the USA has been unwilling to accept Russia as an integral part of a democratic Europe. Russia has considerable apprehensions about US stance on security issues of direct interest to it. In particular, it cannot countenance NATO's eastward expansion into former Soviet republics beyond the Baltics and US backing of Georgia and Ukraine. It regard efforts to make Ukraine a NATO member as crossing a particularly divisive red line.

In turn, Putin's proposal in 2011 of a Common Economic Space from Lisbon to Vladivostok was regarded by the USA as an unacceptable Russian attempt to undermine the Trans-Atlantic alliance and open a path to a more dominant Russia in Europe. With Putin's return as president in May 2012, Russia–US ties re-entered a particularly turbulent phase deriving from prejudices on both sides dating to the Cold War and amplified by US experience in dealing with Putin during his two earlier presidential terms. With its desire to partner with Europe stymied, it was natural that Russia look eastwards and seek to re-balance its ties by strengthening linkages with Asian countries beyond India and China, such as Japan, Republic of Korea, Indonesia, Vietnam and indeed with ASEAN as a whole.

Unlike India–Japan ties, which are close, warm and friendly, Russia's relations with Japan remain constrained by their unresolved dispute over the Kuriles. As a consequence, the two countries are yet to sign a peace treaty to end the Second World War between them. Japan also followed the US lead to impose sanctions on Russia following developments in Ukraine. While for Japan, the protection extended by its ally the USA *vis-à-vis* China is of far greater importance, improved Japan–Russia ties also serve Japanese interests by better balancing China in Asia. In 2013, Russia and Japan commenced confidential deputy foreign minister level discussions seeking to resolve their Kuriles dispute. Progress in that direction would open up new vistas as Japan represents an attractive market for Russian oil and gas and Russia is an appealing option for an LNG-dependent Japan since it would provide it with a short and secure energy supply route. Japan also has the financial capacity to make significant investments in the Russian Far East.

Another area of broadly diverging assessments between India and Russia relates to China. India has long viewed a nuclear armed China as its leading strategic opponent, explaining the conduct of its May

1998 nuclear weapons tests in the context of such an assessment. China's economic growth over the last several decades has expanded its political footprint, enhanced its military clout and made it ambitious, confident and overbearing. Of concern to India is Chinese troop incursions along the Line of Actual Control separating the two countries and China's habit of challenging Indian efforts to upgrade its inadequate border infrastructure. China also regularly finds new ways to irritate India over the status of the Indian state of Arunachal Pradesh, despite being aware of India's strong sensitivities in the matter. China's rising presence in India's maritime neighbourhood, its naval bases at Gwadar and Djibouti and its ambitions in the Indian Ocean also cause unease for India. China's persistent strengthening of Pakistan's defence capabilities by supplying it sophisticated weapons is worrying as it has major strategic implications for India. The China–Pakistan Economic Corridor, funded by China, unacceptably passes through the Pakistan-occupied part of the Indian State of Jammu & Kashmir. China's stance against UN Security Council expansion in both permanent and non-permanent categories is another point of divergence, especially as China has, on occasion, sought to undermine India's aspirations for a UNSC permanent seat. China has also deliberately stood in the way of India's membership of the Nuclear Suppliers Group. It is also constructing hydropower dams on the Brahmaputra River, without adequately addressing India's serious concerns regarding their impact on downstream flood management, agriculture, fishing and ecology, water flows and freshwater availability in north-eastern India. Overall, China needs to show greater consideration for India's core interests and concerns. In contrast, India has been careful to pursue a balanced and productive approach towards China, not letting Chinese irritants stand in the way of maintaining friendly ties and promoting trade, economic, cultural and other linkages with China.

For Russia, its relations with China are not ideology-driven and have never been better in strategic, political and economic terms. Russia does not feel particularly threatened by China's ascendance nor is it averse to China's growing international voice, since both share a similar polycentric world vision. Both independently consider the USA as their main strategic rival. In turn, US 2018 National Defense Strategy identifies the re-emergence of long-term, strategic competition from China and Russia as the central challenge to its prosperity and security. Good relations with China secure Russia a peaceful southern border, enabling it to focus on its primary security challenge from USA/NATO on its European front. It is also attractive for China as it offers it a protected northern flank while it addresses its complex ties with the USA and confronts the USA and its allies on its Pacific Ocean side. Bilateral ties between Russia and China have improved radically over the last two decades, with their border dispute settled and an elaborate institutionalized mechanism in place for regular multilevel exchanges. In 2012, President Putin described China's economic growth as 'by no means a threat, but a challenge that carries colossal potential for business cooperation' and offers a 'chance to catch the Chinese wind in the sails of our economy'. Russia accepts the reality of China as a rising power and profits from cooperating with it, especially in energy, civil aviation and defence. China is one of Russia's top trading partners and investors.

On the other hand, Russia is acutely conscious of potential complications from rising Chinese immigration into its under-populated Siberian and Far East regions, Russian defence IPR violations by China and the lopsided nature of Russia–China bilateral trade. Russia is also fully aware that in changed circumstances China could again become an adversary and bears this in mind while selling sophisticated weapon systems to it.

Yet another broad area where India and Russia have somewhat differing assessments relates to the Indo-Pacific security architecture promoted by the USA. While China and the USA neither share a border nor have a territorial dispute, recent years have seen a reduction in trust between them, *inter alia*, due to stress points in the Indo-Pacific. The USA is concerned that China is leveraging its military and using 'predatory economics' to coerce its smaller neighbours to reorder the Indo-Pacific region to its advantage. It also believes that China will seek 'Indo-Pacific regional hegemony in the near-term and displacement of the United States to achieve global preeminence in the future'. In turn, China views US security strategy in the Pacific as provocative, if not threatening. It is concerned by US 're-balancing' and has interpreted it as reflecting a desire to contain China.

India does not feel threatened by US strategic and military re-balancing towards the Indo-Pacific; instead, it is concerned by China's expanding maritime footprint in the Indo-Pacific, especially into the Indian Ocean. Despite that, India has not directly injected itself into China's maritime territorial disputes with its neighbours in the East and South China Seas. Instead, India has largely limited itself to affirming the importance of safeguarding maritime security and ensuring freedom of navigation and overflight throughout the disputed areas. India would also like to see a less intrusive Chinese maritime presence in the Indian Ocean.

Theoretically, USA re-balancing to the Pacific somewhat reduces the pressure on Russia from NATO expansion threats emanating from the European direction. Russia, however, has neither the desire nor the wherewithal to enhance its competition with the USA in the Pacific Ocean at this stage and would be happy to leave the USA and China to face off there. If anything, it is enhancing its security focus on the Arctic region. Still, in Russia's view, a sustainable security architecture for the Asia-Pacific region can only be achieved on an open-ended, collective basis, building upon the principles of indivisible security, rule of international law, peaceful settlement of disputes and non-use of force or threat of use of force. Nonetheless, ASEAN's enunciation at its 34th Summit in June 2019 of its vision for developing an inclusive regional architecture for the Indo-Pacific has opened up an opportunity to explore and find common ground among all concerned.

Another divergence in approach between India and Russia relates to Afghanistan. Both India and Russia would like to see that Afghanistan, and indeed all Central Asian countries, remain calm and peaceful, do not get destabilized or radicalized by Islamic extremism or serve as a conduit for illicit narcotic drugs and illegal arms. Both countries would like to see that Al-Qaeda, IS or other extremist terrorist formations do not consolidate politically, ideologically and territorially anywhere in the region. Russia is particularly concerned over the flow of illicit narcotic drugs, illegal arms and extremist ideologies out of Afghanistan and coming across Central Asia into its territory. With a stagnant population size, Russia annually loses more youth to illicit narcotics of Afghan origin than it did during the decade-long deployment of the Soviet Army in Afghanistan. Russia's outreach to the Afghan Taliban seeks to cater to its interests in the face of uncertainty about Afghanistan's political future and the possibility of a post-Ghani Taliban dominated dispensation coming to power in Kabul following the exit of USA/NATO forces. Meanwhile, the USA with its 'fight and talk' approach towards the Taliban and conduct of direct negotiations with it continues its search for a workable and inclusive political settlement to the war in Afghanistan. India, on its part, has rejected any dealing with the Taliban, repeatedly voicing instead its support for the government and people of Afghanistan and an inclusive peace process that is Afghan-led, Afghan-owned and Afghan-controlled.

Another area where there have been rumblings of concern in India pertains to Russia–Pakistan defence cooperation. Russia has in the past been attentive to India's sensitivities about weapons deliveries to Pakistan. Pakistan's meagre foreign exchange reserves, and the fact that Russia does not extend credit for its defence sales, circumscribe the potential for such cooperation. Moreover, China has overwhelmingly replaced the USA as the primary supplier of sophisticated weapons to Pakistan. Nonetheless, Prime Minister Narendra Modi must continue to emphatically press the point with President Putin that Russia should step away from progressing its defence ties with Pakistan—a state-long active in abetting, financing, sponsoring and exporting terrorism—as it directly impinges India's security. The informal India–Russia Summit convened in Sochi in June 2018 would have provided an unstructured opportunity to both leaders to confidentially share perceptions and seek understanding on sensitive issues such as this. Beyond the annual summits and bilateral meetings on the margins of multilateral summits (G20, BRICS, RIC, SCO, CICA, etc.), such additional interactions at the highest level would be useful and should be maintained.

As regards the USA, it needs to be encouraged to further ratchet up pressure on Pakistan to make it completely desist from aiding, abetting, sponsoring and providing safe haven to any and every terrorist group. Moreover, while US military supplies to Pakistan have ground to a halt, it should also be encouraged to review its designation of Pakistan as a Major Non-NATO Ally.

Looking Ahead

Russia's GDP is presently growing at a modest +1.5 per cent annually, and its future performance hinges largely on the price of crude oil and, less so, on factors such as the continuation of Western sanctions, the global economic situation and Russia's seriousness in pursuing domestic economic reforms. Seeking to reduce its reliance on the USD, Russia was the largest gold buyer in 2018–2019 and now has the fifth largest gold reserves in the world. Despite Western sanctions, Russia has grown its international reserves over the past five years, from US$361 billion to US$518 billion, into the third largest in the world. Russia currently also has low unemployment and inflation rates, flat population growth, vast and varied natural resource wealth and a hardy and resilient people.

Over the last few years, Russia has worked its way back into the larger strategic game in certain regions, especially West Asia and North Africa; it is gradually increasing its support in Europe. In recent years, greater Russian assertiveness in protecting its interests, particularly along its periphery, is discernible. It is also evidenced by its swift and decisive action in Georgia in 2008, its approach to the crisis in Syria since 2011, and its handling of the Ukrainian crisis since late 2013. It is revealing that the USA, despite being pre-eminent and possessing a dominating global reach, has been largely unsuccessful in dictating outcomes and bringing developments in Afghanistan, Georgia, Iraq, Iran, Libya, Syria, Ukraine and elsewhere to a satisfactory conclusion from its viewpoint. Russia, in contrast, while essentially a major regional power with economic and financial constraints, has an incomparably superior record over the last decade or so. It has seen to it that Abkhazia and South Ossetia have remained independent of Georgia. It has to be ensured that a regime friendly to it has retained power in Syria. It has comfortably re-absorbed Crimea and ensured that developments in Ukraine stay under control and do not harm Russia's interests. It has seriously expanded its influence across the entire West Asia and North Africa region, not only with most Arab states but also with important NATO member Turkey and with Israel.

Indeed, Russia's ties with Israel constitute its most improved bilateral relationship since the dismantling of the Soviet Union. There is regular interaction between Prime Minister Netanyahu and President Putin while quiet Russia–Israel diplomacy has professionally and effectively addressed potential irritants. The first-of-its kind trilateral conference of Israeli, Russian and US national security advisers convened in Jerusalem on 25 June 2019 is an interesting development. As a follow-up, Netanyahu called Putin on 8 July 2019 to discuss Syria, Iran and other issues, including, in particular, the importance of further bilateral coordination between their militaries.

The West too recognizes that despite Western sanctions on Russia over Ukraine, several security crises—Afghanistan, Iran, Syria and Ukraine—are better handled via issue-based cooperation with Russia. This has delivered tangible, positive results in the past. Thus, Putin saved face for Obama by interceding with Bashar al-Assad in September 2013 over the elimination and removal of chemical weapons from Syria. The Minsk-2 agreement of February 2015 on Ukraine was an outcome of cooperation between Russia and other Normandy Group members. Russia's presence contributed to working out of the P5+1 Joint Comprehensive Plan of Action (JCPOA) agreement with Iran of July 2015 on curbing Iran's nuclear weapons programme, though it has since been disowned by Trump. Joint efforts by Russia, the USA and the EU in June 2019 delivered a workable solution to the Moldovan constitutional crisis.

The 2014 and subsequent Western sanctions aimed at punishing Russia over Ukraine have pushed Russia closer to China at a stage when China too was interested in closer linkages. While US Indo-Pacific re-balancing reflected a change in perception, it continued under Obama to treat Russia as a villain whom it needed to continue to block. This may have been partly because Russia is the only country whose nuclear weaponry matches that of the USA and partly because of Obama's larger anti-Putin agenda focused on weakening, subduing and neutralizing Russia so as to undermine Putin's domestic support and create conditions leading to his replacement by a more pliant Russian leader.

However, the USA has no advantage to gain by simultaneously picking a fight with both Russia and China. Indeed, for Trump, there is no automaticity about treating Russia as a primary adversary of the USA. To the contrary, while electioneering, he had highlighted the need to bring the US–Russia relationship back to normal. Given Trump's commitment to improving ties with Russia, he can be expected to pursue a more far-sighted bilateral relationship once an opportunity presents itself and try to bring back ties with Russia back to a more even keel. The challenge before Trump in improving ties with Russia is that it will generate controversy, within both the USA and the EU, against the backdrop of his presidential re-election bid. As a result, Trump is unlikely to quickly or unilaterally withdraw sanctions on Russia. However, he may well be open to seriously considering doing so if a larger arrangement can be worked out that, *inter alia*, matches his expectations for nuclear weapons reduction, addresses cooperation over Syria/Iraq while activating a common front against the IS and incorporates confidence building measures that meet core European security concerns and find broad EU acceptance.

Despite Trump's outward unpredictability, he is astute enough to appreciate that a more cozy Russia–China partnership should be of greater concern to the USA, against whom it may well get directed. It also causes unease for India which, in turn, must nudge USA/EU and Russia back towards a more normal relationship. Improved Russia–US ties meet India's interest and it is hoped that the USA will re-engage with Russia and bring back greater normalcy to their bilateral relationship.

On its part, Russia remains deeply interested in being on good working terms with the USA and would certainly like to avoid a direct confrontation with it. Moreover, it is known that sanctions do not last forever. Russia's countersanctions have added to the bleak economic scenario in some parts of Western Europe. Several EU states are not keen on maintaining sanctions on Russia, and fatigue is setting in. A perceptible shift in European attitude can be gleaned from the Parliamentary Assembly of the Council of Europe voting Russia back as a member on

25 June 2019, five years after its removal over its actions in Ukraine. That reinstatement would have been impossible without the backing of Germany and France. The separate bilateral that President Putin had with all four of his top Western counterparts—Trump, Merkel, Macron and May—on the sidelines of the Osaka G20 Summit on 28–29 June 2019 reflect another step forward in the gradual unravelling of the West's diplomatic isolation of Russia. Given the criticism that Trump faced after his previous meeting with Putin in Helsinki in July 2018, the holding of a Trump–Putin meeting at Osaka was itself significant and showed that Trump no longer feels that constrained about interacting face to face with Putin. No tangible results emerged nor were any expected, yet the atmospherics were good. Putin also invited Trump for the 75th anniversary of the end of the Second World War, to be celebrated in Moscow on 9 May 2020. If Trump attends, it would mark a further improvement in Russia–US ties.

For India, its bilateral ties with Russia and the USA are not a zero-sum game. India's growing engagement with the USA, and indeed drawing closer in the Asia-Pacific to countries such as Australia, Indonesia, Japan, Mongolia, Republic of Korea and Vietnam, must be continued, but not at the cost of its friendship with Russia. Indeed, India's special and privileged strategic partnership with Russia should be carefully and pragmatically nurtured. Any dilution of India's partnership with Russia would weaken a vital building block of India's foreign policy and negatively impact our security scenario by drawing Russia even closer to China and providing a wider opening to Pakistan.

Despite the Indian economy expanding at a healthy pace, India will need considerable time and legroom to catch up with China. Meanwhile, India should be alert about safeguarding its interests and keeping conflict with China at bay while sensibly extending its foreign policy space through a nimble handling of partners and issues. It should not unnecessarily antagonize China by its actions, which should be sensitive yet clear and firm, leaving no scope for misunderstandings. Moreover, India should continue to diligently work with China to define and settle our common border and peacefully resolve our territorial dispute.

India is sufficiently well endowed not to be a camp follower or regional balancing entity for others. It must sustain strong ties with both the USA and Russia as it pursues greater economic well-being and as they work towards normalizing their bilateral relations. Well-prepared, high-level meetings involving India–USA–Russia, may be explored at the opportune moment to identify common ground and bring greater cohesion on specific foreign policy, defence and/or security issues. Consideration could be given in due course to adding others, such as Israel and/or Japan, on specific issues.

As India needs time and space to grow, it should for now partner all countries ready to genuinely contribute to its economic development and well-being. India's multi-directional foreign policy and national security strategy must broaden the developmental space it needs. Indeed, Prime Minister Narendra Modi's catchphrase slogan for India's inclusive domestic growth: *Sabka Saath, Sabka Vikas, Sabka Vishwas* (Together with all; Development for all; Everyone's Trust) also merits application in India's conduct of its foreign affairs. Seeking friendship with all, projecting animosity towards none and earning trust all around must equally guide India's foreign policy. Maintaining close and friendly ties with Russia is integral to such an approach.

Changing Landscape of Central Asia

D. P. Srivastava

British and Russian rivalry shaped the perception of Central Asia in the 19th century. The Great Game epitomized fears of the British Empire builders about the expanding presence of a Czarist Russia in India's neighbourhood. This was given expression in the Anglo-Russian Convention of 1907 relating to Persia, Afghanistan and Tibet. The Convention sought to define spheres of influence, and mute rivalry by freezing the status quo. China was not a player, though it impinged on Tibet which China now claims as part of China. Nor were people of Central Asia consulted.

The Great Game today is being played out between different players. The intervening period saw consolidation of the Soviet hold, and thereafter creation of the Central Asian Republics (CARs) in 1991 with the dismantling of the Soviet Union. The 5 CARs have reasserted their national identity. Their aspiration to play an independent role on an international level was symbolized by Kazakhstan assuming non-permanent membership of the UN Security Council. Its two-year term for 2017–2018 has just concluded. China is a major player. It joined Russia in the Shanghai Cooperation Organisation (SCO). It has created its own instrumentality for augmenting Chinese presence in the area—Belt and Road Initiative (BRI).

The SCO communiques try to present an alternate narrative to Western prescriptions on international issues. They represent drawing together of Russia and China, as they face pressure from the USA. But there is also a subtext of rivalry between the two. Russia maintains groupings such as the Collective Security Treaty Organization (CSTO) and Eurasian Economic Union (EEU), which do not include China.

CSTO is a Russian-led military alliance. Among the CARs, it includes Kazakhstan, Kyrgyzstan and Tajikistan. CSTO was founded in 1992 and preceded the SCO, which came into existence a decade later. There was an idea mooted in Dushanbe, the Tajik capital to merge the SCO with CSTO. The idea is still being debated.[1] The treaty establishing EEU was signed in May 2014 much after the SCO came into being. Though the SCO charter also includes economic cooperation, the fact that Russia saw the need to establish a separate body reflects the subtext of Sino-Russian rivalry.

SCO, BRI, CSTO and EEU

Russia and China have built a multilateral structure, which reflects both the strands of competition and cooperation. CSTO and EEU are Russian-led initiatives, which do not include China. BRI is a Chinese initiative, presented in a multilateral format. The SCO brings together Russia and China to present an alternative narrative to the Western worldview. The CARs have joined one or the other grouping, but do not control them. There is no pan-Central Asia cooperation mechanism consisting of the states of the region.

The prelude to the SCO was a series of agreements between the 'Shanghai 5' including China, Russia, Kazakhstan, Kyrgyzstan and Tajikistan. The grouping endorsed the territorial status quo between China and the CARs, which emerged as independent countries after the breakdown of the Soviet Union. Future political cooperation was to be attempted after ensuring that border disputes were not raised or revived by China. This was a precaution India failed to take in the 1950s with China, or in the 1980s, when SAARC was set up.

The series of border demarcation agreements and troop reduction agreements marked the frontiers of the CARs with China. This did not include some of the intra-CARs issues. Boundary demarcation between Uzbekistan and Kyrgyzstan, for instance, has taken place only last year

---

[1] Available at https://en.wikipedia.org/wiki/Collective_Security_Treaty_Organization#cite_note–11 (accessed on 16 January 2019).

after the death of Uzbek President Islam Karimov. The SCO was not for settling bilateral 'disputes' between member states—what Pakistan has tried to raise within SAARC to block progress in other areas (though the SAARC Charter clearly says that the grouping is for economic cooperation).

The SCO was set up 5 years later in 2001. A Brookings commentary wondered if this was an attempt to counter US influence in Asia.[2] The SCO communiques indeed offered a counter-narrative by Russia and China. But they were not about to limit this to Asia. The SCO summits since inception have taken positions against the doctrine of humanitarian intervention, and human rights and a host of other political issues. Even the Dushanbe statement of the Shanghai Five in July 2000 included a reference to 'oppose intervention in other countries', internal affairs on the pretext of 'humanitarianism' and 'protecting human rights'.[3] The statement also noted the group's opposition to the 'use of force or threat of use of force in international relations without the UN Security Council's prior approval'. There was also 'opposition to US missile defences by stating its strong support to for the Anti-Ballistic Missile (ABM) Treaty of 1972 and its opposition to block based (i.e. US alliance-based) deployment of theatre missile defence systems in the Asia-Pacific region, particularly in Taiwan'.[4]

The SCO's criticism of the West was muted initially. Since then, positions have hardened. The US and EU sanctions against Russia, and China's trade friction with the USA, have brought them closer together. The language has also got stronger. The Qingdao Declaration of SCO Summit of June 2018 reaffirmed that 'unilateral unrestricted build-up of missile defence systems by individual countries or groups of countries will damage international security and destabilize the global situation.'

Does the SCO provide more political space for India? The Qingdao Declaration underlined that the member states *that are signatory to the Non-Proliferation Treaty* (NPT) are committed to 'strict compliance with NPT provisions'. Though India's position is saved by the caveat which limits this formulation to NPT signatories, it does not give any elbow room to us. Similarly, on the issue of *BRI*, the Declaration reaffirms support to the Chinese initiative. It enumerates SCO member states

---

[2] B. Gill, *Shanghai Five: An Attempt to Counter US Influence in Asia?* (Washington, DC: Brookings, 2001). Available at https://www.brookings.edu/opinions/shanghai-five-an-attempt-to-counter-u-s-influence-in-asia/ (accessed on 16 January 2019).
[3] Ibid.
[4] Ibid.

supporting it. Except India, all SCO members are listed. India is not mentioned, and hence is not associated with this declaration of support. On the issue of the Comprehensive Convention on International Terrorism (CCIT), where India has positive interest, the Declaration mentions that the member states 'stand for reaching consensus', implying thereby that this stage has not yet been reached. Pakistan's presence within the SCO means that the organization's support for anti-terrorism would be confined to Central Asia.

As the Russian and Chinese relationship with the USA becomes more tense, harmonizing our positions within the SCO with growing Indo-US relations could become more difficult.

While Russia and China tried to build defences against the expansion of US influence in Central Asia, other members of the SCO often take an independent line. Most of these countries had joined the Partnership for Peace (PfP) programme of NATO in 1994. Initially, this was in tandem with the Russian position, which had also joined the programme. However, as Russia's relations with NATO came under strain, it withdrew from association with NATO. But Uzbekistan remained part of the arrangement and even provided a military base to the USA. It withdrew only after Andijan incident of 2005 when the USA criticized Uzbek human rights record. Uzbekistan resumed cooperation with NATO in 2008. In 2009, Uzbekistan joined the 'northern route' for the supply of non-lethal weapons to International Security Assistance Force (ISAF) in Afghanistan. This route was closed following US sanctions against Russia.

Chinese and Russian Economic Presence in Central Asia

Russia has enough oil and gas, and hence does not need to import them. Chinese energy needs create a complementarity with at least three CARs—Kazakhstan, Uzbekistan and Turkmenistan. By developing an extensive pipeline network, China has broken Russian monopoly over oil and gas transit more effectively than the USA or EU could.

Kazakhstan

Kazakhstan is a member of the Russian-led EEU. In a decade since 2006, China has emerged as bigger market for Kazakh exports than Russia. China is a major buyer of Kazakh oil and gas. The balance of trade is in Kazakhstan's favour so far as trade with China is concerned.

Chinese exports to Kazakhstan's market still lag behind Russian exports, though they are catching up fast. Chinese exports went up by 147 per cent between 2006 and 2017, while the Russian exports increased by 24.6 per cent in this period (Table 18.1).

TABLE 18.1 Kazakhstan's Trade (US$ Million)

Year	Exports			Imports		
	2006	2016	2017	2006	2016	2017
Russia	9,072.9	9,288.3	11,336.5	3,731.1	3,445.2	4,479.3
China	1,924.9	3,668.0	4,692.0	3,592.5	4,228.4	5,773.4
Total (from all sources)	23,708.8	25,376.7	29,139.3	38,257.3	36,777.4	48,348.3

Source: Asian Development Bank Data Library[5]

Uzbekistan

China has overtaken Russia in terms of both export and import in Uzbekistan. Chinese exports went up more than six times (574.4%) between 2006 and 2017. Chinese imports from Uzbekistan have also gone up, though by a slower pace (164%) during this period. Chinese imports account for 40 per cent of Uzbek gas exports.

A decade earlier, China was behind Russia both in exports and imports, as shown in Table 18.2.

TABLE 18.2 Uzbekistan's Trade (US$ Million)

Year	Exports			Imports		
	2006	2016	2017	2006	2016	2017
Russia	1,151.4	2,083.0	2,784.3	1,216.7	716.3	967.3
China	430.5	2,182.6	2,932.6	533.8	1,516.0	1,391.1
Total (from all sources)	4,315.5	10,123.7	12,247.3	5,374.9	7,654.8	9,075.2

Source: Asian Development Bank Data Library[6]

[5] Available at https://data.adb.org/search/type/dataset (accessed on 16 January 2019).
[6] Ibid.

Turkmenistan

In little over a decade since 2006, China has overtaken Russia in terms of both imports and exports. China imports essentially raw material. But from Turkmenistan's point of view, it is a welcome customer for Turkmen gas exports at a time, when both Russia and Iran have stopped buying Turkmen gas, and the balance of trade is in its (Turkmenistan's) favour, as given in Table 18.3.

TABLE 18.3 *Turkmen Trade (US$ Million)*

Year	Export			Import		
	2006	2016	2017	2006	2016	2017
Russia	243	605	365	74	312	80
China	172	361	403	15	5,248.6	6,203
Total *(from all sources)*	1,750	5,215	4,551	5,323	7,546	7,418

Source: Asian Development Bank Data Library[7]

Kyrgyzstan

Kyrgyzstan is a member of Russian-led EEU. Nevertheless, Chinese exports have overtaken Russian exports in little over a decade since 2006. China imports very little. The balance of trade is heavily in its favour, as given in Table 18.4.

TABLE 18.4 *Kyrgyz Trade (US$ Million)*

Year	Exports			Imports		
	2006	2016	2017	2006	2016	2017
Russia	652	800	1,180	154	145	262
China	242	1,465	1,494	38	80	97
Total *(from all sources)*	1,757	3,957	4,599	799	1,424	1,788

Source: Prepared on the basis on author's analysis of statistics from ADB Data library.[8]

---

[7] Ibid.
[8] Ibid.

Tajikistan

Russia is still ahead of China in terms of both exports from and imports to Tajikistan. However, China has nearly doubled its exports (94%) and increased imports by 16 times (1600%). Tajikistan runs trade deficit with both countries, as given in Table 18.5.

TABLE 18.5 *Tajikistan's Trade (US$ Million)*

Year	Exports			Imports		
	2006	2016	2017	2006	2016	2017
Russia	65.4	208.1	199.0	423.7	758.7	800.6
China	9.9	114.2	169.0	148.9	373.8	289.0
Total *(from all sources)*	1,438.6	974.5	1,100.4	1,725.5	2,360.2	2,391.6

Source: Prepared on the basis on author's analysis of statistics from ADB Data library.[9]

Oil and Gas

China has invested in building an extensive network of pipelines to bring oil and gas from Central Asia. China imported 70 per cent of Turkmen gas till recently. This percentage has gone up since then. Russia and Iran, which accounted for the remaining 30 per cent, have stopped buying Turkmen gas. It is set to increase pipeline capacity, and gas imports from that country further. China accounts for 40 per cent of Uzbek gas exports. It buys a substantial part of Kazakh oil exports. Chinese foray in the oil and gas sector in Central Asia *predates the* BRI. It is also more *significant* in terms of integrating Central Asian economies with the Chinese market, despite Russia's initial advantage.

In the wake of the breakdown of the Soviet Union, US and European companies entered Central Asia for oil and gas exploration and production. Under the Clinton Administration, a determined bid was made to break the Russian monopoly on pipeline network. With Shale technology, America first emerged as major gas exporter in the form of LNG. It has since become net oil exporter also reducing its dependence on the Middle East or Central Asia to meet its energy needs. This, coupled with the expected US withdrawal from Afghanistan, has lowered American stakes in Central Asia. This will further increase China's salience.

---

[9] Ibid.

China built Central Asian Gas pipeline (CAGP) to transport natural gas through three parallel pipelines from Turkmenistan, Uzbekistan and Kazakhstan to the border in Western China.[10] Its current gas of 1.9 TCF per year is set to increase further.

China also took share in production in Turkmenistan's massive Galkynysh Gas Field. It is the only foreign country to be awarded a share in Turkmenistan's upstream production. It is expanding pipeline capacity from 1.4 TCF per year to 2.3 TCF per year.

In 2010, the Chinese state company China National Petroleum Corporation (CNPC) signed an agreement with Uzbekistan to deliver 350 BCF per year gas. Three spurs A, B and C of CAGP have been built. Fourth section or Line D is under construction and will increase the pipeline capacity by 880 BCF per day gas, as shown in Figure 18.1.

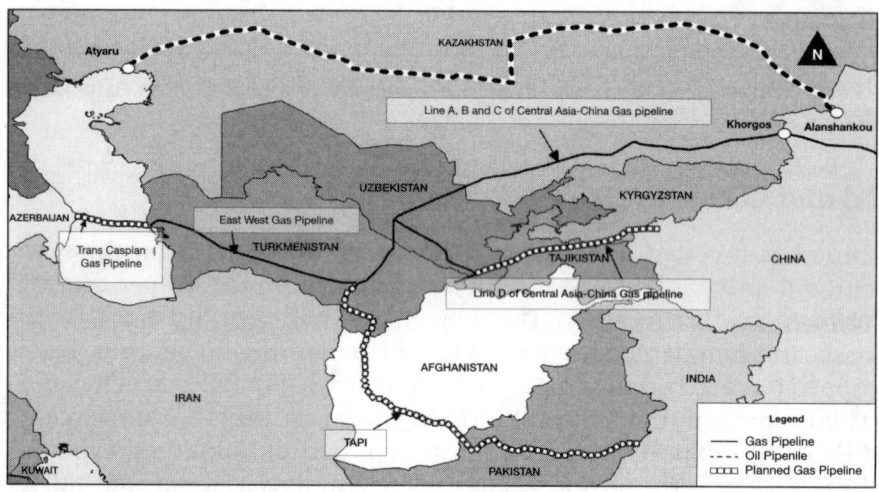

FIGURE 18.1 *Ribbon of Energy Projects in Central Asia*

Map is for thematic representation only, it does not represent a legal survey.
Copyright © 2018: Vivekananda International Foundation/Dt03-10-19

China's pipeline network delivers major part of its gas requirement at lower prices than LNG, apart from serving its geopolitical interest in consolidating its hold over Central Asian countries. Securing its energy needs from its backyard also reduces its dependence on the Middle East oil brought through the Malacca Strait.

---

[10] Available at https://www.eia.gov/beta/international/analysis_includes/countries_long/China/archive/pdf/China_2014.pdf (accessed on 16 January 2019).

India does not have much presence in the Central Asian energy market. Turkmenistan–Afghanistan–Pakistan–India (TAPI) faces serious challenges due to continuing war in Afghanistan, apart from uncertainty of transit through Pakistan in view of that country's deep-rooted hostility against India. In the absence of proximity, India's best hope is to bring petrochemicals, which do not require pipelines and can be imported by overland route. This will require developing the International North–South Transport Corridor (INSTC).

Changing Regional Dynamics

Waning of American influence, emergence of new leadership in Uzbekistan and Kyrgyzstan and increased Chinese presence define changing dynamics of the region. Drawdown of NATO troops in Afghanistan, and closure of Northern Distribution Network following US sanctions against Russia, contributed to reduction in US presence in the region. This included closure of US base in Karshi-Khanabad airbase in Uzbekistan (2005) and Manas in Kyrgyzstan in 2014.

Reduced US presence coincided with launching of BRI by China in 2013. These developments impelled by different geopolitical factors have contributed to greater Chinese inroad in the region.

Uzbekistan

Uzbekistan is the maverick, which has stayed out of the EEU, CSTO, while pursuing an active foreign policy. Unlike Turkmenistan, it did not choose neutrality. It does have the weight to follow independent policies, being the most populous country in Central Asia. It joined PfP and offered base facility to the USA till 2005, when it closed the base in protest against the US criticism of Andijan incident. It has signed *free trade agreement (FTA) with CIS countries* in 2011, but remains wary of the EEU which it considers supranational entity.

While participating in the SCO, Uzbekistan may not want transformation of the organization into a block. It wants to have flexibility in relations with the USA. Last year, President Mirziyoyev visited Washington ending the strained relations since 2005.

Uzbekistan has completed a 19 km tunnel connecting Fergana valley with the rest of Uzbekistan with *soft loan* from China. Uzbek President attended the OBOR Summit. Uzbekistan is discussing with

China construction of a 300 km *rail link* through Kyrgyzstan to China (Andijan-Osh-Kashgar).

Though Uzbekistan attended the OBOR Summit in China, its acceptance of BRI is not unconditional. It expects investment, not credit. The investment should not be in the extraction industries (mining, gas), but in the development and technology sectors.

In 2017, 15.2 per cent of Uzbek exports were to China, while 10.6 per cent were to Russia (Economist Intelligence Unit [EIU]). On the other hand, 23.9 per cent of Uzbek imports were from China, while 22.7 per cent of its imports were from Russia (EIU). Thus, China has emerged as a bigger trade partner than Russia. However, this does not mean complete dependence on these two big neighbours. There are substantial Uzbek exports to Switzerland. Russia will continue to have substantial economic presence. During President Putin's visit to the country, the accompanying business delegation signed agreements worth more than $27 billion.

Islam Karimov's passing away led to the country's opening to the outside world and economic reforms at home. Uzbekistan opened *two border crossings* with Kazakhstan after a long hiatus. President Mirziyoyev visited Kyrgyzstan in 2017, when the two countries reached an agreement on *demarcation of 84 per cent of their common frontier*. In 2018, President Mirziyoyev visited Tajikistan, when he agreed to drop objection to Rogun Dam. President Mirziyoyev also undertook economic reforms at home. This involved 50 per cent devaluation of the Uzbek currency Som.

Kazakhstan

Kazakhstan was the first CAR country to have served as non-permanent member of the UN Security Council. Its term 2017–2018 has just ended. It used its membership of the UN Security Council to highlight issues related to the CARs. It also took the initiative to host the Astana Conference on Syria, which included Russia, Turkey and Iran. This amounted to creating a parallel process to the Geneva Conference on Syria. The difference in thrust was in terms of support to the Bashar al-Assad government. This was closer to the Russian position on Syria.

Kazakhstan is a member of the EEU. It is also part of China's BRI. With 40 per cent of population being of Russian origin, it will continue to have strong links to Russia. President Nazarbayev, who is 78, has been in power since before the collapse of the Soviet Union. This has provided the country strong continuity in policy.

Rise in oil prices also buoyed up the Kazakh economy. Kazakhstan has traditionally enjoyed surplus balance of trade, while it has a negative current account balance as well as budget deficit. Both of these have shrunk with increased oil revenues. The country has high dependence on oil income, which account for more than one-third of the government revenue.

A meeting of presidents of four CARs was hosted in Astana in March 2018—Kazakhstan, the Kyrgyz Republic, Tajikistan and Uzbekistan. This was the first joint meeting in 4 years. Though no agreements were signed, the event was important.[11] It signified an attempt by the CARs to increase intra-CARs cooperation, independent of outside powers.

Kyrgyzstan

Kyrgyzstan among the CARs has the unique distinction of being a Parliamentary democracy. It is a member of EEU. Russia accounted for 26.3 per cent of country's imports, and 14.8 per cent of exports in 2017. Kazakhstan, another EEU member state, accounted for 13 per cent of Kyrgyz imports and 16.7 per cent of exports. The other major trading partner is Switzerland, which accounted for 27.7 per cent of exports.[12]

The Kyrgyz Republic has joined BRI. China is supporting a railway line from China through the Kyrgyz Republic into Uzbekistan and the North–South motor road project. Kyrgyzstan is also a member of CSTO. It hosts a Russian base in Kant, near Bishkek, the national capital. It is also a member of the SCO.

Kyrgyz accession to EEU in 2015 improved mobility for Kyrgyz workers in Russia. Workers' remittances amount for a substantial part of Kyrgyz foreign exchange earnings. But harmonization with EEU regulations also complicates trade with China, particularly re-export of Chinese goods to other EEU member states which are subject to local content rules.

---

[11] Erlan Karin, 'Central Asian leaders meeting represents unity, understanding' *The Astana Times*, 21 March 2018. Available at: https://astanatimes.com/2018/03/central-asian-leaders-meeting-represents-unity-understanding/.
[12] Ibid.

Improvement of Kyrgyzstan's relations with Uzbekistan and Tajikistan improve the prospects of CASA-1000 project, which involves laying a transmission line from Kyrgyzstan to Afghanistan and Pakistan.

The US base in Manas, used as a transit centre for the 'northern route', has been since closed down.

Turkmenistan

Gas exports account for 80 per cent of Turkmen exports. China accounts for 81.7 per cent of its gas exports. Lack of diversification in terms of product mix, and destination, has serious implications for the country's economy. Russia halted gas imports from Turkmenistan in January 2016, and gas exports to Iran stopped in January 2017.

The Country's flagship project—Turkmenistan–Afghanistan–Pakistan–India (TAPI)—faces uncertainty due to unsettled conditions in Afghanistan. With President Trump's decision to halve the US troop strength in Afghanistan, the situation in that country will worsen. This will have a further impact on TAPI.

In case Gazprom decides to resume purchase from Turkmenistan, or exports to China increased, Turkmenistan's economic situation will improve. It is planning to increase gas exports to China from 34 billion cubic meters (bcm) in 2017 to 65 bcm by 2020. This will entail completion of the fourth branch (Line D) of the Central Asia–China pipeline on time. This will have a carrying capacity of 25–30 bcm gas per year. In the long run, as Iran augments gas production from South pars field, and extends the pipeline north-east to Mashhad region, there will be less need for gas imports from Turkmenistan. This essentially means increased dependence on the Chinese market for its gas exports.

Tajikistan

Tajikistan is a front-line state bordering Afghanistan and has endured the spillover effect of the 3 decades' old Civil War in that country. It is member of Russian-led CSTO. Tajikistan hosts Russian troops. A lease agreement for stationing of 201st Motorized Division of Russia in Tajikistan has been renewed in 2012. In 2016, it also joined the China-led counterterrorism alliance, the Quadrilateral Cooperation and Coordination Mechanism, the other members being Afghanistan and Pakistan. China is investing heavily in the country including US$200 million investment in a metallurgical plant, and $1.6 billion investment in 500,000 ton per annum aluminium plant.[13]

ISIS and Hizb ut-Tahrir are active in Tajikistan. The government blames Islamic Renaissance Party of Tajikistan (IRPT) for increasing radicalization and calls them a terrorist organization. It was banned in 2015; before the ban, it was only a legal Islamic party.

The country's GDP is dependent upon remittances from Tajik workers in Russia. GDP showed an impressive rate of growth of 7.1 per cent in 2017.[14] The country suffers from *budget deficit, trade deficit* as well as *current account deficit*.

Agreement with Uzbekistan on Rogun Dam could augment Tajikistan's export of electricity to that country. If the Central Asian Electricity Grid is activated, this will enable it to export electricity to Kazakhstan. The country's electricity exports have already increased by 56.7 per cent in value terms in the first eight months of 2018 as compared to the corresponding period in the previous year.[15] Tajikistan could earn revenue from electricity generation as well as transit once CASA-1000 project is completed. *The success of all the three projects depends upon increased regional cooperation.* Worsening of Afghan situation will set back this process.

Islam

The Central Asian states belong to the Hanafi school of thought, a branch of Sunni Islam. Naqshbandi order emerged in the region near Bokhara in the 14th century. It took its name from Baha-ud-Din Naqshband Bukhari. Taimur considered him his inspiration. Naqshbandi thought influenced Sheikh Ahmad Sirhindi, a major figure in Islam's history in India. He opposed Akbar's views on Hindu and Muslim marriages. He also opposed separation of religion and state.[16]

The search for national identity after the CARs achieved statehood led to the revival of Islam. But official Islam in these countries continued to be under state control even in the post-Soviet period. All five CARs associated with Islam, and joined the Organisation of Islamic Cooperation (OIC). Interestingly, the constitutions of Turkmenistan

---

[13] Ibid.
[14] Ibid.
[15] Ibid.
[16] Available at https://en.wikipedia.org/wiki/Islam (accessed on 6 December 2019).

and Kazakhstan proclaim explicitly that the state is secular (*dunyavi*), though they also joined OIC.[17]

The post-Soviet period saw increased contacts with the Arab world. 'Wahhabism takes the place of Hanafi Sunnism in sectors of society that are suffering an identity crisis'.[18]

Terrorism and Extremism

The governments of CARs are committed to combat extremist philosophies. However, having common borders with Afghanistan has resulted in some manifestations of terrorist movements in Uzbekistan and Tajikistan. Islamic Movement of Uzbekistan (IMU) has links with local conditions.

'In 1997, an off-shoot of the Adalat and IRP, the Hizb-ul Tahrir (Liberation Party), headed by Yuldashev and Namanghani, launched armed actions from Afghanistan'.[19]

AfPak region has played a significant role in spreading extremist philosophy and contributed to the rise of organizations. The linkages work to spread extremism both ways. The Karachi airport attack of 2014 was claimed by Hizb ut-Tahrir, which has presence in Uzbekistan.

Defence and Security

CARs have sought security in a multi-vector foreign policy. With gradual withdrawal of US from the region, their policy options are narrowing. Kazakhstan, Kyrgyzstan and Tajikistan are members of Russian-led CSTO. Given its proximity to Afghanistan, and Wakhan strip adjoining Pakistan Occupied Kashmir, Tajikistan is of particular interest. The country has also witnessed instability and rise of IRPT.

Russia's largest non-naval military facility abroad is in Tajikistan with 7,000 troops. On 27–30 March 2017, Russia and Tajikistan held a joint exercise in the south of Tajikistan, involving 40,000 Tajik reservists, police and special forces and 2,000 Russian troops. On 30 May 2017,

---

[17] O. Roy, *The New Central Asia: Geopolitics and the Creation of Nations* (London: I.B. Tauris, 2007).
[18] Ibid.
[19] Ibid.

Tajikistan hosted Russia and other members of the Commonwealth of Independent States (CIS) to hold joint counterterrorism exercises.[20]

Tajikistan joined China-led counterterrorism alliance, the Quadrilateral Cooperation and Coordination Mechanism, along with Afghanistan and Pakistan in August 2016.[21] Notable absence from the grouping is that of Russia.

In October 2016, China held its first bilateral exercise, involving 10,000 Tajik troops, in Ishkashim district on the border with Afghanistan.[22] Is this a tentative attempt to establish an independent Chinese presence in the security sector in a region where Russia has been the net security provider?

India has invested in the development of Ayni Air Base in Tajikistan. The Gissar aerodrome in Ayni, west of Tajik capital Dushanbe, was a Soviet strategic station in Central Asia during the Cold War. The Border Roads Organisation (BRO) extended the airstrip at Gissar to 3,200 m. The facility was visited by President Ram Nath Kovind in October 2018. It was earlier visited by PM Narendra Modi in 2015.[23] However, any security cooperation between India and CARs would have to be within the parameters of their broader policy orientation.

Afghanistan

The Afghan situation has an impact directly on three CARs bordering the country—Tajikistan, Uzbekistan and Turkmenistan. They are, therefore, concerned with situation in that country. Post-9/11, the US involvement in Afghanistan also increased the salience of Central Asia in American foreign policy. Northern Distribution Network from running through Russia and Central Asia (Kazakhstan and Uzbekistan) was developed as an alternative to supply route running through Pakistan after NATO convoys came under attack in Pakistan. With expected US withdrawal from Afghanistan, this element may lose its importance in the American calculus. But for Central Asian states, geography is a permanent binding force.

---

[20] Economist Intelligence Unit, *Country Report*, 4th Quarter (London: Economist Intelligence Unit, 2017).
[21] Ibid.
[22] Ibid.
[23] Sujan Dutta, 'India Renews Interest in Running Its First Foreign Military Base in Tajikistan', *The Print* (11 October 2018).

Apart from geographical proximity, Uzbekistan and Tajikistan also have overlapping ethnic population with Afghanistan. Tajiks and Uzbeks account for 25 per cent and 11 per cent, respectively, of the Afghan population. It was the Tajik–Uzbek combination under Northern Alliance (NA) which was counterforce to Taliban in the 1990s. Their future orientation will affect the shape of dispensation in Afghanistan after the American withdrawal.

Uzbekistan had launched the initiative of 6+2 in the 1990s, which provided a platform for negotiations on Afghanistan. This incidentally *excluded* India. Uzbekistan is prepared to talk to 'armed opposition groups'. It has also invested considerably in developing a railway line from Termez to Herat. This is to be eventually linked to Iran. While Uzbekistan chose engagement, Tajikistan fell back on Russian protection under CSTO. Uzbekistan has appointed a Special Envoy on Afghanistan. Kazakhstan, though not an immediate neighbour, has taken diplomatic initiative on Afghanistan.

Spread of radicalism and extremist from AfPak region to Central Asia has grave implications for their security, and essentially secular, progressive polity.

India and Central Asia

Prime Minister Modi made a landmark visit to all five CARs in 2015. Smt Sushma Swaraj, external affairs minister (EAM), toured the region in August 2018. First India–Central Asia Dialogue at the level of foreign ministers was held recently in Samarkand, Uzbekistan, on 12–13 January 2019. It was co-chaired by EAM Smt Sushma Swaraj along with H. E. Mr Abdulaziz Kamilov, the foreign minister of the Republic of Uzbekistan. Afghanistan also participated as a special invitee. In April 2019, Defence Minister Smt Nirmala Sitharaman visited Bishkek to participate in SCO's Defence Ministers' Conclave, where she had bilateral discussions with the defence ministers of Kyrgyzstan, Russia and China. SCO Council of Foreign Ministers had its meeting on 22 May 2019 where EAM Smt Sushma Swaraj participated and reiterated India's commitments towards combating terrorism and extremism. She also had bilateral discussions with Kyrgyz President Sooronbay Jeenbekov on the sidelines of the summit. Kyrgyzstan is the host of 19th SCO Summit scheduled to be held on 13–14 June 2019 in Bishkek.

Despite historical ties and initiatives taken at the political level, India's footprint in the region is small. It has a miniscule share (0.54%) in global imports of Central Asia. Its share in Russia's global import is also very small (0.82%). The country-wise break-up is given in Table 18.6.

Indian presence is miniscule in Central Asia and is dwarfed by the Chinese trade with countries of the region. China has the advantage of proximity. But India also needs to do more (Table 18.7).

TABLE 18.6 *India's Share in Global Imports of CIS Countries and Russian Federation (US$ Billion)*

	Global Imports	Imports from India
Kazakhstan	33.6	0.151
Kyrgyzstan	3.8	0.0251
Tajikistan	2.493	0.0222
Turkmenistan	13.875	0.0685
Uzbekistan	3.280	0.0946
Total	67.048	0.3625
Russia	193.0	1.587

India's share in global imports of CIS countries is 0.54 per cent.

India's share in global imports of Russia is 0.82 per cent.

Note: The aforementioned percentage figures are an approximation, as figures of global imports are based on calendar year, while figures of imports from India are based on FY.

TABLE 18.7 *Central Asia's Trade with China and India, 2017 (in US$ million)*

	China	India
Kazakhstan	10,465.4	1,032.8
Turkmenistan	6,606	80.46
Uzbekistan	4,323.7	234.39
Kyrgyzstan	1,591	59.53
Tajikistan	458	74.24

Note: This comparison is only an approximation as Chinese figures are based on ADB data, which lists top 10 trading partners. India does not figure in the list. Indian figures are based on data derived from Indian Department of Commerce.

Absence of connectivity is the major reason for low export volume. This problem could be addressed by developing connectivity. The INSTC and Chabahar port are two important initiatives. Both hinge on transit through Iran. India undertook a pilot run along INSTC, when two containers were sent from Bandar Abbas north to Astara and Amirabad ports on Iran's Caspian Seashore. Bandar Abbas is connected to Astara port by road; a section of rail link between Rasht and Astara remains to be completed. In case of the Amirabad port, there exist both road and rail links with Bandar Abbas. Thus, infrastructure exists. On the other side of the border, road and rail links exist connecting Turkmenistan, Uzbekistan and Kazakhstan. A subsidiary of Russian railway is now offering leasing, as well as transport of containers, to Moscow and St Petersburg.

India is also committed to development of the Chabahar port. An interim operation has been started by India Ports Global Limited (IPGL). The port offers shortest land route to Afghanistan. Transit to Uzbekistan through Afghanistan is possible, though this route has not been used much due to security conditions in that country. Chabahar port is also connected to Inchebaroun and Mashhad/Sarakhs on Iran's northern border for transit of goods to CARs.

Towards a Central Asian Identity

The speeches by the representatives of the five CARs in the 73rd session of the UN General Assembly (UNGA) emphasized the need for regional cooperation *between* the countries of the region.[24] *There was no reference to BRI.*

Except for *Kyrgyzstan, no leader mentioned the SCO either.* President Jeenbekov mentioned: 'we also see a special role and a new mission of such regional organizations as the CIS, the SCO, the CSTO and the EEU'.

The Uzbek PR in his speech referred to the first Consultative meeting of the Heads of State of the Central Asian countries held last March in Astana. He described it as 'the bright symbol of a new era of regional cooperation'.[25]

---

[24] United Nations, *High-Level Meetings of the 73rd Session* (2019). Available at https://www.un.org/en/ga/73/meetings/index.shtml (accessed on 6 December 2019).

[25] Ibid.

Absence of such references does not mean Russia or China, or multilateral fora backed by them, has lost influence on the region. It does, however, express an aspiration for their destiny being decided by the countries of the region.

The other common element in the statements made by the five CARs was concern with the water situation. They also identified the *water problem* and drying up of Aral Sea as major issue. The Kyrghyz speech also underlined the problem of *uranium tailings*. All three—water, Aral Sea and uranium tailings—are legacy of the Soviet days.

Kazakhstan emphasized its strong position on disarmament issues. It mentioned it has signed the Treaty on the Prohibition of Nuclear Weapons. It reiterated its support to NPT and CTBT. It mentioned that the creation of nuclear weapon-free zones remains one of the most effective measures in combating the spread of WMD.

Uzbekistan, Kazakhstan, Turkmenistan and Tajikistan declared their concern about Afghan situation. Tajikistan referred to CASA-1000 as providing electricity to countries of the region. The transmission line project, when completed, will benefit Kyrgyzstan, Tajikistan, Afghanistan and Pakistan.

The quest for regional identity independent of outside presence remains an aspiration. At this stage, intra-regional trade is minimal. According to available World Bank data, in case of Kazakhstan, which has the largest economy in the region, trade with other CARs accounted for 2 per cent of its total trade in 2006. This figure went up to 4 per cent in 2017. In case of Kyrgyzstan, this figure stood at 24 per cent in 2006. This actually went down to 18 per cent in 2017.

Conclusion

The opening of Central Asia after collapse of the Soviet Union presented India with a unique opportunity to expand relations with the CARs. We have, however, lost considerable time. India's exports have a miniscule share (0.54%) of global imports of countries of the region. In the meantime, China has consolidated its presence. This phenomenon predates launch of BRI and goes beyond infrastructure to control natural resources.

Accession to the SCO does not expand India's political space. On core issues such as NPT and CCIT, Qingdao Declaration gives no comfort to Indian positions. This reflects not only Chinese role but also the competing position of Pakistan. India has joined the SCO along with

Pakistan. What is worse is that the SCO is being used to project a world view, which presents difficult choices for India at a time of growing distance between Russia and the USA.

There is still a chance, as speeches by CARs leaders in 73rd UNGA session contained no reference to BRI and with the exception of Kyrgyzstan, no leader mentioned the SCO either. This may reflect their sense of unease with growing Chinese presence, as much as quest for a shared regional identity. Deepening bilateral engagement with CARs countries is much more important than the SCO framework.

Trade, investment and connectivity are key to increasing India's footprints in Central Asia. Without development of the INSTC and Chabahar, this will remain an unfulfilled goal. Both hinge upon relations with Iran. India's presence will also help CARs pursue their multi-vector policy.

India and West Asia
Promoting Security in a Turbulent Region

Talmiz Ahmad

India's ties with West Asia go back several millennia: there is archaeological evidence that during the Harappan civilization, India provided foodstuffs, textiles and items of gracious living such as jewellery to consumers in the Arabian Peninsula. Indian mariners, merchants and intellectuals traversed the Indian Ocean with their Arab colleagues for at least 4,000 years so that over the centuries a shared civilizational ethos was created that persists to this day.

These linkages included the setting up of colonies of Indians in the towns of the Gulf and of Arab communities residing in Indian coastal towns, particularly in the Malabar.

British rule in India was unique in that not only did it extend across the Indian subcontinent, but it also embraced the territories of the Gulf. As James Onley has noted, Britain assumed responsibility for the defence of Oman in 1829, for the Trucial States in 1835, Bahrain in 1861, Kuwait in 1899 and Qatar in 1916.[1]

---

[1] James Onley, 'Britain and the Gulf Sheikhdoms, 1820–1971: The Politics of Protection' (Occasional Paper No. 4, Centre for International and Regional Studies, Georgetown University School of Foreign Service in Qatar, 2009), 1.

The actual implementation of this imperial responsibility was vested in the Government of British India which provided the funding and personnel for this enterprise. This established an extraordinarily substantial and all-embracing political, economic and cultural linkage between India and the people of the Gulf. Onley describes the Gulf–India connection as follows:

> The [Gulf] region's economic dependence on India and India's profound cultural and political influence on the region up to 1947 was such that locals regarded India and Indians as highly as they now regard the West and Westerners. For generations leading up to Britain's withdrawal from India, the sheikhdoms of Eastern Arabia formed part of Britain's Indian Empire. India and Indians represented power and prestige.[2]

India–West Asia Ties

Independent India inherited these substantial links with the Gulf and West Asia. In 1955, the Saudi monarch visited India, while Prime Minister Jawaharlal Nehru was extended a warm welcome in the kingdom next year. However, the political and ideological divide in West Asia with the replacement of monarchies by revolutionary regimes, commencing with Nasser's revolution in Egypt in 1953, soon had an impact on India's ties with West Asia. India moved closer to the revolutionary republics and found a strategic partner in the Soviet Union in the Cold War, while the traditional monarchies in the region affiliated themselves with the US-led Western alliance which also viewed 'Islam' as a 'natural ally' against 'godless communism'.

After the Arab–Israeli War of 1967, as the balance of influence in West Asia shifted in favour of the monarchies, India's political ties with the latter got further diluted, even as the monarchies moved closer to Pakistan, their partner in the Cold War alliance. This partnership between the USA, Saudi Arabia and Pakistan was consolidated during the 'global jihad' organized by them in Afghanistan against the Soviet occupation. This initiative was vigorously opposed by India which backed the Soviet Union as a strategic ally, while decrying the mobilization of religious faith for political purposes.

---

[2] James Onley, 'Indian Communities in the Persian Gulf, c 1500–1947', in *The Persian Gulf in Modern Times: People, Ports, and History*, ed. Lawrence G. Potter (New York, NY: Palgrave MacMillan, 2014), 231.

India's political estrangement from the Gulf monarchies continued after the Soviet withdrawal from Afghanistan, the end of the Cold War and the break-up of the Soviet Union. This was because the monarchies continued to be close partners of Pakistan and turned a blind eye to Pakistan's use of jihadi militants sponsored by its intelligence agency, the Inter-Services Intelligence (ISI), to attack India from 1989 in the state of Jammu and Kashmir, and later in other parts of the country. The Gulf countries were persuaded by Pakistan to view these attacks as reflective not of extremist militancy but of popular anger on account of the unresolved Kashmir issue.

Both during and after the Cold War, India's principal political links in West Asia were with the republics—Egypt, Iraq, Syria, Yemen and Libya. Iraq and Libya generously awarded major infrastructure development projects to Indian companies, even as India had very substantial army and air force training programmes with Iraq that continued up to 1990.

Though through the 1980s and 1990s India's political ties with the Gulf Arab countries (organized from 1981 as the Gulf Cooperation Council [GCC]) were at best lukewarm, this period and beyond saw a remarkable shift in favour of the employment of Indian nationals in these countries at the expense of Pakistan and other Arab countries.

Commencing with just about a million or so in the early 1980s, the Indian community increased to three and a half million by 2005 to six million in 2012, and is over 8.5 million today. The Indian community is the largest expatriate community in every country of the GCC and is the majority community in three countries—the UAE, Bahrain and Qatar.

Besides its large size, it is important to note that Indians are represented in significant numbers at every level of the GCC economies—as business tycoons, professionals, technicians and blue-collar workers. The last 15 years have also witnessed a change in the profile of the Indian presence: where once blue-collar workers were dominant, today there is a marked shift in favour of Indian professionals as engineers, architects, doctors, managers and accountants. Today, several hundred Indians head Gulf and multinational companies in the region.

The commencement of the new millennium marked significant changes in India's political and economic ties with the GCC countries. As India started achieving high growth rates, India's primary energy consumption more than doubled between 1990 and 2012, and by 2013 India had become the third largest consumer of energy in the world.

Given the paucity of domestic production, India became a major importer of energy resources: in 2012, about 70 per cent of India's oil needs were met by imports, rising from 42 per cent in 1990. Over half of India's imports are from the GCC countries; with imports from Iraq and Iran, India's import dependence on the Gulf goes up to 80 per cent. Energy imports have also made the GCC India's leading trade partner as a regional bloc: India–GCC trade was valued at $104 billion in 2017–2018, higher than both India–EU trade ($102 billion) and India–ASEAN trade ($81 billion).[3]

India–West Asia Political Ties

India's political ties with the Gulf monarchies witnessed an upswing in tandem with the rise in India's energy imports from the Gulf and its emergence as a high growth economy. After a long gap, serious political engagement commenced with the visit to India of the Saudi Minister of State for Foreign Affairs, Dr Nizar Obaid Madani, in February 2000 and the visit to Riyadh of Indian External Affairs Minister Jaswant Singh in January 2001.

During this visit, some of the cobwebs from the past, particularly the kingdom's ties with Pakistan that had been an obstacle to the development of Indo-Saudi ties, were swept aside: Saudi leaders now conveyed that the kingdom valued its ties with India on its own merits and would not view relations with India through the prism of its links with any other country. With this breakthrough, between 2005 and 2007, the head of state or government of every GCC country visited India.

The most important visit in this period was that of the Saudi ruler, King Abdullah bin Abdulaziz as chief guest at India's Republic Day celebrations in January 2006. The high point of the visit was the signing of the 'Delhi Declaration' by the Saudi monarch and the Indian prime minister which committed the two countries to realizing a 'strategic energy partnership' and enhanced economic and investment cooperation.

This interaction in Delhi was reciprocated four years later when Prime Minister Manmohan Singh visited Riyadh in February–March 2010. During the four-year period, the regional security environment

---

[3] Rahul Roy-Chaudhury, 'India and the Gulf Region: Building Strategic Partnerships', IISS (29 August 2018). Available at https://www.iiss.org/blogs/analysis/2018/08/india-gulf-strategic-partnerships (accessed on 6 December 2019).

had deteriorated with the expanding presence of the Al-Qaeda in different parts of the region, strengthening of the Taliban in Afghanistan, serious unrest in Yemen, ongoing political uncertainty and sectarian discord in Iraq and increased sectarian violence and terror in Pakistan.

Specifically, in November 2008, Mumbai experienced a violent assault planned and directed from Pakistan. This attack was perpetrated by extremist militants who had been motivated and trained in Pakistan with the aim of spreading widespread murder and mayhem as ends in themselves, with no link with the Kashmir issue. This attack finally made clear to GCC leaders that Pakistan was the fountainhead of jihadi violence that had made the entire region vulnerable. The Mumbai attack played a central role in the shaping of the India–Saudi Arabia strategic partnership enshrined in the 'Riyadh Declaration' signed by the leaders of the two countries during the Manmohan Singh visit.

India–Iran Relations

On 15 March 1950, New Delhi and Tehran signed a friendship treaty which called for 'perpetual peace and friendship' between the two countries. However, their ties were restricted by the fact that they were on opposite sides during the Cold War. This also meant that Iran and Pakistan were staunch political and military allies as members of the Central Treaty Organisation (CENTO). During the 1965 and 1971 wars between India and Pakistan, Iran provided military assistance to Pakistan. Though the Shah of Iran did make overtures to India from time to time and boosted economic and energy links through investments in the Mangalore Refinery and the Irano-Hind shipping line, these initiatives were largely aimed at boosting Iran's stature vis-à-vis its Arab neighbours and did not effect a significant change in bilateral ties with India.

India largely welcomed Iran's 1979 Revolution as an expression of national self-assertion, but differences persisted between New Delhi and Tehran particularly in respect of Afghanistan: Iran was critical of the Soviet invasion of Afghanistan, while India prioritized its strategic ties with the Soviet Union and refused to criticize the occupation in public. Again, during the Iran–Iraq War, India appeared to be more supportive of Iraq due to its close and long-standing political, military and economic ties with the Saddam regime. The two countries moved closer to each other in the 1990s when they both backed the 'Northern Alliance' in Afghanistan against the Taliban.

Reciprocal high-level visits commenced from the early 1990s, culminating in Prime Minister Atal Bihari Vajpayee's visit in 2001 and the conclusion of the 'Tehran Declaration' that envisaged cooperation in a wide range of areas of strategic importance, including defence, which were affirmed and taken forward in the 'New Delhi Declaration' signed by President Khatami and the Indian prime minister in January 2003.

However, bilateral ties were severely constrained by the increasingly harsh sanctions imposed on Iran by the USA and its allies on account of its nuclear weapons programme, culminating in restrictions on Iran's oil exports and international banking and financial transactions from 2010. Though Iran slipped from the second to the sixth position in terms of country-wise oil imports by India, both sides still found creative ways to maintain substantial energy and economic ties.

The conclusion of the nuclear agreement with Iran by the P5+1 powers in January 2016 opened fresh opportunities to reinvigorate bilateral relations. This was done most emphatically during the visit to Tehran of Prime Minister Narendra Modi in May 2016. This visit was particularly significant for boosting bilateral ties and in terms of the projection of India's strategic interests in West and Central Asia. While energy remained central to the bilateral relationship, the leaders of India and Iran envisioned much broader ties. Iranian President Hassan Rouhani noted that his country was 'rich in energy' while India had 'rich minds', factors that, operating in tandem, would yield achievements in frontier areas such as ICT, bio- and nanotechnology, and space and aerospace.

The two countries then signed the Chabahar port development agreement and the trilateral trade and transit pact between India, Afghanistan and Iran. The trade and transit corridors will enable India and Iran to contribute to Afghanistan's economic development and its stability. The corridor will then go across north Afghanistan to all the Central Asian Republics, ending at the Kazakh capital, Almaty.

The Chabahar corridor is complemented by the India-supported International North–South Transit Corridor that goes north-westwards from Chabahar port to Azerbaijan, Russia and Europe. India's outreach to Central Asia and beyond has till now been restricted by the absence of land connections, while global sanctions had prevented Iran from pursuing its interests in the region. The new corridors will change this situation dramatically: they were rightly described by Mr Modi as 'new routes for peace and prosperity'.

President Hassan Rouhani visited India in February 2018. The joint statement issued during the visit applauded the role of the two countries in 'promoting multi-modal connectivity within and across the region'. The two sides agreed to pursue defence cooperation and work together against terrorism. Both countries placed a 'pluralistic, democratic and independent' Afghanistan as central to 'peace and stability in the region' and, in a clear reference to the Pakistani role in hindering free movement of goods from India to Afghanistan, 'called upon countries of the region' to enhance regional connectivity and remove obstacles on land transit.

Sanctions on Iran reinstated by the Trump administration in November 2018 do not embrace the Chabahar project which has great strategic value for India. It is Iran's only deep-water port; it is outside the Gulf and just about 80 km from Gwadar port in Pakistan. Chabahar will give India commercial access to Afghanistan and all the Central Asian Republics. It will also provide the latter with the shortest overland route to the Indian Ocean and thence to markets in Asia and Africa. The Indian company, India Ports Global Ltd, officially started to run the Shahid Beheshti port at Chabahar from January 2019.

The Saudi–Iran Divide

The roots of the current competitions and contentions in West Asia between Saudi Arabia and the Islamic Republic can be traced to events that took place 40 years ago in 1979. This year marked the 1,400th year of the advent of Islam and witnessed three events whose reverberations continue to impact on present-day politics in the region.

The year began with the Islamic Revolution in Iran. Not only did this event overthrow the country's royal order, it also made Islam, as propounded by its leader Ayatollah Ruhollah Khomeini, its ruling doctrine that made Iran a revolutionary force against secular politics and Western political power and cultural influence. Its message, anchored in the region's Islamic traditions, was a powerful allure for the region's Arab youth.

The Islamic Republic's neighbour across the Gulf, Saudi Arabia, viewed the revolution with alarm as it appeared to challenge its leadership of the Arab and Islamic world. These concerns were further aggravated by the second event of that year—the occupation of the Grand Mosque in Mecca by Islamic zealots. They condemned the Saudi royal family for materialism, corruption and licentiousness, and its proximity to the West and declared it unfit to be the guardian of Islam's holy sites of Mecca and Medina.

After the rebellion was crushed with military force, the kingdom confronted the challenge from the possible spread of the Islamic revolution into neighbouring countries through military action. The Saudi leadership encouraged the Iraqi leader, Saddam Hussein, to launch a military attack on Iran. Seeing the Iranian armed forces in disarray, Saddam thought his army would capture large chunks of Iranian territory and dictate terms that would end the Islamic regime and replace it with a more amenable leadership.

But Saddam's plans were foiled as his attack united Iran and encouraged its forces to face the aggression resolutely. The war stretched over eight years and ended only when both sides were exhausted.

The war not only saved the Islamic revolution but also imbued into the Iranian psyche a sense of achievement in the face near-total global isolation when its cities were showered with missiles and its people with chemical weapons, with no protest from the international community and its institutions.

In 1979 itself, in early November, Iran revolutionary youth attacked the US Embassy in Tehran and took its diplomats hostage for 444 days, largely as a reprisal for the long period of Western interventions in Iranian politics, particularly the overthrow of its democratic government in 1953. For the Americans, the diplomats' incarceration and the failed rescue effort laid the basis for an enduring animosity for the Islamic revolution and its leaders that continues to animate the attitude of large sections of the US political, official, media and academic establishments.

Regime Change in Iraq

The end of the Iraq–Iran war was marked by an extended period of camaraderie and positive engagement between Iran and Saudi Arabia when Iran shifted its focus from revolutionary zeal to economic development. Iran stopped questioning the legitimacy of the Saudi royal family, while Saudi leaders proclaimed there were no limits to cooperation with Iran. Asked about the possibility of military conflict with Iran, then Crown Prince Abdullah bin Abdulaziz said, 'This would be strange, since the two countries are linked by ties of religion, history and heritage.'[4]

---

[4] Reza Ekhtiari Amiri, and Ku Hasnita Samsu, 'Security Cooperation of Iran and Saudi Arabia', *International Journal of Business and Social Science* 2, no. 16: 249.

This camaraderie ended with the US assault on Iraq and subsequent regime change and the US commitment to Shia empowerment in the country that overtly privileged the majority Shia community. Saudi Arabia and its GCC partners viewed this approach as opening the doors to the expansion of Iran's influence into one more Arab country. This increased the Saudi sense of strategic vulnerability vis-à-vis its Gulf neighbour, viewing this challenge in sectarian terms: King Abdullah II of Jordan first spoke of the 'Shia Crescent' engulfing the region in 2004, remarks that were later echoed by Egypt's President Hosni Mubarak and Saudi Foreign Minister Prince Saud Al Faisal.

Saudi Arabia set up a regional balance of power by aligning itself with Egypt. But Iraq remained an area of competition in the Gulf: Iran expanded its influence with the support of the regime headed by Prime Minister Nouri al-Maliki who depended on Shia militia funded, armed and trained by Iran. Saudi Arabia retaliated by providing backing for the jihadi insurgency that commenced from 2003 itself under the leadership of the Afghanistan veteran, Abu Musab al-Zarqawi, who proclaimed his formal affiliation with Al-Qaeda by calling his organization Al-Qaeda in Iraq (AQI). After Zarqawi's death in 2006, his successors renamed the body the Islamic State of Iraq (ISI) to affirm their independence from Al-Qaeda and their intention to make Iraq into an Islamic state.

While Saudi Arabia maintained no ties with the Iraqi government in Baghdad, Iran remained the most influential in the country and the principal backer of the government against the ISI.

Arab Spring and After

The balance of power in West Asia ended abruptly with the fall of the Mubarak regime in February 2011 in the wake of the Arab Spring agitations. The Saudi sense of vulnerability increased further with the demand for political reform in Bahrain, a neighbour and GCC member with a Shia majority. The kingdom believed that any reform in Bahrain would empower the Shia and provide a fresh opening for the expansion of Iran's influence to the Saudi border and within the GCC family.

Saudi Arabia brought an abrupt end to the reform agitation in Bahrain by sending its troops into the country and forcibly dispersing the demonstrators. The kingdom then confronted Iranian interests in Syria: it felt that removal of the pro-Iran Bashar al-Assad regime would bring a major Arab country back into the political mainstream and restore the regional balance of power. It would also cut Iran's outreach to the Mediterranean, besides having the additional benefit of ending Iran's ties to the Hezbollah via Damascus, thus bringing one more country into the Arab mainstream.

The kingdom's game plan for Syria stuttered at the outset itself when US President Barack Obama refused to bomb Damascus to effect regime change on the ground that earlier US interventions had brought no advantage to the USA and had only benefitted the jihadis. Saudi Arabia then perforce had to rely on ground action against Assad. It shaped this confrontation on sectarian basis, mobilizing Salafi militants from Syria's Sunni community, in alliance with Qatar and Syria, which were ranged against Shia militia provided by Iran from its Islamic Revolutionary Guard Corps (IRGC) as well as from the Hezbollah and militants from Iraq, Afghanistan and Pakistan.

Though the Saudi-backed militants met with some initial successes, the entry of Russian forces on the side of the Assad government in September 2015 ensured that there would be no military victory for the rebels. The kingdom's efforts received a further setback when Turkey, alarmed by the military successes of the Syrian Kurds and the prospect of their setting up a 'homeland' at the Syria–Turkey border, left the Saudi side and joined Russia and Iran in the Astana peace process, even as Assad's forces continued to take territory from the rebels.

Besides the ongoing conflict in Syria, Saudi Arabia opened another front against Iran, this time in Yemen with which it shares a 1,400-km border. Here, taking advantage of a weak central government in Sanaa after the replacement of long-standing President Ali Abdullah Saleh by his deputy, Abdrabbuh Mansur Hadi, the disgruntled Zaydis of North Yemen had mobilized themselves as a militant movement, informally referred to as 'Houthis' after the family name of their founder.

The Houthis, allied with the former president, occupied Sanaa and then went southwards to take Aden. Based on the Zaydis' Shia identity, Saudi Arabia viewed these successes as providing Iran with a strong military and political base at its border. It launched a military assault on the Houthis from March 2015 and later initiated ground action from the south.

In the four years of war, the Saudis have little to show in terms of achievement on the ground, and, despite widespread death and destruction, the major towns of Taizz, the port city of Hodeidah and Sanaa, the capital, remain with the Houthis.

The Three-Nation Peace Initiative

The doctrinal and strategic competition between Saudi Arabia and Iran is at the heart of the ongoing insecurity in West Asia, manifested through proxy wars in Syria and Yemen, and rivalry in Iraq, and has been shaped largely in sectarian terms. While Saudi Arabia views the expansion of Iran's influence in West Asia as part of its hegemonic intentions, Iran protests that it has no aggressive motives and that the strategic advantages it enjoys at present are entirely unintended consequences of US-led campaigns, first, to destroy the Taliban regime in the east and then the Saddam government in the West. It sees itself as shackled by sanctions and the victim of US hostility for the Islamic revolution. It also robustly denies any role in fomenting the Houthi uprising, pointing out that this is entirely due to domestic contentions.

Setting out the Saudi position, in an essay written in 2016, Prince Abdul Majeed Al Saud said that 'Iran remains the greatest threat to regional peace and security.'[5] According to him, three points define the regime's agenda: developing nuclear weapons, support for terrorist groups and illegitimate leaders (a reference to Hezbollah and Bashar al-Assad), and a desire to divide West Asia along sectarian lines in order to export its revolution to other states.

In their response in the same publication, Iranian scholars Seyed Hossein Mousavian and Mehrdad Saberi accused the Saudis of pursuing an incoherent and inconsistent foreign policy by first backing Saddam Hussain against Iran and then turning against him. Similarly, in Yemen, they had supported the Zaydis in the Civil War in the 1960s but were now at war with the same people. The kingdom, they said, also had a long record of interfering in the affairs of neighbouring countries—Bahrain, Syria, Egypt, Libya and Yemen.[6]

With the advent of the Trump presidency in the USA, the regional security scenario has deteriorated. The president has withdrawn from the nuclear agreement with Iran and has committed himself to effecting regime change in the Islamic Republic. Trump has established

---

[5] HRH Prince Abdulmajeed Al Saud, 'Know Your Enemy, Embrace Your Friends: A Call for Caution in Relations with Iran', *Iran Matters* (18 February 2016). Available at http://iranmatters.belfercenter.org/blog/iran-saudi-conflict (accessed on 18 December 2019).
[6] Seyed Hossein Mouvasian, and Mehrdad Saberi, 'The Iran–Saudi Conflict and the Endgame' (18 February 2016).

very close ties with Saudi Arabia and is promoting a US-Saudi-Israel coalition against Iran in the theatres of its influence, particularly in Syria and Iraq.

There are now serious possibilities of the ongoing proxy conflicts evolving into a direct conflict between them. Given the abiding interests that India, China and Russia have in regional security, it is proposed that these countries shape and promote a diplomatic initiative that will encourage mutual confidence and dialogue between the two estranged Islamic neighbours. Once this has been achieved, it is suggested that the three countries pursue the realization of a regional cooperative security arrangement. The three nations are well placed to shape and pursue this initiative.

India

As Prime Minister Narendra Modi flew out from Doha on 5 June 2016, he completed an unprecedented Indian diplomatic engagement with the countries of the Gulf: in the previous 10 months, he had visited the UAE, Saudi Arabia, Iran and Qatar, and hosted the Abu Dhabi Crown Prince Sheikh Mohammed bin Zayed Al Nahyan in Delhi. In every capital, he was received with the greatest warmth; every country applauded its historic and civilizational links with India, and every interaction yielded substantial agreements which will take bilateral relations to new areas and reshape ties to make them relevant to contemporary times.

Every Gulf country expressed anxiety about the threat from terrorism and pledged to work closely with India to combat it, not only through strong armed action but also by countering radicalization through promotion of a moderate religious discourse espousing peace, tolerance and inclusiveness.

Enhancement of defence ties has been given central importance by all the countries visited by the prime minister. This includes frequent dialogue between senior officers, training, joint exercises by the three arms of the militaries of both countries, joint maritime operations, and supply and joint development of arms and ammunition. Defence cooperation has been complemented by the countries agreeing to intelligence-sharing, counterterrorism operations, capacity building and adoption of best practices and technologies among the security agencies on both sides.

Every one of the joint statements contained a subtext that poses a challenge for India and imposes a new responsibility on it: how to shape an Indian role to promote security in the Gulf?

Most of the countries saw India as their 'strategic partner', a status that represents a high degree of shared values, perceptions and approaches on matters of security concern. Thus, the joint statement with the UAE spoke of 'shared threats to peace, stability and security', and agreed to a 'shared endeavour' to address these concerns, which is founded on 'common ideals and convergent interests'. It spoke of the need for the two countries to establish a 'close strategic partnership' for 'these uncertain times' and called upon them to 'work together to promote peace, reconciliation, stability ... in the wider South Asia, Gulf and west Asia'.

Similarly, the joint statement with Saudi Arabia talked of the two countries' responsibility to promote peace, security and stability in the region. It noted 'the close interlinkage of the stability and security of the Gulf region and the Indian sub-continent and the need for maintaining a secure and peaceful environment for the development of the countries of the region'. In Tehran, Mr Modi noted that India and Iran 'share a crucial stake in peace, stability and prosperity' in the region and have shared concerns relating to 'instability, radicalism and terror'. The two countries agreed to enhance cooperation between their defence and security institutions.

These early interactions were followed by return visits to India of the Crown Prince of Abu Dhabi, Sheikh Mohammed bin Zayed, as the chief guest at India's Republic Day celebrations in January 2017 and of the Iranian president in February 2018.

Prime Minister Modi's interactions with the principal countries of the Gulf have affirmed the acceptance of India as a credible player in the security scenario of this troubled region and have prepared a fertile soil for an initiative to promote regional peace and stability.

China

US disengagement from West Asia and the insistence of President Obama that other countries with an abiding interest in regional security stop being 'free riders' opened opportunities for countries concerned about regional stability to intensify their links with the region. China, with the substantial energy and economic ties with West Asia, has responded to this opportunity with alacrity.

There has been an upswing in its interactions with the Gulf countries in recent years. These have included visits to Beijing of the Bahraini king, the then Saudi crown prince and the Iranian President Hassan Rouhani and the Kuwaiti prime minister in May 2014. China's principal interest has been to consolidate energy links and expand commercial ties, possibly through a free trade agreement with the GCC, on which talks have been taking place since 2004. Now, the 'Belt and Road Initiative' (BRI) has significantly increased interest in China in expanding its trade and investment links and its logistical connectivity with this crucial pathway to Europe through the land route from the Gulf and the sea route through the Red Sea to the Mediterranean and beyond.

China has also been active in Iran. It signed an MOU on defence cooperation with Iran in October 2015, encompassing technical fields, intelligence, cyberspace and terrorism. More importantly, Iran is a junction on the BRI projects, on both the proposed land and sea corridors, and thus its participation is crucial for the success of this ambitious endeavour that, when completed, will transform the economic and strategic landscape of the world. In fact, a significant logistical link with Iran has already been achieved: a train from the Chinese town of Yiwu in Zhejiang province, with 32 containers of goods, covered 9,500 km to reach Tehran in 14 days. This was 30 days less than the journey from Shanghai to Bandar Abbas.

Given its crucial interests, China cannot be indifferent to the turmoil in West Asia. In January 2016, just after the signing of the nuclear agreement with Iran, President Xi Jinping undertook a tour of the Gulf that included visits to Saudi Arabia, Egypt and Iran. Besides his important bilateral interactions, he delivered a substantial address at the Arab League headquarters in which he set out with clarity and eloquence his panacea for the region's ills and the content and direction of China's engagement with the Arab world at least for the next two decades.

To ameliorate the region's security problems, the Chinese president recommended the rejection of the use of force, 'zero-sum' mentality and 'spheres of influence'. He insisted that solutions be sought within the region and not imposed from outside. He suggested a two-pronged approach of 'dialogue and development' within the region, founded on respect for 'national conditions' (i.e., historical, cultural and societal factors that shape the national ethos). In confronting terrorism, he proposed addressing both its symptoms and root causes.

Regarding China's ties with West Asia, he firmly rejected any military intervention by his country. Instead, he offered a broad range of economic and cultural connections: economic ties would be based on the '1+2+3 pattern', with energy as its priority, followed by trade and infrastructure development, and then a move into frontier areas nuclear energy, space and renewable energy. Cultural ties would be anchored in an 'inter-civilizational dialogue', with significant interactions between scholars, youth, clerics, artists, etc.

Russia

Just as the USA seems to be withdrawing from significant military engagements in West Asia, Russia has dramatically entered the regional scenario as a military and diplomatic force that expects to play a major role in shaping the region's security order. The Russian initiative in West Asia is part of its vision of disrupting the 'strategic deadlock' which, in its view, has enabled the West to keep in place a world order that it dominates and ensures it is subject to its rules.

To change this order, Russia is pursuing what Piotr Dutkiewicz and Nikolay Kozhanov have referred to as a 'deadlock-breaking strategy' in terms of which Russia will take a series of initiatives 'to create revisions within the existing regional and global order that are in line with Russia's national interests'.[7] The Russian approach in pursuing this agenda will be based on 'keeping China content, NATO at a healthy distance, and confrontation with the US and the EU at an affordable level'.[8]

Russia's expanding ties with Iran are a part of this strategy. After a series of ups and downs in earlier years, Russia began to court Iran seriously from 2012, at a time when it had no friends in West Asia. Putin and Iranian President Ahmadinejad met at the Shanghai Cooperation Organisation (SCO) summit in June 2012 and anchored the future development of their ties on Iran's nuclear weapons issue; their bilateral nuclear cooperation; expansion of economic relations

---

[7] Piotr Dutkiewicz and Nikolay Kozhanov, 'Civil War in Syria and the Evolution of Russian–Iranian Relations' (Research Paper, Russian Studies Unit, Emirates Policy Center, Abu Dhabi, May 2016), 3. Available at http://www.epc.ae/sites/default/files/publications/Reserach%20Paper—Civil%20War%20in%20Syria.pdf (accessed on 18 December 2019).

[8] Ibid.

and their working together on matters relating to the Caspian Sea. In an unprecedented gesture, Putin referred to Iran as 'an old traditional friend'.

This relationship with Russia suited Iran as well, since it was itself estranged from most of its Arab neighbours, was subject to increasingly harsh sanctions and was looking for a major country as a partner. From then onwards, Russia also exerted considerable effort to get the Iranians involved in negotiations on the nuclear weapons issue with the P5+1, with its leaders and diplomats actively involved in ensuring a successful outcome in early January 2016.

Russian military forces dramatically entered the Syrian conflict in September 2015 on the side of the al-Assad regime, thus boosting the capabilities of the national army. Russian motives in entering the Syrian battleground were to keep Syria intact; preserve the regime from being overthrown through external pressure; promote its interests by annihilating Russians in jihadi ranks; seriously disrupt the increasing capabilities and appeal of jihadi forces, both Al-Qaeda and the Islamic State, and, above all, give a clear signal to Western powers and their regional allies that externally sponsored regime changes were not acceptable.

Western sanctions and the fall in oil prices in 2015–2017 have put considerable pressure on the Russian economy and made it imperative for the country to explore new markets. West Asia has acquired considerable importance in this regard. Bilateral trade between Russia and West Asia went from $2.2 billion in 2010 to $4.2 billion in 2016, with overall trade being in Russia's favour.[9] The principal items that Russia is hoping to export to the region are: oil and gas, petroleum products, equipment and machinery, transport vehicles, precious metals, and metallurgical and agricultural products. Items of long-term interest to Russia in the Gulf are: grain, precious stones and metals and arms; two new areas under consideration are space and nuclear energy.[10]

Russia is a relative newcomer to the West Asian theatre, but now, as Nikolay Kozhanov has noted, it has 'developed its interests in the region as a goal in itself'.[11] It sees its role in the region as part of its conviction that it has a significant role in addressing matters of global

---

[9] Nikolay Kozhanov, 'Russian Policy across the Middle East: Motivations and Methods' (Research Paper, Chatham House, February 2018), 32–33. Available at https://www.chathamhouse.org/publication/russian-policy-across-middle-east-motivations-and-methods (accessed on 18 December 2019).
[10] Ibid., 14–15.
[11] Ibid., 4.

importance. As it has grown increasingly estranged from the West, this conviction has become even more important, as has been the need for it to diversify its global engagements.

Commentators have understood clearly that Russia has a 'strategy and staying power' for its presence in West Asia; as Steven Cook of the Council on Foreign Relations has noted, Russia has 'a strategy to weaken the West, and it starts in the Middle East'.[12] Kozhanov affirms this view by pointing out that Russia's present foray into West Asia is different from its earlier attempts to enter the region; it is now an effort to 'mitigate the negative effects of ongoing confrontation between Moscow and the West on Russia's economy, security and international relations'.[13] In November 2017, during his visit to Tehran, Putin is reported to have assured Supreme Leader Ali Khamenei that Russia would stand by Iran in its confrontation with the USA; Khamenei is said to have told him: 'Our cooperation can isolate America'.[14]

Promoting Confidence-building Measures

Given the substantial ties that the three diplomatic partners—India, China and Russia—have with the major countries of West Asia and the abiding interest they have in regional security, they can shape and pursue a peace initiative in their own interest and in the interest of the region that is so important for global stability and economic benefit. In this regard, they have solid support from historical precedent.

The Thirty Years' War in Europe in the Middle Ages and the Peace of Westphalia that brought it to an end offers diplomatic tools for peace-making that can serve as useful models for the proposed initiative.[15] Among the factors that promoted the peace was the role of a 'Third Party' that was made up of cross-confessional countries that had an abiding interest in peace, were willing to work with other countries

---

[12] Steven A. Cook, 'Russia Is in the Middle East to Stay', *Foreign Policy* (16 March 2018). Available at http://foreignpolicy.com/2018/03/16/the-middle-east-needs-a-steady-boyfriend/ (accessed on 25 May 2018).

[13] Nikolay Kozhanov, 'Russian Policy across the Middle East', 8.

[14] Robin Wright, 'Russia and Iran Deepen Ties to Challenge Trump and the United States', *The New Yorker* (2 March 2018). Available at https://www.newyorker.com/news/news-desk/russia-and-iran-deepen-ties-to-challenge-trump-and-the-united-states (accessed on 25 May 2018).

[15] This is examined in some detail in: Patrick Milton, Michael Axworthy, and Brendan Simms, *Towards a Westphalia for the Middle East* (London: Hurst and Company, 2018).

similarly inclined and had enough clout in terms of legitimacy and geopolitical capability to apply pressure on the parties in contention when needed. The three countries proposed fit the description of the 'Third Party'.

It makes sense for India to lead the three-nation initiative: it has the longest, uninterrupted and substantial ties with all the Gulf countries. It has an established regional standing for its political, economic and technological achievements as also the fact that its conduct in international interaction has consistently been non-hegemonic, non-intrusive and non-prescriptive. It also has the highest stake in regional stability on account of its energy and economic interests. Above all, it has a resident community of over 8 million in the region whose welfare is of paramount importance to all governments in Delhi.

While the three countries leading the peace initiative have close and important ties with each both bilaterally and as members of multilateral fora such as BRICS and the SCO, they also have differences; while Russia and China have a stronger record of cooperative effort in regional and global affairs, India and China have some important differences: they have an unresolved border dispute; India has serious concerns relating to China's close ties with Pakistan and its expanding political and economic influence in other South Asian countries, and India is also unhappy about the Chinese naval presence in the Indian Ocean and views the BRI projects as manifestations of China's regional hegemonic ambitions.

While these are important differences, they need not necessarily come in the way of cooperative efforts in promoting security in West Asia. Both countries have a substantial and abiding interest in regional stability. Again, Russia's presence will ensure that internal balance in the functioning of the three countries as they work together to promote the peace initiative.

Restoration of mutual confidence between Iran and Saudi Arabia will have to be achieved in two steps: first, there will have to be the acceptance of certain basic rules relating to regional conduct. These will include the rejection of sectarian discourse in bilateral interactions and references to domestic issues. Again, the two countries will have to eschew using non-state actors and extremist elements to undermine the political order of the other or interfere in the internal crises in regional entities.

Following this, a climate of trust would be achieved only if the two sides display a genuine desire for compromise and mutual accommodation, particularly in the three areas of present-day competition—Syria, Yemen and Iraq. Given the level of animosity and bloodshed, these accommodations will be very difficult, but they need not be impossible.

In Syria, both countries will have to prioritize the integrity of the country, the accommodation of diverse identities in a multicultural and federal constitutional framework and the setting up of a new leadership after a reasonable transition period. The fact that GCC countries, such as the UAE, Bahrain and Kuwait, are setting up their embassies in Damascus based on their shared 'Arab' (rather than sectarian) identity suggests that acceptance of the Assad regime is not ruled out in Arab circles.

In Yemen, Saudi Arabia would need to accept the need to include the Zaydis in the political process, while Iran would have to recognize that the kingdom has legitimate concerns about the prospect of a dominant Iranian presence in the country. Since Iran has consistently denied that it is providing large-scale military assistance to the Houthis, this should not difficult for Iran to accept.

In Iraq, after the general elections in 2018, the ground has already been prepared for a largely non-sectarian political order in the country. What Iraq needs above all is for its two neighbours—Iran and Saudi Arabia—to end attempts to seek political advantage on sectarian basis, but instead encourage the political consolidation and reconstruction of that devastated nation.

The agenda set out earlier will be contentious, difficult and time-consuming. Perhaps, some ideas relating to promoting mutual accommodation could be discussed at Track-II platforms before governments come into the picture. But once accommodation has been achieved on the lines discussed earlier, there will be a modicum of mutual confidence between the two countries. This will set the stage for the next step in securing peace on long-term basis through an inclusive regional cooperative security arrangement.

Regional Cooperative Security Arrangement

Given the fact that ongoing contentions in West Asia are interlinked, genuine and abiding security in West Asia will be achieved only through pursuing an inclusive approach that embraces all the principal regional and extra-regional players. For the project to be successful, the regional states concerned would need to be assured that they can retain their existing bilateral and even multilateral security arrangements. Thus, the regional security would have to be built up incrementally over many years as levels of mutual confidence increase and existing security agreements become redundant.

The process will involve engagements between regional powers through diverse fora and mechanisms, both bilateral and multilateral, with the leaders of the diplomatic initiative constantly available to manage irritants and promote dialogue.

The diplomatic process has the benefit of two recent models:

- The Council of Security and Cooperation in Europe (CSCE)
- The ASEAN Regional Forum (ARF)

The CSCE, set up at the height of the Cold War, brought together the countries on opposite sides belonging to NATO and Warsaw Pact, and the principal neutral countries of Europe. It was principally a discussion platform but was able to tote up many significant achievements based on a series of important conferences addressing specific issues. The Helsinki Final Act (1975) that founded it included several confidence-building measures (CBMs) pertaining to military exercises. The Stockholm Conference of 1986 agreed on further CBMs regarding these exercises and enjoined the participants to abjure the threat or use of force. The Vienna Document of 1990 provided for exchange of information on existing military forces, and budgets and broad verification procedures. The CSCE process culminated in the Conventional Armed Forces in Europe (CFE) Treaty of 1990, which has been described by Kenneth Pollack as 'one of the most important arms control documents ever signed'.[16]

ASEAN is different from the CSCE process in that it is not a security platform, nor does it include adversaries as members. However, the ARF has some useful pointers for shaping a new security paradigm in the Gulf. It provides for an annual engagement of its members with full dialogue partners; these are countries with an abiding interest in regional security and include: Australia, Canada, China, the EU, India, Japan, New Zealand, Republic of Korea (ROK), Russia and the USA. The formal sessions consist of all the ASEAN countries meeting the

---

[16] Kenneth Pollack, 'Security in the Persian Gulf: New Frameworks for the Twenty-First Century', *Middle East Memo*, no. 24 (Washington, DC: the Saban Center at Brookings, June 2012), 9.

dialogue partners jointly and then separately, one by one. At the same time, several important interactions take place among leaders on the sidelines of the annual meet.

It is interesting to note that the ARF has also set up a 'Track-II' entity, the Council for Security Cooperation in the Asia Pacific (CSCAP), which is tasked with addressing regional security issues through study groups and expert groups to look at issues relevant to regional security. The participants are usually serving and retired diplomats, armed forces officers and academics. The Track-II character of this entity gives it the required flexibility in its deliberations and the opportunity to think out of the box in respect of security issues. Its studies constitute valuable inputs for the more formal dialogue at the ARF interaction.

On the basis of these models, in putting in place the proposed cooperative security arrangement in West Asia, the three leaders of the diplomatic initiative would need to take the following steps:

- They should first meet among themselves to finalize a consensual approach relating to (a) membership, (b) guiding principles, (c) mode of functioning of the new entity and (d) the principal issues to be addressed and entities/mechanisms that will deal with them. To ensure quick interaction between them, a 'Special Envoy for the West Asia Peace Initiative' could be nominated in each country.
- The membership should be made up of (a) the regional entities: the GCC countries, Iran, Iraq and Yemen; (b) the leaders of the initiative: India, China and Russia; (c) the principal extra-regional entities with an interest in Gulf security: the other P5 countries, Turkey and Germany; and (d) the United Nations which could be represented by a 'special envoy'.
- Besides plenary sessions at ministerial level, working groups may be set up to look at the following issues: political, military, economic, social and cultural, and environmental.
- Given the history of discord, the formal governmental interaction could be supported by Track-II discussions and studies on the lines of CSCAP.
- As the main dialogue will be between Saudi Arabia and Iran, political leaders, diplomats and 'troubleshooters' should be on hand to smooth differences. Their role should include the following:
  o Identifying issues that cause discord and mutual suspicion, and define now they could be addressed and
  o Developing mechanisms to promote CBMs, manage conflicts and resolve disputes.

Conclusion

Thirty years after the Cold War ended, while Asian countries have set up several multilateral regional and trans-regional organizations for economic cooperation, they have generally shied away from security alliances or even from platforms for dialogue on security issues. One exception has been the GCC, but even this otherwise small and cohesive body has not evolved into an effective security alliance and is today riven with internal discord. The ARF is a useful platform for dialogue on security issues with a wide variety of dialogue partners, but ASEAN itself has not ventured into setting up its own security alliance.

There are good reasons why Asian countries have not developed intra-Asia security dialogue platforms. First, for most of the second half of the last century, Asia was divided at regional and sub-regional levels based on Cold War allegiances or was non-aligned. These differences created during the colonial period could not be addressed and resolved.

Second, the Cold War itself aggravated historic grievances so that they remain festering sores in the Asian body politic. In fact, free from the constraints placed by the Cold War, some of them have become even more serious. Third, Asian economic resurgence is just a little over 15 years old; in some cases, instead of bringing nations together, it has had the effect of aggravating concerns from some of the resurgent countries which, with their economic success, have now acquired a new assertiveness in political and geopolitical areas.

Finally, the old big powers, the USA, Europe and Russia, continue to be active in their former areas of influence, encouraging allies and confronting foes, thus complicating regional scenarios with the assertions of their own interests.

The Gulf region today reflects all the aforementioned influences. It manifests the historic Arab–Persian and the sectarian Shia–Sunni divides, which, after the Arab Spring, have obtained a new resonance. It has the presence of a superpower, the USA, which took over the hegemonic mantle from the UK and maintained regional security through a massive military presence and intimidation of enemies. The USA has been the traditional ally of the GCC countries against their regional rivals, Iraq and Iran. While the former was crushed militarily in 2003 and is only now experiencing a political revival, the latter is being coerced economically and politically through a tough sanctions regime and threats of confrontation in Syria and regime change at home.

The implications of the Asian economic resurgence affirm that the political status quo in West Asia is not a viable option. Asian countries pursuing economic achievement through high growth rates have come to depend crucially on Gulf energy, even as the Western countries are reducing their dependency. Hence, the security of the Gulf can no longer remain the sole domain of US interests in alliance with the GCC Sheikhdoms; Asian interests are too important, too widespread and too urgent to allow this.

In any case, the USA from the Obama administration onwards has also lost its appetite for military interventions in West Asia: none of the earlier interventions—in Afghanistan, Iraq and Libya—has provided any advantage to the Americans. Trump, sensitive to the concerns of his domestic constituencies, has made the withdrawal of US troops a major aspect of his foreign policy.

The stage is, therefore, set for the consideration of new regional security arrangements that would be less intimidatory and more accommodative, that would be less exclusive and more broad-based, and that would achieve security through consensus building and a peaceful diplomatic approach rather than through regime change and war.

This chapter has proposed that India shapes a diplomatic peace initiative for West Asian security in partnership with China and Russia. Of course, long-standing mutual suspicions and even elements having a vested interest in contention and conflict will ensure that the path forward will be slow and painful, and on occasion there could be even some steps backwards.

But the commitment to Gulf security of major countries with an abiding interest in regional security and the participatory and accommodative character of the proposal will in time wither these obstacles and give the people of the region a chance at peace they have been denied for several decades.

India and Southeast Asia

Anil Wadhwa

Shared historic ties, culture and knowledge have been the basis of Indian interaction and contacts with Southeast Asia. The values and culture of India and Southeast Asia are interconnected, and this is based of contacts through civilizations. Historical evidence shows that there were exchanges through trade, Sanskrit and Indian epics. There is also well-documented evidence of technical innovations between Southeast Asia and India. These commonalities provide the basis for the synergies between India and the region. As the publication by Research and Information Systems (RIS) titled 'Act East: ASEAN–India Shared Cultural Heritage' states:

> These commonalities between India and South East Asia cover cultural values and concepts, structures and artifacts, human habitats, oral or folk heritage, language and literature, traditional arts and crafts, architecture, the performing arts, games, indigenous knowledge systems and practices, myths, customs and beliefs, rituals and other living traditions, written and popular cultural heritage This is where socio cultural issues in ASEAN–India strategic partnership, the policy instrument through which India attempts to promote economic integration and strategic objectives in the region, assume special significance.

From 200 BCE until around the 1500 CE, kingdoms on the south-east coast of the India ventured out to Southeast Asia and the kingdoms in

Burma, Thailand, Indonesia, Malay Peninsula, Cambodia and Vietnam soaked up their Hindu and Buddhist influences, even as their mutual mercantilist, cultural and political ties strengthened. The Pallava kingdom was the most adventurous in exploring the high seas. Even as it died off on the Indian subcontinent, Buddhism caught on in these kingdoms of Southeast Asia. Indian merchants and men of learning started making their presence felt in Southeast Asia, and the trend continued till 1500 CE. The Indian connection in Cambodia can be traced to the Hinduized Kingdoms of Funan (1st Century CE), Chenla (6–9th Century CE) and the Kingdom of Jayavarman II who identified himself as Shiva (850–850 CE) with his capital in Angkor. The Kingdom of Angkor later incorporated the Mon Kingdom of Daryavati in Thailand and the Champa Kingdom of Vietnam, which in turn was established by the Indian-origin Chams in 400 CE. Indian empires also established themselves in Sumatra and Java; the Bujang Valley settlement dating back to 110 CE and the occupation by the Cholas in 11 CE marks Indian presence in Malaysia. While Asoka's Buddhist monks reached in 3 BCE, the cultural and trade links between India and Thailand can be traced back to 6 BCE. During the Sukhotai period (1275–1350 CE), besides the Indian mercantilists, Brahmans were indispensable for their prowess in astrology and conducting rituals. Tamil traders entered Southern Thailand in the Ayutthaya period (1350–1767 CE).

Noted writer David Brewster has observed that despite these close historical ties with Southeast Asia, India disengaged with the region after Independence, diminishing its own influence in the region. This happened primarily because India followed the non-aligned path and did not want to be part of the proposed security architecture in the region dominated by the USA. The conflicts with Pakistan in 1965 and 1971 and the Treaty of Friendship with the Soviet Union, as well as its support for Vietnam, put India in the opposite camp. However, since the 1990s, India has engaged with the region in a much more dynamic manner, starting with economic and cultural ties, and thereafter through security linkages.

Currently, India promotes the centrality and capability of ASEAN in the region; aims to strengthen BIMSTEC in order to promote cooperation in the Bay of Bengal and engages with the Mekong–Ganga Cooperation group, to promote greater linkages between itself and the Indo-China sub-region. It is for the reasons of economics, and the failure of a stalled SAARC, that India has also lent its support to the BBIN grouping, which is meant to enhance connectivity with the immediate neighbours of India to its east. India has also been an active participant in the East Asia Summit, and its related security and economic groupings such as ASEAN Regional Forum (ARF) and ASEAN Defense Minister's Meeting-Plus (ADMM+), with varied membership and many overlaps.

In the early 1990s, India introduced the 'Look East policy'—a novel concept that aimed to turn the country's north-east into the gateway to the Indo-Pacific region and to help build stronger ties with India's extended neighbourhood. The policy remained India's pivot for successive governments. While dividends of the Look East policy can be debated, the Modi government, after its landslide victory in the 2014 parliamentary elections, had different plans altogether for the oil-rich and tea-growing regions of India's north-east, located at the strategic junction of China, Bangladesh, Bhutan and Myanmar. At the Naypyitaw East Asia Summit in 2015, India proposed that it will transform its Look East policy to Act East Policy. The Act East Policy is meant to serve the twin purposes of stronger commercial links with the region and other Indo-Pacific countries and to create development opportunities for the Indian north-east. The three Cs, commerce, culture and connectivity, have since been the pillars of India's Act East Policy.

As the Indian Minister for External Affairs, Sushma Swaraj, stated last year at a conference on Indian Ocean in Hanoi, India's Act East Policy is at the heart of its eastward orientation and ties in with the broader approach to the Indo-Pacific. Over the years, India has made giant strides in its ties with the ASEAN and its related frameworks such as the ARF, EAS and ADMM+ as also with countries further East, including Japan, South Korea, Australia and the Pacific islands. This has now been extended to the Russian Far East and coined 'Act Far East'. The collaboration between India and ASEAN has accelerated across a range of economic and strategic issue, including trade and investment, connectivity, energy, culture, people-to-people contacts and maritime security. It was also in 2014 that PM Modi agreed on a joint vision of the Indo-Pacific with President Obama—signifying that the Indian Ocean and the Pacific Ocean were interconnected as far as security and economics were concerned.

Total 10 heads of state of all ASEAN countries visited India on 26 January 2018 for the 25 Commemorative Summit to mark the relationship with India and also as chief guests at the Indian Republic Day—an unprecedented conglomeration of leaders from ASEAN on this historic occasion. From a dialogue partner in 1996, India has graduated to a Summit level partner in 2002, and to a Strategic Partner of ASEAN in 2012. Today, India is engaged in at least 30 high-level dialogues in varied fields with ASEAN.

PM Modi, in his vision of Security and Growth for All in the Region (SAGAR), enunciated a key security principle in 2015 which is also the bedrock of India's ties with the region. SAGAR recognizes the importance of the oceans in facilitating growth and prosperity in a safe and stable manner. India sees the Indo-Pacific region as an interconnected pathway facilitating the free flow of goods and thoughts. In ensuring this, India sees respect for international law, including UNCLOS, as crucial. South China Sea has emerged as a critical area for the development of the littoral states and is also an important sea route for all the countries for all the ASEAN countries and India. ASEAN has always appreciated India for its support to the central role of the grouping and has sought to actively participate in shaping its shared future. India would like to cooperate with the ASEAN in developing blue economy by providing hydrographic explorations, expanding coastal surveillance, building of offshore patrolling abilities and sharing information for increased maritime domain awareness in order to protect sea lanes of communication to track the deployment of naval vessels and ships in the South China Sea. In this context, the Straits of Malacca, Lombok and Sunda hold a key Indian interest in the region. Collaboration for intelligence sharing between Singapore Information Fusion Centre (IFC) and India's Information management and Analysis Centre (IMAC) for enhanced maritime domain awareness and sharing of movements data for submarines will develop India's maritime surveillance capabilities in the Indian Ocean. It is time that India sets up a regular multilateral naval exercise with ASEAN to keep sea routes, including the Malacca straits free from attacks and piracy in times of need.

India needs deeper economic integration with ASEAN and needs to engage it actively, since it is a grouping of 1.85 billion and possesses a GDP of $3.8 trillion. India's trade and investments with ASEAN have seen an upward trajectory over the past 18 years. ASEAN is India's 4th largest trading partner, accounting for 10.6 per cent of India's total trade. Bilateral trade currently is at US$81.33 billion, and India's exports to ASEAN account for 11.28 per cent of its total exports. ASEAN has invested US$68.91 billion between April 2000 and March 2018 into India, and India has invested US$36.67 billion in ASEAN between 2007 and 2015. While the ASEAN India free trade agreement (FTA) in goods has gone into force, some ASEAN countries like Cambodia are yet to ratify the ASEAN India trade in services agreement. Moreover, India and the rest of ASEAN as well as the other five ASEAN partners—China, Australia, New Zealand, South Korea and Japan—are making slow progress in the negotiations for the Regional Comprehensive Economic Partnership (RCEP) negotiations. India's demand for easing of rules on the movement of professionals has got a cold response from these countries, and India is reluctant to open up its market for targeted goods. India and ASEAN, however, have committed, at the highest level, to swiftly conclude a modern, comprehensive, high quality and mutually beneficial RCEP. Although a trade target of $100 billion was set in 2012, Indian agricultural exports are still facing barriers like high import tariffs from ASEAN countries.

A key aspect of improving the economic relationship is improving connectivity—through land, sea, and air—in order to cut down costs for movement of goods and services between India and ASEAN. India would do well to speed up the construction of the trilateral highway which will connect India, Myanmar and Thailand, and will later expand into Laos, Cambodia and Vietnam. The proposed highway begins at the India–Myanmar border town of Moreh, passing through several Myanmarese towns including Tamu, Kalewa, Yargi, Monywa, Mandalay, Meiktila, Myawaddy and finally ending at Mae Sot on the Myanmar–Thai border. India and ASEAN have already agreed that the highway will then get converted into a four-lane highway, and also connect with the ASEAN Master Plan on Connectivity and the East–West Corridor. A $1 billion credit line has been announced by PM Modi in 2015 to enhance digital and infrastructure connectivity with ASEAN. There is need to identify the constraints in the utilization of this credit facility. The amount of $77 million has also been committed towards developing manufacturing hubs in the Cambodia Myanmar, Laos and Vietnam (CMLV) countries. The trilateral highway can only be a useful venture if economic activity flourishes along the route through Myanmar. India, therefore, needs closer coordination with Myanmar to develop economic hubs and activity along the route which passes through largely difficult terrain. India is repairing 69 bridges in Myanmar, and building stretches of this road. The highway, due to these difficulties, has been delayed by almost 5 years and is now expected to open in 2020. India has, however, utilized this time to work on the soft infrastructure required for the successful opening of the trilateral highway, including a motor vehicles and licensing agreement, and helping Myanmar with some quick impact projects. Most urgently, connectivity development in the north-east itself is important. Construction of a web of roads, establishment of rail linkages, development of necessary infrastructure, opening up of river navigation, removal of impediments like multiple border taxation and by establishment of economic activities like 'Haats' or local markets within the north-east states, India can hope for balanced trade instead of turning into a net receiver of cheaper goods. Home to 3.8 per cent of the Indian population, spread over 8 per cent of India's geographical area, with an international border of 5,300 km, the India north-east is strategic. India has plans for the development of connectivity in the border regions of Arunachal Pradesh, Mizoram and Nagaland with China, Bhutan, Bangladesh and Myanmar. A 4,000 km long ring road connecting the states; railway projects connecting all state capitals by 2020 with extensions to 15 new destinations; last mile connectivity with Myanmar and restoring rail connectivity with Bangladesh are some new initiatives. Total 20 port townships are to be developed along the Brahmaputra and Barak river systems. The augmentation of air connections to and from the region which will give a fillip to commercial ties with ASEAN. At least 50 economic integration and development nodes are to be developed across the region, along with transport pathways so that manufacturing can receive a push.

The Kaladan multi-modal transport project will link Kolkata to Sittwe port in Myanmar, extending into Mizoram by the river and land route. India's involvement in developing port infrastructure in Sabang is significant. Sea links are also vital between the eastern seaboard of India including ports of Ennore and Chennai to CMLV countries and there is need for improving trans-shipment links with partners such as Malaysia, Singapore, Indonesia and Thailand. There is also a proposal to link Dawei port in Myanmar, being developed with Thailand to Chennai port in India, cutting down shipping costs and time. For these proposals to succeed, India and ASEAN must look at shipping joint ventures and related concessions. An agreement on maritime transport between India and ASEAN should cover these essential areas. India needs to work with ASEAN to enhance marine transportation links. Involvement of private players and companies in developing the port projects, and related logistics and service providers there will be crucial. The scope for cooperation in cruise tourism and roll-on roll-off vessels which can carry vehicles between India and some ASEAN states has also been identified. A cruise triangle connecting Kolkata and Andaman Islands with Islands of Myanmar and Thailand could be developed and could be further extended to Indonesia and Malaysia. There is a clear need to develop air links. While flight connections from tier 1 and tier 2 cities in India are well established with Singapore, Thailand Malaysia and now Indonesia, the other countries either lack direct links or have inadequate linkages with India. This is an impediment to tourism as well as trade. Some direct flights, like those to Brunei and Vietnam, have also not fructified. India and ASEAN, therefore, need to work towards an ASEAN India air services agreement which will benefit trade, investments and tourism.

India has been doing its part in enhancing people-to-people connectivity with ASEAN and cultural cooperation and should step up activities such as exchange among diplomats, youth, media, intellectuals and scholarship programmes for ASEAN students. As outlined in the ASEAN India vision document, India and ASEAN must enhance cooperation for preserving each other's heritage and culture. India should continue to align itself with the ASEAN Integration Plan 2025, enhance cooperation in agriculture, energy, tourism, health and SME development in poverty alleviation. Terrorism remains a challenge for both India and ASEAN, and institutional linkages with ASEAN countries, including exchange of intelligence and information, must be strengthened. Indian centres of excellence in English language, IT and software development, etc., have been a huge success and should be ramped up. The additional US$50 million announced for the ASEAN India fund will be useful in conducting these activities, but big ticket items will require timely funding in the future. As far as micro, small and medium enterprises (MSMEs) are concerned, ASEAN and India have agreed to promote stable growth in this area, through technology transfer, capacity building, technical assistance and provision of financing facilities. This will enable SMEs from ASEAN and India to integrate into the essential chains and utilize the funds earmarked by India for project development including those which have a quick impact with smaller amounts.

A notable area of success for India in its relationship with ASEAN has been cooperation in Humanitarian Assistance and Disaster Relief (HADR), including risk reduction—and this needs to be sustained. India has set up a Green Fund with ASEAN which can help in undertaking cooperative projects in climate impact mitigation. India and ASEAN should cooperate in the international solar alliance through closer collaboration in solar equipment and technologies. In 2016, the corpus of the fund meant for enhancing science and technology with ASEAN was enhanced by India to US$5 million, and this will go a long way in supporting technology development initiatives. The sectoral relationship in science and technology with ASEAN will be deepened through cooperation on the ASEAN–India innovation platform, research and training fellowship programme and collaborative research and development programme, in areas aligned with ASEAN Plan of Action on Science, Technology and Innovation 2016–2025. ISRO has supported ASEAN in the development of space technology and its applications. ASEAN and India have agreed that the ASEAN–India space cooperation must be directed towards launch of satellites, their monitoring, setting up of command stations and using of imagery in order to exploit space. Two major space projects with ASEAN for tracking, data and reception/data processing station are located in Ho Chi Minh City, Vietnam, and in Biak, Indonesia. India also needs to enhance cooperation with ASEAN in digitization, especially the financial structure and e-governance. Cybersecurity has emerged as an important subject in the Indo-ASEAN context. Industrial espionage and countering cyberattacks on utilities and commercial establishments are areas where ASEAN has rich experience. The first ASEAN–India Cyber dialogue was held in 2018. An ASEAN–India innovation platform and building of digital connectivity—both Indian initiatives—must be pursued through to their logical conclusion.

India is also looking to partner ASEAN in enhancing blue economy cooperation, investing in development of desalinization technologies, harvesting the biodiversity, and searching and excavating marine minerals in the seas. India and ASEAN have committed themselves, through their joint declaration in 2018, to address threats to their fishery resources. This cooperation covers illegal, unreported and unregulated fishing, the threats faced by their coastal ecosystems and the adverse effects of marine and acid pollution as well as dumping of debris.

India is also contributing to regional maritime security by strengthening the safety and security of maritime traffic through the ocean by developing skills and logistics of its Indo-pacific neighbours, especially those in Southeast Asia. India and ASEAN are engaged in managing and avoiding accidents and incidents and coordinating their activities in rescue and search at sea, and this is all done as prescribed by International Maritime Organisation (IMO) and International Civil Aviation Organisation (ICAO). White shipping agreements exist between India and a number of countries in the region. In addition, Indian ships have undertaken coordinated patrolling and exclusive economic zone (EEZ) surveillance. India is setting up coastal surveillance networks and constantly enhancing the capacity for shared maritime domain awareness with its partners. Another element of ensuring safety of navigation in the region has been the hydrographic support provided to India's partners to chart the waters of the region. This has been augmented with a large training capacity building effort. Launched in 2008 by India, the Indian Ocean Naval Symposium (IONS) has enabled the Indian Ocean littorals to cooperate and enhance their security. The symposium is generating a flow of information between naval professionals to develop a common understanding and cooperative solutions in areas of common interests such as HADR, information security, interoperability and maritime security. India also launched the Indian Ocean Rim Association (IORA) in 1997 with South Africa. This created a platform for the littoral states in the Indian Ocean to come together on issues like traditional and non-traditional security challenges. Many Southeast Asian nations are included in this grouping. The Regional Cooperation Agreement on Combating Piracy and Armed Robbery against Ships in Asia (RECAAP) in which India is a participant is also a well-established mechanism for the region.

Lately, Chinese political and economic influence as well as naval presence in the region has continued to grow, and it has rapidly moved to occupy, militarize in some cases populate and reclaim 32,000 acres in the South China Sea. China's sovereignty claims based on historical forays of its naval flotillas and its so-called nine-dash line have been judged without any legal foundation by the permanent arbitration tribunal set up by the UN Convention on the Law of the Sea (UNCLOS). India and ASEAN have jointly called for full and effective implementation of the Declaration on the Conduct of the Parties in the South China Sea (DOC) and have expressed the hope for an early conclusion of the code of conduct (COC) in the South China Sea, but the fact remains that Chinese action over the disputed islands in the South China Sea has not faced any opposition, other than verbal, mainly by the USA which carries out freedom of navigation operations in the area. The countries of Southeast Asia, and the international community in general, would not like to see China convert the South China Sea into a 'Beijing lake'.

The Malacca Straits connect the Indian Ocean to the South China Sea, and it is through these straits that over 40 per cent of India's seaborne trade passes. India also has energy interests in the region and is involved in exploring for oil in the South China Sea in Vietnam's oil block, which is disputed by China due to the claims based on its nine-dash line. Notwithstanding all the steps India is taking on its own and jointly with others to promote maritime security, its security challenges are set to increase. China's 2015 White Paper on military strategy enunciated 'open sea protection' for which its naval capacity to protect its interests overseas and sea lanes of communication away from its shores is projected to increase. China is contracting additional aircraft carriers, a powerful nuclear-powered fleet of submarines and has moved to strengthen its air power. China's energy supplies are vulnerable and it is, therefore, seeking access to the Bay of Bengal though Myanmar in order to have an alternative supply line through the Malacca Strait. However, this can only partially offset its Malacca dilemma since the energy to be transported for China will grow further. In future, therefore, the People's Liberation Army (PLA) Navy is bound to deploy more ships in the Indian Ocean region to defend its own sea lanes of communication. The presence of Chinese naval ships and submarines will raise new dilemmas for India. China's conduct in the South China Sea and its belligerent reaction to the award of UNCLOS established permanent Court of Arbitration on its maritime claims is a precedent which India would not like to see repeated in the Indian Ocean. China today possesses enormous economic resources and increasing military prowess. While so far, there are no maritime territorial disputes involving China in the Indian Ocean, China's demonstrated reservations on the UNCLOS provisions in full makes India, like others, wary of its behaviour. India, the USA, Japan and Australia, along with ASEAN, therefore, have a shared interest in maintaining a strategic balance in the Indo-Pacific. Indonesia is a key ASEAN state in this endeavour, because to avoid the Malacca straits choke point, the Sunda and Lombok straits provide an alternate route from where Chinese naval assets can pass into the Indian Ocean.

The ASEAN will be happy to see India playing a larger role in Southeast Asia in order to balance the geopolitical situation which has emerged in the region. India has the political and economic instruments to further strengthen ties with ASEAN. The Indian navy is playing a notable role, not only to build maritime bridges through joint exercises and visits but also to protect the sea lanes of communication and well as Indian interests in the region. India has moved to strengthen the naval presence in the Andaman and Nicobar Islands at the mouth of the Malacca Straits and it is from here that the Indian navy can play a vital role in the maritime domain. However, despite India's support for ASEAN institutions, ASEAN has a limited role in regional security and, therefore, India has concentrated on defence arrangements at a bilateral level. In 2003, Singapore and India entered into a comprehensive defence cooperation agreement that has facilitated annual defence policy dialogues, joint exercises, intelligence sharing and cooperation in defence technology. The Singapore Air Force has long-term use of the Indian Kalaikunda airbase and India has agreed to the storage of Singaporean equipment and training of its army personnel at Babina and Deolali firing ranges. With Vietnam, India signed a comprehensive defence agreement in 2000, which provides for regular exchange of intelligence, joint coast guard training to combat piracy, jungle warfare, counter-insurgency training, repair of Vietnamese MiG aircraft, training of Vietnamese pilots and Indian assistance in small and medium arms production. This has since expanded to naval cooperation, maritime domain awareness and missile cooperation. In June 2011, Vietnam announced that it would provide regular access to the small port of Nha Trang near Cam Ranh Bay to the Indian navy. Aside from Singapore and Vietnam, with whom defence ties are strong, India in future will have to move firmly in securing and strengthening defence ties with countries such as Indonesia, Malaysia, the Philippines, Myanmar and Thailand, with whom bilateral cooperation has also gained steady ground. India carries out the SIMBEX exercise with Singapore navy, the Ausindex with the Australian navy. According to the Defence Minister of Australia Marise Payne, in 2014, Australia and India conducted 11 major defence activities together; in 2018, this figure had climbed to 38. Since 1995, the Indian navy conducts the biennial Milan exercise with navies of the Indian Ocean region at the Andaman and Nicobar islands.

Overall, the Chinese actions in the region have led to a natural reaction and pushback. A notable development in the region is the revival of the informal grouping of the Quad—comprising India, Japan, Australia, and USA—to coordinate positions in the Indo-Pacific. The Quad members have never specifically stated that the Quad targets any country, and this was made clear by PM Modi at Shangri-La, who also called for an inclusive Indo-Pacific, based on the rule of law. At the heart of the new security paradigm in Southeast Asia is the interest of the US to engage with the region, and also its capabilities. The gap between the Chinese and the US capabilities in areas that will be future determinants such as artificial intelligence, robotics and new technologies in civilian and military use seems to be narrowing. In the circumstances, the Quad, or some other mechanism, which pools the strengths of other like-minded countries is seen as the best hope of sustaining a rules-based order in the region. There is a feeling within Japan that that the Japan–US security alliance is the cornerstone of national security in Asia, that the free and open Indo-Pacific strategy must be region wide in scope and based on shared values to respond effectively to the new challenges. To succeed, it must be implemented in partnership with other members of the Quad. As the asymmetries vis-à-vis china have grown, smaller states in the Indo-Pacific have started hedging against China. Many commentators in the USA have expressed the view that the ASEAN needs to step up the plate and articulate how it could subscribe to the broader Indo-Pacific concept and a rules-based order if it needs to remain central to the policies evolving in the region. An attempt has been made by Indonesia on behalf of ASEAN to articulate the ASEAN response to the Quad and the Indo-Pacific concept which has found favour with the rest of ASEAN.

India approaches the region from an overarching vision. PM Modi, speaking at the Shangri-La Dialogue in May 2018, spoke of this vision, highlighting a free and inclusive Indo-Pacific. This is a region where some of the largest and smallest nations of the world have coexisted in harmony. This harmony exists because of economic cultural ideological and civilizational commonalties. This is precisely the collective approach that is required in order to truly develop this region to its fullest potential. The region, he said, cannot just be a growth engine; it has to be a community of ideas and commitments. India has committed itself to work with countries of the region towards an inclusive rules-based order, espousing freedom of navigation, equality under international law, peaceful resolution of disputes and equitable distribution of the benefits of globalization.

The ambitious BRI plans of China, some of which have resulted in debt traps for some nations due to unsound principles of economics and are unsuited to the host country—but serve Chinese geopolitical ends—also need an alternative. Japan has announced that it will boost the $110 billion fund it had created in 2015 for a five-year period in Asia to a sum of US$200 billion that would be offered for the same period. In addition, Japan's concessionary Yen loans have been doubled to 1 trillion yen since 2015. This provides access to large sums of financing for economic and social projects on terms more favourable than the market. Japanese foreign direct investment (FDI) in ASEAN is growing, and the ADB has been funding a number of projects in the region. With the help of Japan International Cooperation Agency (JICA), ADB has created Leading Asia's Private Sector Infrastructure Fund (LEAP) in 2016 so that it could leverage and complement money to non-governmental projects which can range from public private partnerships to joint ventures and power finance. The focus has been on energy, water, transport and health. Japan has been playing a significant role by itself or through ADB in some connectivity projects like the East–West Economic Corridor, linking Da Nang port in Vietnam with north-east Thailand through Laos. A southern economic corridor links Bangkok with Ho Chi Minh City through Cambodia. If India and Japan can cooperate with each other in ASEAN and use each other's capabilities, the effects can be exponential. If both India and Japan can cooperate with each other in ASEAN, they could remain confident that their investment in rail, roads, highways, ports would be put to good use, and the local economies could also benefit from the special economic zones, manufacturing and trading hubs. India could use its niche area of IT to power customs and risk management. India and Japan could partner other governments or the private sector there to mitigate risk and shorten lead times. India and Japan could also work in Africa; and the Asia-Pacific growth corridor for one has the potential to rival the Chinese BRI since it stretches from Japan to Southeast and Southeast Asia towards Africa. There is a need to ramp up these efforts.

There have been steps taken by the other countries such as the USA and Australia also to counter the Chinese BRI narrative. The US

Development Finance Initiative (DFI) is meant to help 'developing countries prosper while advancing US foreign policy goals and enhancing US national interests'. OPIC, which currently implements the US DFI, has seen its commitments soar to $70 billion in 2014 from $10 billion in 1971 when it was founded. In November 2018, after a parliamentary consensus was reached in both houses, mainly in response to the Chinese BRI, the USA created a new US International Development Finance Corporation (USIDFC) with a $60 billion funding—which is expected to become operational later this year—through the passage of the Better Utilization of Investment Leading to Development (BUILD) Act. This has been done mainly to obtain private and market-based investments in low-income countries. The new agency will also work in middle-income countries on grounds of national security or on grounds of development in an underdeveloped part of any country. Secretary Pompeo has welcomed this initiative, which he said, will add to the financial capacity of the US government for development purposes. This can be contrasted with the Chinese financial model which does not cater to small and medium enterprises.

By the end of 2018, US President Trump had also signed the Asia Reassurance Initiative Act (ARIA) which is also directed at enhancing US security, economic goals and values in East and Southeast Asia, authorizing an appropriation of $1.5 billion a year up to the next five years for an array of projects and acts. These include joint maritime training and freedom of navigation operations in support of a rules-based order in the Indo-Pacific, South China Sea and the East China Sea. The USA will work with its treaty allies, strategic partners and security partners in implementing this goal.

In November 2018, an infrastructure initiative of Australia worth AUD2 billion aimed at the Pacific was also unveiled by Australia. The initiative will set up the Australian Infrastructure Financing facility for the Pacific. In addition, Export Finance and Insurance Corporation (EFIC), Australia's export financing agency will have at its disposal AUD$1 billion as capital which could be called upon any time. It will use grant funding combined with loans to support the development of high priority infrastructure.

Despite pronouncements from the USA of initiatives such as the BUILD Act and the ARIA for infrastructure projects in the region, the vulnerability of ASEAN countries such as Cambodia, Laos, Myanmar and Thailand to the lure of Chinese-funded projects and their deeper incorporation into Chinese economic system remains the foremost likely possibility. It would, therefore, be simplistic to see the Act East

Policy of India just as an outcome of the regional situation, where SAARC is stalled, and India's desires to derive economic benefits out of its engagement with countries to its east, and develop its north-east. India's Act East policy has now added a strategic dimension. In future, India will have to be nimble and quick in completing its connectivity projects with ASEAN, will have to develop strong defence, political, cultural and socio-economic ties and create interdependencies with countries of Southeast Asia. It will need to work with like-minded countries to keep its neighbourhood secure, to keep its sea lanes of communication open and ensure a stable and peaceful external environment for its own economic development, which has become crucial for its 1.25 billion people. Southeast Asia will drive the future economic growth and will be the driver of the 'Asian Century'. It is imperative that India is an inevitable part of this developing story.

India and the European Union

Gulshan Sachdeva

Introduction

In the last one decade, the European elite has been struggling to deal with one crisis after another. These include Greek crisis, troubles in some of the Eurozone economies, conflict in Ukraine (and tensions with Russia), terrorist attacks, rise of populism, migration and refugee influx, British exit from the EU (Brexit), stand-off in Catalonia, rift with Trump and so on. This is in sharp contrast to its earlier successful projects such as the EU enlargement and introduction of single currency, the Euro. Despite facing crises and challenges on multiple fronts (including broader decline of the West and rise of China, etc.), the EU is still one of the major economies of the world. It has huge capacities and linkages to influence core institutions of global political and economic governance. The EU and its member states (MS) have played a key role in climate change negotiations. As a result of policy initiatives, Europe is going to play a significant role in emerging green technologies. Traditionally, Europe has been the largest donor of development finance and a leading player in global development architecture. Although the EU was normally seen by outsiders as mainly an economic bloc, it has also started playing a significant role in international peace and security. European role was clearly evident in the Iranian nuclear deal. So despite difficulties, in 2016, a *Global Strategy for the European Union's Foreign and Security Policy* was announced. The idea has been to make the EU 'more effective in confronting energy security, migration, climate change, violent extremism, and hybrid warfare'.[1] There is also a possibility that after Brexit, the EU may be able to implement some of its ambitious integration projects. The plan has already been laid down for covering all MS with Schengen Area, Eurozone and the banking union.

As the largest trader and investor, the EU is also deeply integrated in the global economy. Productivity levels are still pretty high. Due to various integration measures over the decades, most EU MS have achieved unprecedented prosperity. In 2018, the EU economy was about $18 trillion with average per capita income of about $40,000. With less than 7 per cent of world population, the EU produced about 17 per cent global economic output in 2016. If 28 states are considered a single trading partner, the EU trade exceeds that of China or the USA.

Till recently, the EU project was considered a very successful model of integration around the world including India. Due to various crises, however, the image of Europe/EU in Indian media and policy circles in the last few years has taken a beating. Even earlier, most Indian policymakers and analysts have been somewhat sceptical of the EU's role as a major strategic player in Asia. In fact, the EU has hardly been a factor in India's foreign policy debates in the last 25 years. Many Indian analysts believed that the EU provided limited value addition to New Delhi's major strategic challenges related to China and other neighbouring regions.[2] In 2011, an Indian think tank made a comparative assessment of India's major strategic partners. In the study, it did not even include the EU in the list.[3] There has also been a perception in

---

[1] European Union Global Strategy, *Shared Vision, Common Action: A Stronger Europe: A Global Strategy for the European Union's Foreign and Security Policy* (2016). Available at https://eeas.europa.eu/archives/docs/top_stories/pdf/eugs_review_web.pdf (accessed on 10 December 2019).

[2] Dhruva Jaishankar, 'Europe in Indian Strategy', in *Grand Strategy for India 2020 and Beyond*, ed. K. Venkatshamy and P. George (New Delhi: Institute for Defence Studies & Analysis, Pentagon Security International, 2012); C. Raja Mohan, '*India and the Balance of Power*', *Foreign Affairs* (2006, July–August); Bernd Von Muenchow-Pohl, *India and Europe in a Multi Polar World* (Washington, DC: Carnegie Endowment for International Peace, 2012).

[3] Foundation for National Security Research, *India's Strategic Partners: A Comparative Assessment* (New Delhi: Foundation for National Security Research, 2011).

policy circles that what matters in the context of Europe is bilateral ties with major European players, rather than linkages with the EU. This, to some extent, reflects lack of Indian understanding of EU institutional processes, their competencies as well as major changes, which have taken place in the last three decades.

Strengthened Institutional Linkages

The pre-colonial and colonial history of Indo-European linkages is well documented.[4] During the Cold War, New Delhi followed policies of self-reliance and non-alignment. In addition, its closeness to the USSR limited its interactions with Europe.[5] Still, trade, investment and people-to-people contacts with major European countries remained important. Since the establishment of diplomatic ties with the European Economic Community (EEC) in 1962, many agreements have been signed to facilitate trade and development cooperation. India also became beneficiary of EU's Generalised Scheme of Preferences (GSP).

In the 1990s, rising India's global vision of a democratic and multi-polar world largely coincided with Europe. Many EU statements and agreements looked bilateral ties beyond economic issues. The EU also realized that through a solid partnership with India, it may be able to influence economic and security architecture in Asia, which is still evolving. This led to annual summit meetings in 2000, the EU–India Strategic Partnership in 2004 and Joint Action Plan (JAP) in 2005. In 2006, India also became member of the Asia–Europe Meeting (ASEM), an informal and multidimensional process of dialogue between Asia and Europe. In 2007, negotiations for a Broad Based Trade and Investment Agreement (BTIA) were initiated. The JAP was further revised in 2008. Although regular summit meetings continued till 2012,[6] the relationship somehow lost its earlier momentum after 2009. This resulted due to a global economic slowdown, deadlock in trade negotiations; difficulties in some of the Eurozone economies and also 'policy paralysis' in India.

In 2014, with the new leadership in India and the EU, renewed possibilities emerged to improve bilateral relations. Economic and

---

[4] Gulshan Sachdeva, ed., *Challenges in Europe: Indian Perspectives* (Singapore: Palgrave Macmillan, 2019), Chapter 19.

[5] J. N. Dixit, 'India and Europe: Perceptions and Misperceptions', in *India and the European Union in the New Millennium*, ed. Rajendra K. Jain (New Delhi: Radiant, 2000).

[6] Bhaswati Mukherjee, *India and EU: An Insider's View* (New Delhi: Vij Books, 2018).

development issues became a top priority within Prime Minister Modi's foreign policy agenda. As Europe was India's major trade, investment and technology partner, it was expected that the EU would become a new focus of engagement. New Delhi also announced several new initiatives—'Make in India', 'Clean India', 'Digital India', '100 Smart Cities' and 'Clean Ganges'. Many EU MS were expected to become significant partners and contributors to these new initiatives.[7] These developments brought some momentum back in relationship. After a gap of four years, two bilateral summits took place in 2016 and 2017. Both have also agreed for an ambitious *Agenda for Action 2020*.[8] In 2017, at the 14th bilateral summit, separate joint declarations on counterterrorism, urban partnership, and clean energy and environment were issued. Meanwhile, bilateral relations with major EU MS have further improved. Since 2014, Mr Narendra Modi has made bilateral visits to about a dozen European countries including multiple visits to France and Germany. All these meetings both at the bilateral as well as at the EU level have somehow brought the EU back to New Delhi's foreign policy agenda.

Core Is Economics but FTA Is Deadlocked

Despite expanding into many areas, the central pillar of bilateral ties is still economic partnership. With more than €125 billion combined trade of goods and services, the EU is New Delhi's single largest trade partner. While goods trade has grown from merely €25 billion in 2000 to about €92 billion in 2018, services trade became $33 billion in 2018. Unlike earlier years, when it was in favour of the EU, trade is now balanced. Still there are some worrying trends. Over the years, trade has grown in absolute terms. Still, as a percentage of total Indian trade, it has declined almost every year.[9]

Despite large variations in various official and unofficial estimates, all of them indicate a strong EU–India investment partnership. Between 2000 and 2017, as per Indian authorities, the EU companies invested

---

[7] Gulshan Sachdeva, *Evaluation of the EU–India Strategic Partnership and the Potential for Its Revitalization* (Brussels: Foreign Affairs Committee, European Parliament, 2015).

[8] Ministry of External Affairs, *EU India Agenda for Action 2020* (2016). Available at mea.gov.in/Images/attach/EU_India_Agenda_for_Action_post_VC.pdf (accessed on 10 December 2019).

[9] Gulshan Sachdeva, *Evaluation of the EU–India Strategic Partnership and the Potential for Its Revitalization*.

about $80 billion in India. This amounted to about one-fourth of total investment into India. In fact, this was higher than combined investment from the USA, Japan, China and Russia during this period.[10] By 2017, the EU foreign direct investment (FDI) stock in India amounted to about €77 billion. Similarly, Indian companies invested about €12 billion in the EU (Eurostat Database). Some independent studies indicate even larger investment figures. The Europe India Chamber of Commerce (EICC) study shows that European companies invested more than €180 billion in India till 2014.[11] Earlier, another EICC study showed that Indian firms had invested about €50 billion in Europe till 2012.[12] These investments were both greenfield and mergers and acquisitions. A close look at the technical and financial collaborations signed by Indian firms also clearly indicates that EU firms are a major source of technology transfer.[13]

These strong economic factors led to the start of negotiations on BTIA in 2007. The agenda was very comprehensive and ambitious. It included goods and services trade, investment, public procurement, intellectual property and competition. There are indications that India was in favour of step-by-step approach. However, the EU was pushing for a deeper and comprehensive agreement. The Indian economy was doing very well at that time and New Delhi was a bit aggressive on trade deals. In the first two–three years, a significant progress was made, particularly on goods trade. However, later negotiations became more difficult, particularly in the area of services. From 2009 onwards, political economy climate in both the EU and India became unfavourable. So far, 12 full rounds of negotiations and many technical meetings have taken place. Besides, expert-level inter-sessional meetings, chief negotiator meetings and meetings at a higher level have also taken place. As per EU official information, 'the negotiations were brought to a *de facto* standstill in the summer 2013 due to a mismatch of the level of ambitions'. Following the 2017 EU–India Summit, EU and India

---

[10] Ministry of Commerce and Industry, Department of Industrial Policy & Promotion, Ministry of Commerce and Industry, Government of India, *FDI Factsheet,* April 2000 to June 2017. Available at http://dipp.nic.in/publications/fdi-statistics (accessed on 10 December 2019).

[11] A. Charlie, *European Companies in India: Reigniting Economic Growth* (Brussels: Europe India Chamber of Commerce, 2014).

[12] A. Charlie, *Indian Companies in the European Union* (Brussels: Europe India Chamber of Commerce, 2012).

[13] Gulshan Sachdeva, 'India–EU Economic Ties: Strengthening the Core of the Strategic Partnership', in *The EU–India Partnership: Time to Go Strategic?* ed. Luis Peral and Vijay Sakhuja (Paris: EUISS, 2012), 39–54.

had extensive exchanges to evaluate whether conditions were right to resume negotiations. Both sides are now in the process of assessing the outcomes of those talks.[14]

The negotiations are deadlocked because of EU's concerns about high tariffs on cars and wines as well market opening in insurance, banking, retail, legal services, geographical indication and public procurement. Similarly, main Indian concerns are about services trade. Reports indicate that the EU also demands civil society monitoring of FTAs, about which Indian policymakers are not very comfortable.[15] New Delhi favours liberalization in terms of movement of professionals as well as better market access for pharmaceuticals, textiles and agricultural goods. India has been pushing for liberal visa regime under the Mode 4 quota of services trade. This will allow IT professionals to stay and work temporarily in the EU. Broader sectoral definitions, longer stays, movement flexibility within the EU markets under Mode 4 are India's major demands.

A couple of years back, there were some indications that new Delhi may take a 'flexible approach' on tariffs for wines and spirits, and auto components in exchange for a 'data secure nation' status being provided to India by the EU. As India is still not considered data secure by the EU, it affects many Indian IT companies. As a result of very long negotiations, Indian industry's positions have been changing. Some of them have started advocating against a possible FTA. Federation of Indian Chambers of Commerce & Industry (FICCI) earlier suggested expansion of scope of the pact to cover 95 per cent of merchandise goods.[16] There was also a serious campaign by some European NGOs which argued that trade agreement may affect flow of cheaper drugs to many countries in the developing world.[17] The Society of Indian

---

[14] European Commission, *Overview of FTA and Other Trade Negotiations* (2018). Available at http://trade.ec.europa.eu/doclib/docs/2006/december/tradoc_118238.pdf (accessed on 10 December 2019).

[15] Shruti Srivastava, 'European Union Intensifying Efforts for Negotiations on India FTA', *Financial Express* (9 March 2015). Available at http://www.financialexpress.com/economy/european-union-intensifying-efforts-for-negotiations-on-india-fta/51476/ (accessed on 10 December 2019).

[16] Press Trust of India, 'FTA with EU Must Cover 95 Per Cent Goods for Real Benefit to India', the *Economic Times* (26 September 2008). Available at https://economictimes.indiatimes.com/news/economy/foreign-trade/fta-with-eu-must-cover–95-pc-goods-for-real-benefit-to-india/articleshow/3531664.cms?from=mdr (accessed on 10 December 2019).

[17] Sarah Boseley, 'Does EU/India Free Trade Agreement Spell the End of Cheap Drugs for Poor Countries?' *The Guardian* (10 February 2012). Available

Automobile Manufacturers (SIAM) felt that the proposed deal may negatively affect investments, and technology inflow will affect Indian plans to indigenize car industry.[18] Lately, the car industry has argued that trade deal with the EU is against Make in India initiative by the government.[19] Difficult global economic conditions and some domestic opposition in India have negatively affected possibility of a trade deal.[20] A few sectors like textiles, however, continue to argue in favour of a trade deal with the EU.[21] This sector has become particularly vulnerable after the EU signed a trade deal with Vietnam in 2019.

Some academic studies earlier outlined potential benefits from the FTA.[22] Now the Indian government has provided some estimates. Its *Economic Survey* has estimated that by separately signing two FTAs with the EU and the UK, the apparels, leather goods and footwear sectors will result in a benefit of $3 billion extra exports. Estimates also indicate that as a result of these two agreements, about 150,000 new jobs will be created.[23]

As a result of global and European economic slowdown, India–EU economic ties were affected negatively between 2009 and 2015. Still, the impact was limited as Germany, India's largest trade partner in Europe, was doing relatively fine. Overall, Indian trade and investment with most MS declined marginally or stagnated. When Narendra Modi became Indian prime minister in 2014, he gave priority to foreign economic relations in his foreign policy. It was hoped that bilateral

---

at https://www.theguardian.com/society/sarah-boseley-global-health/2012/feb/10/hiv-infection-pharmaceuticals-industry (accessed on 10 December 2019).

[18] Pankaj Doval, 'Auto Industry against Inclusion in India–European Union Free Trade Agreement', the *Times of India* (16 May 2012).

[19] Zee News, *Auto Sector Inclusion in India–EU FTA against 'Make in India'* (13 April 2015). Available at http://zeenews.india.com/business/news/economy/auto-sector-inclusion-in-india-eu-fta-against-make-in-india_123338.html (accessed on 10 December 2019).

[20] For a summary of some major issues, see Ritesh Kumar Singh and Prachi Priya, 'What's Holding Back the India–EU FTA?' *The Diplomat* (17 June 2014). Available at https://thediplomat.com/2014/06/whats-holding-back-the-india-eu-fta/ (accessed on 10 December 2019).

[21] Amiti Sen, 'Commerce Minister Reviews Free Trade Pacts', *Business Line* (12 June 2019). 12 June. Available at https://www.thehindubusinessline.com/economy/commerce-minister-reviews-free-trade-pacts/article27891028.ece (accessed on 10 December 2019).

[22] For details of these studies, see Gulshan Sachdeva, ed., *Challenges in Europe*, Chapter 15.

[23] Ministry of Finance, *Economic Survey 2016–17* (New Delhi: Government of India, 2016), 26.

trade negotiations could be restarted. Despite very high expectations from the European side, the movement has been limited. Contrary to expectations, the Modi government has been very cautious about trade agreements. In fact, hardly any new trade agreement has been signed by India in the last five years. Most of the agreements were signed before he came to power. At the 13th India–EU summit (2016), there was hardly any movement on restarting negotiations on EU–India BTIA. Narendra Modi did not even mention FTA in his official statement.[24] The European Commission President Jean-Claude Juncker after the summit said that it is 'high time' for an FTA between India and the EU. However, he asserted that 'once the circumstances are right—and only once the circumstances are right—we will resume'.[25] This indicated that there was hesitation even to restart negotiations.

In the meanwhile, New Delhi has terminated bilateral investment treaties (BITs) with many countries. The list also includes more than 20 EU MS.[26] The changes in government policy were brought as India faced many arbitration claims internationally under BIT. It also lost a few cases due to 'excessive judicial delays' in India. To counter this, New Delhi adopted a model BIT from 2015 with more restrictive definitions. It expected that all nations must sign new investment agreements based on 2015 model BIT. Since investments are part of proposed FTA with the EU, many European nations argued that model BIT could have waited till negotiations are completed. So this Indian move has created further uncertainty for European investors, particularly when there is almost no progress in FTA negotiations.

Trade negotiations are also going to be affected by the Brexit outcome. In case of hard Brexit, India–EU trade deal will be minus Britain. Britain is also keen to start negotiations for a separate trade deal with India. As UK is important export market and investment destination

---

[24] Narendra Modi, *English Translation of Press Statement by Prime Minister during India–EU Summit* (6 October 2017). Available at http://www. mea.gov.in/Speeches-Statements.htm?dtl/29007/English_Translation_of_Press_Statement_by_Prime_Minister_during_IndiaEU_Summit_October_6_2017 (accessed on 10 December 2019).

[25] J. C. Juncker, *Statement at the 14th India–EU Summit* (6 October 2017). Available at https://ec.europa.eu/commission/news/president-juncker-eu-india-summit-2017-oct-06_en (accessed on 9 October 2017).

[26] Nicholas Peacock, and Nihal Joseph, 'Mixed Messages to Investors as India Quietly Terminates Bilateral Investment Treaties with 58 Countries', *Arbitration Notes* (16 March 2017). Available at http://hsfnotes.com/arbitration/2017/03/16/mixed-messages-to-investors-as-india-quietly-terminates-bilateral-investment-treaties-with-58-countries/ (accessed on 10 December 2019).

for Indian companies, Indian policymakers are informally preparing for these negotiations as well. Still, they will have to wait for the final outcome of UK–EU Brexit deal. So in the present circumstances, even if negotiations are relaunched, it will take a couple years to finalize a deal. Although never acknowledged officially, both India and the EU seem to have practically given up the possibility of a bilateral trade deal, at least for the next couple of years.

Moving into Strategic Areas

Since movement on FTA is stalled, both EU and India are moving into other areas including defence and security. On defence matters, traditionally, India has dealt mainly with individual MS. It has worked out a solid framework of security and defence cooperation with major European countries. Many of these issues are covered under bilateral strategic partnerships established with France (1998), Germany (2001) and the UK (2004). During the Cold War period, India also had close defence cooperation with some of the key countries from Central and Eastern Europe (CEE).

Upon independence, major weapon systems of Indian Armed Forces were of British origin. In the 1960s, these were diversified with acquisitions from France. Although the USSR became a major source of defence imports in later years,[27] yet India imported the Anglo-French Jaguar aircraft in the late 1970s, Mirage 2000 from France and submarines from Germany in the 1980s. The European defence industry from the UK, France, Germany, Spain, Italy, Poland, the Czech Republic and Bulgaria has significant linkages with the Indian military. A large number of European defence companies are also operating in India. They are eager to participate in Indian defence modernization and have given proposals under 'Make in India' programme.[28]

The decision by the Indian government to buy 36 Rafale jets for €7.87 billion in flyaway conditions will have long-term implications for

---

[27] Gulshan Sachdeva, 'India's Relations with Russia', in *Handbook of India's International Relations*, ed. David Scott (London: Routledge, 2011), 213–222.

[28] Sameer Patil, Purvaja Modak, Anil Chopra, Kunal Kulkarni, Aditya Phatak, Sharmila Joshi, Shefali Virkar, and Manjeet Kripalani, *India–EU Defence Cooperation: The Role of Industry* (Research Paper No. 12, produced by Gateway House Mumbai and Istituto Affari Internazionali, Rome under EU-India Think Tank Twinning Initiative, 2016). Available at https://euindiathinktanks.com/wp-content/uploads/2018/04/India-EU-defence-cooperation-and-the-role-of-industry-min.pdf (accessed on 10 December 2019).

India–Europe defence relations. In addition to more purchases and joint production, the successful implementation of the deal may further open Indian market for spares and services from Europe. Defence deals are also a reflection of political and strategic trust between countries as well as an indication of close understanding of geopolitical environment. So positives could overflow into other areas. In recent years, there has also been relatively better appreciation of Indian regional security concerns in Europe. As a result, cooperation with individual EU MS has definitely moved further. With the EU, New Delhi has established five security-related dialogues. These include dialogues on security, counterterrorism, counter-piracy, cybersecurity and cybercrime, and non-proliferation and disarmament.[29] There has also been serious engagement in the area of maritime security. A working relationship has also been established between Europol with India's National Investigation Agency. Since 2016, the annual security dialogue has been merged with foreign policy consultations.

Brexit Complications for India

The UK is scheduled to leave the EU. At the moment, the withdrawal agreement negotiated with the EU has been rejected by the British parliament. It is still difficult to predict what is going to happen in the coming months. Political developments in the UK may lead to hard Brexit, some compromise deal, another referendum and no Brexit at all. Although the UK joined the EU in 1973, the whole Brexit drama shows that they never tried to fully understand or internalized working of the EU. Otherwise, they would not have been in a place where they are today. The EU is more about rules, values, procedures and consensus. Although this is also a political project, it is less about geopolitics and strategy. Otherwise, the EU would have made many more compromises when they were losing an important member with nuclear weapons and permanent seat in the UN Security Council. This also has some lessons for Indian policymakers who are dealing with the EU institutions and negotiating trade and investment deal with Brussels. Any EU trade deal without some clauses related to human rights and labour standards is not going to be ratified by the European Parliament easily. India's increasing geopolitical importance may not automatically facilitate a bilateral trade deal with the EU.

---

[29] Rajendra K. Jain, and Gulshan Sachdeva, 'India–EU Strategic Partnership: A New Raodmap', *Asia Europe Journal* (2019). Available at https://doi.org/10.1007/s10308-019-00556-0 (accessed on 10 December 2019).

Businesses in Europe are more or less ready to adjust with the existing Brexit deal. It gives them enough time to prepare for new realities. Except for the hard Brexit scenario, Indian companies operating in the EU and the UK will not face any major difference, at least for the next couple of years. In any case, both the UK and the EU would like to avoid 'no-deal scenario' at any cost. They know that this is going to harm both of them very seriously. The British Parliament has repeatedly voted against the 'no deal' withdrawal. Still, both of them are also now preparing for a no-deal scenario as well.

For Indian companies operating from the UK, the hard Brexit scenario will create many challenges. Specific sectors, which are going to be affected, include automobiles, auto components, pharmaceuticals, gems and jewellery, education and IT-enabled services. They will have absolutely no time to adjust to new realities. Indian investment in the UK may see a declining trend in the next few years. Main focus of a large number of Indian companies investing in the UK has been primarily British market. Still, some of them have been using Britain as a gateway to Europe. A few may need to relocate their businesses.[30]

Any clarity on Brexit will help India–EU FTA negotiation process. Brexit uncertainty has been one of the reasons responsible for the delay in restarting negotiations. Depending on the outcome of Brexit process, the UK and India may also start formal negotiations for a bilateral trade and investment agreement. Earlier, it was thought with British exit, it might be easier for India to negotiate on Mode 4 services with the EU. However, with the refugee and migration crisis in Europe, it is not going to be easy with either of them. Although Brexit process is going to create some new complications, Indian companies and policymakers will have enough time to understand its implications and prepare for possible changes.

EU, China and India

Rapid economic growth and opening up of the Chinese economy led to EU–China strategic partnership in 2003. Initially, the EU officially declared that its objectives in China were (a) to engage China further, both bilaterally and on the world stage, through an upgraded political dialogue; (b) to support China's transition to an open society based upon the rule of law and respect for human rights; (c) to support China's

---

[30] Gulshan Sachdeva, *Adjusting to Brexit May Not Be Tough for India Inc.*, Moneycontrol.com (26 December 2018). Available at https://www.moneycontrol.com/news/politics/opinion-adjusting-to-brexit-may-not-be-tough-for-india-inc–3319851.html (accessed on 10 December 2019).

transition to an open society based upon the rule of law and respect for human rights and (d) to raise the EU's profile in China. China's own *EU Policy Paper* (2003)[31] argued 'there is no fundamental conflict of interest between China and the EU and neither side poses a threat to the other'.

This was the period when economic relationship was booming and it coincided with one of the worst periods in transatlantic relationship (Iraq War, unilateral foreign policy stance of Bush administration). The EU's 'honeymoon' with China, however, was over within a few years. Contrary to Chinese expectations, the lifting of arms embargo and granting of market economy status to China did not materialize. With the arrival of Angela Merkel and Nicolas Sarkozy in Germany and France, the relationship became more realistic as both of them put transatlantic relations top of their agenda. Similar to India, the core of EU–China relationship has been economic.[32] The EU–China goods and services trade, which was just $6 billion in 1980 has grown to $650 billion in recent years. Still, the EU foreign policy to a large extent is also driven by normative principles, including human rights. So China provides a formidable challenge to normative identity represented by the EU. Meanwhile, China has taken full advantage of the EU institutional mechanism through close to 60 sectoral dialogues to promote its geopolitical goals and also to neutralize European concerns about democracy and human rights.

Earlier, European dealings with China and India were part of their broader engagement strategy in Asia in which bilateral ties were more or less independent of each other. To some extent, this is changing in the last few years, particularly after Chinese assertiveness in the neighbourhood and announcement of the Belt and Road Initiative (BRI). This provides a new opportunity for India and the EU to work together. In the context of changing scope of the BRI, European and Indian perceptions are also evolving. Due to different locations and interests, there are some similarities and few significant differences the way India and Europe have approached the BRI. The sovereignty-related issues concerning the China–Pakistan Economic Corridor (CPEC) and broader geopolitical implications within the Indian Ocean region have overshadowed other aspects of the BRI in the Indian narrative. A broad

---

[31] Ministry of Foreign Affairs of the People's Republic of China, *China's EU Policy Paper*, 13 October 2003. Available at: https://www.fmprc.gov.cn/mfa_eng/topics_665678/ceupp_665916/t27708.shtml (accessed on 23 January 2020).

[32] Gulshan Sachdeva, 'The European Union–China Relations', in *China and the Eurasian Region*, ed. C. V. Ranganathan and Sanjeev Kumar (New Delhi: ICWA & Vij Books, 2018), 141–167.

consensus seems to have emerged that the BRI is primarily a Chinese initiative and that it is difficult for New Delhi to endorse the CPEC. India's participation in the AIIB, SCO and BRICS had relatively little impact on New Delhi's perception of the BRI.[33]

As the EU also promotes connectivity and regional integration, initially it welcomed the BRI and an EU–China connectivity platform was also established. Of late, however, the EU approach is becoming more strategic and it has also outlined its own EU–Asia connectivity strategy. It is also felt by many analysts that through the BRI and 16+1 initiative, China is dividing Europe.[34] Meanwhile, however, many EU members (Bulgaria, Greece, Hungary, Italy, Luxembourg Poland, Portugal, etc.) have joined the initiative. Already 60 Chinese cities are now connected through rail with 50 European cities (including 18 Russian cities) in 15 countries. As per Chinese statistics, over 14,000 trains have travelled on these routes since 2011.[35] Frequently exported goods from China through rail include electronics, vehicle parts, machinery, textiles, foods and beverages. Limited imports include wine, tobacco products and automobile spares, etc.

In March 2019, the European Commission released a strategy paper called *EU–China: A Strategic Outlook*.[36] In the paper, the EU recognized that rising China is an important global partner. However, it was asserted that China is also 'an economic competitor in the pursuit of technological leadership, and a systemic rival promoting alternative models of governance'. To counter this, the EU needs a 'policy shift towards a more realistic, assertive, and multi-faceted approach'. One of the major messages of the strategy is that 'neither the EU nor any of its Member States can effectively achieve their aims with China without full unity'. The key principles of the European engagement on connectivity are 'financial, environmental and social sustainability,

---

[33] Gulshan Sachdeva, 'Indian Perceptions of the Chinese Belt and Road Initiative', *International Studies* 55, no. 4 (2018): 285–296.

[34] Gulshan Sachdeva and Karine Lisbonne de Vergeron, *Developing EU & Indian Cooperative Responses to the Belt & Road Initiative. EU–India Think Tanks Twinning Initiative* (New Delhi: European Union, 2018). Available at https://euindiathinktanks.com/2019/publications/european-and-indian-perceptions-of-the-belt-and-road-initiative/ (accessed on 10 December 2019).

[35] Zhang Xinyuan, *Data Tells: China–Europe Freight Train Continues to Expand in Scope* (19 April 2019). Available at https://news.cgtn.com/news/3d3d774d3263444d34457a6333566d54/index.html (accessed on 10 December 2019).

[36] European Commission, *EU–China: A Strategic Outlook* (12 March 2019). Available at https://ec.europa.eu/commission/sites/beta-political/files/communication-eu-china-a-strategic-outlook.pdf (accessed on 10 December 2019).

transparency, open procurement and level playing field'. The strategy paper clearly outlines European concerns about China, which provide ample scope for India and the EU to work together in many areas. As the BRI, 5G, market access, etc., affect both the EU and India, wider bilateral consultations may facilitate better understanding and response.

EU–Russia Tensions

Europe has been a pioneer in regional integration model. It also promoted regional integration all over the world. The Ukrainian crisis, however, showed its limitation. The competitive integration attempts both from the EU and Russia created a crisis in Ukraine. Both the EU and Russia had devoted a lot of time and energy to build a strategic partnership. The Ukrainian crisis, however, resulted in damaging the strategic understating with Russia built over years. The European elite may not consider Russian Federation as an enemy today. However, certainly Moscow and Brussels are not 'strategic partners' anymore. Tensions between the EU and Russia may create some complications for India in the post-Soviet space. Due to broad rift with the West, Russian ties with Beijing have further strengthened. As the EU is trying to diversify its energy resources away from Russia, this may provide some new opportunities for India. As Chinese economy is also slowing down, Russia may need new customers in Asia in the coming years.

The EU's New Strategy for India

In November 2018, the EU announced its new strategy towards India for the next decade.[37] It has recognized that since 2004, when a bilateral strategic partnership was signed, the 'commonalities have grown'. These include areas of climate change, sustainable development goals and effective multilateralism. Many specific actions are proposed in the areas of shared approach at the multilateral level; India's sustainable modernization; clean energy transition and development cooperation.

The EU has clearly acknowledged that India's economic growth and modernization have been impressive; its engagements with diverse partners have grown significantly; and it has acquired an

---

[37] European Commission, *Joint Communication to the European Parliament and the Council: Elements for an EU Strategy on India* (2018). Available at https://eeas.europa.eu/sites/eeas/files/jc_elements_for_an_eu_strategy_on_india_-_final_adopted.pdf (accessed on 10 December 2019).

important geopolitical role. While adopting the strategy, the EU High Representative for Foreign Affairs and Security Policy, Federica Mogherini, said, 'India is a key player in our interconnected world'.[38] The strategy advocates India playing a bigger role in a multi-polar world, 'which requires a multipolar Asia'.

To make strategy attractive to Indian policymakers, it seems the EU is keen to focus more on 'strategic' component of the relationship with New Delhi. It wants to engage New Delhi 'at a strategic level' with Indian Ministries and institutions. Specific areas include maritime and cybersecurity and military-to-military relations. It asserts that both the EU and India have significant stakes in the security and stability in the Indian Ocean, West Asia, Central Asia and Africa. This reflects the results of a large number of official and unofficial bilateral dialogues in the last 10–15 years. There is also an advice for New Delhi. It argues that improved India–Pakistan relations will unlock huge potential for the region. Indirectly hinting Chinese BRI, the strategy asserts that connectivity plans in Asia should be 'environmentally, economically, socially and fiscally sustainable'.

Without underestimating potential for cooperation in the foreign policy and security issues, it must be clearly understood that basic competence of the EU is in trade, investment and related matters. Although policy coordination in many other areas has increased significantly in the last 10–15 years, many of these issues are still dealt at the national level. Recognizing this limitation, the EU has urged its MS to coordinate their bilateral initiatives with the EU strategy.

Despite ambitious strategy, the major EU frustration is reflected in the areas of trade and investment. Although the EU has shown its commitment to trade agreement in the strategy, it wants high level of investment protection. Besides, Brussels would like to include a chapter in the agreement dealing with social and environmental impacts. The new EU strategy on India reflects European recognition of India's rise and willingness to work with New Delhi on areas much beyond trade and commerce. To some extent, this is the result of Prime Minister Modi's visits to various European capitals in the last four years and re-engagement through summit meetings, which were stalled for a few years.

---

[38] European Commission, *Press Release: EU Shapes Its Ambitious Strategy on India* (2018). Available at http://europa.eu/rapid/press-release_IP-18-6481_en.htm (accessed on 10 December 2019).

The Indian government has formally welcomed the new strategy. The MEA statement says that India looks forward 'to engaging with the EU not only a robust bilateral agenda, but also on regional and global issues of shared concern and for reforming the multilateral system and institutions to better reflect contemporary global realities'.[39]

Emerging and Possible Areas of Cooperation

India–Europe relations have already become more strategic in the sense that many discussions are taking place in the areas beyond trade and investment. The strategic partnership institutional mechanism now spans over 30 dialogue mechanisms. If focused properly, the following few areas have the potential to make this relationship more meaningful.

Energy: Despite huge differences in their level of development, Europe and India are somehow facing similar energy security challenges. These include rise in global demand; instability in energy producing regions; diversification of energy mix and sources of energy supply. There is also a growing need to shift towards renewables in order to address climate change issues. The Many European countries have been investing heavily in the renewable energy sector and established a regime of binding commitments. Earlier, the perception was that Europe and India somehow hold opposite views concerning climate change, energy and environment. This is changing radically. Many new opportunities are now emerging for both of them to work together. As India plans to achieve renewable energy targets of 175GW by 2022 and 500GW by 2030, there is a huge scope of cooperation with the EU.[40] A solid beginning has already been made through International Solar Alliance; water partnership and smart grid cooperation. Both are working together on clean energy and climate partnership through joint projects in renewable energy, clean technology and energy efficiency. The European Investment Bank (EIB) has made significant investment in green energy projects in India.

---

[39] Ministry of External Affairs, *India Welcomes Joint Communication by the European Commission on India–EU Partnership* (26 November 2018). Available at https://www.mea.gov.in/press-releases.htm?dtl/30643/India+welcomes+Joint+Communication+by+the+European+Commission+on+IndiaEU+partnership++A+Partnership+for+Sustainable+Modernisation+and+Rulesbased+Global+Order (accessed on 10 December 2019).

[40] Gulshan Sachdeva, 'Indian Energy Security and the Role of Renewables: Possibility of Cooperation with the EU', in *India's Emerging Energy Relations: Issues and Challenges*, ed. Girijesh Pant (New Delhi: Springer, 2015).

Development cooperation: Development cooperation activities are becoming a significant aspect of Indian foreign policy discourse and strategic thinking in recent years. Although India has been active in this area for decades, the scale and geographical coverage has expanded significantly in the last 15 years. Current Indian development activities abroad are implemented through Lines of Credit (LoC); capacity-building particularly Indian Technical and Economic Cooperation (ITEC) programme and bilateral grant assistance projects. A significant part of these activities are concentrated in the neighbourhood and Africa.[41] As the EU and its MS are major players in development activities, both India and Europe can develop some triangular cooperation in third countries. A beginning can be made in places such as Afghanistan, Myanmar, Central Asia and Africa.

Migration and mobility: As migration-related issues are going to be politically relevant in Europe, the EU and its MS are keen to develop cooperation with all third countries including India. India is a country with the largest number of its people living outside its borders. For the last few years, India is also the top remittance-receiver country in the world. Although the EU is the second largest destination of global migrants, Indian migration to the EU is relatively small. Due to their demographic profile, most EU MS will need people from outside. Now European migrant numbers have come down and most EU economies are recovering. Over the years, India has emerged as a leading source of high-skill migration. Through some of the schemes like Blue Card, the EU MS have attempted to attract skilled migration from India. The success, however, has been limited. Since 2016, India–EU Common Agenda on Migration & Mobility (CAMM) has been established. The major focus is on establishing a framework for attracting talents and students to the EU and also on finding ways to improve orderly mobility and checking irregular migration. India is already the largest beneficiary of the EU's Erasmus+ programme for higher education scholarships and cooperation between Indian and European universities.

Central & Eastern Europe: The CEE region is becoming geo-strategically important. Traditionally, this erstwhile 'Eastern Europe' was a friendly area with significant political, economic, cultural and defence ties. After the Soviet break-up, region moved towards the EU and NATO. As

---

[41] Gulshan Sachdeva, 'India, South–South Cooperation and International Development Architecture', in *Contemporary Asian Perspectives on South–South Cooperation*, ed. Anthea Muleaka (Seoul: Korea Development Institute and the Asia Foundation, 2016).

a result of their economic and political transformation as well as move towards Europeanization, Indian trade and economic ties declined considerably. Since 2012, China is engaged in the region through its 16+1 initiative. Under this format, Beijing has intensified its ties with 11 EU MS from the region and five Balkan countries. In the region, it has signed strategic partnerships with Poland, Hungary and Serbia. Apart from Greece, many of the infrastructural projects under the BRI are implemented in CEE. So long as these countries were becoming part of the EU institutional framework, New Delhi was relaxed. However, Beijing's increasing influence in the region cannot be ignored. Some of the countries from the region, such as Poland, are traditionally close to India and have significant weight within the EU institutions. Still, India has no strategic partnership in the region. With a clear strategy, India has the potential to regain its influence.[42] Similar to the India-Nordic summit, New Delhi must initiate formal institutional engagements. At the moment, these countries are covered under the India–Europe 29 Business Forum (IE29BF). These 29 countries are part of the MEA's central Europe division, which covers not only the CEE but also the Nordic and Baltic regions as well as Turkey. This is too large and diverse a platform for any meaningful engagement. The initial engagement in the region can begin with Visegrad Four (the Czech Republic, Hungary, Poland and Slovakia), which could be extended to others later. Although Mr Modi has made many visits to Europe, he has not visited a single nation in the CEE so far. Apart from an annual regional summit, there is also a strong case for engaging one or two key countries through strategic partnership.

Conclusion

The unique experiment of economic and political integration among sovereign nations, which brought peace, stability and prosperity to Europe, is facing multiple internal and external challenges. Still, political and economic capacities of the EU and its MS have shown resilience to somehow muddle through many of the present crises. This has been evident in dealing with Greek and Eurozone crises. However, rise of populism in addition to evolving security situation in Europe is making things very difficult for Europe to go for rational policy choices. This

---

[42] Gulshan Sachdeva, *India Must Rediscover Its Ties with Central and Eastern Europe*, Moneycontrol.com (26 September 2018). Available at https://www.moneycontrol.com/news/politics/opinion-india-must-rediscover-its-ties-with-central-and-eastern-europe-2985811.html (accessed on 10 December 2019).

was clearly evident during Brexit referendum. At the end, both may still find some workable solution. Despite populist parties gaining in various elections, a reasonable political stability is expected in major countries as well as EU institutions. The rise of China, tensions with Russia and rift with the US under Trump administration are pushing Europe for other reliable partners. Despite its limitations, emerging India with all its political and economic strengths could develop a serious partnership with Europe. The way various competencies are divided between the EU and its MS, India has to carefully devise its European engagement strategy. As the core of this partnership is still economics, the EU institutions are extremely important for India for a meaningful partnership. For trade and economic matters, it is not possible to bypass EU and its concerns related to labour and environmental standards and human rights. India should also use EU capacities in the areas of climate change, sustainable development goals, development cooperation, disaster management, human rights, etc. The EU's statements on matters related to counterterrorism, etc., are useful but its competencies in these matters are limited. With a new leadership at the helm of affairs in the EU, this is the right time for the Modi government to work out its European strategy for the next five years.

India and the Indian Ocean

Yogendra Kumar

Introduction

There is a universal realization that global turbulence is deepening. Different countries, especially the big powers, have incompatible—and essentially aspirational—perspectives as to how this turbulence would end. The turbulence has been created by the compaction of external and domestic factors, specific to individual countries. Externally, there is growing ineffectiveness of global multilateral institutions originating at the end of the Second World War, failure of parallel institutions to emerge as their replacements, gathering clash of competing 'visions' of the global futures, increasing frequency of global financial economic crises and the destabilizing nature of global challenges such as climate change, large-scale and unregulated migrations, religious extremism and terrorism, rise of non-state actors empowered by technology, especially cyber, and an expanding gyre of state and regional instability. Domestically, state institutions are coming under increasing stress due to the state having lost the monopoly over public narrative and political fractiousness fed by rising societal and sectional aspirations. The countenancing of external challenges and exploitation of opportunities would depend, crucially, on the internal cohesion and resilient institutions of any nation state.

Situated in a troubled and unstable neighbourhood, challenges for India span a wide spectrum representing, practically, a microcosm of the problems of the world at large. The difficult relationships with its neighbours, especially Pakistan and, to a considerable extent, China, are acquiring a maritime dimension. The South Asian region, affected in varying degrees by the different aspects of this global turbulence, also faces serious threats of political instability in certain parts, scorching terrorism, internal political and economic frailties, daunting challenges of sustainable and demographically balanced economic growth, and low economic integration notwithstanding significant cultural similarities; nor does it have an effective pan-regional multilateral organization to address these common challenges which makes it vulnerable to manipulation by extra-regional powers. Many of these challenges are, further, compounded by the circumstances prevailing in the surrounding Indian Ocean and the other adjacent seas on which all the South Asian countries depend in some form or the other. The onset of globalization has meant that overwhelming proportion of global trade is carried at sea. The state of the oceans, the conducive circumstances prevailing there, safety and security of navigation routes, the health of these waters, the oceanic resources, etc., concern all countries. For littoral states, India being the primary one in South Asia, the maritime zones under UNCLOS are critical aspects of the national life in terms of security, wealth of resources and good order at sea. The challenges in the maritime sphere are but a subset of the overall global and regional challenges for their mutually reinforcing character even though the former are not identical to the latter.

For India, the Indian Ocean has been, historically, a part of its national being and a defining feature of its identity. The Asokan rock edicts of the 4th century BCE refer to India as *Jambudwipa* (Island of the *Jamun*—or the Indian blackberry—tree), an expression found as early as the Mahabharata texts. The security environment prevailing in the Indian Ocean has, through the millennia, shaped the highs and lows of its history on land. Thanks to it being a facilitative medium for long periods of history, the influence of Indian civilization spread far and wide throughout Eurasia and large parts of the African continent. For the leaders of the Indian freedom struggle during the colonial period, India's civilizational decline has been synchronous with the arrival of the European maritime powers, and in the eventual conversion of the Indian Ocean into a 'British lake' controlled by the Royal Navy headquartered at Singapore. The incessant effort of the Indian leaders, since Independence, has been to shed the country's resultant 'maritime blindness' and to use the Indian Ocean for the country's socio-economic and civilizational progress. In the 21st-century circumstances, India seeks to achieve this progress through the renewal of its enduring civilizational linkages but with a different set of tasks at hand.

Challenges Affecting the Nature of India's Relationship with the Indian Ocean

India as the Largest Country on the Indian Ocean Littoral

As the largest country on the Indian Ocean littoral, India's stakes in the conditions prevailing there have been high. The country has a long coastline and its coastal areas host huge populations and industrial centres which provide the locomotive power for its economic and cultural growth. It also has several islands across the coastline and deeper in the Indian Ocean in the Andaman and Nicobar Islands as well as the Lakshadweep and Minicoy Islands groups; both of these latter island groups have, in the past, been objects of strategic contestation and their strategic salience in the wider Indo-Pacific geopolitics has once again assumed high significance. Thus, the security of the peninsular, as well as the island formations, is part of India's national security calculus. The Mumbai terror attacks, in November 2008, are a grim reminder about the country's security vulnerabilities in the maritime domain. In addition, India has a huge exclusive economic zone (EEZ), covering an area of nearly 2.02 sq. km, which is a source of hydrocarbons and other minerals and of fish stock; the anticipated addition of approximately 1.2 sq. km of its Continental Shelf region under the UNCLOS provisions would make the country's seabed and sub-seabed area almost equal to its land area of 3.3 sq. km. As a responsible member in the comity of nations, India also covers a search-and-rescue zone of 3.9 sq. km following its ratification, in 2001, of the International Convention on Maritime Search and Rescue. India's utilization of the maritime resources has been suboptimal and tapping the full potential of these resources is a major thrust area in India's economic and technological growth plans. The range of 'traditional' and 'non-traditional' security challenges for India is vast and meeting them effectively remains a daunting national task for both security and progress.

These challenges are being met in a variety of ways. The Indian Navy, the Indian Coast Guard and the coastal police are the key agencies in providing security and supportive environment for trade and economic activities consistent with the UN-mandated Sustainable Development Goals (SDGs) for conservation of marine ecology and scientific research. Whilst the Indian Navy has overall responsibility in national defence in the maritime domain, the Coast Guard supervises, and coordinates, offshore security where several national and state agencies are involved: these relate to security of offshore installations for hydrocarbons, drugs and weapons smuggling, illegal, unreported and unregulated (IUU) fishing, armed robbery at sea, marine pollution, search and rescue, assistance in scientific research, etc. Capacity-building, in terms of infrastructure and weapons/equipment upgradation, has several dimensions, including power projection capabilities of the Indian Navy. The Indian Navy is strengthening capabilities in the Andaman and Nicobar Islands for enhanced constabulary functions in the Bay of Bengal as well as to meet contingencies arising from the likely spilling over of the tensions from the South China Sea into the Indian Ocean; similar upgradation is under way in the Lakshadweep and Minicoy Island group. The Indian Navy's Maritime Security Strategy publication (October 2015) has identified key choke points for Indian Ocean Region (IOR) security as the Ombai-Wetar Straits, Lombok Strait, Sunda Strait, the Malacca Straits, the Strait of Hormuz, Bab al-Mandab, the Mozambique Channel and the Cape of Good Hope. As it aims to be the 'net maritime security provider' in the Indian Ocean, it is developing by necessity significant maritime domain awareness (MDA) capabilities, on its own and in concert with other countries/organizations; in this effort, it aims to play a lead role in the region. The Indian Navy is also part of the overall national security capacity having formally launched deterrence patrols by its nuclear weapons capable submarine INS *Arihant* in October–November 2018, thereby completing the country's nuclear triad covering the capabilities on land, in air and at sea.

Proximity to IOR Sea Lanes of Communications

Major navigation routes across the Indian Ocean, as the arteries of global trade, are located in proximity to the Indian peninsula. The Nine Degree Channel, passing through the Lakshadweep and the Minicoy Island groups, is used by most of the merchant shipping traffic between Europe, Middle East and Western Asia with South East Asia and East Asia. The Six Degree Channel, between Aceh (Indonesia) and Great Nicobar (India), is also a major shipping route to the Malacca Straits. The Ten Degree Channel, between the Nicobar Islands and the Andaman Islands, is used for commercial traffic for the Bay of Bengal. India has strategic interest in the safety of these navigation channels but this interest extends far beyond in the Indian Ocean given its dependence on them for merchandise, passenger traffic and energy supplies. The declared Indian Navy interest in the various choke points controlling ingress and egress for smooth movement across the entire stretch of the Indian Ocean has earlier been referred to. As its geographical location gives it the capacity for power projection over these navigation routes and farther beyond, the importance of India's role in the Indian Ocean affairs is recognized by all countries. For the same reason, India remains vulnerable to attempts by state, as well as non-state actors, to make these shipping lanes a target of their domination or, in the case of the non-state actors, disruption. This being a perennial feature of the geopolitics of the Indian Ocean, it has implications, from India's point of view, about the balance of power in the Indian Ocean region and beyond.

These strategic concerns translate into heightened attention to the political and security conditions affecting the freedom of navigation through various choke points. Somali piracy off the coast of Africa and the Gulf of Aden, peeking between 2005 and 2010, expanded up to the Straits of Hormuz and beyond Seychelles and required a major international effort to suppress it at considerable cost to the participating countries, including India, and resulted in the high insurance premium. Even as this threat has not been completely eliminated, naval operations by diverse countries are having a significant effect on the strategic equilibrium in the Indian Ocean. The disturbed conditions in the Indonesian province of Aceh also led to piracy in that region which finally ended after the political settlement there following the 2004 Indian Ocean tsunami. The safety of IOR sea lanes of communications (SLOCs) is also contingent upon the level of political stability in the states located around the choke points as also the relationships among the key countries; the disturbed conditions in Somalia and state fragility in Myanmar, Maldives, Yemen have negative implications; the tense relationship between Iran and Saudi Arabia and other Gulf Cooperation Council (GCC) countries have similar implications if one were to remember the Persian Gulf 'tanker war' of the 1980s between Iran and Iraq. From the Indian point of view, the construction of the port infrastructure by China, under its 'Maritime Silk Road' (MSR) programme, portends instability along the IOR navigation channels given their economic unviability and location in countries experiencing political fragility; illustratively, these projects are located in Myanmar, Sri Lanka, Maldives and Pakistan. Thus, the challenges to the IOR balance of power inhere not only in the security downside of fragile states but also the activities of states, including China which is, at present, perceived more as a 'disruptive' power in this context. While the Indian Navy has a declared policy of monitoring the security situation at the various IOR choke points, the aforementioned complex challenges require both power balancing and creation of robust governance mechanisms for the Indian Ocean.

Ramifications of Shifting IOR Geopolitics

With the end of the Cold War and the onset of globalization, the increasing salience of the Indian Ocean region, and growing attention to its shipping lanes, a shift in geopolitics in the Indo-Pacific is also manifest in the presence of the big powers from outside the region. Even as the US military presence has been a constant feature, the 'Global War on Terror' (GWOT) and the subsequent Somali anti-piracy operations have witnessed a large number of extra-regional navies in northern and western Indian Ocean regions on account of the participation in Shared Awareness and De-Confliction (SHADE) activities and the US Navy-led multinational Combined Task Forces (CTFs), namely numbers 150, 151 and 152. The UK and France have strengthened their presence in the western Indian Ocean as well as the Gulf region. There has been a recent rush in setting up of naval bases in the Horn of Africa region which has been partly due to the ongoing war in Yemen and also conflicting geopolitical ambitions and Gulf tensions; these bases have been set up in Djibouti (Saudi Arabia, China, Italy, Japan, the USA and France), in Suakin in Sudan (Turkey), in Mogadishu in Somalia (Turkey and UAE), in Berbera in Somaliland (UAE) and at Assab in Eritrea (UAE).[1] With no abatement of the Yemen War in sight and the tensions in the Red Sea, the maritime rivalry there is expected to intensify with increasing interest in facilities in the region on the part of Israel, Egypt, Russia and Iran.[2] The growing tension between Qatar and the other Arab countries on the Persian Gulf littoral has also led to extra-regional interest there, the most recent being Turkey (Qatar) and Russia (Fujairah, UAE). One of the most significant trends is the growing Chinese naval presence in the Indian Ocean region. The presence of Chinese naval ships, including submarines, along with the opening of the 'Logistics base' in Djibouti, in August 2017, has led to the debate as to whether China's entry is disruptive of the existing strategic equilibrium which, by and

---

[1] David Brewster, 'With Eyes on the Indian Ocean, New Players Rush into the Horn of Africa'. *The War on the Rocks* (7 February 2018). Available at https://warontherocks.com/2018/02/with-eyes-on-the-Indian-ocean-new-players-rush-into-the-home-of-africa/ (accessed on 3 March 2018).

[2] Elionora Ardemagin, *Gulf Powers: Maritime Rivalry in the Western Indian Ocean* (Milano: Italian Institute for International Political Studies, 13 April 2018). Available at Ispionline.it/en/pubblicazione/gulf-powers-maritime-rivalry-western-indian-ocean-20212#references (accessed on 30 May 2018).

large, suits Indian interests due to strategic convergence with the USA. The growing presence of foreign navies and the increasing geopolitical fluidity has also led to the acquisition of naval platforms by the littoral countries. The contract for supply of eight Chinese submarines (Yuan-class Type 041 diesel-electric) to Pakistan can, by itself, lead to a major disturbance in the existing equilibrium in IOR. Moreover, given Pakistan's declared policy of placing nuclear weapons on naval platforms, the experience of the PNS *Zulfikar* incident (September 2014), when the Al-Qaeda attempted to capture the Pakistani ship, raises the frightful prospect of a situation of the 'loose nukes at sea' for the IOR at large, and not just for India alone. Although the Chinese Navy is not in a position to alter the balance of power in the Indian Ocean, it maintains a constant presence complemented by its Belt and Road Initiative (BRI)/MSR projects in strategically important countries; it is also using its navy for diplomatic signalling as it did by means of a 'live' exercise in the western Indian Ocean at the height of the Doklam India–China military stand-off.

India is already taking several steps to respond to the effects of the IOR geopolitical shifts on the strategic equilibrium such as it is. These are in the nature of building naval capabilities, including infrastructure, arrangements for port access in different island countries and the wider littoral, having coordinated patrols (CORPATs) with some key countries, and bilateral and multilateral naval exercises with the littorals and non-littorals. One of Indian Navy's flagship multilateral exercises is the biennial MILAN series which aims at interoperability capabilities and comfort, at a modest tactical level, among the participating navies from the larger 'Indo-Pacific' region; the latest, the 'MILAN 2018', was joined by 16 countries and was conducted from 6–13 March 2018. The 'Malabar series' of trilateral exercises, between India, the USA and Japan, are seen as having strategic ramifications due to their scale and tactical sophistication covering a range of joint operations; the 'Malabar 2017' exercise, in the Bay of Bengal, occasioned the participating US Fleet commander to say that he was confident that the US force could operate 'for real' should the situation so demand. These exercises, held alternately between the Bay of Bengal and the Western Pacific, represent a certain diplomatic signalling that the participating countries have stakes in the strategic equilibrium prevailing in the Bay of Bengal and the Western Pacific; all these countries have a complex relationship with China, with their individual peculiarities, and China watches these exercises closely, even deploying surveillance ships for this purpose. Although Australia is a participant in the recently launched 'India–Australia–Japan–US Consultations' (the Quad) on the

'Indo-Pacific', it is not a participant in the 'Malabar Series' despite its desire to do so; however, parallel sets of separate strategic discussions on regional issues are being carried out among the four partners in these 'Consultations'. Japan and Australia are also building naval relationships with key Indian Ocean island countries, besides India, and Japan has a base in Djibouti alongside China and other countries. The scope for joint diplomatic initiatives, including naval, with these countries will continue to grow as they develop an alternate 'Indo-Pacific vision' for regional safety and security, connectivities and shared values.

The Indian Ocean and the Pacific Ocean do not have an interlocking security architecture even though it is being recognized that geopolitical developments in one affect the situation in the other; this is largely the result of growing strategic interests of major regional powers, namely India and China, in the security milieu prevailing in Western Pacific/South China Sea and the Indian Ocean, respectively. The Indian Navy is the strongest force in the Indian Ocean after that of the USA which is supportive, as stated in the US National Security Strategy (NSS) released by US President in December 2017, of India's—and, by extension, the Indian Navy's—'leadership role in the Indian Ocean security and throughout the broader region'.[3] Yet the Indian Ocean waters are divided between the four US theatre commands, lacking a unified perspective for the entire IOR, thereby injecting divergences with that of India; the renaming of the US 'Pacific Command', covering the area from 'Hollywood to Bollywood' unlike India's definition of the 'Indo-Pacific', into the 'Indo-Pacific Command' represents a certain China focus with which India goes along to a considerable extent. Given this 'Indo-Pacific' connect, the naval infrastructure commanded by the USA in the Straits of Malacca, troop rotation facilities at Darwin (Australia) and Australian facilities at Cocos and Christmas Islands covering the Sunda Strait have implications for force equilibrium at least in the Bay of Bengal.[4] As mentioned earlier, force balance in the Horn of Africa region is fragile and under threat in the Gulf region; the developments in these two regions, hosting large Indian diaspora and sources of

---

[3] National Archives, 'National Security Strategy of the United States of America', 45–46. Available at https://www.whitehouse.gov/wp-content/uploads/2017/12/NSS-Final-12-18-2017-summary.pdf (accessed on 26 May 2018).

[4] Zack Cooper, *Security Implications of China's Military Presence in the Indian Ocean* (Washington, DC: Asia Maritime Transparency Initiative, 4 April 2018). Available at https://amti.csis.org/security-implications-China's-military-indian-ocean/ (accessed on 2 June 2018).

energy supply, can, potentially, upset the strategic equilibrium in the Indian Ocean as a whole.

Climate Change

Historically, an important factor in India's national wealth creation, the importance of the Indian Ocean has increased in recent times for two critical reasons. The impact of climate change on the Indian Ocean, like oceans elsewhere, has an important bearing on national security and well-being. Second, the ocean resources present a new frontier for the country's economic and technological growth since these have remained largely untapped hitherto due to lack of national capacities.

The UN-sponsored global integrated marine assessment on the state of the world's oceans states that human activities have 'so many and great impacts on the ocean that the limits of its carrying capacity are being (or, in some cases, have been) reached'.[5] Applicable no less to the Indian Ocean, the warming of the oceans is causing serious damage to coral reefs, seagrass beds, etc., representing a far serious climate change threat than the depletion of the world's temperate and tropical forests. The Indian Ocean warming[6] is resulting in the decline of phytoplanktons that provide food for various marine lifeforms, including fish; continuous warming is inhibiting vertical mixing, necessary to bring nutrients into upper ocean layers for photosynthesis; reduction in tuna stock will have negative impact on fish catch, thereby increasing overexploitation in the near future; changes in freshwater inflow into the ocean would affect temperature and salinity content, related to thermohaline dynamics at sea affecting air–sea interaction mechanisms and Indian monsoon rainfall; and sea-level rise combined with increasing intensity of cyclones can seriously affect coastal cities and coastlines subjecting them to major socio-economic stresses. These phenomena would affect coastal infrastructure complicating institutional capacities to mount disaster response efforts. Coastal zone management systems are required to be put in place to meet these challenges, environmental

---

[5] United Nations General Assembly, 'Summary of the first global integrated marine assessment' (UNGA document A/70/112 dated 22 July 2015), p. 48, under agenda item on Oceans and the law of the sea. Available at daccess-dds-ny.un.org (accessed on 31 January 2016).

[6] Ajay Mathur, Saurabh Bharadwaj, and Nitya Nanda, 'Non-Traditional Security Challenges to the Maritime Order in the Indian Ocean Region', in *Whither Indian Ocean Maritime Order?* ed. Yogendra Kumar (New Delhi: Knowledge World, 2017), 96–97 passim.

degradation and coastal pollution; the government has declared several areas covering approximately 10,000 sq. km, such as the Sundarbans, the Gulf of Mannar and the Gulf of Khambhat, as marine protected areas (MPA) due to the vulnerability of the fauna and flora.

India has been somewhat slower in taking full advantage of the abundant resources from the sea for its economic growth. Although large communities in peninsular India and its island territories depend on the ocean, their activities are largely confined to fishing which is also primarily low tech. 'Blue economy' dimension of the country's overall economic activity is still in its infancy; India's assumption of responsibility to achieve UN-mandated SDGs, including SDG 14 (life below water)—with its cross-linkages with goals dealing with poverty, zero hunger, decent work and economic growth, sustainable consumption and production and climate change—orients these activities into a new direction within a limited time frame of just one decade. SDG 14 is focused on the maritime sector, including the coastal and the marine ecosystem. Sustainable and high-tech mechanized fishing in the oceanic waters remains a government objective as also its processing at sea comparable to the practices followed by the developed countries. Mining technology, including deep sea mining, for extraction of polymetallic nodules and polymetallic massive sulphides, that is, copper, iron, copper silver, gold, zinc, titanium and zirconium, is still way off. There is increasing attention towards exploitation of oil and gas hydrate reserves in India's EEZ. Apart from fisheries, there are estimates of Myctophid, as potential food for livestock, poultry and aquatics, to the tune of 100 million metric tonnes (MMTs) within Indian territorial waters and a mari-culture potential of 7 MMT.[7] Other potential resources being tapped, although on a trial basis, are freshwater, tidal energy (17,300 MW), wave energy (45,000 MW), ocean thermal energy conversion (180,000 MW) and wind energy (350,000 MW).[8] Marine micro-algae are being tapped as a promising source for renewable energy.[9] The Indian government has a 2013 integrated and multidisciplinary National Plan for Conservation of Aquatic Ecosystems for a holistic conservation, restoration and sustainable use of resources of lakes and wetlands. There is an ambitious programme, with emphasis on Blue Economy, to promote port-led development and sustainable

---

[7] K. Somasunder, and M. N. Rajeevan, 'Diplomatic Role for Ministry of Earth Sciences', in *Whither Indian Ocean Maritime Order?* no. 5., 198–199.
[8] Ibid., 199.
[9] Ibid., 205.

development of coastal communities through skill development and livelihood generation activities, fisheries development, coastal tourism, etc. Launched in 2016, the SagarMala programme envisages strengthening of the port infrastructure, port connectivity through rail corridors, freight-friendly expressways and inland waterways, development of adjacent industrial clusters and coastal economic zones and sustainable development of coastal communities. Verily, the scale of national effort to enhance the country's security, as well as set it on a course for socially equitable and environmentally sustainable growth, is just about beginning to be grasped even as the time horizon is shrinking.

The Indian Ocean is also being studied, and not by India alone, to understand the dynamics of the monsoons and as to how climate change is impacting its evolving relationship with national economies and life–nature balance as a whole. Indian experts are engaged in atmospheric sciences and services, ocean science and services, and cryosphere/geoscience and technology. Cyclones, geo-engineering approaches, earth system science and climate constitute critical dimensions of their pioneering work. Studies are ongoing about the role of the oceans in monsoons including the nature of interaction between the weather phenomena such as El Nino–Southern Oscillation (ENSO) in the Pacific, Atlantic Multi-decadal Oscillation (AMO), Indian Ocean Dipole (IOD) and the monsoon. These scientific studies, accompanied by appropriate technologies, are a vital necessity for improvement of weather services bringing enormous benefits to the beneficiary communities as well as for climate change adaptation and mitigation.

The Indian Approach

A holistic maritime system for the Indian Ocean is lacking as the existing one is a legacy of the Cold War if the disposition of armed forces and their supporting infrastructure is looked at. It is incapable of coping with the geopolitical flux, as well as the multitudinous challenges, of both 'traditional' and the 'non-traditional' variety, arising from the seas for the littoral countries and communities as, indeed, for the world at large. While the existing force equilibrium, by and large, suits India by virtue of strategic convergence with the USA and the strength of the Indian Navy, a pan-IOR governance mechanism, capable of inspiring confidence among all stakeholders, is a vital and pressing necessity given the deteriorating trends overall. To address the entire spectrum of these challenges, Prime Minister Modi conceptualized the Indian approach in two seminal articulations.

SAGAR Speech

On the occasion of the handing over of an offshore patrol vessel to the Mauritius Coast Guard, on 12 March 2015 at Port Louis, Prime Minister Modi spoke of SAGAR, an acronym formed by his vision of 'Security and Growth for All in the Region'. Its main elements are as follows[10]:

- India has national responsibility for safeguarding the mainland and the islands and to defend its national interests. This includes commitment to help others during natural disasters, and search and rescue so as to 'ensure a safe, secure and stable Indian Ocean Region that delivers us all to the shores of prosperity'.
- Indian policy aims at deepened economic and security cooperation, including strengthening the maritime security capacities and economies.
- India will work for collective cooperation for peace and security within the region, the better preparedness for emergencies through multilateral mechanisms such as the Indian Ocean Naval Symposium (IONS) and bilateral maritime security cooperation.
- The Indian objective is promotion of greater regional integration on the basis of sustainable development and 'Blue Economy' where the Indian Ocean Rim Association (IORA) is an instrument for this purpose, including for combating climate change.
- The IOR littoral states have primary responsibility for peace, stability and prosperity of the Indian Ocean. India seeks a climate of trust and transparency, respect for international maritime rules and norms by all countries, whilst remaining sensitive to each other's interests, peaceful resolution of maritime issues and increase in maritime cooperation.

Shangri-La Speech

In his keynote address at the Shangri-La Dialogue, on 1 June 2018, at Singapore, Prime Minister Modi articulated, as follows,[11] his vision for the 'Indo-Pacific' region as a whole which he defined, in contrast with that of the USA, as stretching from the western coast of the Americas up to the eastern coast of Africa. Although looking largely at the Pacific Ocean, including the South China Sea, it has relevance for the Indian Ocean too.

---

[10] Yogendra Kumar, Unpublished article for *SP's Military Yearbook 2018–2019* (2019).
[11] Ibid.

- The Indo-Pacific is a natural region. The destinies of the people living in this region are linked.
- The Indian vision is one of 'free, open, inclusive region which embraces us all in a common pursuit of progress and prosperity'.
- ASEAN has been and will be essential to its future.
- Common prosperity and security require, through dialogue, of a 'common rules-based order for the region'. It applies to all individually as well as to the global commons on the basis of the belief in sovereignty and territorial integrity as well as equality of all nations. International commitments by nations must be upheld.
- There is need to have equal access as right under international law to the use of common spaces on sea and in the air that would require freedom of navigation, unimpeded commerce and peaceful settlement of disputes in accordance with international law.
- India is against growing protectionism and is for a level playing field and for open and stable international trade regime and for rules-based, open, balanced and stable trade environment in the Indo-Pacific. Connectivity is vital but needs to be based on respect for sovereignty and territorial integrity, consultation, good governance, transparency, viability and sustainability.
- Nations must turn their back on rivalry, especially great power rivalry, and a special responsibility devolves both on existing and rising powers. India will work with the countries individually or in formats of three or more but these friendships are not alliances of containment. India aims to promote a democratic and rules-based international order in which all countries thrive as equal and sovereign.

An Assessment

These two articulations sum up India's diplomatic objectives in the IOR and, now, in the wider 'Indo-Pacific' region. This diplomacy is in bilateral, plurilateral and multilateral formats with the objective of sustaining the existing IOR strategic equilibrium but to help develop 'ground rules' and habits of cooperation to fashion a regional mechanism in which all countries, within and outside the region, can develop sufficient stakes for it to function effectively.

In its bilateral relationships, India has aimed to facilitate naval and Coast Guard outreach to important countries for sustaining this strategic equilibrium. This has been by means of port access, intelligence sharing, developing infrastructure for better domain awareness in various countries as an enabler for exploitation of their EEZ resources, coordinated patrols, humanitarian and disaster responses, other forms of capacity building such as training and think tank networking. It is also involved in several infrastructure and economic cooperation projects with strategic partner countries. It is paying close attention to the activities of the Chinese Navy, including the docking of its submarines in ports closer to India, and conveying its concerns to the relevant countries should these appear to be crossing the 'red lines' in terms of its own security; these concerns also cover those BRI/MSR projects which entail the recipient countries entering into a debt trap of China because of their implications for the use of such projects for a possible strategic purpose. India's attention has been particularly on the economically vulnerable and politically fragile countries in this regard due to the location of some of them on shipping lanes passing through close to India or on navigation routes of its strategic interest; these countries, especially Pakistan, are in India's close neighbourhood, on the Persian Gulf littoral, the East African littoral and in the Indian Ocean island countries. This objective also underlies its growing relationship with the USA for its own capacity building and extension of the Indian Navy's reach through the sharing of logistics arrangements, a policy being extended to France, and Japan; it is also in agreement with Indonesia for the development of the Sabang port not far from the Malacca Straits. It carries out regular dialogues on maritime issues with all the major powers and neighbours, including China as well, for sharing of views about their respective priorities. It also engages with different regional and sub-regional groupings such as the African Union and Southern African Development Community (SADC), East African Community, the Gulf Cooperation Council, Bay of Bengal Initiative for Multi-Sectoral Technical and Economic Cooperation (BIMSTEC), and ASEAN and related organizations.

India is a strong supporter of both IORA and IONS, of which it has been a founding member. As an organization dedicated to the promotion of economic integration in the IOR, its Charter responsibilities have an expanded to include maritime safety and security and the 'Blue Economy'. India made a major contribution to the IORA Summit, in Jakarta on 7 March 2017, in the elaboration of the work programme, in short-, medium- and long-term, under the 'Jakarta Concord'; India is operationalizing summit commitments, including an Information Fusion Centre for coordination on MDA. IORA has a Maritime Safety and Security Working Group which is currently engaged in developing various procedural frameworks and capacity-building; it is also developing cooperation programmes in 'Blue Economy' sphere. IONS is a useful platform for raising, through its various working groups, interoperability capabilities and strategic trust levels among the littoral navies and the other stakeholder extra-regional navies, including those representing adversarial countries, such as Pakistan; its current chairmanship is held by Iran.

There is much work ahead for India for it to shape a supportive maritime system in the Indian Ocean for securing peace, stability and conditions for its rapid socio-economic growth. Apart from the growing presence of the Chinese Navy and increasing interest among the IOR countries in receiving Chinese funds for their development needs, the strategic equilibrium in the Horn of Africa region is weakening and it is under threat in the Gulf region. India would have the naval capability to intervene in certain situations to protect its security interests but not to stabilize the equilibria in these sub-regions. Like India's, the 'loiter' and other operational capabilities, for maritime system defence roles, of the other navies, such as the USA, France and Japan, are also being expended in IOR through logistics-sharing agreements. Its ability to mount Humanitarian Assistance and Disaster Relief (HADR) operations in different parts of the IOR and beyond as well as to carry out evacuations of civilians from different conflict situations, including in hostile environment, does project it as a significant power to reckon with. Its appeal as a benign power capable of buttressing stability in the region, however, needs to be burnished through capacity-building, intelligence-sharing, developing individually and in concert a pan-IOR MDA, assisting vulnerable countries in checking illegal fishing and other incidents of transnational crime, building capacities in partner countries in operational oceanography, etc. The development of ground rules and operational procedures in maritime and 'Blue Economy' by IORA would, alone, encourage a large majority of Indian Ocean countries to develop stakes in the functioning of such a maritime system. Similarly, IONS needs to demonstrate on the ground the interoperability comfort among the participating navies and also develop some 'communication' with the IORA bodies to strengthen the latter's capacity-building efforts, given that these are two separate organizations with the own structures and institutional cultures.

Concluding Remarks

India has existential stakes in the stability of the Indian Ocean. The absence of a holistic maritime system for the Indian Ocean is an opportunity in that the process of its shaping does not involve the dismantlement of any existing one. The pan-IOR organizations need to be sufficiently strengthened to carve out a role for themselves for countries to develop stakes in their success. Due to its extensive network of relationships and largely benign image, India is well placed to play a lead role, including a thought leadership role which needs to be enhanced through an effective media policy of participation in the mainstream discourse in important littoral countries. Effective steps are required by the four consulting powers of the 'Quad' to make their 'vision' credible for the littoral countries. Foregrounding cooperation in 'non-traditional' challenges will increase comfort level even among the adversarial countries for finding common grounds even over divergent strategic perspectives. In the Middle East, where India has very high stakes, the Indian and the US strategic perspectives do not converge four-square requiring a more nuanced diplomacy to secure its interests.

The window of such opportunity may not remain open for too long. The Paris accords consider 2030 as an inflection point in the climate change trajectory if those commitments are not met. The substantial realization of the SDGs is also benchmarked to the same year. Several observers feel that the Chinese Navy would not be capable of altering the balance of power in the Indian Ocean for another decade or more. These three statements are meant to convey that these diverse challenges, for India in the Indian Ocean region, are likely to conflate around the same time. This timeline brings out the complexity of these challenges requiring multi-pronged strategy on the part of India. The challenge, therefore, lies in India being able to leverage the current favourable circumstances to realize the road map offered by Prime Minister Modi in his SAGAR and Shangri-La speeches.

India's Tryst with Africa
India–Africa Contextualized

Anil Trigunayat

Africa is on a defining cusp in this 21st century. For centuries Africans were subjected to colonialism, racism, loot and then neocolonialism compounded by sophisticated plunder of their natural resources in cohort with the myopic and occasionally corrupt leadership, which was often installed through military coups or external intervention. Consequently, poverty disease, crime, underdevelopment and hopelessness ensued. They were afflicted by corruption, conflict and coups (3Cs). This is an irony and a paradox since the continent is replete with vast natural and human resources. There have been many leaders who have had a vision for their country and the continent. But neither Africa is a single nation nor has each one looked at the prospective routes through the same prism. This is normal since Africa is not only 54 nation states but a kaleidoscope of culture, traditions, tribes and colourful diversity with unique aspirations and methodologies. Hence, in appreciating and interacting with them, it is essential to understand that Africa is not a 'single' entity but a kaleidoscope of intermingling strategic space.

Africans have made sincere efforts to unite and evolve multilateral institutions such as the African Union (AU), the African Development Bank (AfDB) and several effective regional organizations mostly related to financial, banking, customs or developmental priorities. Despite the slow and occasionally wavering processes, they have been working hard to create a pan-African economic space which could provide them the requisite levers for international negotiability and protection. They established an Agenda 2063 at the AU Summit in 2015 which seeks to achieve a more prosperous Africa through an inclusive growth and sustainable development embracing Pan-Africanism. Since they identified the basic problems afflicting the continent a 'Call for Action Plan' sought to eradicate poverty, provide affordable housing, education and skill development, equitable industrialization, modernizing agriculture, creating infrastructure across the spectrum, mobilization of domestic resources for development and conflict prevention across Africa. These are the key issues that are faced by any developing country. 'Trade and not aid' surely not the conditional aid has been the driving force for achieving these objectives.

One of the key recommendations has been to establish a Continental Free Trade Area since the Agenda 2063 had set the target of enhancing intra-regional trade to 50 per cent by 2050 from the current 18 per cent. It estimated an eventual growth and share of 12 per cent for Africa in the global trade from 2 per cent. Despite roadblocks and divergences, the project is moving smoothly as it seeks to establish a Prosperous Africa, a Peaceful Africa and a Just Africa. Earlier, in 2008, an African Free Trade Zone was created with the participation of sub-regional groups such as East African Community (EAC), Southern African Development Community (SADC) and Common Market for Eastern and Southern Africa (COMESA). However, in March 2018, at the Kigali Summit, 44 countries signed up to the African Continental Free Trade Area (AfCFTA) encompassing 1.2 billion people with a combined GDP of $2.3 billion. This happens to be the largest trade agreement since WTO and seeks to establish 'a single continental market for goods and services with free movement of business persons and investments'. It would end up reducing the average export tariffs of 6.1 per cent on over 90 per cent of the items. A closer integration continues even though the biggest economies like Nigeria are yet to come on board and scotch their apprehensions while South Africa did finally join in. President Buhari, in order to protect their industries and manufacturing, does not want Nigeria to become a 'dumping ground'. But undoubtedly Africa is slated to be the next big thing in the later half of the 21st century as it would provide consumer market with 1.7 billion people of over $6.7 trillion consumer and business spending by 2030 and investment opportunity of over $100 billion a year after discounting for the domestically generated funds for the infrastructural needs across 55 countries. According to the AfDB Economic Outlook report 2018, Africa now collects $500 billion in tax revenues; $50 billion in foreign aid and $60 billion in remittances and almost the same in foreign direct investment (FDI). This is further sweetened by the UNCTAD 'World Investment Report' that stated:

> Foreign investment in sub-Saharan Africa rose 13% last year to $32 billion, bucking a global downward trend and reversing two years of decline. Development of new mining and oil projects, a new U.S. development-finance institution and the ratification of an agreement to create a continent-wide free-trade area could further boost foreign direct investment (FDI) in 2019.[1]

Yet the inherent sub-regional, administrative, bureaucratic and logistical, as well as security challenges that have stunted the integration and growth so far, will have to be addressed in a more concerted manner.

During 2001–2016, out of the 10 fastest growing countries, 6 have been African. Having been somewhat in disconnect with the developed world, they could easily absorb the shocks of the economic downturn. Their share of FDI also increased to 11.4 per cent in 2016 from 9.4 per cent in 2015. Spending by consumers and businesses also grew to almost $4 trillion and the household consumption is expected to grow on an average by 3.8 per cent to reach $2.1 trillion in 2025. By some estimates, Africa's working-age population will grow by approximately 450 million people—about 3 per cent per annum—between 2015 and 2035. By 2050, Africa will have 362 million young people between the ages of 15 and 24 years old. This goes to confirm that significant opportunities exist for global investors and businesses.

And as the World Bank estimates, the challenges and variation in growth remain.

> Growth in Sub-Saharan Africa is estimated at 2.3 percent for 2018, down from 2.5 percent in 2017. Economic growth remains below population growth for the fourth consecutive year, and although regional growth is expected to rebound to 2.8 percent in 2019, it will have remained below three percent since 2015.[2]

---

[1] Available at https://www.africanews.com/2019/06/13/africa-13-percent-boost-in-fdi-flow-south-africa-ghana-ethiopia-big-winners/ (accessed on 17 December 2019).

[2] World Bank, *The World Bank in Africa* (11 April 2019). Available at https://www.worldbank.org/en/region/afr/overview (accessed on 17 December 2019).

But 'Non-resource-intensive economies such as Kenya, Rwanda, Uganda, and several in the West African Economic and Monetary Union, including Benin and Côte d'Ivoire, recorded solid economic growth in 2018'.[3]

But for that to succeed, it is imperative that there is a conducive domestic and external environment. The region is made up of a combination of low, lower middle, upper middle and high-income countries. Total 18 countries are fragile and conflict-affected states. Africa also has 13 small states, characterized by a small population, limited human capital and a confined land area. Moreover, the current impending and ongoing trade wars and decimation of the international institutions pose a threat to Africa. The biggest economy USA is intent on a conflict path with China and European Union which are Africa's major partners, and any adverse developments or slowdown in growth there would also impact Africa's nascent dreams adversely. North African countries such as Libya, Tunisia, Sudan and Algeria are still suffering from the ravages of the Arab Revolution and the militancy and extremism, as well as external interventions, are compounding the instability in the region. Africa might also degenerate into their theatre of trade wars and the 'gold rush' and mutually decimating strategies employed by the major powers will have consequences difficult to gauge. Consequently, the global governance, being under threat, could impact African countries in an unpredictable and volatile manner at least in the medium term. Alternatives need to come up like the BRICS Summit in South Africa where the theme was 'BRICS in Africa: Collaboration for Inclusive Growth and Shared Prosperity in the Industrial Revolution 4.0'. How far BRICS financial and other institutions are able to deliver on the African expectations is a moot point even though at least two of its major constituents China and India are heavily invested in the continent and third one South Africa is a driving economy in the region.

The Gold Rush—Chinese Advantage

China had early on realized the potential and consequent strategy to ensure its presence in Africa. It had seen the resource control and primacy by Western MNCs, especially in the mineral and hydrocarbons by virtue of their long-standing colonial presence or trading relations with the help of the African leaders who though were looking for some viable alternative found it most convenient for their own benefits

---

[3] Ibid.

and continuity. Besides it was convenient as most of the leaders had close relations with their benefactors. Beijing was ready with its fat chequebook diplomacy apart from efficiency and speed of its project delivery mechanisms. Chinese engaged the African leaders extensively both bilaterally and regionally with long-term loans and credits or gifted iconic buildings be it sports stadiums, hospitals, railways, roads and bridges, government offices or agricultural equipment in record time. These edifice became the landmark of Sino-African friendship and commitment. In turn, they secured oil and mining concessions. Their China–Africa Forums became a model of cooperation for others to follow but the Chinese secured the early bird advantage much to the chagrin of others who were still crafting their focus and policies, despite the fact the Western countries remain the largest donors for humanitarian purposes and investors in select areas of their interest. Witnessing the Chinese expanse and its growing strength in Africa and the fact that Africa is subjected to a debt trap a new narrative is being advanced that Beijing is the new neocolonialist power. Unfazed Chinese have continued apace with their injection of capital, loans and credits and cornering major projects and assets in the process threatening a shrinking space for the rest of the world.

China's second coming in Africa—the first being a short-lived intervention during the wars of liberation in the 1960s and 1970s—has transformed the image of the continent from largely one of a problem to be solved to a commercial prospect. As a result, China's trade relationship with Africa has grown in this century from just $10 billion to nearly $200 billion, and its continental investment stake is now greater than that of the USA at $35 billion by 2017, with over $140 billion in Chinese loans committed to date. Center for Strategic and International Studies (CSIS) in Washington, DC, also assessed that during 2000–2014, China provided a total of $354 billion in loans, grants and other assistance to countries around the world. Just over a third of this was provided to Africa. China gave $121.6 billion for 2,390 projects, with 60 per cent of these being in the transport and energy sectors. In comparison, the USA provided $100 billion of aid to Africa during the same period but 80 per cent of it was dedicated to health care and humanitarian assistance. In Ethiopia, the second largest African recipient of Chinese developmental financing, about half of the funding was used for transportation projects reflecting the country's strategic location in the Horn of Africa. In Angola, however, 40 per cent of the funding was used to exploit the country's large oil resources. Other analyses have shown correlations between Chinese development finance and the foreign policies of the recipients. Aid data looked at how closely aid recipients, especially in Africa, voted in favour of China in the United Nations. They found a 10 per cent increase in voting convergence went with an 86 per cent Official Developmental Assistance (ODA) increase, according to CSIS.

China is also changing its perception management style and taking more recourse to investments and joint ventures while writing off several unrecoverable loans and debt. This was clearly evidenced during the 7th Forum on China–Africa Cooperation (FOCAC) Summit held in Beijing on 3–4 September 2018 where 53 African heads of states participated. FOCAC that began in 2000 at ministerial/summit levels every three years has evolved into main driving force for Sino-African cooperation even though bilateral formats like China–Kenya Industrial Capacity Cooperation Forum also exist. In addition, China regularly undertakes high-level visits to its African partner countries when huge bilateral projects and financing are announced. At the 7th FOCAC, China reiterated its commitment to develop and enrich the comprehensive strategic and cooperative partnership. The Beijing Declaration clearly ingrained the Chinese president's pet Belt and Road Initiative (BRI) into the fabric of their Sino-African engagement. They underscored the synergy between the BRI, Agenda 2063 and UN's Agenda 2030 for sustainable development. In keeping with its futuristic engagement, China announced a financial package of $60 billion for next three years which might support the existing and newer areas of cooperation, especially in industrial promotion, capacity-building, infrastructure and connectivity as well as social development among others. The break-up of $60 billion package is quite interesting as it entails $20 billion in Line of Credit (LoC); $15 billion in aid and interest-free loans, $10 billion in development finance; $10 billion in investments through private sector and $5 billion in import financing. They have written off several debts and loans of the poorer countries. Maritime and ocean development cooperation became the key area for mutually beneficial cooperation. China has already set up a base in the Horn of Africa in Djibouti which fits well into its blue water strategies including the 'Pearl of String strategy'. Hence, through its investments and loans in strategic assets in infrastructure sector, it has acquired a long-lasting comparative advantage.

Even 2019 began with Chinese Foreign Minister Wang Yi visiting Ethiopia, Burkina Faso, Gambia and Senegal from 2 to 6 January. This was in continuation to 29-year-old tradition that first international visit of the Chinese foreign minister has to be to Africa, Wang said that China–Africa friendship is unbreakable and the one-China principle has been consolidated and strengthened in Africa. But the context of their cooperation might come under some stress with the Western countries, especially the USA looking at the Chinese expanse as a zero-sum game strategy.

USA and Others—Catching Up Game

On 13 December 2018, the USA decided on a new Africa policy to counter Chinese influence and 'predatory' practices of China and Russia which is part of its global strategy. Speaking at the Heritage Foundation, John Bolton, national security advisor, accused it of wielding 'bribes, opaque agreements, and the strategic use of debt to hold states in Africa captive to Beijing's wishes and demands'. Russia, he alleged, is also 'seeking to increase its influence in the region through corrupt economic dealings'. Russia and China's efforts across the African continent, he said, 'stunt' its economic growth. Under the new 'Prosper Africa' strategy, Bolton said, 'we will encourage African leaders to choose high-quality, transparent, inclusive, and sustainable foreign investment projects, including those from the United States'.[4] The USA is one of the largest providers of developmental assistance, and to Africa it gave US$8.7 billion in 2017. This is another matter that President Trump was quoted referring to Africa as a 'shithole' that obviously irked the proud continent.

There are few buyers of the Western argument as several Africans remind them of the exploitative Western practices and unfavourable financial terms while lamenting the poor and vindictive projection of Africa in the Western media. On the other hand, they often acknowledge that China has extended assistance without any strings attached, especially on the human rights issues. China is there to stay. While some African countries welcomed renewed US interest in the continent, they urged the USA to follow a policy of soft power projection and support China–Africa cooperation and not rivalry. Former Nigerian President Olusegun Obasanjo wrote that 'Africa is likely to resist making a choice between China and the United States. The US is asking African countries to choose sides at a time when many don't have this luxury'. He warned that 'the history of superpower rivalry in Africa is messy, destructive and occasionally bloody'.[5]

---

[4] Available at https://amp.detroitnews.com/amp/38730489 and https://www.heritage.org/event/webcast-only-the-trump-administrations-new-africa-strategy (accessed on 17 December 2019).

[5] Available at https://qz.com/africa/1501023/president-obasanjo-says-trumps-africa-strategy-cant-rival-china/?utm_source=email&utm_medium=africa-weekly-brief (accessed on 17 December 2019).

In order to provide the requisite impetus, the 12th US–Africa Business Summit was held in Maputo from 18 to 21 June 2019 which was attended by a large number of African leaders and over 1,000 businessmen and industrialists from Africa and the USA with a theme 'Advancing a Resilient and Sustainable US-Africa Partnership' as a follow-up to the US-Africa Business Summit of 2017. However, the USA has a lot of ground to cover.

Russia is also staging a comeback after its first foray into infrastructure and steel plants as well as oil and gas collaboration with several countries. Having learnt a bitter lesson during NATO's Libyan experiment in 2011, Putin has become far more active and cautious, and going its own way to acquire and ensure strategic relationships and assets. Western sources assert,

> ... documents leaked to the Mikhail Khodorkovsky funded Dossier Center, reports that Russia is seeking to bolster its presence in at least 13 African countries—having already signed military deals in 20 states—'by building relations with existing rulers, striking military deals, and grooming a new generation of "leaders" and undercover "agents"'.

And

> Ensuring his escalating African efforts aren't missed, Putin and Egyptian President Abdel Fatah al-Sisi will convene 50 African leaders at the first-ever Russian-African Summit in Sochi this October. Russian Foreign Minister Sergei Lavrov, a frequent traveller to Africa, says its purpose will be to cement 'Russia's active presence in the region'.[6]

India's Extensive Outreach and Engagement with Africa

India and Africa have a historic and umbilical relationship. It is not a cliche'. It makes a good talking point during speeches and political interactions but will need an objective assessment of the extant and depth of our engagement to stand up to scrutiny for devising better policy choices. It is also a fact that India has consistently, even if occasionally in ad hoc manner, engaged with the African countries. It emerged as a strong voice for their emancipation from the colonial

---

[6] Available at https://www.cnbc.com/amp/2019/06/14/vladimir-putin-muscles-into-africa-which-is-bad-news-for-us-interests.html?__twitter_impression=true (accessed on 17 December 2019).

yoke and from then on through Non-Aligned Movement (NAM) and has stood for and advocated the core concerns of the African countries, especially the least developed countries (LDCs) in the international fora be it GATT/WTO, UN/CHOGM or the Climate Change negotiations. This has been widely appreciated and has earned India an immeasurable affection quotient across Africa. This was further enriched by the Indian diaspora and enterprise which had helped the respective countries of their residence in economic upliftment, progress and development. In many countries, they emerged as major economic players and were widely respected as they also imbibed and attuned the African ethos and requirements. Besides, India through its extensive capacity building assistance and 'share and care' approach helped a great deal in creating skilled manpower, modern institutions in the fields of both education and defence. Indian teachers and professors were widely respected, especially by those who studied during the 1960s–1980s; unfortunately, this very effective mode of engagement dried out and needs to be revived. Several African leaders fondly recall their Indian teachers even after 40–50 years. Several military officers were trained in India and rose to become heads of government and heads of state in their countries like former President Olusegun Obasanjo of Nigeria who were singularly instrumental in expanding cooperation with India. At least six current or former African chiefs of armed forces were trained in Indian military institutions and not less than 13 current or former presidents, prime ministers (PMs) and vice-presidents attended educational or training institutions in India. During my own tenures, I met several of them including President Obasanjo of Nigeria and PM Ali Zeidan of Libya. This is an extremely important dimension of the soft power which should be nurtured in a more focused manner. Thousands of Africans have been trained under the fully funded Indian Technical and Economic Cooperation (ITEC) programme and have risen to responsible positions. Another important capacity building effort is to train about 80 women every year to work on solar panels who are fondly popular as 'solar mamas' as they, on return, electrify the communities and at least 50 houses each.

One of the most important connectivity and capacity-building programme launched by India pursuant to the vision of former President A. P. J. Abdul Kalam was the Pan-Africa e-network initiative that focused on tele-medicine, tele-education and e-governance or connectivity among heads of states across 48 countries. It entailed five Indian ace universities offering courses and 12 super specialty hospitals providing consultations and medical education and was fully funded by Indian government under New Partnership for Africa's Development

(NEPAD). Reportedly, over 7,000 students completed their studies. To take it to the next level on 10 September 2018, the Ministry of External Affairs and Telecommunications Consultants India Limited (TCIL) signed an agreement for the implementation of e-VidyaBharti and e-ArogyaBharti (e-VBAB) to create a digital bridge of knowledge and health between Africa and India in accordance with India's enhanced Africa focus. Through technological upgrade, it will provide free tele-education to 4,000 students and free continuing medical education for 1,000 students every year. Earlier, in 2004, India had launched the Techno-Economic Approach for Africa–India Movement (Team-9) with eight West African countries which subsequently became part of the India–Africa Forum Summit in 2008. India had also launched a Cotton Technical Assistance Programme in 2012 that is being implemented in Benin, Burkina Faso, Chad, Malawi, Nigeria and Uganda. Under the International Solar Alliance initiative, several African countries have become our partners and this provides a window of green-energy future since large part of Africa literally remains dark and has power cuts occasionally due to the powerful diesel and other lobbies. India has ambitious plans in renewable energy and can easily share its assistance and expertise in an efficient and expeditious manner.

Diaspora versus Racism

The diaspora normally helps a great deal in building the bridges at people-to-people level and, in turn, contributes to the growth of bilateral relations, especially in the economic field as well as through the leadership positions acquired by them as a result of exposure and experience in a particular country. India has approximately 3 million people of Indian origin across the African continent who are highly successful. Even if many of them had migrated or were forcibly taken as indentured labour, they have become highly successful as professional entrepreneurs and business leaders and in many countries they are the prime movers of industrial activity. One hardly sees any blue-collar Indian workers in Africa which provides India an advantage since it does not take away bulk of the jobs from the locals unlike China. However, over the years, some successful Indians have indulged in showing off their wealth much to the chagrin and frustration of the local communities and gave rise to anti-India sentiments in Africa that even made the Indian government wary of utilizing the diaspora asset. However, this has been rectified to a great extent even though the identity of Indian diaspora in Africa remains somewhat complex as they feel far more attuned to their African heritage rather than Indian origin but with India's resurgence as a regional power their perception has changed. The Indian community has begun to synthesize with the socio-economic needs of the local communities by rendering various services such as education, medical treatment, job creation and employment. No wonder the former president of Nigeria stated more than once 'That the Indian industrialists are the second biggest employment providers after the federal Government in Nigeria'. The Government of India also recognized their potential and has been engaging them through Pravasi Bharatiya Divas (PBD), and India–Africa Forum summits and other bilateral and B2B formats need to be pursued in a more concerted and comprehensive manner so that the maximum goodwill and mutual benefit could be generated through the diaspora dividend.

Since the 1950s, India has been encouraging African students through scholarships for higher education, training and capacity-building in Indian Institutions. According to estimates, currently, there are more than 55,000 students from various African countries in India. However, unfortunately several incidents of racial attacks against the African students and various difficulties being faced by them in their day-to-day existence in India have created a big furore resulting in image deficit for India in their own countries. The representative of the association of the African Students Union in India (AASI) in an interview mentioned that

> racism is two-way street; what if they went back and treated Indians the same way in their continent. Don't tell us about the age old Indo-Africa relations. If there is that long relationship than why do people stare at us and perhaps they don't care because they think that they will never depend on Africa but things are changing there is always pay back. If I don't do it 'someone else will'.

He further added with a warning: 'World is turning. The generation in power back home is old. That means the generation that you are discriminating against now will be future leaders who you will have to deal with in ten years to come'.[7] This trend and perception needs to be nipped in the bud by proactive action on the part of security outfits in the country as negative perception can cause more harm than the abhorrent reality. Therefore, it is imperative that every effort is made through institutionalized and attitudinal changes among the Indians that Africans are our guests and must be treated with respect and

---

[7] *Patriot* (30 November–6 December 2018), 9.

affection so that our national interests are served and not undermined by the occasional negativity and errant behavioural patterns.

Defence and Security Imperatives

India has a long history of cooperation in the defence capacity-building in various African countries and participating in the UN Peacekeeping Operations since 1960 in Congo. Their role has been broadly appreciated, especially in preventing genocide in South Sudan. Similarly, Indian women police personnel did a remarkable job in Liberia that was rather unique and President Sirleaf was all praise for them. Currently, India trains a large number of Africans not only in its defence institutions but also in the peacekeeping operations and manoeuvrability in addition to conducting counterterrorism and insurgency operations. India had set up national defence colleges in several countries including Nigeria. It would also be useful to align our engagement with the African Peace and Security Architecture (APSA) devised by the then Organisation of African Unity (OAU) to deal with African problems such as genocide and ethnic cleansing.

India has also been very active in anti-piracy operations on the East Coast of Africa, especially Somalia and Gulf of Aden to Mozambique Channel to ensure free lines of trade and communications. Indian navy successfully escorted around 2,500 vessels. Like the US Africom, it needs to also strategically look at Gulf of Guinea. While in the context of India's aspirations for a permanent seat at the UNSC peacekeeping counts for one of its major credentials, from its presence in Africa the concrete manifestation of support to India is yet to be seen, especially when pitted against Chinese machinations to the contrary. Japan is also another strong aspirant and competitor for Asian presence at the UNSC and with its immense ODA assistance and consistent engagement with Africa through Tokyo International Conference on African Development (TICAD), etc., has made better inroads into the African mindset. Africans themselves are looking for at least two permanent seats; hence, negotiations are not going to be that easy and some mutual accommodation will have to be found.

Africa is also infested by violent terrorist groups such as Boko Haram, Al-Shabaab, Al-Qaeda and Al-Qaeda in the Islamic Maghreb (AQIM) with linkages in Pakistan, Afghanistan and Iraq, and, hence, counter-terrorism cooperation and capacity building assistance to Africa in this context assumes a much deeper significance. Given the limitations of local expertise in countering these ferocious groups, which may have implications for India's security, it is important for us to have a sustained security and strategic dialogue to address these mutually affecting concerns.

Current Africa-Centred Policy

PM Narendra Modi, while speaking at the Parliament in Kampala in July 2018, outlined his Africa vision through his 10 guiding principles which include the following: Africa is among top priorities for India and momentum of cooperation will be sustained through regular exchanges; development partnership as per African priorities; preferential access to Indian markets for African products; assist in harnessing digital revolution in Africa; improve Africa's agriculture potential; fight climate change together; work together to keep oceans and maritime lanes free for all; Africa instead of becoming a theatre of competition should become nursery for its youth; and aspire and work together for a just, representative, democratic global order. These are ideal, achievable and collaborative policies that dictate a paradigm shift compared to other big powers who are trying to get into the 'Gold Rush' for exploitation by way of neocolonialist approaches.

In the past, there have been sporadic efforts to enhance the bilateral trade and investment which had limited success. The bilateral trade in recent years had peaked at close to $70 billion in 2013–2014 but came down to around US$56 billion in 2016–2017 which in any case is way below potential and needs to be perked up through diversification of the trade basket and addressing the structural bottlenecks. Trade deficit remains in favour of Africa due to imports of oil and other minerals but this, inter alia, helps generate more growth in the Continent. Nigeria occasionally surpassed Saudi Arabia in exporting almost 12 per cent of our crude requirements. It is imperative that with the unpredictability in the Middle East region, we should secure long-term supplies, concessions, contracts to ensure our energy security in a mutually beneficial matrix and could be linked with some desirable investments in those countries. Likewise, Indian investments in Africa range around 17 billion even though over two decades it has invested a cumulative $55 billion becoming the fifth largest investor but that is much less compared to other Western countries and China.

Efforts to engage Africa at the bilateral and multilateral levels both at the G2G and B2B level continues. Almost 30 visits at the level of president, PM and vice-president have taken place during the tenure of Modi government which is unprecedented and has bridged the much lamented hiatus by the African countries. India has also focused on reviving defence collaborations including maritime cooperation. It was also the first time that an Africa Day was celebrated at the Vibrant Gujarat with the participation of 25 African countries and Morocco and South Africa being the lead partners. Similarly, the South African President Cyril Ramaphosa was the chief guest at the Republic Day 2019.

India's outreach is not limited merely to bilateral context but also to trilateral and multilateral mechanisms. India and Japan—the two powerful economic giants in the region—have achieved an exceptional sophistication for mutually beneficial cooperation in the last decade or so and more importantly under PM Modi and PM Abe in the past couple of years as their strategic space is increasingly constrained by a rising China even if this is not a direct reaction to it. It is not only limited to the bilateral context in the Indo-Pacific but is aimed at expanding the benevolent footprint into South East Asia as well as Africa. India has been engaged with Africa for centuries in one way or the other, while Japan has been a liberal spender by way of a tremendous ODA and investments. Hence, it is natural that both decided to work closely in Africa as an offshoot of their camaraderie in the Indo-Pacific. Recently, a meeting of 'India–Japan Act East Forum' was held in New Delhi to fine-tune and chart out the nuts and bolts of the collaborative strategy.

In November 2016, Japan's PM Shinzo Abe and Indian PM Narendra Modi in their Summit joint statement reiterated the resolve of the two countries to 'develop industrial corridors and industrial network for the growth of Asia and Africa'. India–Japan economic engagement with Africa, under the aegis of Asia Africa Growth Corridor (AAGC), is based on the premise that the direction of global economic activities is indeed shifting towards the Indo-Pacific region. India and Japan as two democracies and robust economies are committed to evolve a sound economic, political and security architecture of the Indo-Pacific region. Collaboration in Africa and ASEAN are a natural corollary. The vision document clearly highlights that the AAGC would be based on four pillars: 'enhancing capacity and skills; quality infrastructure and institutional connectivity; development and cooperation projects and people-to-people partnership'. PM Modi while inaugurating the AfDB annual meeting in Ahmedabad said that India is working with the USA and Japan to support development in Africa. Talking about the vision document, the PM said that 'the idea is that India and Japan, with other willing partners, would explore joint initiatives in skills, health, infrastructure, manufacturing and connectivity'.

Similarly, the EU and the USA are eager to work closely with India in Africa. India has an entirely non-reciprocal beneficiation approach towards Africa aimed at their development, while all others have their own special interests and approaches that may not be so easily aligned with ours and even could work at cross purposes which India can ill afford at this juncture. More importantly, cultural dynamics of the respective businesses are significantly different. Africa and India can jointly address food security issues of many countries, especially in the Middle East since significant arable land is available there. Countries from the GCC like UAE and Saudi Arabia have expressed desired to work with India in Africa which should be explored in a trilateral format. Hence, despite the political will and pronouncements by leaders, it will be useful to have a critical SWOT analysis of these ventures and intentions.

Lines of Credit and Capacity-Building Assistance—Promises versus Delivery

Fresh commitments have been made during the successive India–Africa Forum summits and similar other high-profile outreach efforts. In fact, the 3rd India–Africa Partnership Summit in 2015, with the participation at the highest level from all 54 countries, was a great achievement that underscored the depth and potential of a partnership that has become a priority for the Indian foreign policy establishment that is looking to imaginatively garner the impact of its robust engagement through trade, technology, training, capacity building and development partnership. PM Modi even announced a fabulous package of concessional credit of US$10 billion, grants-in-aid of US$600 million and 50,000 slots for training and higher education over the next five years. India has already extended 180 LoCs amounting to $8 billion to over 40 countries. Fantastic figures of the credit lines are offered to various countries where high-level visits take place often to add content to the outcomes and more often to provide a reliable and attractive conduit for collaboration that eventually helps Indian project and other exports. The dictum with regard to Indian technologies is that they are available, adaptable and affordable, and fit in with the stage of development a country or its constituents are in. It has generated tremendous goodwill over time since these are demand driven according to African preferences.

While Indian assistance, both technical and financial, is sought by a large number of development partners and India has readily provided the requisite help, the fact remains that there are still many gaps that continue to stunt the desired outcome both for donor and the recipient. It has virtually become a given that during the VVIP visits some announcement on extension of a LoC is made. However, very often, the announcements do not materialize into projects with the same pace and enthusiasm for several reasons. One is being non-availability of budgeted funds, second being procedural uncertainty and, third, the inability of recipient country to comply with the cumbersome prescribed procedure. Also, the requirement of sovereign guarantees from the recipient government in most cases is a non-starter. As such, India's terms and conditions of LIBOR+ or the interest rates and tenures per se are not the most attractive as at times the governments compare with what China and other countries happily offer. Hence, while the LoCs remain unutilized, there is a great demand for government grants rather the LoC.

In Vivekananda International Foundation's recent Task Force Report entitled 'India–Africa: A Partnership for Growth' (2018), the following areas were identified for undertaking more efforts: establishment of direct shipping line between India and Africa; making Chabahar a transhipment port for trade with Africa; establishing direct banking facilities to bring down the cost of doing business through European banks; making the premium charged by Export Credit Guarantee Corporation of India more competitive; and reviewing and augmenting the Exim's capacity.

In order to address some of the underlying issues and constraints perhaps, we can consider the following:

- Pronouncements of assistance should only be made if funds have been made available to the line ministry.
- Government may also consider a revolving and non-lapsing fund for its economic diplomacy so that seeking approvals and budgeting funds every year could be avoided that will also provide the necessary certainty for the line ministries to complete the projects in time.
- Although India is not a capital exporting country, we have to decide to what extent are we willing to fund the strategic development projects as grants-in-aid since most countries prefer this route and do not want to provide a sovereign guarantee that further aggravates their debt burden.
- We need to recognize that we are not alone and must devise packages that are better than our competitors.

- It will be useful to shortlist credible and reliable companies with their own manufacturing and turnkey project execution capacity from private and public sector which can be tapped by the recipient countries. Of course, due diligence of any company is a prerequisite. Any unfair practices or semblance of corruption should debar them permanently.
- While bidding for projects is desirable, the companies with niche projects and products in the strategic domain must be given precedence. Perhaps time has come to abdicate the L1 approach and adopt the highest quality deliverables.
- We must acknowledge that the Africans and others know what kind of projects is best for them. Imposition of any preferences may recoil. All stakeholders must be on board and above board.
- Above all, the delivery mechanisms must be pruned and fine-tuned and the gap between commitment, and execution and implementation should be reduced to the minimum.
- Our ambassadors and missions should be made accountable for the timely implementation through close monitoring, and their recommendations and comments must be given due credence.

Strategic Choices and Leap Forward

- India should be proactive and not reactive in its strategy and approach, and should not make pro forma gestures.
- Promise and delivery should match with highest quality, efficiency and execution. A standing project monitoring mechanism should be constituted which should also seek the inputs from the resident African ambassadors.
- Africans need to be aligned with the Indian outreach efforts and offerings. Likewise, capacity-building should correspond to short-, medium- and long-term requirements of the continent. Skill India could be replicated in a realistic manner in accordance with the Continent's developmental needs.
- Defence, security and counterterrorism collaboration should be expanded and deepened for security and stability of both through capacity, and institution and confidence building.
- Closer cooperation and periodic interactions at bilateral, sub-regional, regional and multilateral level through specified joint working groups, task forces and frequent consultations should be instituted and revived. An ongoing perceived and real momentum should be discernible from the past. African governments could be assisted in building requisite ecosystems for enabling

entrepreneurship, employment generation, especially to prepare for AI-driven Industrial Revolution 4.0 as an equal partner.
- Irritants restricting trade and investment should be addressed and removed forthwith. Special dispensations such as duty-free preferences, faster visa processing and work visa and residence permits could continue as a mark of goodwill for another decade to the least developing countries. Indian investments should be enhanced through PPP model in core sectors of infrastructure, agriculture, food processing, renewable energy, ICT and financial services. Greater focus on SMEs be given through information, technology, expertise and credit availability.
- A fresh look for bilateral and trilateral collaborative mechanisms to cater to food and energy security issues is given and necessary arrangements be evolved for mutually beneficial partnerships.
- A reliable updated database of ITEC and other African alumni be maintained and kept in close touch with. Every effort to be made that racist incidents are dealt with severely. The relevant educational institutions should be made responsible if innocent students are subjected to indignity. On completion of their studies, if needed, some internships could be arranged in government and private organizations with the help of trade and industry associations.
- Retired Indian professors and teachers could be deputed to the African universities and colleges.
- It would be useful to have sub-regional level Track-II mechanisms in place with the former Indian ambassadors in Africa, defence attaches, think tanks and prominent NRIs and citizens who can regularly interact with their counterparts and government organizations, interlocutors and think tanks to provide a constant feedback for tweaking the policy, where and if necessary.
- India has decided to open 18 new missions but they should be manned by senior-level ambassadors as far as possible who should be provided with adequate manpower and funding with a clear mandate.
- Finally, perception management and soft power projection should be a clear priority to regain the confidence of Africans at the grassroots level.

Africa and India are destined to grow together through a mutually sustainable partnership for development and growth in this 21st century. We need not draw the solace that some other countries such as China will be discounted due to debt traps and yield us space but work upon the strategies that will spin the mutually beneficial outcomes in the short and long term. High-level exchanges must accord priority to Africa with intermittent interactions in the interim. Let's remind ourselves what Vivekananda said a century ago: 'Whenever you promise to do any work, you must do it exactly at the appointed time, or people lose their faith in you'. In any case, India can ill afford to let the African opportunity slip by.

Latin America
A Long-term Partner for India

R. Viswanathan

Some Indians might think that Latin America is less important for India's trade on the assumptions that the region is too far and the cost and time for shipping should be very high. They would be surprised to know that India exports more to some Latin American countries than to neighbouring countries or traditional trade partners. Here are some examples:

- India's exports (2017–2018) of 160 million dollars to the distant and small Uruguay (15,000 km away; population 3.4 million) are more than the exports of 133 million to Uzbekistan which is just 3,000 km from Delhi and has a larger population of 31 million.
- India's exports of 292 million dollars to the remote Guatemala are more than double the exports of 121 million to Cambodia, a close neighbour.
- India exports more to Central America (956 million dollars) than to the Central Asian Republics (365 m), although the latter is close by and has more population (70 million), while Central American population is just 46 million.
- India's exports to Mexico (3.78 billion) are more than the exports to neighbouring Iran (2.65 billion) and Thailand (3.65 billion), and the

traditional partners such as Russia (2.13 billion), Canada (2.5 billion) or Egypt (2.4 billion).
- India's exports to Colombia (787 million dollars), Peru (699 million) and Chile (676 million) are more than the exports to some West European countries such as Austria, Ireland or Scandinavian countries.
- India's trade with Dominican Republic (900 million) is more than the trade with Portugal, Greece and some other European countries.

Latin America is the leading destination for India's vehicle exports at 3.76 billion. Mexico is the largest market for India's vehicle exports with 2.02 billion. Colombia is one of the top 3 global markets for Indian motorcycles and used to be the No. 1 market few years back. Hero, an Indian motorcycle firm, has invested 80 million dollars in a production unit in Cali, Colombia. In some countries such as Guatemala and Colombia, Indian motorcycle brands are the leaders with the highest market share.

India is the third largest supplier of textiles and the fourth largest supplier of ready-made garments to Latin America.

For those who think that it is very difficult for India to compete with the Chinese exports, here is another piece of information: India has consistently beaten China in the export of pharmaceuticals to Latin America. India's exports were 651 million dollars in comparison to China's 404 million.

Latin America is a large market of 19 countries with a total population of 615 million, GDP of over 5 trillion dollars and imports of about 1 trillion dollars. It is a relatively homogeneous market in which 18 countries speak Spanish and one country (Brazil) speaks Portuguese. The macroeconomic fundamentals of the region have become more stable and stronger in the last two decades with the exception of Venezuela. Average inflation of the region is in single digit, while the ratio of external debt to GDP is just about 28 per cent. Over 60 million people have come out of poverty in the first 15 years of this century, thanks to the inclusive development policies of the governments in the region. Millennials, who form a significant portion of the people, drive the market growth with their new mindset and ambitions. The economies are set on a growth trajectory, and the region is poised to become more prosperous offering potential for significant increase in India's exports.

There is also good scope for project exports in areas such as renewable energy, pipelines, transmission lines, airports, ports, power and other infrastructure projects. Some companies such as Sterlite, Suzlon,

Praj, KEC and Shapoorji Pallonji have got such contracts. A Bengaluru firm is doing mini hydel projects in Central America.

India's exports and imports in 2017–2018 (in million dollars) are in the following table:

Country	Exports	Imports	Total Trade
Mexico	3,783	3,930	7,713
Brazil	3,064	5,498	8,562
Argentina	709	2,229	2,938
Colombia	939	593	1,532
Peru	761	2,377	3,138
Chile	764	2,092	2,856
Venezuela	79	5,866	5,945
Ecuador	280	194	474
Bolivia	105	667	772
Paraguay	168	167	335
Uruguay	160	25	185
Panama	227	43	270
Guatemala	292	16	308
Dominican Republic	197	646	843
Costa Rica	134	67	201
Honduras	146	13	159
El Salvador	70	9	79
Nicaragua	87	4	91
Cuba	42	2	44
Total	**12,007**	**24,438**	**36,445**

Imports

Chile maintains its position as the top supplier of copper and Argentina as major supplier of soy oil.

Energy Security

Latin America has become a regular new source for India's imports of crude oil in the last 15 years. The Latin American share of India's crude imports is around 15 per cent. In 2014–2015, the region supplied 36

India's Main Exports (in Million Dollars)

Vehicles	3,759
Equipment and machinery	1,007
Organic chemicals	973
Iron and steel products	805
Pharmaceuticals	779
Chemical products	630
Synthetic fibres	635
Textiles	591
Plastic products	483
Cotton	363
Dyestuff	327
Rubber articles	243

Source: Ministry of Commerce of India, https://commerce-app.gov.in/eidb/default.asp

Notes: Major destinations of vehicle exports: Mexico = 2,027 million dollars; Chile = 284 m; Brazil = 278 m; Colombia = 255 m; Peru = 218 m; Argentina = 142 m; Guatemala = 98 m; Ecuador = 75 m; Costa Rica = 66 m and Bolivia = 59 m.

Major destinations of pharma exports: Brazil = 229 million dollars; Chile = 65 m; Colombia = 55 m; Venezuela = 55 m; Peru = 40 m; Dominican Republic = 35 m; Guatemala = 32 m and Ecuador = 32 m.

million tonnes and held a 19 per cent share in India's global imports of 189 million tonnes. Out of the 700,000 barrels per day (bpd) imported from the region, typically 400,000 bpd comes from Venezuela, 100,000 bpd each from Mexico and Brazil, and about 50,000 bpd each from Colombia and Ecuador, depending on prices and availability at any time. Reliance continues to be the leading importer of Latin American crude with 400,000 bpd, while Essar and the public sector oil companies import about 150,000 bpd each.

The total crude imports of India have doubled in the last decade from 99 million tonnes in 2005–2006 to 202 million tonnes in 2015–2016. According to a 2015 report of International Energy Agency, India's imports are projected to reach 358 million tonnes by 2040. While India's crude imports are relentlessly increasing, Latin America is blessed with huge reserves, large production capacity and surplus for exports. Venezuela has more oil reserves (292 billion barrels) than Saudi Arabia which has 266 billion barrels. Argentina has the world's second largest reserves of shale gas and the fourth largest shale oil and

India's Major Imports (in Million Dollars)

Crude oil	1,0490
Gold	3,663
Copper	3,007
Vegetable oil	2,649
Raw sugar	920
Equipment and machinery	861
Aircrafts	464
Wood pulp	503
Iron and steel	350

Source: Ministry of Commerce of India, https://commerce-app.gov.in/eidb/default.asp

Notes: Gold imports which started three years back have increased steadily reaching the second position last year. The raw sugar is imported from Brazil for refining and re-exports. Peru was the top supplier of gold with 1.78 billion dollars, followed by Bolivia (663 million), Dominican Republic (584 million), Colombia (308 million), Brazil (289 million) and Mexico (37 million).

Venezuela is the top source of imports of crude oil with 5.86 billion dollars, followed by Mexico (2.77 billion), Brazil (1.56 billion), Colombia (177 million) and Ecuador (85 million).

production from these have just started. Brazil has started commercial production of its new-found pre-salt reserves. Mexico is discovering new reserves after the historic opening of the energy sector to private and foreign investment in recent years. With all these, Latin America has the capacity to double its crude exports from the current export of about 5 million bpd.

It is important to note that crude oil is the number one global export of Latin America (115 billion dollars in 2015) and it is also the largest import item for India. The USA, which was the principal market for Latin America, has substantially reduced its imports of crude from Latin America after the game-changing shale revolution. So the Latin Americans are now keener to diversify and penetrate large oil importing markets such as India and China. This fits in perfectly with India's strategic energy security policy to diversify its import sources and reduce over-dependence on the volatile Middle East. In any case, the Latin American crude option has put pressure on the suppliers from the Middle East (who had enjoyed undue monopoly in the past) to better their prices and terms of supply to India.

Food Security

While India has achieved self-sufficiency in the case of cereals, it is facing perpetual and growing shortage of vegetable oil and pulses whose imports are increasing in the same way as in the case of petroleum crude. India's domestic production of oil seeds and pulses has not been able to cope with the growing demand. India's imports of vegetable oil have jumped from 0.1 million tonnes in 1992–1993 to 8.8 million tonnes in 2009–2010 reaching 15.75 million tonnes in 2015–2016. Consumption has doubled from 10.1 million tonnes in 2001–2002 to 20.08 million tonnes in 2014–2015 and is projected to reach 26.8 million tonnes by 2025. India's imports of pulses have reached about 5 million tonnes in 2015–2016 from just 0.56 million tonnes in 1998–1999.

India has been importing soy oil worth over 2 billion dollars from Argentina and also small quantities from Brazil and Paraguay. The South American region comprising Brazil, Argentina, Paraguay and Uruguay have become the largest soya producer in the world. These countries want to increase their share of the vegetable oil market of India which is dominated by the monopoly suppliers of palm oil from Malaysia and Indonesia. Here again, India can play off South America against the South East Asian suppliers to get better prices. Some Latin American countries have also started palm plantations and export of palm oil. This is also helpful for India to lessen the excessive dependence on Malaysia and Indonesia who have been dictating prices.

India is the largest importer of pulses in the world accounting for 50 per cent of the global trade. In 2015–2016, India's imports were 5 million tonnes and these are expected to increase in the future. Bulk of the imports come from Canada, Australia and Myanmar. India has just started importing small quantities of pulses from Brazil and Argentina. The South Americans are interested in increasing their exports and becoming a regular supplier. Production of pulses has become an attractive idea for the Mercosur region which has realized the risks of having become over-dependent on soya, the predominant crop in the region. The emergence of South America as a supplier of pulses will make the other supplier countries to become more competitive in prices. So India should actively encourage South Americans to grow more pulses for exports to the Indian market.

Chile, Peru and Argentina have started supplying fresh fruits and vegetables to India. These are not considered as competition to domestic production but seen as complementary since they come during India's off season from South America which is in the Southern Hemisphere.

Indian agriculture faces daunting challenges caused by the increasing diversion of agricultural land for other purposes (residential, commercial, industrial and infrastructural uses), shortage of water and low productivity due to inadequate investment by most farmers whose land sizes are small. On the other hand, South America has vast tracts of fertile land, abundant water, advanced technologies and best practices with which the region has emerged as a global agricultural powerhouse. Argentina and Brazil are global leaders in some areas of agricultural research and agribusiness. The region has the potential to bring in another 40 million hectares of land into agriculture and feed an extra 500 million people.

Minerals for Make in India

India has been importing copper and other minerals from Latin America, which has huge reserves. These imports go into the 'Make in India' manufacturing programme. India's imports of copper concentrates have seen an increase of 20 times from 0.08 million tonnes in 2000–2001 to 1.8 million tonnes in 2015–2016. Latin America is an important source.

Lithium has become crucial in this era of electric cars and batteries used in many devices. The Argentina–Chile–Bolivia triangle has the largest deposit of lithium reserves in the world. Indian companies could invest and source lithium from this region for India's needs in the future.

In recent years, India has started sourcing gold and precious and semi-precious stones from Latin America, which has considerable reserves. India has been importing gold mostly from non-producing third countries such as Switzerland and UAE. It is only in the last few years that India has started direct imports from Latin American producers such as Colombia, Peru, Bolivia, Ecuador, Dominican Republic, Mexico and Brazil. The imports from the region will go up in the coming years. India's total imports of gold have had a fourfold increase from 245 tonnes in 1997–1998 to 957 tonnes in 2015–2016.

India Is More Important for Latin American Exports than Germany, UK and France

Indian love for the Latin American market is not unrequited. The Latin Americans too have started reciprocating and valuing India as a long-term large and growing market for their exports.

India has become more important as an export destination for Latin America than their traditional European trade partners such as Germany, UK or France. In 2016, Latin America exported 16.7 billion dollars of goods to India, while their exports to Germany were 14.4 billion, Spain 13.5 billion, UK 10 billion, Italy 9.3 billion and France 7.2 billion.

India was the sixth largest export destination for Latin America in 2016, after the USA, China, Netherlands, Canada and Japan. In 2014, India was in the third rank with 29 billion dollars ahead of Japan, the Netherlands and Canada. The main reason for the drop in Latin American export to India in 2016 is the sharp fall in prices of oil, the main Indian import from the region.

India is the number one destination of Latin America's vegetable oil exports, the second largest importer of Latin American crude oil, third for the region's exports of copper and fourth for gold and minerals.

The China Factor

China has become the second largest trading partner (overtaking European Union) of Latin America with a trade of 270 billion dollars, the largest provider of credit to the region with a cumulative amount of 150 billion dollars and a top investor with over 100 billion dollars in the region. The Chinese president has pledged to take China–Latin America trade to 500 billion dollars and investment to 250 billion by 2020. India's figures with Latin America look very modest with trade of 30 billion dollars, investment of 12 billion and credit of just under 200 million dollars. However, the Latinos are wary of the non-transparent and sometimes high-handed business practices of Chinese firms and hidden agenda of Chinese government owned enterprises. The Latin American manufacturing has been hit hard by the dumping of Chinese goods. While admiring the spectacular economic growth of China, the Latin Americans dislike the communist dictatorship, recalling their own experience of sufferings from dictatorships till recently. So they see the great growth story of China as a 'Cuento Chino', which in Latin America means an 'exaggerated and unbelievable story'. The Argentine movie *Cuento Chino* brings out this lack of trust and gap in culture and communication with China.

Realizing the need to reduce the risks of over-dependence on China, the Latin Americans are keener on India, which they perceive as a non-threatening and benign economic partner. India's inclusive growth model within a large, diverse and sometimes chaotic but vibrant democracy resonates with Latin American aspirations and realities. The

Indian culture and traditions of yoga, meditation, wisdom and gurus are comfort zones for them. The Indian companies have a positive image in the region. The Latin Americans appreciate the contribution of Indian pharma companies to lower the cost of medicines and increase the share of affordable generics in their markets. They are inspired by the success story of Indian IT companies which have helped human resource development by employing over 25,000 young Latin Americans in their operations in the region.

The USA is alarmed by the overwhelming presence of China in Latin America and see it as a 'Pivot to Americas' intrusion into their backyard. They have been provoked especially by the Chinese proposals of grandiose projects such as the 50 billion dollar Nicaragua Canal and the Bi-Oceanic railway connecting Brazilian Atlantic port with Peruvian Pacific port. So they are going all out to trash China accusing them of harming the environment and being insensitive to issues such as good governance and human rights. The US think tanks highlight and contrast the Chinese predatory exploitative approach with the benign presence of India in the region.

Investment and Joint Ventures

Indian companies have invested around 12 billion dollars in Latin America in sectors such as energy, agrochemicals, metals, pharmaceuticals and auto parts. Latin American firms have invested close to a billion dollars in India in areas such as food processing, multiplexes, soft drinks and auto parts.

New Paradigm of Synergies and Complementarities

In the past, the economists saw Indian and Latin American exporters as competitive for the same consumer markets of the developed world. In the old days, Indian and Latin American raw materials went to the developed market which processed them and exported the finished products back to the raw material exporters. But these theories and practices have been upended with a new paradigm of business between India and Latin America.

Here are some examples of the new paradigm of business with Latin America:

- Indian firms import raw materials from Latin America, process them in India and export the finished products. Reliance imports crude oil from Brazil, refine it in Jamnagar and export diesel to Brazil besides other countries. Renuka Sugars imports a billion dollar worth raw sugar from Brazil, refine it in Kandla and Haldia, and then export the refined sugar to Asia and the Middle East. A Brazilian firm Surya Brasil imports henna ingredients from India, makes its own brand of products and export them to 20 countries in the world.

- Two dozen Indian IT firms have been using the distance and different time zone factors as advantages by developing a new 12/12 business model in which they do near-shore delivery of services to their US clients for 12 hours from the same time zone in Latin America and shift to India for the next 12 hours. They employ 30,000 Latin American staff from Mexico to Chile. The Indian companies have also started getting IT projects from Latin American banks and companies. Three Latin American IT firms have set up global delivery centres in India to service their clients in Europe and North America. An Argentine steel company employs 200 Indian engineers in Mumbai to provide offshore services for their global projects.
- UPL, the largest Indian agrochemical company, does more business in Latin America (1.2 billion dollars) than in India (less than a billion).
- Advanta, the global seeds firm owned by the UPL group, does research and development in Argentina and introduces the new seeds in India.
- A Mexican company Cinepolis has invested over 100 million dollars and become the fourth largest owner of multiplexes in India.
- Aje, a Peruvian company, has bet on the Indian cola market with production of Big Cola brand of soft drinks in Maharashtra.
- Tata Marcopolo buses made by the Brazilian-Indian joint venture are ubiquitous in the Indian cities.
- A Mahindra group company is exporting Peruvian grapes to US and Europe.

Petroleum crude, copper, gold, ores and vegetable oil are among the top global exports of Latin America. At the same time, these are the major imports of India from the world. India is going to increase its imports of these items in the future both globally and from Latin America in view of the growing gap between domestic demand and production. The increasing Indian population (15 million a year) and consumption power of the new middle class as well as the need for fuelling the high growth of the economy will continue to drive the rise in imports. This Indian need is matched by the potential for supplies from Latin America which has ample resources.

Latin America has surplus of what India lacks and needs. And India has what the Latin Americans seek. India perceives Latin America as a contributor to its energy and food security and as a new market for its exports. On the other hand, Latin Americans look at India as a large and growing new market for their exports. This is the new paradigm of the emerging long-term complementarity.

Entertainment Business

There is growing collaboration between India and Latin America in the entertainment business. Indian film producers have shot scenes in Latin America and have cast Latin American actresses in Indian films. Prabhakar Sharan from Bihar has acted as hero in a Latin American film in Spanish made in Costa Rica.

An Argentine director Pablo Cesar made a feature film *Unicorn—The Garden of Fruits* in 1996 as a co-production with India. His new film *Thinking of Him* based on the romantic story of meeting of Tagore with Victoria Ocampo in Buenos Aires was premiered on 28 November 2017 in the Goa Film Festival.

The Argentine musician Gustavo Santaolalla composed music for Amir Khan's film *Dhobi Ghat* directed by Kiran Rao. This was released in January 2011.

Globo TV of Brazil produced and telecast a soap opera *Caminho das Indias—Passage to India* in 2009. It was partly shot in India and there were Indian characters and Indian costumes. It got the highest ratings during the eight months of its telecast and stimulated Brazilian interest in India. It has been dubbed in Spanish and telecast in other Latin American countries. Bollywood films are being shown in more and more Latin American TV channels.

Spiritual Relations

Latin America has added value to Indian spiritual business. Several hundred thousand Latin Americans practice yoga, meditation and follow Indian gurus. The Argentine band Yoga Rave sings in pure Sanskrit in their shows performed sometimes in nightclubs. During their performance in the nightclubs, meat, alcohol, smoking and drugs are not allowed. Janderson Fernandes de Oliveira de of Sao Paulo came to India for spiritual enlightening. But he went beyond learning and became an authentic guru himself anointed as 'Sri Prem Baba' and as head of the Sachcha Dham Ashram in Rishikesh. He has ashrams in 12 countries around the world where he preaches Indian spiritualism with a Brazilian touch.

Evolution of Political Relations

The political relations of India with Latin America have evolved in three stages: in the 1950s, 1960s and 1970s, it was a period of mutual ignorance and indifference. India was grappling with its own survival as an independent country in the process of consolidating itself as a democracy with diverse languages, religions, ethnic groups and cultures. On the other side, Latin America was mired in military dictatorships and economic instability. The two sides did not feel the need to reach out to each other.

The second stage of occasional interaction was in the 1980s and 1990s when the two sides probed each other tentatively. In the 1980s, the Latin American region was coming out of dictatorships and transitioning to democracies, which started taking tentative interest in India. There were some exchanges of visits, signing of cooperation agreements and trade transactions. But these were ad hoc and were not systematically sustained.

Since 2000, the third phase of relations has started with mutual attraction between the two sides. Latin America has become politically stable with strengthening of its democracies. The region enjoyed unprecedented stability and prosperity in the first decade of this century termed as the 'Growth Decade' when millions of poor were uplifted to middle class by the Leftist governments helped by the commodities boom. At the same time, India had also transformed into an emerging power with high economic growth and aspiration to become a global player. The New India and the New Latin America of the 21st century started courting each other seriously and systematically. They discovered mutual complementarities and synergies.

Brazil and India became strategic partners during President Lula's presidency. A number of bilateral cooperation agreements were signed and high-level visits were exchanged. The two countries took the initiative to form IBSA along with South Africa. India, Brazil and South Africa (IBSA) caught the imagination of the world as a promising alliance of the three leading democracies in their continents with regional and global leadership. They started doing technical assistance projects in third countries as part of South–South cooperation. The three powers also coordinated their campaigns to become permanent members of

UN Security Council. India and Brazil collaborated vigorously in multilateral fora such as UN and WTO.

Mexico and Argentina started courting India which they perceived as an emerging power in the 21st century. Other Latin American countries had also started taking India more seriously with unprecedented number of exchanges of visits and signing of cooperation agreements. Trade has started growing; investments are flowing and joint ventures and collaborations are flourishing. These have reached a critical mass, laying a solid foundation for a long-term win-win partnership.

Challenges

The recent political developments in some Latin American countries pose some challenges for Indo-Latin American relations.

Bolsonaro, the new president of Brazil, has downgraded the strategic partnership with India, established by President Lula. President Bolsonaro and his foreign Minister Araujo have never mentioned India in their foreign policy statements. They have the least interest in South–South cooperation. Their priority is the USA and Europe. They are undermining even Mercosur, with which India has a Preferential Trade Arrangement (PTA) and is negotiating for an expanded PTA. India cannot, therefore, count on Brazil as a partner under the Bolsonaro administration. India needs to wait till such time the new Brazilian government realize the importance of India. The Brazilian foreign ministry and the defence ministry do not support the aberration of Bolsonaro's policies and they hope to convince the president to do course correction at an opportune time.

India's relations with Mexico, the second largest country in the region after Mexico, are also becoming less substantive under the new President Lopez Obrador. He is fully absorbed in his domestic priorities and does not have time for foreign policy. He is not interested in foreign travel or pursuit of any regional or global agenda.

Venezuela, the top supplier of crude oil to India from Latin America, is in a disastrous and pathetic situation under President Maduro. He started his second term for six years as president on 10 January. But the political drama of his rigged re-election, the economic collapse of the country and the traumatization of the society resemble the story of 'one hundred years of solitude' by the Colombian Nobel Prize winner Gabriel Garcia Marquez. The Venezuelan reality is even more bizarre than the magical fiction of Marquez in which the people of Macondo are cursed to suffer one disaster after another. The country has two presidents. The president of the National Assembly Guaido claims to be the president on the ground that Maduro's re-election was illegitimate. Guaido has been recognized as the president by the USA, EU and most Latin American countries. The Trump administration is threatening with military options and openly encouraging the Venezuelan armed forces to revolt against Maduro regime.

The GDP of Venezuela has contracted consecutively for the last five years to over 50 per cent. It is forecast to shrink by another 10 per cent in 2019. The country has the highest inflation in the world running into six digits. The government has stopped publishing inflation and other economic statistics. Since most of the domestic manufacturing industry and agriculture have been destroyed, the country has become desperately dependent on imports. But there is severe shortage of foreign exchange reserves which are inadequate to cover even essential imports. The Venezuelan currency Bolivar has lost 99.9 per cent of its value and has become worthless. The government keeps changing currencies and exchange rates, which has given rise to huge black market for dollars and goods.

Poor people scavenge for food in the rubbish bins. Long queues are common in front of super markets and shops which are often empty and running short of medicines, food and essential items such as toilet paper and soap. There are frequent power cuts and shortage of water. Most international airlines have stopped flights to Venezuela due to payment issues.

Crime and violence is rampant in Caracas which has one of the highest murder rates in the region. The city has become unsafe even for diplomats who need to use bullet proof cars.

According to UNHCR, 3 million Venezuelans (10% of the total population) have fled to other countries to escape the poverty, misery and crisis. This has become the biggest migration and humanitarian crisis in the history of Latin America. In the past, over a million South Americans (most of them Colombians) used to work in Venezuela which offered better prospects than their countries.

The country's oil production has come down from 3 million bpd to 1.5 million bpd due to mismanagement and lack of investment. Neither the company nor the government publish figures of oil exports and revenue which are kept as secrets. A significant part of oil is sent to China as barter payment for the 60 billion dollar plus debt. The Trump administration has imposed sanctions against the Venezuelan oil company and has cut off oil payment from US buyers.

It is just a matter of time the Maduro administration collapses sooner than later.

But India need not worry about oil supply even if there is any change of regime in Venezuela. The next government and their successors will have no choice but to continue to attach importance to India, the second largest market for their oil exports. The USA, the number one destination of Venezuelan oil, is reducing imports after the shale revolution and the increase in domestic production. So Venezuela needs India more than the other way.

Suggestions for Action

Given the political challenges arising from the new foreign policy orientation of Brazil, the indifference Mexico as well as the crisis in Venezuela, India should keep a low profile with these countries but continue to strengthen the economic relations with Latin America.

India should pursue trade agreements with Mexico, Colombia and Peru which are major destinations for exports.

India should extend large lines of credit to Latin American countries as it is doing in the case of Asia and Africa. While China has extended about 150 billion dollars of credit to Latin America, India's credit is just under 200 million dollars.

India could become a member of the Inter-American Development Bank in whose projects Indian companies can participate. China and South Korea are already members.

India should set up cultural centres in more Latin American countries to project its soft power. At the moment, only Brazil and Mexico have Indian cultural centres.

There should be more visits of Indian prime minister, president and external affairs minister to the region. The Chinese dignitaries make frequent, regular and extensive visits to the region.

The Ministry of Commerce and Industry of India should revive its Focus LAC programme which had helped in the past in encouraging and supporting Indian exporters to explore the business opportunities in Latin America.

The annual India–Latin America Business Conclave needs to be scaled up and organized regularly by pooling and coordinating the efforts of Confederation of Indian Industry (CII) and Federation of Indian Chambers of Commerce & Industry (FICCI), and other trade bodies and export promotion councils with substantive financial support by the government.

Indian universities need to be encouraged to open Latin America study centres and Spanish and Portuguese language courses. China has 65 Latin America centres. India has only three centres: one in JNU, another in Jindal University and the third in Goa University.

India should open more embassies in the region. India has embassies only in 10 out of the 19 countries in Latin America.

About the Editors and Contributors

Editors

Arvind Gupta is the Director of Vivekananda International Foundation (VIF), a Delhi-based independent, non-partisan think tank focusing on research on foreign policy, defence and security-related issues from the Indian perspective.

During 2014–2017, he was the Deputy National Security Advisor and Secretary, National Security Council Secretariat in the Government of India. He was associated with the National Security Council Secretariat as Joint Secretary from 1999 to 2007.

During 2012–2014, he was Director General of the Institute for Defence Studies and Analyses (IDSA), an autonomous institute set up by the Indian Ministry of Defence. He was Lal Bahadur Shastri Chair on National Security at the IDSA during 2008–2014. He was the managing editor of *Strategic Analysis,* IDSA's flagship academic journal.

A former diplomat, Dr Gupta joined the Indian Foreign Service (IFS) in 1979. He has served in Indian Mission in Moscow, London and Ankara, and worked on several desks in the Ministry of External Affairs (MEA).

He is also an Honorary Professor in the Department of Defence and National Security Studies, Panjab University, Chandigarh. His interests are in India's foreign policy, national security, history, governance, culture and civilization. He also writes articles on popular science.

Having 20 years of policy-level experience in national security issues, he has been a part of several official and Track-II discussions on security. He has written and edited several books and articles on global, regional and national security issues as well as foreign policy.

His latest book *How India Manages Its National Security* was published in 2018.

Anil Wadhwa was a member of the IFS from July 1979 till May 2017. In his 37-year career, he has been ambassador of India to Italy, San Marino, Thailand, Oman, Poland and Lithuania, and has served in Hong Kong, Beijing (twice), permanent mission of India in Geneva and worked on deputation with the Organisation for the Prohibition of Chemical Weapons in The Hague where he headed their media and public affairs and government relations branches. Ambassador Wadhwa was head of the East Europe division in the MEA in New Delhi and looked after relations with Russia and Eastern European countries. As Secretary (East) in the MEA, he oversaw relations with ASEAN, South East Asia, Australia, New Zealand and the Pacific, the Gulf Cooperation Council (GCC), the Middle East and West Asia. He has attended a host of international conferences and was Indian delegate to the conference on disarmament in Geneva, first committee in New York, as well as to the ASEAN, ASEM, ADMM and Small Island States meetings such as Forum for India–Pacific Islands Cooperation (FIPIC). Ambassador Wadhwa has contributed a number of articles on foreign policy, disarmament and international security. He is fluent in Chinese and knows French. He has been a senior fellow (January–October 2018), and since then, a distinguished fellow with the VIF, New Delhi. He also serves as an independent Director/Advisor on some corporate boards.

Contributors

Talmiz Ahmad joined the IFS in 1974. He served as Ambassador to Saudi Arabia in 2000–2003 and 2010–2011, Oman in 2003–2004 and the UAE in 2007–2010. After a stint in the corporate sector (2011–2015) in Dubai, he is now a full-time academic and holds the Ram Sathe Chair for International Studies, Symbiosis International University, Pune. He has authored three books on West Asian affairs and comments regularly on the politics and economics of West Asia, Eurasia and the Indian Ocean, political Islam and transnational jihad, and energy security issues.

Prasenjit K. Basu is the author of *Asia Reborn: A Continent Rises from the Ravages of Colonialism and War to A New Dynamism*, which won the Best First Book award (non-fiction) at the Tata Literature Live! Mumbai LitFest in 2018. He also co-authored *India as a New Global Leader* (2005). He was Chief Economist for India and South East Asia at Credit Suisse First Boston (1998–2003), Chief Economist at Khazanah Nasional (Malaysia, 2004–2006), Chief Asia Economist at Daiwa Securities (2007–2011), Global Research Head at Maybank group (2012–2013), Chief ASEAN Economist at Macquarie Securities (2015–2016) and has held senior economist roles at Wharton Econometrics and UBS Securities. He has taught Economics and Global Affairs at the SP Jain School of Global Management and is currently an Adjunct Professor at ESSEC Asia-Pacific Business School (Singapore). Mr Basu has dual master's degrees in International Relations and Public Administration from the University of Pennsylvania, and a BA (Hons) in Economics from St. Stephen's College, Delhi.

Ashok Behuria is a Fellow and Coordinator of the South Asia Centre at IDSA. He holds PhD on 'India–Pakistan Relationship during the Eighties' in International Relations from Jawaharlal Nehru University (JNU), New Delhi, India. He joined IDSA in 2003 and before that he worked as Assistant Director at the International Centre for Peace Studies, New Delhi. Dr Behuria has also been Editor of *International Studies*, the prestigious research journal from JNU, and has been in the Editorial Boards of *Journal of Peace Studies* and *Strategic Analysis*, the flagship journal from IDSA. He has taught at the University of Delhi and Jamia Millia Islamia, New Delhi. He is a close observer of developments in South Asia and has been awarded the prestigious K. Subrahmanyam Award for excellence in strategic studies for his work on Pakistan in 2009. He has published many research articles on strategic issues related to Pakistan, India–Pakistan relations, Sri Lanka, Nepal and South Asian security environment in Indian and foreign journals. He has edited several books on South Asia and continues with his research on internal politics in Pakistan, evolving strategic scenario in the AfPak region, radicalization of religious discourse in the region, India's engagement with the neighbourhood, regional security and interstate cooperation.

Satish Chandra is the Vice Chairman of the Executive Committee of VIF, with which he has been associated since its inception in 2009. He was President of the Association of Indian Diplomats in 2010. Mr Chandra Joined the IFS in 1965 and till 1989 was posted in various capacities in Indian missions in Vienna, Karachi, Washington, DC, Algiers and Dhaka as well as at the headquarters.

Subsequently, he served as India's Ambassador to the Philippines (1989–1992), its Permanent Representative to the UN Offices in Geneva (1992–1995) and its High Commissioner to Pakistan (1995–1998).

He set up the NSCS in 1999 and headed it as Secretary till demission from office in February 2005 concurrently holding the post of Deputy National Security Advisor from February 2002.

Apart from representing India at a variety of multilateral fora such as the IAEA, WHO, ILO, the UN Human Rights Commission and the Disarmament Commission, he served as the President of the Conference on Disarmament during his assignment in Geneva.

Sujit Dutta is a Distinguished Fellow and the Head of the China Cluster at the VIF, New Delhi. He is also the founding Editor of the VIF Quarterly journal *National Security*. He was formerly senior Professor at the Nelson Mandela Centre for Peace and Conflict Resolution, Jamia Millia Islamia, and held the UGC M. K. Gandhi Chair in peace and conflict studies. He was Senior Fellow and Head of the East Asia Centre at the IDSA, New Delhi, before being invited to join Jamia Millia Islamia. He has also been a Senior Fellow at the prestigious United States Institute of Peace, Washington, DC. He was a member of the India–China Eminent Persons' Group set up by the two governments (2001–2005).

Professor Dutta is a political scientist and international affairs specialist. His work over the past three decades covers teaching, research, guidance and mentoring younger scholars and students, and editing the journal *Strategic Analysis*. His areas of expertise and current work include conflict studies, world order, Indian strategic thought, India–China relations, Chinese politics, foreign and security policies and the Indo-Pacific. He has published widely in these fields.

Yogendra Kumar retired from the IFS in 2012 in the rank of Secretary to the Government of India. At the time of his retirement, he was Indian Ambassador to the Philippines, with concurrent accreditation to the Pacific Island countries of Palau, Micronesia and the Marshall Islands. Earlier, he has been High Commissioner to Namibia and Ambassador to Tajikistan (2000–2003) during which period he also handled Afghanistan affairs. He has served on the faculty of the National Defence College and, in the MEA, handled multilateral organizations/dialogues such as G8–G5 Dialogue, ASEAN, EAS, IBSA and IORA. Since retirement, he has been writing and speaking on foreign policy and security affairs. His book *Diplomatic Dimension of Maritime Challenges for India in the 21st Century* was published in 2015. He has edited and contributed to the book *Whither Indian Ocean Maritime Order?* containing presentations/articles by eminent security and Foreign Service experts at a seminar organized by him in November 2016 on Prime Minister's landmark speech on Indian Ocean policy. Published in 2017, this book was presented by the Indian delegation to the participating delegations, headed by their respective heads of state/government at the first Indian Ocean Rim Association Leaders' Summit in Jakarta in March 2017.

Ajai Malhotra served at Embassy of India, Moscow, during 1982–1985, 1993–1996 and 2011–2013, besides heading from 1996–1999 the Division handling Russia at MEA, New Delhi, and holding other important positions at that Ministry and Indian missions in Bucharest, Geneva, Kuwait, Nairobi, New York and Washington, DC. He retired on 30 November 2013 as Ambassador of India to the Russian Federation. His current appointments include Member, Advisory Committee, UN Human Rights Council, Geneva; Distinguished Fellow & Senior Advisor (Climate Change), TERI; Independent Director, ONGC and ONGC Videsh Limited; and Chairman cum Managing Trustee of Chikitsa, Shiksha and other Indian NGOs.

Asoke Kumar Mukerji is a Distinguished Fellow of the VIF, New Delhi. He was India's Ambassador and Permanent Representative to the United Nations in New York from 2013 to 2015 when the UN adopted Agenda 2030 on Sustainable Development. He led the Indian team which got implemented within 75 days and with 177 co-sponsoring countries Prime Minister Narendra Modi's proposal to the United Nations to declare an International Day of Yoga. He has been awarded a Doctor of Civil Laws (honoris causa) degree in 2018 by the University of East Anglia (UK) for his contributions to diplomacy.

S. D. Muni is Professor Emeritus at the School of International Studies JNU, and also a member of the Executive Council of the IDSA, New Delhi. For nearly 40 years, he taught, conducted and supervised research in International Relations and South Asian Studies at JNU (1974–2006), National University of Singapore (2008–2013), Banaras Hindu University (1985–1986) and University of Rajasthan (1972–1973). He served as India's Special Envoy to South East Asian countries on UNSC Reforms (2005) and represented India's Minister of External Affairs at the 50th anniversary celebrations of the Paris Peace Conference, held in Phnom Penh, Kampuchea. He also served as India's Ambassador to Lao

People's Democratic Republic (1997–1999). Professor Muni was nominated to the first-ever constituted National Security Advisory Board (NSAB) of India during 1990–1991. He was the founding Executive Member of the Regional Centre for Strategic Studies, Colombo, Sri Lanka. In 2005, he was bestowed with 'Sri Lanka Rathna' award, Sri Lanka's highest national honour for a foreign national. The Institute of National Security Studies Sri Lanka, Colombo, offered him affiliation as Honorary Distinguished Fellow in 2016.

In October 2014, he received the 'Lifetime Achievement Award' from Shri Venkateshwara University, Tirupati, Andhra Pradesh, and was also honoured by University of Delhi in March 2017, for his contribution to India–Nepal relations. He was invited to address the UN Special Committee on Indian Ocean as a zone of peace at Sochi (Soviet Union) in 1985. He is the author and editor of nearly 30 books and monographs and more than 200 research papers. His latest book *India's Eastward Engagement: From Antiquity to the Act East Policy* was released in January 2019. Professor Muni was also the founder editor of two prestigious quarterly journals in India: The *South Asia Journal* (renamed as *South Asian Survey*) and *Indian Foreign Affairs Journal*.

Vivek Prahladan has written a book *East Asia and Detente: A Cold War Diplomatic History* (2019). He has received a PhD in Modern History from JNU, India. He has been Visiting Researcher, Keio University, Japan (2014–2017), and a Visiting Research Scholar at Department of History, King's College London (2012). He has written for Asteion (Japan), Nuclear Proliferation History Project of the Woodrow Wilson International Center for Scholars, the *National Interest*, the *Diplomat*, *Economic & Political Weekly* and Asia Sentinel. He recently authored a book *The Nation Declassified: India and the Cold War World* (2017).

P. S. Raghavan is Chairman of the NSAB, which advises India's National Security Council on security and strategic issues of immediate and long-term relevance.

In his diplomatic career (1979–2016), he was Ambassador of India to Russia, Czech Republic and Ireland, and had other diplomatic positions in USSR, UK, Poland, South Africa and Vietnam.

He was Joint Secretary in the Prime Minister's Office (2000–2004), dealing with foreign affairs, nuclear energy, space, defence and national security. As Secretary (2013–2014) in the MEA, he handled India's external economic relations and oversaw administration, security and e-governance in MEA. He also headed the Development Partnership

Administration, which coordinates India's economic partnership programmes in developing countries.

As Chairman of NSAB, he engages with government departments and think tanks in India, the USA, Russia, Europe and Asia, on initiatives to promote understanding of India's strategic perspectives. He writes widely on these issues.

Gulshan Sachdeva is Jean Monnet Chair; Coordinator, Jean Monnet Centre of Excellence for EU Studies in India; and Chairperson, Centre for European Studies, School of International Studies, JNU. He is also Editor-in-Chief, *International Studies* (SAGE). He headed the ADB and the Asia Foundation projects at the Afghanistan Ministry of Foreign Affairs in Kabul (2006–2010). His research is focused on the EU, Eurasian integration, Afghanistan, development cooperation and energy security. His recent publications include *Challenges in Europe: Indian Perspectives* (2019), *India in a Reconnecting Eurasia* (2016) and *Evaluation of the EU–India Strategic Partnership and the Potential for Its Revitalization* (2015). He holds PhD in economics from the Hungarian Academy of Sciences, Budapest.

Rajiv Sikri, in his diplomatic career from 1970 to 2006, served in Moscow (twice), New York, Paris and Kathmandu as India's Ambassador to Kazakhstan. He held many senior positions in India's MEA, including as Secretary (East), Special Secretary for Economic Relations, Additional Secretary for Strategy and Research, Head of the Soviet and East Europe Division and Head of West Europe Division.

He is the author of *Challenge and Strategy: Rethinking India's Foreign Policy* (which has been translated into Hindi and Marathi too), and has contributed several chapters in edited books as well as articles in scholarly journals.

Veena Sikri is a Professor and Ambassador, Founding Trustee and Convener at South Asia Women's Network (SWAN).

Professor Sikri's career and experience straddle the worlds of academia and diplomacy. She has served for 37 years (1971–2008) as a career diplomat with the IFS. She has been India's High Commissioner to Bangladesh and Malaysia, India's Consul General in Hong Kong, and Director General of the Indian Council for Cultural Relations (ICCR), New Delhi. She has held challenging and prestigious assignments at the Indian embassies in Moscow, Kathmandu, Paris and at the Permanent

Mission of India to the UN in New York, where she represented India in the UN Security Council, ECOSOC and at Summit meetings of the Non-Aligned Movement (NAM).

After retiring from the IFS, Professor Sikri joined academia as Professor, holding the Ford Foundation endowed Chair, Academy of International Studies, Jamia Millia Islamia, New Delhi, from February 2009 to October 2013. She was concurrently Visiting Senior Research Fellow with the Institute of Southeast Asian Studies (ISEAS), Singapore (November 2008 to October 2011).

She is the Founding Trustee and Convener of the SWAN. While at Jamia Millia Islamia, Professor Sikri conceptualized and created this organization, which was established in March 2009. With its unique focus on gender empowerment as the key to sustainable economic growth, social development and environmental sustainability in South Asia, SWAN brings together women leaders from nine South Asian countries: Afghanistan, Bangladesh, Bhutan, India, Maldives, Myanmar, Nepal, Pakistan and Sri Lanka.

Her publications include *India and Malaysia: Intertwined Strands* (2013), and she co-co-edited the volume (together with Professor Muchkund Dubey and Professor Imtiaz Ahmed) *Contemporarising Tagore and the World* (2013).

Arun K. Singh is Distinguished Senior Fellow at German Marshall Fund of the USA, Distinguished Halle Fellow at Emory University and Visiting Faculty at Ashoka University. He completed his assignment as Ambassador of India to the USA in 2016, after a career spanning nearly four decades in the IFS. Earlier, he had served as Ambassador to France during 2013–2015 and to Israel during 2005–2008.

His other diplomatic assignments have included tours of duty in Soviet Union and later in Russia, Japan, Ethiopia and in the Indian mission to UN in New York.

In the MEA in New Delhi, he was involved for nearly a decade in the formulation and implementation of India's policies related to Afghanistan, Pakistan and Iran, including in the period following 9/11.

In Spring 2017, he was Diplomat in Residence at the School of International Service of American University in Washington, DC, teaching a course on US Foreign Policy in South Asia. He was also visiting faculty at School of Advanced International studies (SAIS) of Johns Hopkins University, teaching a course on current global trends and challenges. During this period, he was invited as Distinguished Visiting Fellow by Emory University (Atlanta, Georgia, USA), and Center for the Advanced Study of India (CASI) at University of Pennsylvania. Aside from intense interactions with students and faculty, he spoke at public platforms on US–India relations, Indian economic and technological trends, US foreign policy in South Asia, and diplomacy and statecraft.

Uttam Kumar Sinha is a Senior Fellow at the Nehru Memorial Museum and Library and on leave of absence from the IDSA. He holds an adjunct position at the Malaviya Centre for Peace Research, Banaras Hindu University, and is an honorary Senior Fellow at the Institute for National Security Studies Sri Lanka, Colombo. He is also the Managing Editor of *Strategic Analysis*. A doctorate from JNU, his research areas include international politics, climate change, transboundary water issues and the Arctic region.

He was a visiting fellow at the Peace Research Institute Oslo in 2006, a Chevening Scholar at the LSE in 2008 and a visitor at the Harvard Kennedy School in 2015. He is actively engaged in Track-II dialogue process and was India's representative to the Council for Security Cooperation in the Asia Pacific (CSCAP) Working Group on Water Resources Security. He chaired the Working Group on Water Dispute Resolution Mechanism of the Strategic Studies Network, National Defense University (NDU), Washington, DC.

He is the author of the book *Riverine Neighbourhood: Hydro-politics in South Asia* (2016) and editor or co-editor of the following volumes: *The Modi Doctrine: New Paradigms in India's Foreign Policy* (2016), *Non-Traditional Security Challenges in Asia: Approaches and Responses* (2015), *Arctic: Commerce, Governance and Policy* (2015) and *Emerging Strategic Trends in Asia* (2015).

Vikram Sood is Advisor at the Observer Research Foundation, an independent public policy think tank based in New Delhi. He was a career intelligence officer and served in the Research and Analysis Wing (R&AW), India's external intelligence agency, till his retirement in March 2003 after heading the R&AW. For over a decade, he has been regularly writing on intelligence, terrorism, security, foreign relations and strategic issues in journals and newspapers.

He has contributed chapters related to security, China, intelligence and India's neighbourhood to various books published in the last few years. He is the author of *The Unending Game—A Former R&AW Chief's Insights into Espionage* published in 2018.

D. P. Srivastava is Independent Director, GAIL and India Ports Global Ltd (IPGL), tasked with development of Chabahar port. He is Distinguished Fellow in VIF. He has coordinated VIF Task Forces on 'India–Africa Relations' and 'Nuclear Power: Imperative for Development'. He got retired as Indian Ambassador to Iran in 2015. He was also Ambassador to Libya, Czech Republic and High Commissioner to Malta. He has served in Cairo, Jeddah, Riyadh, Washington, Karachi and Brussels. He has extensive experience of UN peacekeeping, human rights and energy issues. His area of specialization is the Middle East. He knows Arabic, French and Farsi.

Anil Trigunayat has been a member of the IFS. He has served in the Indian missions in Côte d'Ivoire, Bangladesh, Mongolia, the USA, Russia, Sweden, Nigeria, Libya, Malta and Jordan. In the MEA, he worked in the Economic, West Asia and North Africa, Gulf and Consular Divisions. He also served as Director General/Joint Secretary for the Gulf and Haj Divisions in the MEA, New Delhi. Thereafter, Mr Trigunayat worked as Deputy Chief of Mission in the rank of Ambassador in the Embassy of India, Moscow.

Prior to his superannuation in May 2016, he served as Ambassador of India to Jordan and Libya and High Commissioner to Malta (June 2012–May 2016).

He is a postgraduate in physics from the Agra/Kumaun University and also studied Russian history, culture and Language at JNU, New Delhi. As a Visiting Fellow, he conducted research work on 'WTO and Regional Trading Blocs' at the Oxford University.

He is a member of the All India Management Association/Delhi Management Association as well as that of Oxford and Cambridge Society of India and Secretary of the Association of Indian Diplomats (former Ambassadors). He is also the Honorary Member of the International Trade Council, Brussels, and of Centre for International Relations and Community Well-Being (CIRCW) and Board Member of Peaceful Mind Foundation as well as Confederation of Education Excellence, New Delhi. He also serves on the Board of Advisers of BRICS Chamber of Commerce and Asian-African Chamber of Commerce & Industry and also the President of MIICCIA Chamber of Commerce Industry and Agriculture.[1] He is the Distinguished Fellow at VIF.[2] Recently he has joined the National Cooperative Development

---

[1] See www.miiccia.com (accessed on 19 December 2019).
[2] See www.vifindia.org (accessed on 19 December 2019).

Corporation as Advisor International[3] and as Co-President of Uni disaster Management and Rural Development Society.[4] He is a regular contributor and commentator on foreign policy and education-related issues.

Ambassador Trigunayat is closely associated with the interfaith dialogue, peace and harmony efforts in the society, especially through the U Dialogue by Unity Earth[5] and World Congress of Religions at Kazakhstan. Ambassador Trigunayat knows French, Russian and Spanish languages.

R. Viswanathan worked as Lecturer in chemistry at Bishop Heber College, Trichy (1974–1975) and at Pachaiyappa's College, Madras (1975–1977). MSc chemistry from Pachaiyappa's College Madras, 1974, BSc chemistry from Pushpam College, Poondi High School studies—Government Secondary School, Mariamman Kovil, Mr Viswanathan is the former Indian Ambassador to Argentina, Uruguay and Paraguay (2007–2012). He was earlier the Ambassador to Venezuela and served as the first Consul General of India in Sao Paulo, Brazil. He has headed the MEA's division on Latin America and the Caribbean as well as its Investment and Trade Promotion Division. He is specialized in Latin America since 1996 and has been a regular contributor to newspapers and business journals, besides giving lectures on the subject at think tanks and universities across India, Latin America and the USA. He speaks Spanish and Portuguese. A self-confessed Latinophile, Ambassador Viswanathan is an avid reader of Latin American literature and admirer of Latino culture. He is fluent in Tamil, Spanish, English, Portuguese and Portuñol.

Deepa Gopalan Wadhwa is Chairperson of the India–Japan Friendship Forum, Member Governing Council of the Institute of Chinese Studies and is on the Governing Council of the Asian Confluence based in Shillong. She also serves as independent Director and Advisor on a few boards of companies. She has been a distinguished career diplomat who joined the IFS in 1979 and retired in December 2015.

She has served as Ambassador of India to Japan (2012–2015), Qatar (2009–2012) and Sweden (2005–2009). She was concurrently accredited as Ambassador to Latvia (from Stockholm), and Republic of the Marshall

---

[3] See www.ncdc.in (accessed on 19 December 2019).
[4] See www.udmrd.org (accessed on 19 December 2019).
[5] See www.unity.earth (accessed on 19 December 2019).

Islands (from Tokyo). During her career, she has also held other significant assignments in Geneva, Hong Kong, China, the Netherlands, the International Labour Organization (ILO) and the MEA.

In the course of her career spanning over 36 years, she has handled a wide swathe of issues and subjects related to India's relations with key countries such as Pakistan, China and Japan; participated in international conferences and negotiations related to climate change, sustainable development, disarmament and human rights; and was instrumental in the active promotion of India's economic interests in areas of trade, technology, investments and energy security during postings in Europe, the GCC and Japan.

Index

Act East Policy of India, 336
African Continental Free Trade
    Area (AfCFTA), 374
African Peace and Security
    Architecture (APSA), 384
African Students Union in India
    (AASI), 383
Agenda 2030, 73–74
    world leader's emphasis, 76
agreements with China, 234
Al-Qaeda in the Islamic Maghreb
    (AQIM), 384
American Grand strategy, 104
Annual Average Losses (AAL), 124
Arab Revolution, 376
Arab Spring, 309–310
Argentina–Chile–Bolivia triangle,
    398
Arthashastra, 45
asana, 46
Asean Defense Minister's Meeting-
    Plus (ADMM+), 326
ASEAN Integration Plan 2025, 330
ASEAN Regional Forum (ARF), 320,
    326
Asia Africa Growth Corridor
    (AAGC) project, 230, 386
Asia Reassurance Initiative Act
    (ARIA), 336

Asia
    Japan and India, 107–108
    Nehru's world historical
        perspective, 113
Asian conflict system, 100
Asian containment strategy, 112
Asia–Europe Meeting (ASEM), 340
Atlantic Charter, 66

Banaras Hindu University (BHU),
    135
Bangladeshi politics, 35
Bay of Bengal Initiative
    for Multi-Sectoral
    Technical and Economic
    Cooperation(BIMSTEC),
    123
Beijing Declaration, 378
Belt and Road Initiative (BRI), 281,
    349, 378
Bengal Initiative for Multi-Sectoral
    Technical and Economic
    Cooperation (BIMSTEC), 38
Better Utilization of Investment
    Leading to Development
    (BUILD), 336
bhai–bhai relationship, 184
bheda, 46
Bhutanese territory, 234

bilateral investment treaties (BITs), 345
bilateral trade investment, 385
border management issues, 12
Bretton Woods Agreements, 66
Brexit complications for India, 347–348
Britain's economic impact on India, 133
British imperial system, 101
Broad Based Trade and Investment Agreement (BTIA), 340, 342
business process outsourcing (BPO), 137

caste-based reservation policies, 180
Central and Eastern European (CEE), 354
Central Asia, 281
   Afghanistan, 295–296
   BRI, 282–284
   Chinese and Russian economic presence, 284
   CSTO, 282–284
   defence and security, 294–295
   EEU, 282–284
   identity, 298–299
   India share, 296–297
   Islam, 293
   Kazakhstan, 284
   Kyrgyzstan, 286
   oil and gas, 287–289
   regional dynamics, 289
      Kazakhstan, 290–291
      Kyrgyzstan, 291
      Tajikistan, 292–293
      Turkmenistan, 292
      Uzbekistan, 289–290
   SCO, 282–284
   Tajikistan, 287
   terrorism and extremism, 294
   Turkmenistan, 286
   Uzbekistan, 285

Central Asian Republics (CARs), 281
Chabahar project, 188
China, 181
   assertive nationalism and geo-political thinking, 234
   economic growth, 181
   friendship with Pakistan, 182
   important neighbour of India, 36
   Indian analysis of relations and security challenges, 245
   Indian relations and security challenges
      BIMSTEC summit, 247
      engagement, 246
      internal and external balancing, 247
   software services, 138
   strategic alliance with Pakistan, 184
   strategy, 185
   Tibet, occupied in 1950, 182
   trade relationship with Africa, 377
China–Africa Forums, 377
China–Kenya Industrial Capacity Development Forum, 378
China–Latin America trade, 399
China–Pakistan Economic Corridor (CPEC), 3, 182, 349
China's presence in the Indian Ocean, 182
Chinese foreign policy, 233
Chinese imports, 233
Chinese violation, 233
climate change, 123, 165
   ADP forecasts, 125
   Himalayas, 126–128
   need for climate diplomacy, 125–126
code of conduct (COC), 332
Cold War
   map, 101
   navalization, 105

security, 116
Collective Security Treaty Organization (CSTO), 282
colonial policy, 134
Combined Task Forces (CTFs), 362
commercial diplomacy, 144
conflicts with Pakistan, 325
containment, 106
Continental Free Trade Area, 374
Conventional Armed Forces in Europe (CFE) Treaty of 1990, 320
Council for Security Cooperation in the Asia Pacific (CSCAP), 321
Council of Security and Cooperation in Europe (CSCE), 320
Countering America's Adversaries Through Sanctions Act (CAATSA), 39
Covert Autonomous Disposable Aircraft (CICADA), 168
culture, 11
cybersecurity, 331

Dalai Lama, 183
dana, 46
danda, 46
Declaration of the Conduct (DOC), 332
Decolonization Resolution, 72
defence and security imperatives, 384
democratic traditions, 180
Diamond Pitt, 134
diaspora versus racism, 382–384
dvaidhibhava, 46
Détente, 107

e-ArogyaBharti (e-VBAB), 382
E-commerce technologies, 87
e-VidyaBharti, 382
Earth Summit, 73
East Coast of Africa, 384

Economic and Social Council (ECOSOC), 70
economic growth, 375
education, 135
Elihu Yale, 134
energy security, 394
  crude imports of India, 395
  crude oil, 396
entertainment business, 402
Eurasian containment, 106
Eurasian Détente versus Asian Détente, 106–107
Eurasian Economic Union (EEU), 282
Europe
  approach to Russia and China., 219–220
  Brexit process, 218
  political and economic cultures, 219
European Economic Community (EEC), 340
EU–China strategic partnership, 348
  institutional mechanism, 349
EU–Russia tensions, 351
EU's new strategy for India, 351–353
exclusive economic zone (EEZ), 359

Federation of Indian Chambers of Commerce and Industry (FICCI), 343
First Industrial Revolution, 134
food security, 397
  consumption, 397
  global agricultural powerhouse, 398
  India as importer of pulses, 397
  Indian agriculture, 398
  production of oil seeds and pulses, 397
  production of pulses, 397
  South American, 397

422   *India's Foreign Policy*

foreign direct investment (FDI), 375
foreign policy of country, 34
foreign policy of India
　strategic autonomy, 43
Foreign Secretaries to National Security Advisor–Vice Premier, 234
Forum on China–Africa Cooperation Summit (FOCAC), 7th, 378

General Assembly
　destructive scenario, 81
　faltered momentum on Security Council reforms, 79
　second scenario, 81
　traditional scenario, 80
Generalised Scheme of Preferences (GSP), 340
Generalized Scheme of Preferences (GSP)
　privileges to India, 188
global economic environment, 10
global environment, 4–8
global geopolitics turbulences, 40
Global Governance
　commission, 118
Global War on Terror (GWOT), 362
globally connected India rebirth, 136–140
Government of India Act of 1919, 63
Great Archipelago, 106
Great Game, 281
Group of 77 (G77), 72

Helsinki Final Act (1975), 320
Himalaya and the Hindu Kush (HKH) mountain system, 126
Himalaya
　hot spot of climate change, 126–128
Human Development Report, 118

Humanitarian Assistance and Disaster Relief (HADR), 330, 371

impact assessment matrix, 60
India and India's relations with SAARC neighbours
　Bhuta, 198–201
India and Russia friendship, 267
　bilateral trade, 267
　Comprehensive Economic Cooperation Agreement, 270
　cumulative oil and gas investment, 268
　defence cooperation, 268
　import items, 270
　nuclear energy, cooperation, 268
　Pharma 2020 strategy, 269
　polycentric world, 270–276
　scientific and technological cooperation, 270
India foreign policy, 2, 34
　domestic priorities, 12
　implementation, 13
　internal security issues, 12
　neighbourhood, 8–10
　overview, 153–155
India Ports Global Limited (IPGL), 298
India
　Afghanistan, relationship with, 36
　China, 36
　Digital India programme, 75
　entry of software, 138
　export strategy, 139
　exports of goods and services, 136
　globalized economy, 137
　interests in West Asian region, 41
　rebirth of globally connected, 136–140
　tensions with Pakistan, 35

Index   423

world's largest economy, 134
world's largest importer of arms, 42
Indian economy
   alliances in remaking, 145–148
   BRICS grouping, 142
   commercial diplomacy, 144
   economic failure, 139
   exporter of services, 141
   flow of Indian labour, 142
   imbalance in trade, 143
   international pecking order challenge, 140–145
   international trader, 141
   market exchange rates, 140
   Modi government, 140
   strategic importance of manufacturing, 148–151
   substantial presence, 142
Indian foreign office
   critical dilemma, 101
   overestimate, 105
Indian foreign policy, 112
   domestic drivers, 155–158
   elements, 154
   objectives, 154
Indian Ocean, 358
   assessment, 369–371
   climate change, 365–367
   littoral, 359
   ramifications of shifting IOR geopolitics, 362
   SAGAR speech, 368
   sea lanes of communications (SLOCs), 360–362
   Shangri-La speech, 368
Indian Ocean Naval Symposium (IONS), 331
Indian Ocean Rim Association (IORA), 123, 331
Indian renaissance, 103
Indian Technical and Economic Cooperation (ITEC) programme, 354
India–Afghan ties, 196
   future, 197
India–Africa Forum, 383
India–Bangladesh relations, 201
   Awami League, 202
India–Bhutan bilateral trade, 200
India–Bhutan relations, 198
   economic cooperation, 199
India–China conflict, 183
India–China relationship, 184
India–Europe relations
   emerging and possible areas of cooperation, 353
      CEE, 354
      development cooperation, 354
      energy, 353
      migration and mobility, 354
India–Iran relations, 305–307
India–Japan Act East Forum, 386
India–Japan Global Partnership, 254
India–Maldives ties, 204–205
   future prospects, 205–207
India–Nepal relations, 207–208
   future propsects, 208–210
India–Pakistan relations, 210–212
India–Russia relationshipis, 39
India–Sri Lanka relations, 212–214
   future prospects, 214
India–US relations, 188
   defence cooperation, 39
   resurgence, 38
India–West Asia ties, 302–304
   political, 304–305
India's Act East Policy, 326
India's domestic jurisdiction, 233
India's exports, 392
India's freedom of manoeuver, 181
India's international political economic interests, 222
   ASEAN, 227
   China, 226
   Europe, 224–225
   Russia, 225
   USA, 223–224
India's knowledge base, 133
India's neighbourhood policy, 152

tracing domestic roots, 158–163
India's post-Cold War, 246
India's relations with SAARC
neighbours, 194
    Afghanistan, 196–198
    Bangladesh, 201–204
    Maldives, 201–204
    Nepal, 207–210
    Pakistan, 210–212
    Sri Lankan, 212–214
    volatility, 194
Indic civilizations, 131
Indo-European linkages, 340
    moving into strategic areas, 346
    negotiations, 343
    new initiatives, 341
Indo-Pacific, 6
    maritime domains, 235, 236
    region, 386
    strategy, 37
Indo-Persian language family, 132
information and communication technology (ITC) revolution, 48
infrastructure initiative Australia, 336
Institute of Defence Studies and Analyses (IDSA)
    analysis of India's neighbourhood policy, 158
Intellectual Property Rights (IPRs)
    battle over, 85
intelligence and foreign policy, 164
    China and India, 166
    cyber warfare, 168
    hackers, 169
    missiles, 168
    nano-technology, 167
    robotic, 168
    talks about 1990s, 165
    technological revolution, 169
intelligence leaks, 167
international cooperation
    challenges, 86–88
    Indian efforts, 88–89

    role in improving S&T, 86
International Day of Non-Violence, 75
International Day of Yoga (IDY), 59, 75
International Energy Agency, 395
International Labour Conference (ILC), 64
International Labour Organization (ILO), 63
    India's participation, 63–64
International North–South Transport Corridor (INSTC), 298
international relations (IR)
    search of Indian narrative, 24–29
    Westernized studies, 21–24
International Solar Alliance (ISA), 127
investment and joint ventures, 400
Iraq–Iran
    regime change, 308–309

Japan and India partnership
    bilateral congruences, 255
    cultural and historical ties, 253–254
    economic engagement, 260–263
    political convergence, 255
    relations, 254
    strategic convergence, 256–260
    structural complementarities, 252
Japanese Peace Treaty, 109

Kaladan multi-modal transport project, 329

Ladakh and Arunachal Pradesh, 235
Lakshman rekha, 184
Latin America
    China, 400
    market, 398

Leading Asia's private Sector Infrastructure Fund (LEAP), 335
least developed countries (LDCs), 381
Line of Actual Control (LAC), 183, 246
lines of credit (LoCs), 354, 387
  issues and constraints, 388–389
  strategic choices and leap, 389–390
  Task Force Report, 388
lithium, 398
Look East policy, 326

MALABAR naval exercises, 38
Maritime Silk Road (MSR) programme, 361
Mekong–Ganga Cooperation group, 325
member states (MS), 338
micro, small and medium enterprises (MSMEs), 330
minerals for make in India, 398
Ministry of External Affairs (MEA), 382
  report, 154
  statement, 353
Missile Technology Control Regime, 187
Mon Kingdom of Daryavati in Thailand, 325
multilateral diplomacy
  achievements of India, 76
multilateralism
  core principle, 62
  engagement of India, 76
  India's participation, 62–66
Muslims invaders, 133

Narendra Modi, 1
  India's foreign policy, 2–4
  proposal at the UN General Assembly, 75
National Security as an Ambiguous Symbol, 116

National Security Council Secretariat (NSCS), 44
national security management objective, 34
National Security Strategy (NSS), 364
national security
  holistic approach, 43
NATO's Libyan experiment in 2011, 380
Natya Shastra, 52
NDA government, 1
new age security, 120
Nixon Doctrine, 104
Non-Aligned Movement (NAM), 136, 381
non-state security, 115
non-traditional security, 10
North African countries, 376
Nuclear Non-Proliferation Treaty (NPT), 76, 182
Nuclear Suppliers Group, 187

Organisation of African Unity (OAU), 384

Pallava kingdom, 325
Panchamrit, 155
Panchsheel, 154
  principle, 108
People's Republic of China, 232
political independence, 136
political relations of India, 403
positive multilateralism, 82
post-Mao period, 234
power over opinion, 46
Pravasi Bharatiya Divas (PBD), 383
Prosper Africa strategy, 379
public diplomacy
  activities, 47
  moving towards cultural diplomacy, 47
  squarely in realm of cultural diplomacy, 47

Quad, 187

Regional Comprehensive Economic Partnership (RCEP), 327
Research and Information Systems (RIS), 324
Responsibility to Protect, 119
riverine neighbourhood
 treaties/arrangements on water sharing, 129
Robotic armies, 168
Russia, 39, 189
 Chinese influence, expansion, 220–222
 India
  defence partnership, 191
  friendship, 190
  trade and economic relations, 191
  territory and rich natural resources, 189
Russian foreign policy, 266
Russia–India–China trilateral dialogue, 190

sadgunya and samdhi, 46
Samdhi and Sama, 46
samsraya, 46
Sarva Dharma Sambhava, 54
Saudi–Iran divide, 307–308
science & technology (S&T), 85
 achievements, 97–98
security, 115
Security and Growth for All in the Region (SAGAR), 327
Security Council
 decisions on Iran, 77
 Indian influence on process to reform, 78–79
 India's interest in participating, 77
 issues relevant to India, 76–77
 reform, faltered momentum in General Assembly, 80
security
 broadening, 121–122

climate change, 123
Cold War, 116
environmental issues, 117
Human Development Report, 118
neighbourhood, 122–125
new age, 120
post-Cold War times, 117
regional institutional, 123
sedentary civilizations, 133
Shanghai Cooperation Organisation (SCO), 281, 318
Shangri-La Dialogue, 334
share and care approach, 381
Shared Awareness and De-Confliction (SHADE) activities, 362
Sino-African friendship, 377
Sino-centric world order, 188
Sino-Pak alliance, 245
Society of Indian Automobile Manufacturers (SIAM), 344
soft power, 45
 dimensions, 50–55
 heritage, 55
 importance, 45–48
 projection
  diplomacy, 57
  strategizing projection, 55–61
Soft Power 30 Index, 58
Southern Thailand in Ayutthaya period (1350–1767 CE), 325
spiritual relations, 402
string of pearls, 246
structure of peace, 105
Summit joint statement, 386
Sushruta Samhita, 52
Sustainable Development Goals (SDGs), 359
synergies and complementarities, new paradigm, 400–402

Taliban smell victory, 197
Tata group, 137

Index 427

Techno-Economic Approach for Africa–India Movement (Team-9), 382
technology, 10
Telecommunications Consultants India Limited (TCIL), 382
the United States of America (USA)
   intelligence, collection and analysis, 167
Third Pole, 127
three-nation peace initiative, 311–312
   China, 313–315
   confidence building measures (CBMs), 317–319
   India, 312–313
   regional cooperative security arrangement, 320–321
   Russia, 315–317
Tibetan refugee population in India, 183
traditional security, 118
trans-Himalayan states, 235
transboundary rivers, 129
Treaty of Friendship with Soviet Union, 325
true strategic partnership, 188
Trump Administration, 188

Ukrainian crisis, 351
UN Charter, 67–68
   India's participation, 68
UN Convention on the Law of the Sea (UNCLOS), 332
UN Millennium Declaration, 119
UN Security Council, 182
United States (US), 185
   Africa Business Summit, 12th, 380
   Development Finance Initiative (DFI), 335
   foreign policy, 188
   helped India, 187
   India, relations, 186
   military equipment, 187
   power, 186
   relationship, comprehensive approach, suggestions, 227
   GSP withdrawal, 230
   international political, 227
   new trade and investment, 228
   opportunities, 229
   policy and decision-making, 228
   transactional compromises, 229
   Republican and Democratic Administrations, 186
United States(US)
   China strategy, 185
   fundamental values, 186
Universal Declaration of Human Rights (UDHR), 69
upaya is sama, 46
US International Development finance Cooperation (USIDFC), 336

Vasudhaiva Kutumbakam, 53
vigraha, 46

West Asia, 41
   India's initiatives, 41
World Development Report, 119
World Trade Organization (WTO), 70
Wuhan reset, 250

Xi's new era, 236
   core interests, 239–240
   great power status, 240
   military build-up, 244–245
   one belt and one road, 240–242
   peaceful rise to striving for achievement, 238–239
yana, 46